D1564334

AMERICAN

INTELLECTUALS

AND AFRICAN

NATIONALISTS,

1955–1970

AMERICAN

INTELLECTUALS

AND AFRICAN

NATIONALISTS,

1955–1970

Martin
Staniland

Yale University Press

New Haven and London

To the memory
of Jim Coleman

Published with assistance from the Mary Cady Tew Memorial Fund.

Copyright © 1991 by Yale University.

Designed by April Leidig-Higgins.
Set in Meridien type by Brevis Press.
Printed in the United States of America by Vail-Ballou Press, Binghamton, New York.

Library of Congress Cataloging-in-Publication Data

Staniland, Martin.

American intellectuals and African nationalists, 1955–1970 / Martin Staniland.

p.   cm.

Includes bibliographical references (p.   ) and index.

ISBN 0-300-04838-6

1. Africa—Foreign public opinion, American—History—20th century.   2. Africa—Relations—United States.   3. United States—Relations—Africa.   4. Public opinion—United States—History—20th century.   5. Intellectuals—United States—Attitudes—History—20th century.   6. Africa—Politics and government—1945–1960.
7. Africa—Politics and government—1960–   8. Nationalism—Africa—History—20th century.   I. Title.
DT2925.S73   1991
303.48'27306—dc20   90–44756
                          CIP

10 9 8 7 6 5 4 3 2 1

CONTENTS

v

PREFACE

The writing of this book extended over a ten-year period, but the experiences that stimulated it go back to September 1963. At that time, I arrived in Ghana as a very green graduate student at the Institute of African Studies, directed by the late Thomas Hodgkin. Over the next two years, I lived in a dormitory at the University of Ghana during the sometimes tense but always exciting period when the Nkrumah government was in decline. Subsequently I spent four years exploring the rich world of local politics in Benin and the Ivory Coast and in the early seventies worked in northern Ghana on a political conflict centered on the Dagomba kingdom.

During this period, I became increasingly aware of how little of the cultural and imaginative experience accumulated in academic research ever finds expression in the books and papers that appear in a vita. I became fascinated by the cultural underworld of the fieldwork enterprise—particularly by the ways in which very specific experiences and personal idiosyncrasies seemed to affect the public face of research. I began to find the impact of Africa on foreigners as interesting as what these foreigners had to say formally about Africa.

At this point, radical critics also became interested in lifting the curtain of objectivity separating the scholar from his or her subject. But what these critics had to say about the political and personal worlds of African studies turned out to be narrowly polemical—limited to lifeless and very sweeping labeling of individuals and ideas as "conservative," "progressive," "racist," or whatever. The rich and complicated dilemmas of people I had known disappeared under these caricatures, which were as partial as they were impersonal.

At a more analytic level, it seemed to me that the polemics of the time were discouraging the proper investigation of an important and dramatic piece of intellectual history—the "discovery" of Africa by Western academics and journalists as a result of the rapid collapse of the colonial empires and the establishment of new states. As an immigrant to the United States, I became particularly interested in the American side of this encounter and in how writers in American journals had tried to construe and communicate the meaning of African nationalism and self-government to their readers. (Some of the writers I quote are not in fact American, at least by birth; but they are a minority, and my concern in any case is with the commitments of the editors and the readers.)

The direction of the research and the organization of the book were determined by a fairly simple interest in the remarkable variety of incompatible interpretations that I found of particular cases. I then began to search for patterns of interpretation and evaluation and to identify the larger preconceptions and beliefs that gave consistency to these patterns. The identifications of these ideological "templates" at least helped to explain the sometimes grotesquely disparate accounts published in different sources on particular countries and crises.

The heart of this study concerns the adventures and misadventures of Western ideologies in Africa. My interest in these picaresque goings-on has, however, led me into more serious (or at least solemn) thinking about their implications for the way we go about understanding international relations. Starting out in a continent which has nurtured and lately rejected anthropology, I end by suggesting that this discipline may find a satisfying new enterprise in reconstructing the study of international relations. But this is only a suggestion.

The long and frequently-interrupted conception of this book has tried the patience of relatives, friends, and colleagues. These are not always exclusive categories and the person who has helped me most falls in all three: my main debt is to my wife, Alberta, who, as she frequently says, "never got to see California because of this book." I doubt if in the end the book is any consolation, but its completion is certainly due as much to her determination as to any incidental contribution of mine. Paul and Laura, who believe that the only idea that matters is dessert, also helped enormously.

For helping to get the writing done at all, I owe a particular debt to four institutions—the Center for International and Strategic Affairs, University of California, Los Angeles; the Institute of International Studies, University of California, Berkeley; the Center for International Affairs, Harvard University; and the University Center for International Studies, University of Pittsburgh. The first three enabled me to survive academically (and even physically) for three years, and I am particularly grateful to those involved in the African Studies programs at each institution—

Dick Sklar at UCLA, Carl Rosberg and Bob Price at Berkeley, and Dov Ronen at Harvard.

At the University of Pittsburgh, I want to thank Burkart Holzner and Tom McKechnie, who helped me over the last lap by granting me a Faculty Fellowship in the winter semester of 1989. For their kindness in commenting on this and related writing, I want to thank Harvey Glickman, Lou Picard, and M. Crawford Young, all of whom commented in detail on earlier drafts. For her unstinting advice, friendship, and skill, I want to thank Kendall Stanley, who actually produced the final draft. Michelle Egan deserves my thanks for the hard work she put into the bibliography.

The book is dedicated to a man who died before it was finished, but whose life was devoted to the understanding and recognition of the continent with which it deals.

All of these people contributed to the writing of this book. I hope that they will be tolerant of the defects I have contributed to it.

ONE

Ideologies and International Affairs

This book is only indirectly about "international relations" in the conventional sense of relations between states. Rather, it is about the images of foreign societies that shape our attitudes and policies toward them. Specifically, it is an exploration of attempts by opinion makers in the United States to construe the meaning and implications of African independence for their readers.

While it is impossible to prove that policymakers were influenced by writings of the kind reviewed in this book, common sense suggests that "foreign policy" must be framed by assumptions about the character of foreign societies. At one level, foreign policy-making may consist of setting general goals and asserting broad principles, but in application such goals and principles have to be related to conceptions of foreign reality.

Yet foreigners are oddly absent from scholarly work on foreign policy. More exactly, such work often shows little interest in examining the views of particular societies that were in circulation among both the more and the less informed members of the public when the societies in question were significant subjects for policy-making. Yet surely it is of interest, if only as background, to be told how, for example, Vietnamese or Nicaraguan societies were being portrayed in the more influential media when American foreign policymakers were preoccupied with these countries. Intellectual and diplomatic historians have certainly investigated such imagery, but their work seems to have little impact on the political scientists who write about foreign policy.

This indifference is itself surprising. For some years, textbooks on international relations have been stressing the importance of "perception" and "cognition," as well as the connection between domestic politics and

I

foreign policy. But this emphasis has not led to any broadening of focus in scholarship. The "domestic connection" is usually interpreted as referring to political and economic pressure groups, while the cultural and intellectual strand in this connection is ignored. Yet we have only to look at op-ed articles about a current foreign policy issue to see the evidence of sustained competition among entrenched ideological interests, which are struggling not just to influence specific decisions, but also to assert and establish notions about fundamental identities and values, domestic and foreign. No matter how much pundits deplore the influence of "ideology" on foreign policy, the fact is that foreign policy provides a major battleground for fighting between the more articulate advocates of radically dissimilar "worldviews"—in the nonpejorative sense, "ideologies."

Since this work is about American intellectuals and about Africa, it would be a distraction to go into the reasons for the indifference of scholars to the cultural and intellectual dimensions of arguments over foreign policy. More positively, I have tried to show the value of identifying and scrutinizing competing views of foreign societies as an approach not only to understanding the cognitive undergrowth of foreign policy, but also to illuminating rival views about what is valuable and basic in the domestic society itself. An African proverb I quote says: "The stranger sees what he knows." The material in succeeding chapters shows just how determinedly American visitors and commentators did see what they knew and judged what they saw according to what they valued—behaving like so many mirrors walking down bush paths.

Critics have relentlessly branded such intellectual performances as "ethnocentric." I would argue that much criticism of this kind is superficial, question-begging, and illogical. Everybody acquires a set of mental templates in growing up which enable them to construct meaning from the bewildering, complex, and ambiguous supply of information that their senses provide. How an individual constructs meaning is affected by inherited sets of rules about meaning that social institutions provide. Such sets of rules constitute "ideologies," each of which provides "an interrelated set of convictions or assumptions that reduces the complexities of a particular slice of reality to easily comprehensible terms and suggests appropriate ways of dealing with that reality."[1] Using this nonpejorative

---

1. Hunt, *Ideology and U.S. Foreign Policy,* xi. Elsewhere, Hunt writes: "[Ideologies are] integrated and coherent systems of symbols, values, and beliefs [that provide] an indispensable guide to an infinitely complex and otherwise bewildering pres-

definition, the term *ideology* simply refers to available frameworks of interpretation and evaluation. They may be extremely simplistic or quite sophisticated: they may be backed by political authority (as the pejorative use of the term implies) or they may compete (as, say, conservative and liberal or Catholic and Protestant ideologies do in the United States). But if an ideology is not politically imposed or necessarily adopted in toto, neither is it chosen like a cereal in a supermarket. The most fundamental framework concerned is acquired early in life: it may function like a disk operating system, but it is not as easily removed.

Indeed, it or something like it had better not be removed, since without some framework we literally cannot make sense of the physical and social world in which we find ourselves.[2] A problem necessarily arises, however, when frameworks formed in one cultural context are applied to interpreting phenomena in other cultures. Such encounters give rise to charges of "ethnocentrism." The logic of such criticisms is weighed in the last chapter: I only state here that this book is not another critique of "Western ethnocentrism," but rather a portrayal of the efforts of writers fired by different convictions to make sense of societies that were quite strange to most of them.

In depicting these efforts, I have tried strenuously to remain within the assumptions and logic of each framework and not to impose extraneous judgments of my own. As a reaction against the heavily polemical tone of much writing about Africa, this posture may (as some readers have suggested) have taken me to the opposite extreme, that of excessive agnosticism. In response to this criticism, I have tried to take a more evaluative approach to certain important writers without sacrificing balance.

In exploring the role of ideology in international affairs, we often encounter the belief that a society has a single or clearly dominant framework of values and concepts that constitutes (say) an American ideology. Michael H. Hunt's recent excellent book *Ideology and U.S. Foreign Policy* falls

---

ent, and . . . a basis for moral action intended to shape a better future" (ibid., 12). According to Julius Gould and William L. Kolb, an ideology is "a pattern of beliefs and concepts (both factual and normative) which purport to explain complex social phenomena with a view to directing and simplifying socio-political choices facing individuals" (*A Dictionary of the Social Sciences*, 315).

2. According to Clifford Geertz, ideologies play a vital role in political life "by providing the authoritative concepts that render it meaningful, the suasive images by means of which it can be sensibly grasped" ("Ideology as a Cultural System," 63).

within an established tradition of attempting to identify "an ideology of U.S. foreign policy" (or, in earlier works, to trace "American national character" in foreign policy). Such an approach makes sense as long as we continue to believe that the cultural identity embodied in nationality is bound to be expressed in foreign relations. It is also empirically sound, since (as Hunt's work demonstrates) there are enduring patterns in the kinds of symbols and values used to justify and criticize foreign policies.

But an emphasis on national ideology tends to overshadow the battles that occur very close to the White House, sometimes within Congress, and widely in the country at large. Such contestation has been marked since 1975. Even if (as is obvious) it is highly unequal—the opinions expressed in *Monthly Review* are unlikely even to be noticed in Washington—the competing traditions are resilient, enjoy their own, often devoted followings, and reflect the diversity and pluralism of American society. As I hope this study shows, each contains a coherent set of fundamental assumptions and commitments which are fully deployed and sturdily defended in efforts to come to terms with involvements abroad.

In the section that follows I distinguish in a very general fashion between the assumptions, values, and political preoccupations of four groups—American liberals, African-Americans, the American left, and American conservatives—discussing where appropriate each group's previous contacts with Africa.

The categories in question are broad and obviously rough. I use them because they do correspond to camps that are both recognizable to a reader of the main journals of opinion and (just as importantly) are generally accepted and invoked by the contestants themselves. I do not claim that these categories are philosophically watertight, much less that all Americans belong to one or other of them. I use them because they reflect the accepted battlefield terminology, the idiom according to which friends are identified and enemies are spotted.

Liberalism

Conservative and socialist critics have often complained about the control that liberals have exercised over American commentary on African affairs—a control amounting in the critics' eyes to a suffocating tyranny.[3] In 1961, for example, a traveler recently back from Africa noted: "So strong is the sympathy of Americans for the anti-colonialism of Africans that one able and responsible reporter remarked to me in private that it is virtually impossible to place any piece of reporting on Africa unless the piece has a 'liberal' slant."[4] The complaints became louder during the sixties and seventies, finding a particularly influential sympathizer in Chester A. Crocker, subsequently President Reagan's assistant secretary of state for African affairs. According to Crocker, the liberal orthodoxy was so strong in Washington under the Carter administration that it was impossible for nonliberals (Crocker meant, in fact, conservatives) to get a hearing on African issues, both in policy-making circles and in those in which opinions were shaped and exchanged.[5]

The strength of the liberal orthodoxy makes it important to establish what it was that the orthodox believed. At the risk of great oversimplification, we can say that American liberals in this period held to some or all of the following general assumptions and beliefs:

1. an emphasis on the individual and on individual rights;
2. a belief in progress, sustained by an optimistic view of human nature;
3. a belief in equality and in social mobility, the latter to be achieved through individual effort and talent;
4. a belief in the possibility of general harmony and prosperity arising from the individual pursuit of individual interest;
5. a belief in democracy, conditional upon the majority not infringing upon individual and minority rights.

3. In 1968, for example, Michael Lofchie, a UCLA Africanist, noted among his American colleagues "a pervasive disinclination to produce a conceptual terminology which, by even the most remote stretch of the imagination, could be construed as 'conservative'" ("Political Theory and African Politics," 6). Lofchie, it should be said, was not complaining about this liberal dominance, but merely noting its existence for purposes of explaining some features of American academic work on African politics.

4. McConnell, "Africa and the Americans," 42.

5. In particular, there was (Crocker observed) "universal deference" to the views of UN Ambassador Andrew Young, a deference reinforced by Young's "close identity of view" with a group of staffers serving the relevant congressional committees ("Lost in Africa," *New Republic*, 18 February 1978, 16).

In respect of foreign affairs, such tenets typically implied the following positions:

1. a belief in freedom of trade, expression, and movement of peoples across borders;
2. a hostility to monarchies and aristocracies, as undemocratic, responsible for perpetuating inequality, and likely to drag people into wars undertaken in pursuit of individual glory, military prestige, or dynastic advantage;
3. a hostility to "special interests" thought to depend upon or cause wars, notably professional soldiers, professional diplomats, and makers of armaments;
4. a belief that warfare is irrational, wasteful, and productive of heavy taxation and tyrannies;
5. a belief that "the people" are naturally (and by self-interest) peaceable;
6. a belief that lack of democracy and lack of self-determination (notably for nationalities) are major causes of war.

The very expansiveness of these principles points to the main problem in using the label "liberal": that it is claimed by people of quite different political affiliations. In the United States, conservatives lay claim to the individualism associated with "classical liberalism," while Democrats of the post–New Deal persuasion conceive liberalism more in terms of democracy and equality.

The real problem may then be to identify what liberals do *not* believe in. A distinguished economist once remarked, in a suitably puzzled tone, that liberalism "used to signify individual liberty, and now means rather state paternalism."[6] But, as Kenneth Minogue points out, even that analysis is too simple: the problem is that liberalism stands for both. It has, following a curious ideological odyssey, transformed itself and expanded to the point that it now "provides a moral and political consensus which unites virtually all of us, excepting only a few palpable eccentrics on the right and communists on the left."[7]

This statement may seem exaggerated, in view of the sharpness of more recent divisions between conservatives ("classical liberals") and liberal

---

6. Frank Knight, quoted in Minogue, *The Liberal Mind*, vii.
7. Ibid. Liberalism, Minogue remarks, is now "an intellectual compromise so extensive that it includes most of the guiding beliefs of modern Western opinion."

Democrats. Even so, it is probably best to regard liberalism as a continuum, with wings that emphasize certain elements rather than others (or that, indeed, reject the others). At the extremes of the continuum, liberalism overlaps with and shades into sets of positions which we would normally identify as "socialist" or "conservative," respectively. Thus, at the "left" end of the spectrum, many self-styled liberals share with socialists a belief in state intervention to assure social progress, and also share with them a suspicion of nationalism and tradition. Liberals at the "right" end of the spectrum emphasize individual freedom and dislike of "big government" to such an extent that their positions are hardly distinguishable from conservatives of the more libertarian variety.

In commenting on foreign affairs, liberals across much of the spectrum tend to see their principles as global in scope and, potentially, in application. They see rationality, progress, and freedom as values that are acceptable or at least desirable anywhere: they therefore tend to treat historical and cultural idiosyncrasies as of secondary importance and as derivative and malleable. The main question for liberals tends to be what institutions and policies might best serve the values they consider important.

This commitment gives rise to problems, however. For while believing firmly in the universal relevance of their values, liberals also believe in individualism and the right to self-determination, whether it is that of a person or of a nation. What, however, should liberals do if an individual or a nation exercises its self-determination illiberally? This problem arose for liberals with the new states of Eastern Europe between the wars, and it was to face them again as a result of African self-determination.

Liberals' belief in the universality of their principles is also complicated by their belief in a duty to correct or compensate for inequality. This means that individuals (or countries) should be judged according to their situations, and similar discrimination should be exercised in allocating benefits and penalties. As Minogue notes, liberals are apt to regard those suffering from inequality as victims of a "suffering situation" and as therefore entitled to special consideration, both in the allocation of rights and resources and in the assessment of responsibility.[8] Others not subject to the disabling effects of a particular environment (for example, colonial rule) are held to be fully responsible both legally and morally.[9]

8. Ibid., 9.
9. Minogue writes: "Environmentalism is an essential element in all suffering

Whether applied through domestic "affirmative action" programs or in dealing with third world countries, this approach has invariably aroused conservatives to furious denunciation of "double standards." Some liberals have, indeed, also rebelled against what they see as misapplication or abuse of this notion of a sliding scale in the weighing of rights and responsibilities. In the present case, critics protested that liberals were far too ready to cast all Africans as victims, as products of a "suffering situation." "Explaining" (critics claimed) all too easily and simplistically became "explaining away"—blaming all kinds of African behavior on some form of deprivation or oppression, whether perpetrated by identifiable oppressors—slave-traders, colonialists, Western businessmen, Cold Warriors, even missionaries—or (more impersonally) by "environment."

Radicalism

Before the mid-sixties, little writing about Africa appeared in self-styled socialist and radical journals in the United States. Similarly, little academic and journalistic writing about Africa showed explicit sympathy for socialist principles. From the mid-sixties onward, however, "radicalism" or a "radical" approach became an increasingly common and explicit feature of writing about Africa—especially of academic writing.

But this change did not of itself mean that the left's concern with Africa (compared, say, to its concern with East-West relations, Southeast Asia, Latin America, or domestic issues) actually increased during this period. Applying the admittedly crude test of numbers of articles and words devoted to African issues, we find in leftist journals much the same curve of rising and falling interest in the continent that is apparent in liberal and conservative (but not black) journals.

The writers and journals examined here can be described as "of the left" either because they so described themselves or because they used concepts and expressed sympathies conventionally associated with the

---

situations. Victims are be definition the products of their environment, and sometimes put to the test the purity of our rational concern by exhibiting unsavory characteristics" (ibid., 9). He also remarks that in this view "the delinquency, or even the downright nastiness, of victims is an index of their suffering." As with so many generalizations about liberalism, this one is clearly more applicable to one wing (the post–New Deal wing) than to the older, more individualistic wing, which has indeed taken a stand on rejecting just this kind of argument.

left. Often (and certainly in the sixties) such expression took a largely negative form, characteristic of a period when the rather staid noun *critique* became transformed into the highly transitive, even aggressive verb "to critique," and a whole new occupation, "critiquing," was invented.

The values and concepts preferred by the authors of such critiques were usually assumed or implicit in their polemics. Some identified themselves simply as "radicals"—a broad church that included democratic socialists (to be found, for example, in *Dissent, Studies on the Left,* and the *Nation*), populists, orthodox Marxist-Leninists (such as those contributing to *Political Affairs,* the journal of the Communist party of the USA, and *World Marxist Review*), pacifists (prominent among writers for *Liberation*), neo-Marxists, "plain Marxists" (such as Paul Baran and Paul Sweezy, the coeditors of *Monthly Review*), and world-system theorists.[10] (The latter were represented most originally by Immanuel Wallerstein, who in the late sixties developed an eclectic theory of capitalist development much more historical and global in character than the "nation-building" approach of his earlier work.)

Most of the writers in question showed both a hostility to capitalism and a preference for the collective control of the major means of production and distribution in society. They saw such control as the condition for achieving improved opportunities and living standards for working people and their families, for reducing inequalities, and for giving substance to the values of "freedom" and "democracy" proclaimed—but nowhere achieved—by liberals under capitalism.

Beyond this broad program, real and often bitter differences existed over priorities and strategy. Many of these differences appeared in arguments about how socialists should interpret and react to events in Africa—over such issues as the correct attitude to adopt toward movements for self-determination (both before and after independence), the relation between democracy and socialism in the new states, the character of class conflict in Africa, the value of pan-Africanism, and the proper role of non-African states (especially, of course, socialist or "progressive" states). There was less disagreement about other matters, such as the nature of imperialism, colonialism, neocolonialism, the value of religion and custom, and the significance of race.

10. The term *plain Marxists* is taken from Peter Clecak, *Radical Paradoxes: Dilemmas of the American Left, 1945–1970* (New York: Harper and Row, 1973).

African-Americans

Because of the history of slavery, the African-American relationship with Africa is deeper and more complex than that between any mainly white group and the continent. This is not to say that all African-Americans who have written about Africa have done so explicitly or exclusively as African-American writers, rather than as writers with some prior ideological or religious loyalty. Yet African-Americans have a sufficiently distinct history and a sufficiently distinctive set of problems that most African-American writers at some level embrace the agonizing issue of what it is to be black in a mainly white society. Often, in grasping this issue, they face the question of African heritage, asking in effect the question Countee Cullen posed to himself: "What is Africa to me?"[11]

Although active African-American interest in and communication with Africa can be traced back to at least the late eighteenth century, such interest was for a long time the preserve of a small group of intellectuals, missionaries, and professionals. Apart from organized attempts to arrange the repatriation of African-Americans to Africa (most notably that led by Marcus Garvey), distinguished African-American intellectuals such as William Leo Hansberry, Carter G. Woodson, and W. E. B. DuBois worked to increase outsiders' knowledge of African achievements and to stimulate African-American interest and pride in them. African-Americans went as missionaries to Africa (sometimes in the face of opposition from European colonial governments).[12]

Yet the general level of interest in and information about Africa among most African-Americans seems to have remained low until the advent of African nationalist movements in the late forties and fifties. A poll published in April 1957 (a month after Ghana became independent) revealed that 70 percent of African-Americans questioned "could name no coun-

11. "Heritage," in *On These I Stand* (New York: Harper and Row, 1925).
12. On Garvey, see Edmund D. Cronon, *Black Moses: The Story of Marcus Garvey and the Universal Negro Improvement Association* (Madison: University of Wisconsin Press, 1968) and Robert A. Hill, ed., *The Marcus Garvey and University Negro Improvement Association Papers*, 2 vols. (Berkeley: University of California Press, 1983). On W. E. B. DuBois, see Elliot M. Rudwick, *W. E. B. DuBois: A Study in Minority Leadership* (Philadelphia: University of Pennsylvania Press, 1960); Francis L. Broderick, *W. E. B. DuBois: Negro Leader in a Time of Crisis* (Stanford: Stanford University Press, 1959); W. E. B. DuBois, *The World and Africa: An Inquiry into the Part Which Africa Has Played in World History* (New York: Viking, 1947; repr. Millwood, N.Y.: Kraus, 1965).

tries or territory in Africa" (as compared with 55 percent of whites questioned).[13]

Ignorance was often accompanied by a superior and patronizing attitude on the part of African-Americans toward Africans. As early as 1895, John Smyth, an African-American and a former minister to Liberia, remarked: "[Negroes] are averse to the discussion of Africa, when their relationship with that ancient and mysterious land is made the subject of discourse or reflection."[14] Smyth suggested that the remoteness of Africa and the influence of disparaging white attitudes toward Africans contributed to this indifference. These factors, he concluded, "make the subject of Africa discordant and unmusical to our ears."

Smyth admitted that this situation was an embarrassment. Yet his own attitude was clearly more guarded than such admirers of African culture as DuBois and Woodson would have wished. African-American views, he commented, were "derived" from "current opinion in the minds of the Caucasians," and indeed until the 1950s the posture of some African-American writers did reflect the dismissive, condescending attitude common among whites.

The contrary view, that an African heritage was something to be cherished, enjoyed a limited audience. Moreover, those promoting it, such as DuBois, Paul Robeson, and Alphaeus Hunton, were often doubly suspect since their political affinities tended to be with the left, through such bodies as the Council on African Affairs (CAA).[15] In the era of Mc-

---

13. "Only one per cent of Negroes, contrasted with six percent of whites, could name as many as five countries, colonies, or other territories on the African continent" (Alfred O. Hero, Jr., "American Negroes and U.S. Foreign Policy: 1937–1967," *Journal of Conflict Resolution* 13, no. 2 [June 1969]: 223, 235).

14. Smyth continued: "The illiteracy, poverty, and degradation of the Negro, pure and simple, as known in Christian lands, may be of a reason in connection with *the partially true and partially false* impressions that the Negroes, or Africans, are pagan and heathen as a whole, and as a sequence hopelessly degraded beings" (quoted in Skinner, "African, Afro-American, White American," 382; emphasis added). On Smyth, see Peter Duignan and L. H. Gann, *The United States and Africa: A History* (Cambridge: Cambridge University Press and Hoover Institution, 1984), 119–20; and Edwin S. Redkey, "The Meaning of Africa to Afro-Americans, 1890–1914," in "The Meaning of Africa to Afro-Americans: A Comparative Study of Race and Racism," *Black Academy Review* 3, nos. 1 and 2 (Spring/Summer 1972): 19–20.

15. DuBois was heavily influenced by Marxism and actually joined the Communist party in 1961; Hunton and Robeson were also Marxists; and DuBois,

Carthyism, any such association was sure to alienate the centrist leadership of the NAACP and other middle-class African-American leaders.[16]

The change in attitudes toward Africa increasingly apparent in African-American journals during the 1950s was not, in fact, the result of any significant ideological or political change among African-Americans. At least to begin with, it seems to have expressed pride in the fact that Africans had achieved integration, in the sense of obtaining self-government and admission to international citizenship. This achievement provided the broadest and most enduring appeal of African nationalism to African-Americans, an achievement readily intelligible within the civil rights tradition and, indeed, within that of American liberal nationalism.

The more explicit forms of cultural nationalism—with their rejection of integrationist goals—were to come later, largely in the sixties, and originated among academics, writers, and political organizers of a younger generation. In the fifties, it was such solidly moderate periodicals as *Ebony* that publicized the emergence of new African nations and announced that it was time for African-Americans to reassess their attitudes toward Africa.

Conservatives

Because of the strength of "the liberal consensus" in American political debate on Africa and other issues until at least the mid-sixties, conser-

---

Hunton, and Robeson constituted, as one observer put it, "the staunchly anti-imperialist" wing of the CAA, which was set up by Robeson and Max Yergan (later a fervent anticommunist) in 1937. The historians Duignan and Gann claim that the CAA "subscribed to Marxism and was friendly with the American Communist Party and the Soviet Union" (*The United States and Africa*, 340).

On Hunton, Robeson, and DuBois, see Doxey A. Wilkerson, "William Alphaeus Hunton: A Life That Made a Difference," *Freedomways* 10, no. 3 (Third Quarter 1970): 257; Robert S. Browne and John Henrik Clarke, "The American Negro's Impact," *Africa Today* 14, no. 1 (December 1966): 16. On the CAA, see Hollis R. Lynch, *Black American Radicals and the Liberation of Africa: The Council on African Affairs, 1935–1955* (Ithaca, N.Y.: Cornell University, African Studies and Research Center, 1978), Monograph Series, no. 5.

16. The leaders of the Council on African Affairs did in fact have to devote much time to ensuring their political survival and defending themselves against accusations of being treasonable.

vatives claimed that they had difficulty both in establishing a distinct identity and in making their views heard.[17]

Conservatives profited, however, from the political disturbances associated with the Vietnam War and the civil rights movement. Among intellectuals, indeed, the movement toward the right seems to have begun before the wartime buildup began.[18] Unlike the parallel excursion on the left, this movement struck roots within the electorate, realizing its potential in the defeat of Jimmy Carter in 1980.

The essential question for conservatives, before and after coming to power, was how to distinguish themselves from the liberal orthodoxy. One response was to say that, while American conservatism did cherish certain ideas and values usually labeled "liberal," its identity was drawn from much broader sources—from a distinctive heritage of beliefs and attitudes that could be traced as far back as the ancient Greeks and that, indeed, constituted a disposition to be found in all Western societies.[19]

Conservatism thus, despite its label, represented not an absolute, unconditional attachment to all existing institutions, but rather a recurrent agenda of questions to be asked about change. This agenda differed in its inspiration from the liberal agenda in that it treated historical experience as an indispensable arbiter of what was practical, an essential brake to counteract the accelerator of liberalism, which, Houdini-like, saw historical experience as an encumbrance to be escaped from.

The major assumptions and convictions shaping the conservative agenda and expressing "the conservative disposition" were broadly as follows:

17. In the fifties, as George H. Nash remarks in his excellent survey of American conservative thought, "theirs was the outlook of a minority, of a movement that was self-consciously challenging many entrenched interests and powerful trends in American life" (*The Conservative Intellectual Movement in America since 1945* [New York: Basic Books, 1976], 218).

18. In 1961, Koil Rowland remarked in the radical right journal *American Mercury* that in intellectual circles, to be anything else than conservative was "fast becoming *gauche*" (no pun apparently intended) ("A Creed for Conservatives," November 1961, 39).

19. Regarding the similarities between American conservatism and American liberalism, conservatives can often be found arguing for limited government, for the protection of minorities, and for individual property rights against the state. But they can also be found arguing for the primacy of national or community interest over individual rights (including voting rights).

1. *An assumption of human imperfectibility,* both in individual behavior and in social institutions. "Human sin is a fact," and it is a standing threat to all institutions and a limit on all attempts to improve them.[20] (Liberals, on the contrary, assume an immanent potential for improvement.)
2. *A belief in order as a condition for liberty:* since sin is a reality, "the only social unit in which any very great or profound change is possible is the human heart."[21] Individuals must accept responsibility for their actions (rather than blaming them on "society"), and institutions can help them to do so by ensuring a stable, consistent pattern of rewards and penalties. (Contemporary liberals, on the other hand, emphasize the conditioning of behavior by institutions and therefore stress change in institutions as essential to improving behavior.)
3. *A belief in religion and traditions* as providing touchstones for the evaluation of behavior and as sources of inspiration to improve it. Since sin (rather than social organization) is the source of trouble, religion provides the relevant principles for improvement. Since sin is a permanent source of trouble in society, tradition represents a valuable accumulation of ideas and actions to deal with it. (Liberals envisage progress as achieved through the application of reason, which is seen as demolishing the myths, superstitions, and oppressions associated, in liberal minds, with both religion and tradition.)
4. *A belief that sentiment and emotion, rather than intellect and reason, are the main determinants of behavior and the main sources of social cohesion.*
5. *A belief in the strength and values of communities* (as distinct from the liberal emphasis on the individual). Conservatives, following Burke, value emotional richness and firmness of identity, which they see as provided for individuals by the traditions and personal interdependence characteristic of long-established communities. This disposition naturally leads to:
6. *A particular belief in the value of communities founded on ties of birth, blood, and culture.* Conservatives tend to have an inherent respect for ethnic, tribal, national, and even racial communities, for the

20. Rowland, "A Creed for Conservatives," 41.
21. Ibid.

"irrational" ties they create, and the emotional demands they make. (Liberals tend to be skeptical of the value and, indeed, the reality of such entities, regarding them as havens of superstition and obstacles to the freedom and mobility of individuals.) Respect for such communities leads to:

7. *A particular respect for nationalism and for the cultural and political diversity it expresses.* Conservatives are skeptical of attempts to impose global ideologies and institutions upon the existing variety of nation-states. Attaching greater political and emotional significance than liberals (and socialists) to the claims of nationality on individuals, conservatives also take the idea of "national interest" more seriously. Protection of national interest (and the values it represents) may involve either isolation from international affairs or aggressive intervention in them. But even intervention requires reference to national interest, whereas liberal interventionism typically rests on the premise of some supranational interest (for example, the protection of human rights).

8. *A belief in leadership and a skepticism about claims made on behalf of democracy and equality.* Holding that "the only true equality is moral equality," conservatives argue that differences of natural endowment, compounded by differences in individual effort, make attempts to enforce equality of reward and status unrealistic and harmful. They tend to be hostile to democratic processes insofar as their outcomes are determined by ethically irrelevant factors (for example, how many votes a candidate can gather) rather than by appropriate criteria which reward individual talent and merit.[22]

Within the broad conservative tradition represented by this summary, it is useful to distinguish (as George H. Nash does) three broad strands within American conservatism.[23] One group consists of the true heirs to nineteenth-century liberalism—people who are primarily concerned with

22. Conservative attitudes toward democracy fluctuate. Sometimes, as in the writings of William F. Buckley, Jr., and Erik von Kuehnelt-Leddihn (and others), conservatives clearly incline toward aristocratic or meritocratic forms of government. But (especially on the radical right) there is also a strong populist tradition, which sees a conservative democracy betrayed by a liberal, typically capitalist conspiracy.

23. See Nash, *The Conservative Intellectual Movement*, xiii.

the defense of free enterprise from state intervention. In relation to Africa and the third world, this position has most often been expounded by Elliot Berg, the British economist Peter Bauer, and Milton Friedman.

The second group (the so-called new conservatives) has been mainly concerned with the cultural impact of secularism and the phenomenon of the "mass society." In emphasizing the moral and emotional value of tradition and community, it continued the European "organic" tradition in conservatism. Led in the United States by Russell Kirk, Robert Nisbet, and Peter Viereck, this perspective has been represented in American writing on Africa and the third world by Peter Berger and the British writer Elspeth Huxley.

The third group is more directly a product of the Cold War. Led by such writers as James Burnham, Frank Meyer, and Whittaker Chambers, it has been marked by a preoccupation with the global struggle against communism. Where the first group has been mainly economic and the second cultural in focus, Burnham and his associates concentrated on the international arena, working to unmask and defeat communist expansion both in foreign countries and within the United States. Their "globalism" has corresponded (though obviously with very different ideological content) to the globalism of liberal interventionists and the "internationalism" of socialists.

In subsequent chapters, we shall examine the application of the ideas and commitments identified here to the task of understanding and evaluating African nationalism and the new states it brought about. Chapter 2 gives a brief history of the American discovery of Africa in the 1950s, with all the cultural incongruities and personal terrors that accompanied it. This chapter also describes the literary and intellectual legacy of existing writing about Africa—the preconceptions about the continent's climate, geography, and social institutions that visitors were likely to take aboard their planes. Finally, it introduces three countries—Ghana, the Congo, and Nigeria—which were to become politically and symbolically important in ensuing arguments about the problems and achievements of the new African states.

Chapters 3 through 7 examine interpretations and assessments that appeared in journals addressed to the four groups identified in the Preface. In each case, the procedure has been to select journals which in their editorial positions represent themselves as addressing and acting as a mouthpiece for the group concerned.

Such a procedure has its logical and political problems. To what extent is it reasonable to regard someone who happens to write on Ethiopia in, say, the *Progressive* as "representing" radical opinion on this issue? Is the *Progressive*, for that matter, itself either "radical" or in any demonstrable manner "representative" of radical opinion? Both kinds of question are fair, and difficult to answer unequivocally in particular instances. The first is, however, a lesser problem if we accept that most journals do have an "editorial consensus," however tacit in ordinary circumstances. The second is actually unanswerable in any absolute sense, such terms as *radical* or *conservative* being essentially ideological and inevitably contested: who is judge or jury in such cases?

Each chapter deals with a broadly common sequence of issues, referring as appropriate to the three "archetypical" countries and others. Since I am mainly concerned with the engineering of arguments, I have not applied any kind of formal content analysis to the sources used. While the occurrence of key words or terms clearly has indicative significance, the real question to me is that of conceptual assembly. How well do concepts and analogies developed in one context fare when applied in another? Where do stresses appear and how do the ideological engineers respond to such stresses? Since these questions deal with the structure of arguments and relations between them, the enumeration of specific elements, however revealing, did not seem to me to be helpful in answering them.

The order of the five central chapters was determined partly by considerations of length, partly by an ideological hierarchy apparent in the material. In this field, at least, a liberal orthodoxy has prevailed, though severely challenged and, indeed, undermined during the period in question. It seemed to me reasonable to begin with the liberal orthodoxy, and then to examine the tensions that developed within the liberal camp and the contending camps that benefited from these tensions. In addition, it seemed logical to place the conservatives last, not out of any inherent disrespect, nor to imply a more recent growth of interest in the continent, but rather because their advocacy has been most influential in recent years. Though the book does not cover developments after 1970 systematically, conservative positions were beginning to acquire a more general following in the early seventies, while those of the radicals, white and black, already had their greatest followings and were shortly to go into eclipse.

The concluding chapter asks the necessary "so what" question. What can we learn from a study of this kind about the role that ideologies play in both political argument and intercultural relations? How far does such a study help us to understand the relationship between ideologies and political culture and, indeed, the relationship between political culture and foreign policy? And—less abstractly—what, if anything, does this study suggest is peculiar about American attitudes to and relations with Africa?

TWO

"Jungle Neighborhoods"

The problems of Africa first invite, then mock,
comparisons with our own experience, whether
the problem be that of subduing the wilderness,
uplifting the backward, mingling races or proclaiming freedom.—*Life,* 4 May 1953

American responses to African nationalism offer a specially interesting case study of the intellectual-cum-editorial process
because in the late 1950s the established foreign policy sages,
as well as the American intelligentsia at large, were generally ignorant
about the continent. In horse racing terms, very few of the established
tipsters knew anything about the horses, their form, the riders, or—for
that matter—even the location and shape of the course.

When Americans tried to understand politics in the Soviet Union or
Western Europe, they usually had to hand well (if crudely) marked form
cards. They had some images of national histories and some acquired
political experience from dealing with the countries concerned, and the
major newspapers, if not the journals of opinion, had resident correspondents in their capitals.

Few such images and resources were available at independence for outsiders trying to gauge the future of African states. African independence
was, in fact, a serious challenge to the authority of sages (as the many
worried remarks about "mysterious Africa" testify). As one journalist
wrote of the Congo, "Totally unknown men, representing undisclosed
goals, leading movements with unpronounceable names, had suddenly
burst into everyone's life."[1] Many writers, required to comment in avowed
ignorance by a public and a government anxious about possible anarchy

---

1. Gonze, "Katanga Secession," 6.

19

and communist penetration in African states, cast about for precedents and analogies—for horses, races, and tracks that were more familiar and might provide clues to African form.

Much comparison with American history therefore occurred in commentary on Africa. Much of it was longer on ingenuity than on pertinence. Inevitably, many poor tips were given and many bets were lost. But a study of the process reveals exceptionally well the degree of ideological arbitrariness characteristic of commentary on foreign affairs, as well as the extreme imaginative and logical difficulties involved in practicing the empathy so generously preached by so many commentators.

American Relations with Africa, 1919–1955

American views of Africa have been shaped by the kinds of contact that earlier generations have had with the continent, as well as by the channels through which information, ideas, and impressions currently flow back to the United States.

Until the mid-fifties, such contacts and channels were very limited and largely informal. Before World War II, most of the Americans who visited sub-Saharan Africa were missionaries or merchants. Some visitors were tourists or hunters, a few were propelled by scientific interest, and a very small number were on government business.

American commercial interest in Africa had faded after the end of the West African slave trade. As American foreign trade and investment began to expand in the late nineteenth century, they were directed more toward the Pacific and Latin America than toward Europe, and the imperial partition of Africa in the eighties and nineties created serious barriers to trade between colonies and countries other than the colonial powers themselves. This situation persisted after 1919, despite pressure by the United States government for application of the "open door" principle in Africa and despite the popularity of individual American products such as Ford automobiles.[2] In the late 1930s, only 4.1 percent of American exports went to Africa and only 3.2 percent of American imports were African in origin.[3] Even this trade, and much American investment, was

2. On this period, see Edward H. McKinley's excellent study *The Lure of Africa.*
3. Calculated from figures in Emerson, *Africa and United States Policy,* 32.

heavily concentrated in three countries—South Africa, Ethiopia, and Liberia (all territories normally outside European colonial control).[4]

Official relations were similarly restricted. By 1939, there were forty U.S. consulates and other posts in Africa, and in 1937 a State Department official was, for the first time, given full-time responsibility for Africa. But American interest, again, was concentrated on Liberia, South Africa, and (to some extent) Ethiopia. In deference to the colonial powers, matters concerning other territories were usually handled "by some junior officer of the West European division."[5]

American diplomatic representatives in colonial Africa often received responsibility for huge areas. (At one point, the American consul in Lagos was threatened with having to add to his jurisdiction the Belgian Trust Territory of Ruanda-Urundi, two thousand miles away, on the far eastern border of the Congo.) American influence was slight, as was shown by the great difficulty that American representatives had in persuading British merchants to stop selling American flags to Africans for use as loincloths.[6]

World War II increased American diplomatic and strategic interest in Africa. Not only did the United States discover the strategic value of northern and western Africa, but the war exposed and aggravated the fragility of European power in Africa and elsewhere. It also enabled (or forced) many Africans to travel abroad in colonial armies, giving them a chance to experience at first hand the frailties and prejudices of Europeans. The war both created an opportunity for African nationalism and bred the hopes, disappointments, and frustrations that inspired it.

After the war, however, American interest in and relations with sub-

4. South Africa was the main source of imports and the country in which over half of American capital in Africa was invested. Such investment was mainly in mineral production. In the late thirties, the Belgian Congo began to become important as a source of uranium: the value of American mineral exports from the Belgian Congo and Ruanda-Urundi rose from $1,039,000 in 1938 to $25,495,000 in 1950 (Rudin, "The Past and Present Role of Africa in World Affairs," 36). Other figures on American trade and investment can be found in Wallerstein, "Africa, the United States, and the World Economy," 21.

5. Van Essen, "The United States Department of State and Africa," 845, 847. In 1937, responsibility for African affairs in the State Department was transferred to the Division of Near Eastern Affairs.

6. McKinley, *The Lure of Africa*, 59, 60. Accommodation was also meagre: in the thirties, the American consul in Nairobi held court in a room over a vacant auctioneer's showroom.

Saharan Africa developed fairly slowly. Diplomatically, the United States government made reinforcement of Western Europe against the Soviet Union a priority and was unwilling to challenge its allies in their colonies. Officials made few statements about colonial Africa, and such statements usually balanced recognition of "the legitimate aspirations of the African people" against insistence on the need to support "[America's] friends and allies in the world-wide contest between the Free and Communist worlds."[7]

Being regarded as "free" and "stable," African territories received relatively little aid directly from the United States, although some Marshall aid found its way to the colonies through the British, French, and Belgian exchequers. Between 1945 and 1955, African territories received only $71 million in U.S. aid (0.15 percent of total foreign aid in this period). Of this amount, $70 million went to four countries: Egypt, Libya, Liberia, and Ethiopia.[8] As late as 1956, direct financial aid to African states amounted to only $2 million—considerably less than the total financial support given by Catholic and Protestant churches in the United States to their African missions.[9]

American trade with and investment in Africa did not expand greatly or become more diversified between 1945 and 1960. By 1960, the proportion of U.S. exports going to Africa was the same as in 1930—4 percent.[10]

Even in the late sixties, only between 2.5 and 4.9 percent of American imports originated in Africa, although then and later particular countries were important as sources of minerals, including latterly oil. American investment in Africa (half of it in South Africa) represented in 1960 only

7. These phrases were used in a speech by George V. Allen, assistant secretary of state for Near Eastern, South Asian, and African affairs, in April 1956. On this occasion, Allen emphasized the need to maintain harmony with "the so-called colonial powers" (quoted in Nielsen, *The Great Powers and Africa,* 262–63).

8. In addition, only 2.12 percent of government-backed loans went to African countries, principally to South Africa and the newly created Central African Federation (comprising the territories now called Malawi, Zambia, and Zimbabwe) (Emerson, *Africa and United States Policy,* 36).

9. "Foreign Aid," *Commonweal,* 6 January 1956, 344.

10. A large proportion (61 percent) of American exports consisted of manufactured goods (mostly machinery and transportation equipment). In many countries and for many commodities, American market share was under 15 percent. See Bertolin, "U.S. Economic Interests in Africa," 30, 34; Wallerstein, "Africa and the World Economy," 21; and West and West, "Conflicting Economic Interests of Africa and the United States," 160, 243.

2.8 percent of all American private overseas investment. Roughly eight times more American money was invested in Canada than in the whole of the African continent.[11]

American academic and journalistic interest in Africa was equally limited, outside a minute group of academic specialists (including several notable African-American scholars). Until the 1950s, American images of the continent were in fact largely shaped by reports furnished by missionaries, explorers, and hunters.

Of these groups, the missionaries were numerically the largest, as well as the most permanent and dispersed.[12] But (as Edward H. McKinley has noted) the contribution of missionaries to American knowledge of Africa was less than might have been expected. Few of them actually wrote for publication, and when they did so, they usually published only in mission journals.[13] Further, the very purpose of their work led them to disregard or to treat disparagingly the values and customs they encountered.[14] While missionaries in fact wrote some well-informed and dispassionate monographs on African cultures, the natural focus of their writing was on the problems and tactics of conversion. As a result, the converts themselves usually provided the main African dramatis personae.

Scholars—and particularly anthropologists—might have been expected to provide more empathetic accounts of African societies. But money for fieldwork was limited.[15] Moreover, American anthropologists were mainly interested in North American Indian cultures and in those of South America and the Pacific.[16]

11. Ostrander and Armstrong, "U.S. Private Investment in Africa," 38; Emerson, *Africa and United States Policy*, 34.

12. In 1925, there were roughly three thousand American Protestant missionaries in sub-Saharan Africa and a substantially smaller number of Catholics (Emerson, *Africa and United States Policy*, 49). By 1939, three-quarters of all Americans living in Africa south of the Niger and west of the Great Lakes were missionaries (McKinley, *The Lure of Africa*, 173). In 1956, there were over twelve thousand American Protestant missionaries in Nigeria alone, and nearly the same number in the Belgian Congo.

13. McKinley, *The Lure of Africa*, 7.

14. As McKinley notes: "When the indigenes were described in their natural state, it was in such horrified and deprecating terms as to emphasize the need for immediate evangelization, which usually required more missionaries, more money, and another Ford" (ibid., 6).

15. Many anthropologists were in fact expected to collect animals in order to finance their dealings with human subjects.

16. Textbooks reflected these preferences, as did the synthetic works of major

Individual scholars produced occasional works on Africa, but their interest was sometimes fleeting and inspired by casual encounters.[17] In the twenties, Harvard University sponsored a major survey of colonial policies in Africa, which led to a well-known book by Raymond L. Buell, with the revealing title *The Native Problem in Africa*.[18] African material only started to find its way into American anthropology textbooks in the thirties, and the same decade saw the first serious investigations of African societies by American scholars, notably William Bascom, Jack Harris, Lorenzo D. Turner, and—above all—Melville J. Herskovits.[19]

---

scholars. Lewis H. Morgan's *Ancient Society*, for example, had only one index entry for an African people—and that one (''the Ashangoes'') was hard to identify (McKinley, *The Lure of Africa*, p. 154; Daniel F. McCall, ''American Anthropology and Africa,'' 20). McCall points out that ''not until 1959, when G. P. Murdock's *Africa* was published, did an American enter the field of African culture history.'' Harvard University began an African studies series in 1917, but ''there were so few Americans who could meet the stipulation of 'original work'. . . that most of the contributors were non-American'' (pp. 23, 25).

17. Frederick Starr's work *Congo Natives* (1912) was reportedly inspired by a display featuring Africans from the Congo basin and their crafts mounted at an exhibition commemorating the centennial of the Louisiana Purchase.

18. Under the auspices of Harvard University (where he was an instructor and assistant professor), Buell conducted extensive fieldwork in Africa in 1925–1926 on ''financial and political questions'' relative to colonialism. He subsequently worked as a lecturer and as research director of the Foreign Policy Association. In addition to twenty other works on a wide range of foreign affairs topics, Buell wrote a book entitled *Liberia: A Century of Survival* (published posthumously in 1947). His two-volume work included a number of criticisms of specific colonial practices, though (as McKinley notes) his most stringent comments were reserved for Liberia and ''he found little to criticize in the presumed necessity of prolonged white rule'' (*The Lure of Africa*, 149). In the climate of the time, however, the book was regarded as liberal and for many years it enjoyed immense authority because of the sheer detail it contained and the lack of any other equally comprehensive source on the current state of colonial administration.

19. Herskovits was rightly regarded as the father of African studies in the United States, not just because of his early entry into the field, but also because of his work as an institution builder (mainly in founding the first African studies program in the United States, at Northwestern University in 1948) and his intellectual influence.

Along with black American scholars such as Carter G. Woodson and W. E. B. DuBois, Herskovits challenged the prevailing assumption (flowing from the idea of the ''natural'' African) that complex social institutions, such as the state, encountered in Africa must have been the result of external influence. His two-volume study of the kingdom of Dahomey depicted in convincing detail the in-

"Area studies" and international studies generally gleaned many supporters as a result of World War II and the subsequent tensions of the Cold War. But Africa did not noticeably benefit.[20] As late as 1953, there was only one African studies center in the United States (that set up by Herskovits at Northwestern).[21] According to different estimates, in 1950–1951 there were only between ten and twenty African specialists in American universities.[22] As a result, when conferences on "the African revolution" began to take place, many of the speakers were European.[23]

The American press also paid little attention to Africa until the 1950s. Although there seems to have been a rising interest in the continent during the thirties, it was essentially nonpolitical in focus. An exception was Ethiopia (the only country to receive extensive coverage in, for ex-

---

digenous origins of kingship and the sophistication of the social and political systems on which it rested. On Herskovits's work, see the useful monograph by George Eaton Simpson, *Melville J. Herskovits* (New York: Columbia University Press, 1973).

20. For example, by 1951 there were twenty-nine "non-Western" programs in American universities and colleges.

21. Herskovits, a skillful grantsman, had established his own program in 1948. McCall notes the "population explosion" in American anthropology stimulated by the wartime involvement of American forces in Asia, but remarks that none of this had affected texts when he was a student: "We read a good deal more by British and European anthropologists on Africa than we did works by Americans. Americans had gone to Africa as professional anthropologists about as early in this century as British or continental Europeans, but they had not gone, till then, in sufficient numbers, or stayed long enough, or given enough of their total interests to the ethnography and ethnology of the continent" ("American Anthropology and Africa," 27).

For some interesting comments on the relationship between anthropology and government after World War II, see Pye, "Culture and Political Science," 65.

22. Dressel, "The Development of African Studies in the United States," 66–67.

23. Curtin, "African Studies," 358. In one symposium (C. Grove Haines's *Africa Today*), at least twelve of the thirty-nine contributors and discussants were non-Americans (and of the Americans, three had formal connections with missionary organizations). In the other (Calvin W. Stillman's *Africa in the Modern World*), five of the sixteen contributors were foreign. Curtin points out that even in 1969, 80 percent of those of full professor rank teaching African history in the United States had been recruited from abroad: similar proportions could be found among those teaching African literature, languages, and linguistics (Curtin, "African Studies," 362). The dominance of foreigners among the journalists reporting on Africa for American newspapers was even more striking.

ample, *Time* magazine) because of the Italian invasion. In this case, criticism of Italian imperialism was sometimes mixed with general praise for colonialism ("proud obscenity and ignorant insanitation" were, *Time* commented, "on the wane wherever whites [had] colonized").[24]

On the eve of independence, the American press was as little prepared to deal with African politics as were American diplomats and academics. In 1955, only three American correspondents were based in Africa—one for *Time-Life*, one for the *New York Times*, and one for the *Christian Science Monitor*.[25] The *Monitor*'s man was, however, an Englishman (John Hughes) —another example of dependence on non-Americans apparent also in academic African studies.[26]

Making Contact

Institutions

By 1955, it was clear that a number of African territories were moving toward self-government and ultimately independence. The independence of Ghana on 6 March 1957 epitomized this movement. By this time governments, scholars, and the media were becoming interested in, and sometimes alarmed about, the arrival of a large number of sovereign African states in international politics.

Official interest in Africa, spurred by concern about possible Soviet influence in the new states, grew substantially in the late fifties (though not quickly enough for some critics). The number of speeches and statements on African issues by State Department officials went up from eight

24. *Time*, 28 October 1935, 14 (quoted in Roberts, "The Changed Images of Africa in Some Selected American Media from 1930 to 1969," 170).

25. Payne, "American Press Coverage of Africa," 47–48. The *Times* had started sending correspondents to Africa after World War II. In the sixties, it usually had at least two correspondents in Africa, one based in Nairobi, the other in Lagos or Accra: by 1972 it had four full-time correspondents in Africa and nine stringers. The *Monitor* began regular coverage in 1955, though it had used stringers in Africa as far back as the twenties.

26. Although by 1964 the body of correspondents representing the American media in Africa had grown to fifty-nine, only twenty were actually native Americans. The majority were, like Hughes, British by origin (Payne, "American Press Coverage of Africa," 46, citing survey by John Wilhelm of the McGraw-Hill News Service).

Africa (July 1970)

TUNISIA (1956)

Algiers

Tunis

Rabat

MOROCCO (1956)

Tripoli

Cairo

SPANISH SAHARA

ALGERIA (1962)

LIBYA (1951)

UNITED ARAB REPUBLIC (EGYPT)

El Aoun

MAURITANIA (1960)

MALI (1960)

NIGER (1960)

Khartoum

FRENCH TERRITORY OF AFARS AND ISSAS

SENEGAL

Nouakchott

CHAD (1960)

SUDAN (1956)

Djibouti

GAMBIA (1960)

UPPER VOLTA (1960)

Niamey

GUINEA (1958)

Dakar

Bamako

Ouagadougou

PORTUGUESE GUINEA

Bissau

Conakry

GHANA (1957)

NIGERIA (1960)

Fort Lamy

Addis Ababa

Freetown

Monrovia

Abidjan

Accra

Porto Novo

Lagos

CENTRAL AFRICAN REPUBLIC (1960)

ETHIOPIA

SIERRA LEONE (1961)

LIBERIA (1847)

IVORY COAST (1960)

TOGO (1960)

DAHOMEY (1960)

CAMEROON (1960)

Bangui

UGANDA (1962)

SOMALIA (1960)

Bata

Yaounde

Kampala

KENYA (1963)

Mogadiscio

EQUATORIAL GUINEA (1968)

GABON (1960)

DEMOCRATIC REPUBLIC OF THE CONGO (1960)

RWANDA (1962)

Nairobi

Libreville

Brazzaville

Kigali

BURUNDI (1962)

REPUBLIC OF CONGO (1960)

Kinshasa

Bujumbura

TANZANIA (1961)

Dar es Salaam

Luanda

MALAWI (1964)

ANGOLA

ZAMBIA (1964)

MOZAMBIQUE

Zomba

Lusaka

Salisbury

Tananarive

SOUTH WEST AFRICA

RHODESIA

Windhoek

BOTSWANA (1966)

MALAGASY REPUBLIC (1960)

Gaborone

Lourenço Marques

Pretoria

Mbabane

Dependent territories shaded

● = Capital

Dates of independence in parentheses

Maseru

SWAZILAND (1968)

SOUTH AFRICA (1910)

LESOTHO (1966)

in 1955 to 152 in 1961: their content showed an ever greater anxiety to win the favor of African states.[27] Aid levels rose sharply. Compared with a total (in loans and grants) for the four years 1953–1957 of only $120.3 million, the allocations for 1958, 1959, and 1960 were $100 million, $159 million, and $211 million, respectively.[28] The percentage of American aid going to Africa rose from roughly 1.6 percent in FY 1957 to a peak of 10.1 percent in FY 1962.

The expansion of American diplomatic representation necessarily kept pace with the granting of formal independence to African states. It started from a low level: in 1956, the State Department had only 100 employees in post in the whole of Africa, and by late 1957 the total number of Foreign Service officers in African embassies and consulates was still (at 248) smaller than the number in West Germany (256).[29] In 1956, a semi-autonomous Office of African Affairs was set up in the State Department, and in 1958 the first assistant secretary for African affairs was appointed. By the summer of 1960, the United States had eight embassies and twenty-five consulates-general in Africa (in the same year, seventeen African countries became independent).

Critics (particularly Democratic critics) nevertheless argued that the United States had been sluggish and unimaginative in responding to African independence. They were particularly upset by the (French-inspired) delay in setting up an embassy in Guinea (which broke with the French Community in September 1958). The *New Republic* painted an alarming picture of Soviet encroachment in Conakry, even after an American mission had been established there: "Our diplomatic mission . . . consists of a middle-grade *chargé d'affaires,* who keeps his office in a small rear room of the Texaco Company's headquarters. He rooms at the *Hôtel de France,* yet manages to isolate himself from most of the goings-on in the lobby."[30] The Hôtel de France, readers were given to understand, was Conakry's equivalent of Shepheard's Hotel in Cairo—a crossroads for world travelers, among them the entrepreneurial opportunists, spies, and

27. Figures from Roberts, "The Changed Images of Africa," 115–22.

28. Figures drawn from Emerson, *Africa and United States Policy,* 26, 37; Nielsen, *The Great Powers and Africa,* 279; *Africa Report,* 29 March 1957, 14. By 1959, over seven hundred American personnel were working on aid projects related to Africa (compared with 179 in 1953).

29. Vernon McKay, cited in Emerson, *Africa and United States Policy,* 25.

30. "Guinea—Balance Wheel in West Africa?" *New Republic,* 15 June 1959, 9.

intriguers who nightly thronged the lobby, while upstairs their nation's representative lurked timidly under his mosquito net reading the *New Yorker* or the *Washington Post*.

No such timidity plagued the academic community. For academics (particularly social scientists), the appeal of Africa was that it offered an opportunity to expand the range of material upon which they could draw to investigate broad questions of social and political development and to test theories. Between 1953 and 1961, ten new African studies programs and centers were established: by 1967, there were approximately forty such programs in the country.[31]

The federal government underwrote expansion of the main African studies centers with funds provided under the National Defense Education Act.[32] The largest foundations were, however, very important as supporters of the development of African studies. By far the largest donor was the Ford Foundation, which gave approximately twenty million dollars in support of African studies between 1954 and 1974. This aid included both direct institutional support (notably in the early years to Northwestern, Boston University, and Harvard University) and the award of Foreign Area Fellowships, mainly to younger scholars. The Foreign Area Fellowships program was crucial to the intellectual development of African studies not just because of its size, but also because it allowed stu-

---

31. Carter, "African Studies in the United States," 96. By 1967, there were, by one conservative estimate, 260 faculty specializing in Africa in American universities and colleges and over 1,000 graduate students involved in African studies and research. Philip Curtin suggests that by 1970 the number of African specialists in the United States had reached 1,800 ("African Studies," 358). By 1970, the total number of African studies programs (not all of them attached to centers) had risen to 78.

32. The federal government invested some $76 million in roughly four hundred research and training projects concerned with Africa between 1949 and 1964 (Lystad, "African Studies in the United States," 50). This funding was particularly helpful to expansion in the teaching of African languages. In 1961, teaching in only three languages was available. Between 1961 and 1966, the number of student semester-hours provided in African language teaching rose from 322 to 2,780, and the number of languages went up to at least eighteen (Dressel, "Development of African Studies in the United States," 69; Stevick, "The Teaching of African Languages in the United States," 17). Stevick gives the number of languages taught as nine in 1961–1962 and either eighteen (p. 17) or 28 (p. 18) in 1965–1966: see also Joseph Axelrod and Donald N. Bigelow, *Inventory of NDEA Title IV and Title VI Language and Area Centers* (Washington, D.C.: American Council on Education, July 1961).

dents to spend a year or more in fieldwork. Indeed, an entire generation of specialists owed their start in the field or their professional development to this program. Between 1954 and 1976, roughly 350 Foreign Area Fellowships were awarded for study in Africa.[33] Apart from Ford, a major donor was the Carnegie Corporation, which provided some grants for visits to Africa after 1945. Its contribution was central to the establishment of the Northwestern African Studies Center in 1948.

For the foundations, their advisers, and some politicians, Africa represented a significant new battleground in the Cold War. Officials of the Ford Foundation, for example, stressed that American scholarship should contribute to sound policy-making in a period of increased American involvement in world affairs and intense competition between the superpowers. Rowan Gaithier, president of the Ford Foundation, declared in 1954: "Any program directed toward human welfare in this period of history must be concerned with the increased involvement of our country in world affairs, with our new responsibilities of international leadership, and, above all, with the deadly threat to any hope of human progress posed by wars and communism. More knowledge about foreign areas available to and shared by more people, is essential for the successful response of a democracy to the problems of avoiding war and promoting peace."[34]

33. On the history of the Foreign Area Fellowship program, see Sutton and Smock, "The Ford Foundation and African Studies," 69; and "Training and Career Opportunities for the American Specialist on Africa," *African Studies Bulletin* 2, no. 4 (December 1959): 21–22, statement by Melvin Fox of the Ford Foundation.

34. Quoted in Sutton and Smock, "The Ford Foundation and African Studies," 68. For another example of a foundation representative stressing the relationship between area studies and "effective international policies," see Melvin Fox's contribution in "Training and Career Opportunities for the American Specialist on Africa," 21. In 1959, the idea of a "national policy" for African studies was mooted by a representative of the Carnegie Corporation, and in September 1958 a group of Africanists themselves proposed the establishment of "at least one national center of African studies," which would concentrate on the social sciences and stress "an interdisciplinary approach to contemporary problems" (ibid., 24, statement by Alan Pifer; Drake, "African Studies Association Meets," 2).

Similar reasoning was used by politicians and their advisers. Thus in 1955 Chester Bowles, an associate of John F. Kennedy, supported a call for new African studies programs by pointing out that the Soviet Union had recently set up "a major center" in Tashkent (Bowles, "Africa," 44).

Specialist associations, conferences, and journals concerned with Africa multiplied from the mid-fifties on.[35] The main academic body—the African Studies Association—was founded in March 1957, its stated functions being "to facilitate communication among scholars interested in Africa and to stimulate research on Africa by specialists in various scientific disciplines and the humanities."[36] By 1959, the ASA had a total membership of 597, which by 1966 had reached 1,400.[37] The ASA began to issue an *African Studies Bulletin* in April 1958 and later started publishing the *African Studies Review*.

Other periodicals also began life at this time. In 1953, the American Committee on Africa launched *Africa Today,* a periodical with a circulation of around three thousand that contained specialist articles and reflected the ACOA's aims ("to keep the conscience of Americans alive to the issues at stake in Africa" and "to gain sympathetic support for the aims of self-government and equality"). In 1956, the Institute of African-American Relations, Inc. (later the African-American Institute), began publishing *Africa Special Report,* which bloomed into the glossy photomagazine *Africa Report.*[38]

Coverage of Africa in the nonspecialist media also increased substantially in the late fifties.[39] According to one study, the number of column

35. At least four special conferences were held between 1954 and 1956 to review developments in Africa.

36. Even in 1957, the numbers involved were tiny: only twenty people had responded to an earlier proposal for an "African institute," and only thirty-five attended the two-day founding meeting of the ASA in New York (Cowan, "Ten Years of African Studies," 1). According to a report in *Science,* "The continually increasing importance of Africa in world affairs, and the attraction of an ever-growing number of specialists to African research, convinced those attending the conference that a clearing house was needed for the cross-dissemination of information on Africa" ("African Studies Association," 998). Melville Herskovits was elected as the first president of the association. In 1958, the association held its first full conference and elected an entire slate of officers and directors, headed by Gwendolen M. Carter of Smith College.

37. Over 250 participants attended the ASA's annual conference in 1959. The association's membership peaked at 2,062 in 1968.

38. By 1971, *Africa Report* had a circulation of twelve thousand, but it fell sharply thereafter. In the early sixties, several more strictly academic journals appeared, notably the *Journal of African History* and the *Journal of Modern African Studies* (1963), both published in Great Britain but representing important outlets for the work of American scholars.

39. For more than seventeen hundred dailies, the main source of news on

inches devoted to Africa in the *New York Times* rose from 232 in 1950 to 1,038 in 1959, and on to 3,608 in 1961.[40] The amount of news printed varied greatly from one newspaper to another. In a sample of coverage from 1965–1966, William A. Payne found that only the *New York Times* printed some African stories every day (an average of five items), while the *Washington Post* carried an average of 3.4 items, and the *Christian Science Monitor* 2.37 items.[41] Overall, reporting tended to concentrate on a small number of countries, led by the Congo (Zaire), South Africa, Rhodesia, and Nigeria.

Individuals

Statistics on personnel, grants, and column inches convey no sense of the experiences and impressions of individuals sent—or drawn—to Africa for the first time. Because of the strangeness and fearsome reputation of the continent, many such visitors prepared for their trips to what *Time* once called the world's "jungle neighborhoods" with an apprehension that often seemed in retrospect exaggerated or even ludicrous. A *New Yorker* correspondent, for example, recalled stopping off in London en route to Ghana in 1957 to buy a pair of mosquito boots, which he assumed would be necessary to traverse downtown Accra: "I put them on only once, in the privacy of a hotel bedroom, and noted that when they were worn with khaki drill shorts they made me look like some grotesque Balkan

---

Africa was still the wire services, AP and UPI. The former had by 1973 six or more full-time correspondents in Africa, the latter five. Agence France Presse at the same time had twenty-four full-time correspondents and Reuters twenty-two (Payne, "American Press Coverage," 48; Segal, "Africa and the United States Media," 49). For an examination of the work of the two European agencies, see Bishop, "How Reuters and A.F.P. Coverage of Independent Africa Compares."

40. Roberts, "The Changed Images of Africa," 139–46. The number of editorial column inches on African issues went up from zero in 1955 to 22 in 1959 and 50 in 1961. *Time*'s coverage went up even more dramatically, from 70 inches in 1950 to 748 inches in 1961 (ibid., 125–36). Between 1955 and 1976, both *Time* and *Newsweek* usually had two full-time correspondents in Africa, based mainly in Nairobi (Segal, "Africa and the United States Media," 49).

41. The *Post* had its own Africa correspondent by 1965: in the period surveyed, African news provided between one and 15 percent of all foreign news covered. The *Monitor* actually exceeded the *Post* in terms of column inches and carried longer features (Payne, "American Press Coverage," 47, 48). With its own correspondent from 1965 on, the *Los Angeles Times* also provided substantial African coverage, with an average of one column of African news in each issue.

dancer. After that I packed them away."[42] Marguerite Cartwright, a college teacher who visited Africa often in the late fifties, confessed to getting a tetanus shot (to add to the ten obtained before her first trip to Asia) before a trip to West Africa ("chance of accident or forced landing in out-of-the-way spots").[43]

Newspaper editors sometimes expressed their own view of the continent by selecting reporters with a taste for the exotic or deviant. During the Stanleyville episode in the Congo in 1964, for example, *Time* noted that its "front-line men" there included an Oxford graduate who had stayed in Africa because (in his own words) "I am interested in abnormal psychology."[44]

The visitors' apprehension and unfamiliarity meant that first impressions, typically received at airports or hotels, were not only vivid, but were quickly loaded with immense significance and portentous symbolism. Visiting Nigeria during civil war, Lloyd Garrison of the *New York Times* noted how forcefully the continent attacked all the senses:

> As with the opening of a furnace door, the first thing that strikes you when you step from your plane in West Africa is the initial blast of hot, humid air. All senses are alerted to the change. The night seems darker but more alive with earth sounds—the chorus of crickets, the humming of the moths, the whine of the mosquito. The earth itself smells different; a dank, spongy perfume wells up, evoking an impression of something timeless and primeval, like Rousseau's dreamy, moonlit African landscapes in which the lion, not man, is the only innocent in the forest.[45]

42. Norman Lewis, "A Highlife or Two in Ghana," 134.
43. "African Odyssey: Ghana," 176. Such preparation did not save her and others from surprise and embarrassment. Cartwright, who liked to boast of her closeness to several West African leaders, described in great detail the hospitality offered her at the inauguration of Nnamdi Azikiwe as governor-general of Nigeria in 1960 ("Dinner at Maxim's as guest of industrialist Bank-Anthony followed the private reception at the home of Mrs. Aduke Moore"). But disaster befell her at the state luncheon. It started well enough ("The superb menu began with Dry Pale Amontillado sherry, Chateau Climens 1950, and iced double consomme"). But then "a waiter dropped a red cherry tart on my chair during one of the toasts, and I, resplendent in white, sat in the middle of it, and it was, alas, necessary for me to back out of the door even before Their Excellencies."
44. "A Letter from the Publisher," 4 December 1964, 3.
45. "Biafra vs. Nigeria," 38–39.

Most reactions were more prosaic, and more irritable. Incidents while eating and experiences at airports in fact provided a large amount of supporting evidence for many reporters' hastily formed judgments about Africa. For some, hotel service became a preoccupation. David Reed, reporting for *U.S. News and World Report*, suffered serious indignities in Khartoum before moving on to the Congo, for all journalists a major center of culinary outrage and uncivil service.[46] And this was before independence. After 1960, life became increasingly grim, especially, it seemed, for correspondents of *U.S. News and World Report*.[47] As Peter Ritner (a South African) remarked, the effects of such experiences could be detected in "the superciliousness that [marred] the reports of many American journalists who [had] been rebuffed once too often at some wretched African border-station by an opera-bouffish customs clerk."[48]

Some Americans, however, arrived in too much of a hurry to notice their surroundings or to take offence at their reception. One such was the Foreign Service officer designated to open relations with the Republic of Mali in August 1960, who presented his credentials and set up an embassy within twelve hours of arrival.[49] His colleague in the neighboring

46. "I've been complaining to the hotel management for a week [Reed wrote] that the air conditioning in my room is no good. But the people just throw up their hands in despair. Seems as though the job of repairing air conditioners has been Africanized" ("A Different Kind of Report on Africa," 96).

Of Khartoum, Reed wrote: "Sometimes . . . it is impossible to get the hotel servants to be even civil, let alone offer anything like ordinary service. In the dining room, you're at their mercy. They just seem to bring anything that happens to be handy—say, a meat course first, followed by soup, then dessert. If you complain you get little more than a frosty stare."

47. Reed's colleague Albert Meyers illustrated the "rock bottom" state of the Congolese economy in 1966 by pointing to the inflated cost of eating out: "You can easily pay up to $14 for a meal which more often than not is served by a Congolese waiter who is wearing a dirty uniform and has his thumb in the soup" ("The Congo after 6 Years and a Billion in Aid," 65).

48. "Many Pictures but No Patterns," 14.

49. As U.S. consul-designate to Bamako, Mali, this official who was vacationing in Switzerland, abandoned his holiday on hearing of the break-up of the Mali Federation, rushed to Geneva, and was told to fly immediately to West Africa to open diplomatic relations with the new Republic of Mali. He "stopped at the United States embassy in Paris and picked up two American flags, a typewriter, government stationery, and code equipment." Reaching Bamako at seven in the morning, the consul secured two rooms at a hotel, a car, and a flagpole. After some adventures with the Malian posts and telegraphs department, he visited the

republic of Upper Volta (now Burkina Faso) began his ambassadorial career making do "with an unused cot and a mosquito net in the local customs office" and subsequently had to sleep every Sunday night "in a former chicken house on the [Central Hotel] grounds which had been redecorated in pink and green."[50]

Nor were all reporters' experiences bad. Some journalists received breathtaking hospitality, which was all the more unexpected when they disliked the government concerned. One such experience was that of Edwin Newman who, on a visit to Guinea in 1958, asked the newly installed president some critical questions about the country's pretensions to independence and sovereignty. Sekou Toure replied that he was trying to cut costs, by, for example, maintaining a small army. Toure then offered to make Newman a general—a gesture Newman apparently refused. On his return to the United States, Newman reported, rather ungraciously, that Guinea was "the sort of country that the word 'backward' might have been invented to describe."[51]

Images of Africa

Newcomers to Africa from the United States were certain to carry with them some preconceptions about the continent as a whole. They, in turn, added to the preconceptions of those at home by reports which attempted to convey a sense of the physical character of Africa and which usually offered some generalizations about "the African" and African society.

Among the sources of established American views, none could match— for better or for worse—the twenty-six novels and sixteen films springing from the imagination of Edgar Rice Burroughs. They featured a child of the English aristocracy who escaped the rigors of the British public school system only through the good fortune of getting himself abandoned in the jungle as a baby. Ray Bradbury was perhaps exaggerating when he

---

chief of protocol in the afternoon, and met some American missionaries and businessmen. "By sundown, the consulate was in business. That night, and for two months thereafter, [the consul] took his code equipment to bed with him to safeguard it" (G. Mennen Williams, "Diplomatic Rapport between Africa and the United States," 58).

50. The hotel required him to vacate the room every Sunday to make room for a regular customer (ibid.).

51. "Independent Guinea's Morning After," 24.

said, "I don't know what would have happened to the world if Edgar Rice Burroughs had never been born," but the town in which he was speaking—Tarzana, California—would certainly not have existed.[52]

Burroughs neither visited Africa, nor expressed any wish to do so. (This was perhaps just as well, given the rather limited amenities depicted in his works.) But the influence of the Tarzan opus can be gauged by the fact that by 1970 some thirty million copies of the books and ten million Tarzan comic books had been sold.[53] The success of the Tarzan epic made it a target for angry criticism by African nationalists and intellectuals, who claimed that it gave a degrading view of African society, confirming colonial stereotypes of the superiority of whites and the inferiority of blacks.[54] Philip Quigg has pointed out that such criticism is misconceived, since in the Burroughs oeuvre, "Europeans in Africa were invariably evil and out to exploit Africans in the most devious and criminal ways; Africans were innocent and good; and Americans, who were also innocent and good . . . would save the Africans from the ruthless Europeans." Tarzan, despite his English antecedents (and his eventual marriage to a white hunter's daughter), thus begins to emerge as the archetypically outraged American anticolonialist. Moreover (Quigg noted), it was not the Africans, but Tarzan himself who, cutting short a potentially promising career in the colonial service, preferred to spend his time swinging and whooping through the trees.[55]

The Tarzan opus and much journalistic and academic writing—both before and after 1955—contained some strikingly similar assumptions about Africa as an environment for social and political organization. The vast size and emptiness of the continent were its most widely noted physical characteristics. Typically, writers fell back on American geography to convey its size ("three times the size of all fifty of the United States")

52. Opubor and Ogunbi, "Ooga Booga," 344.

53. Figures given in Roberts, "Changed Images," 9. As early as 1929, a New Orleans newspaper commented on the popularity of Tarzan, suggesting that he could probably win as many votes as Herbert Hoover (McKinley, *The Lure of Africa*, 68).

54. See, for example, the comments of Opubor and Ogunubi: "There's no doubt about the fact that Tarzan films were employed to legitimize ideas about the 'superior' race, and the implied notions of the civilizing mission. . . . In the kingdom of Tarzan, the black man is always stupid, and his society in confusion. If he is cast as intelligent, he uses his brains for mischief making" ("Ooga Booga," 350).

55. "The Changing American View of Africa," 8.

and the scale of its natural features.[56] Countries were almost invariably introduced as physical analogs of American states: Ghana was usually "the size of Oregon," while Nigeria was "almost as big as Texas and New Mexico combined."[57]

Viewed from the air (the usual first encounter in the fifties), Africa seemed huge and monotonous.[58] It was also empty ("You can fly for hours over Africa without seeing any evidence of human life. The land looks untouched, primeval"). But such imagery was at least based on direct personal experience and it allowed for more variety than the stereotypes inherited from the age of explorers. These stereotypes had established a physical image of Africa as a continent covered by jungle. Previously, it had been assumed to be mainly desert (desert, according to one writer, infested by a kind of boa constrictor which could move "with such incredible swiftness that no animal can escape from it").[59] After H. M. Stanley's trip to Africa, the continent officially became jungle, and the boa constrictors were moved to South America.

Its image, however, remained primarily a physical one. To Americans and other outsiders, "Africa was more a land of animals and scenery than a land of people."[60] The physical character of the continent, moreover, was invoked both as a metaphor for the human condition in Africa and as a determinant of African manners and morals. This was, travelers often reported, a world in which nature not only was beyond man's control but indeed was still controlling man.

56. Mildred Adams wrote in the *New York Times*: "The Sahara makes our 'great American desert' look like a child's sand box, the Congo jungle dwarfs Louisiana's thickest bayou" ("Key Pieces in the African Puzzle," 18).

57. Oakes, "Africa—A Continent Afire," 16.

58. As Stewart Alsop noted: "After many hours the seemingly endless rain forest may give way to drier bush country, and then, perhaps hours later, to open savanna land" ("Africa: The Riddle without an Answer," 82).

59. Paul Rosenblum, "Boa Constrictor in the Desert," 5. The desert, Rosenblum points out, was seen as a barrier against invasions by uncivilized Africans. A parochial school textbook published in 1902 said that the Sahara had been "a benefit to man as a barrier, or protection, from enemies." The savages from the "black" continent "were kept in check by the Sahara Desert, which for centuries seemed to stand guard on the southern line of civilization."

60. McKinley, *The Lure of Africa*, 6: "Scenery, animals, the bustle of African cars, the vagaries of colonial social life—these were what interested most American travelers, and, consequently, their readers—not the indigenous population and its problems."

Such emphasis on the power of the physical environment created an intimidating, even mystical idea of the continent as a place possessed by forces beyond the mastery and even the understanding of human beings. Seen from thirty thousand feet, the Sahara's surface was "fearful," the succeeding rain forest "a dense and solid mat of uninviting green." After sunset, such impressions could be even stronger, the land below taking on a deeper silence, becoming even more inscrutable: "Three minutes after we lifted at midnight from the Nairobi airport to fly north," reported James Burnham, "though the night was clear there was darkness below— unbroken for hundreds of miles."[61]

To American conservatives, and some liberals, the darkness and emptiness were psychological as well as physical. The vast and implacable terrain, the hostile fauna, the pitiless climate, all imposed themselves on man, mocked his powers, and ridiculed his achievements: "Add the live volcanoes in the eastern highlands," Mildred Adams declared, "the Great Rift Valley more than a thousand feet deep, the fevers, the insects, and the animals, and one begins to understand why humans have moved so gingerly about this continent and done so little with it that has endured.[62] In the face of this environment, civilization was bound to exist on sufferance and for the most part man was still, in Burnham's words, "part of the landscape."[63] Even writers in liberal journals were impressed by the menace of aggressive, encircling natural forces, symbolized by the jungle. As Milton Bracker put it in the *New York Times Magazine*: "The jungle—In the Congo, it is never more than minutes away; and the feeling is everywhere that, given a chance, vegetation often too thick for the sun to penetrate would soon entwine and bury the glittering but transient islands of urbanization."[64]

Where the grip of human reason was so tenuous, the visitor could meet up with much that was mysterious and, in European terms, inexplicable. Here, Robert Coughlan warned his readers, "strange concepts [would] be encountered, and complications sinuous as the jungle creepers, and fan-

---

61. "The View from the Outside," 128.
62. "Key Pieces in the African Puzzle," 18.
63. "A short distance from the intermittent towns the earth-colored, foundation-less native huts, the straggly patches of maize and banana trees, the few scrawny goats and cows, the native Africans themselves are swallowed up by the landscape" ("View from the Outside," 128).
64. "The Congo Is Like This," 16.

tastic unpronounceable names."[65] The jungle, indeed, was everywhere, adding to the impenetrable mystery of Africa. "A long drive on a jungle road," reported Stewart Alsop, "is a curious experience. There is never a view—only the road ahead, and the jungle high on either side, a furiously competing tangle of shrubs, and vines and trees. . . . After a while, you begin to feel that behind that jungle wall are things you don't understand and never will."[66]

Even liberals, less susceptible than conservatives to romance and mystery, found Africa intellectually daunting. Along with a guilty sense of being ignorant about Africa, liberal writers suffered a kind of intellectual despair over the impossibility of summarizing current developments in Africa. "At moments," wrote Mildred Adams in the *New York Times Magazine*, "in the villages or on the long dirt roads, the only dependable constants seem to be that Africa's peoples are mostly dark-skinned and have problems."[67] Other visitors came back, like Congresswoman Frances P. Bolton, overwhelmed by the contrasts they found in Africa:

Africa is so vital, so personal and yet so impersonal. There are moments when one says "she" unhesitatingly, so great is the sense of maternity, of the creative, passive, waiting forces that seem to surround one, that seem to well up out of the earth one walks on. And then again Africa is all male—aggressive, powerful, ruthless, invincible. Above all else Africa is a land of extremes, of such beauty by day and night that one stands breathless before it; of such ruthless cruelty that only the bravest can support it. . . . It is as if a great giant stirred for the first time in many centuries, stretching himself, opening his gentle eyes upon an unknown and very disturbing world.[68]

65. "Black Africa Surges to Independence," 102. Africa, declared Coughlan in 1959, was even now the continent "of apes and ivory . . . of Stanley and Livingstone, of crocodile and lion, and of 125 million people still living in or at the edge of savagery" (ibid., 101).

66. Alsop, "Africa: The Riddle without an Answer," 84.

67. "Key Pieces in the African Puzzle," 18. John B. Oakes remarked in a similar vein: "In a half-continent so vast as sub-Saharan Africa, generalizations are even more dangerous than usual" ("Africa's 'Ordeal of Independence,'" 7).

68. Speech to the Ninth Annual Foreign Policy Conference, Colgate University, quoted in *Africa Special Report* 2, no. 7 (30 July 1957): 3. Congresswoman Bolton had spent four months on a tour of twenty-four African countries on behalf of the House subcommittee on the Near East and Africa. At the conclusion of her trip, she submitted a 151-page report. Another veteran member of Congress, Sen.

Africa's problems were usually attributed by liberals and conservatives alike to the environment. Specific behavioral traits were explained by reference to physical and climatic conditions. Even Colin Legum, an exceptionally knowledgeable African correspondent, sometimes resorted, at least in his early days, to such explanation: "Africa is a naturally suspicious continent: in the past every man has felt his neighbor's hand to be threateningly against him; the forests make for suspicion; the slave trade has seared the unconscious mind; the part played by the imperialist powers has inevitably caused Africans to view all change as being motivated by selfish interests; the security of tribal society and the power of familiar magic have been weakened or destroyed."[69]

The climate was often regarded as a major factor explaining African mores. Many observers concluded that the climate in fact directly affected African attitudes and habits.[70] Noting the "inefficiency and jolly indolence" of Africans, one visitor remarked: "Old Africa hands swear that after some time in the tropical heat and humidity, the brain stops working sensibly."[71] As independence drew near, several outsiders warned of the threat that the African climate represented to the works of civilization. Stuart Cloete wrote: "The climate is a factor that can never be forgotten in tropical Africa. A palm oil plantation must be cleared every nine months if the palms are to survive. In less than a year well-built houses are overwhelmed if abandoned, crushed in the arms of lianas. Mold grows

Theodore Francis Green, Democrat of Rhode Island, conducted a similar, if shorter, odyssey in 1956, visiting thirteen countries in six weeks and celebrating his eighty-ninth birthday in Leopoldville (Kinshasa). Green was less effusive than Bolton, remarking on his return that he had found Africans "largely illiterate but very intelligent" (quoted in John McStallworth, "News Briefs," *Africa Special Report* 1, no. 7 [19 November 1956]: n.p.).

69. "The Future of Africa, II," 14. Insularity, remarked another writer, was a direct product of Africa's remoteness from the major currents of world history and of Africans' remoteness from each other: "Thus isolated by their surroundings and their history, this island of men survived in small groups jealous of their own ways and understandably suspicious of others" (Adams, "Key Pieces in the African Puzzle," 18). Stuart Cloete remarked likewise that "the love of a neighbor, if he came from a different tribe, [was] an emotional impossibility to the African in the bush" ("End of Era with Threat of the Jungle Taking Over," 14).

70. In 1933, for instance, the Berkeley political scientist Raymond Gettell asserted that "[a] tropical climate tends to relax the mental and moral fibre, induces indolence, self-indulgence, and various excesses which lower the physical tone of the population" (cited in McKinley, *The Lure of Africa*, p. 168).

71. Alsop, "Africa," 83.

on shoes overnight. Only unremitting supervision can arrest these elemental forces, can hold them back in the endless war against the terrible fecundity of the forest."[72]

The alleged abundance of nature was also said to be a cause of African "indolence."[73] The idea of the jungle-as-supermarket endured down to the 1960s, defying evidence of malnutrition and hunger, and surviving the growth of cities and industries, to reappear, incongruously, in an apologia for the Nkrumah government in Ghana written by an African-American writer in 1966. Thus, Shirley Graham, the wife of W. E. B. DuBois, declared, in contradicting those who accused the regime of causing starvation among its citizens: "There is too much food growing wild by the roadsides! Prices were high, but actual food shortages existed in the imported items considered essential only by Europeans."[74]

While this remark showed extraordinary ignorance of Ghanaian diets (and Ghanaian roadsides), it exemplified the rosier view of Africa to be found in some African-American writing. Of all the continents, it was (declared a writer in *Freedomways*) "the most generously endowed by nature and [possessed of] the greatest potential for providing an abundant life for its people." Africa was "bathed in the life-giving energy of the sunlight and a climate generally more conducive to human health and comfort than that of any other continent; abundant in rivers and lakes . . . endowed with millions of miles of tropical and sub-tropical highlands. [It was] a continent less frequented by hurricanes and other natural disasters than any other; a continent beneath whose soil lies the world's largest known reserves of copper, uranium, gold, diamonds, cobalt and other metals . . . the continent most capable of sustaining a large population at high standards of living." Given such resources, the writer concluded, it was "quite conceivable that within little more than a generation the African continent could become the garden-spot of human civilization and culture in the modern world."[75]

72. "End of Era with Threat of the Jungle Taking Over," 14.

73. "To get food," one school geography explained, "the black man has only to gather the wild fruit or to hunt and fish" (quoted in Wilson, "Taking Tarzan out of the Textbooks," 42).

74. "What Happened in Ghana?" 210. Her husband had written in rather similar vein of "the African": "He can be lazy, engaging in work as a pastime rather than for the income it brings" (DuBois, "Black Africa Tomorrow," 109).

75. J. H. O'Dell, review of Kwame Nkrumah, *Consciencism*, *Freedomways* 6, no. 1 (Winter 1966): 57.

A similar difference of view was apparent in assessments of African societies. The environmentalism of much liberal and conservative writing had the effect of denying diversity and individuality to Africans and to African societies. The environment being a vast, unchanging tract of featureless jungle and grassland (the assumption ran), so the people living in it were essentially similar and their societies unchanging. "The African" was "reduced to an exemplar of single traits"—a person dominated by environment and custom, incapable of individual thought or action, living in societies without histories and without a capacity for innovation.[76] As late as 1953, a writer in *Life* magazine introduced a special issue on Africa with the following description which epitomizes this tradition (ironically enough, in a feature urging a reconsideration of American attitudes to Africa): "For centuries the rhythm of Africa remained unchanged. It was not slow, as in lands where the sun swings wide, but sharp and savage as the tom-tom beat. Enormous brooding silences were broken by the shrill squeak of leopards. The yellow snout of a crocodile slid silently over a pool to end in an abrupt snapping of jaws. Men's activities were molded by the environment. Life was dominated by the witch doctor prancing in his devil mask and swaying headdress; peace was abruptly stopped by the stabbing spear."[77]

Similar images of primitivism (redeemed by colonialism) were projected in schoolbooks in use at this time. In a world history published in 1950, the authors declared: "The Dark Continent is an unexplored wilderness, with an unbearable climate, a Negro population largely barbarous, and deserts and jungles quite impenetrable. . . . The people are dark of skin; many of them are even darker of mind."[78] A geography book

---

76. As Dorothy Hammond and Alta Jablow remark, Africans are seen in such writing as "representative of their tribe, or they are faceless units in the collectivity called 'The African.' . . . As the individual is reduced to 'The African,' so 'The African' is reduced to an exemplar of single traits; and for the most part these single-dimensioned descriptions are pejorative" ("'The African' in Western Literature," 8).

A general weakness of liberal and radical critiques of stereotyping such as this one is that the writers rarely say whether it is the use of collective categories (such as "Africans" or "the African") or just the pejorative character of the stereotypes to which they object. If it is the former, the critique should in fairness be extended to *all* collective categories and *all* formulations of "national," "racial," and "ethnic" character, including those used by black and African nationalists.

77. Alexander Campbell, "Africa: A Continent in Ferment," 9.

78. Carlton J. H. Hayes, Parker T. Moon, and John W. Wayland, *World History*

issued in 1949 remarked that, despite great advances under colonial tutelage, "many difficult problems remain to be solved before the guiding hand of temperate-zone peoples can be safely withdrawn from the governments of the peoples of the rainy low-latitudes."[79] This appeared in the very year that the British were preparing to withdraw their "guiding hand" from Ghana, the independence of which was to be the major symbol of the advent of African self-determination, as well as a stimulus to the arguments examined in the following chapters.

Images of Countries

With independence, the generalized images of Africa identified above were gradually and partially supplemented by more specific images of particular countries. But this process was very slow and related to a very small number of states: it is absolutely safe to say that even now, Lesotho, Mali, and Rwanda have very few associations in the minds of American citizens and few enough in the minds of journalists.

Certain countries did, however, acquire fame or notoriety. They typically became symbols of particular kinds of problems, to the extent that we find African analogies ("another Congo," "another Nigeria," "another Chad," or "another Uganda") beginning to occur in American writing, alongside the more familiar and worn analogies of American domestic history and international politics. Some, admittedly, were transient (for example, how many nods of agreement would be prompted these days by describing a problem abroad as "another Zanzibar"?). But others have become part of the permanent allegorical inventory of American political rhetoric.

Three countries—Ghana, the Congo (Zaire), and Nigeria—are mainly used for purposes of illustration in this book.[80] They were selected not just because at least three of them became relatively familiar to American

---

(New York: Macmillan, 1950), quoted in Wilson, "Taking Tarzan out of the Textbooks," 42. Wilson notes that in world history books examined by her, on average 2.8 percent of pages were devoted to Africa (and a half to four-fifths of such space concerned Egypt): in elementary geographies, 9.7 percent of all pages were devoted to African material.

79. E. C. Case and D. R. Bergsmark, *College Geography* (1949), quoted in Rosenblum, "Boa Constrictor in the Desert," 5.

80. Angola and Rhodesia (Zimbabwe) were originally to appear also as cases: for reasons of space, comparative use of them was dropped, but Angola is referred to here in two chapters.

readers, at least as symbols or cases of what writers portrayed as generically African problems, but also because they provided foci for arguments between the schools described in subsequent chapters. Each school justified general positions by reference to these cases and used them to attack the prejudices of their rivals. But reference to the cases is useful in another way that has less to do with the intentions of writers: considered comparatively and retrospectively, they reveal changes in position and, indeed, internal contradictions.

Ghana

The night of 6 March 1957 was, for witnesses of Ghana's independence celebrations, "even by West African standards . . . a steamy night, the kind when foreigners dream of northern winters."[81] But discomfort did not tarnish the magic of the event for Africans and foreigners alike. One generally laconic journalist reported that what he had seen that night left the observer "with the right to believe in the impossible, and above all to believe in the unlimited capabilities of the human being."[82] "This historic event," the NAACP's board of directors proclaimed even before it occurred, "presages the complete reclamation of the Continent of Africa by its indigenous peoples."[83]

On that day and for several years afterwards, Ghana became (in Immanuel Wallerstein's words) "the most scrutinized country in Africa."[84] Such scrutiny was partly due to its novelty as an early case of decolonization. But novelty alone does not explain the intensity of outsiders' interest in Ghana, much less the intensity of the arguments that events there provoked. The Sudan became independent in 1956, but it never received such attention, at least after independence.[85] Nor do physical

81. Reed, "The Rocky Road to Freedom," 212.

82. Russell Warren Howe, "Gold Coast into Ghana" (July 1957): 155.

83. Reported in the *Crisis* 64, no. 3 (March 1957): 163. "African-Americans had long recognized the significance of developments in the Gold Coast. In 1950, the historian Rayford W. Logan declared that 21 December 1950 (the date of the approval of the new Gold Coast constitution providing for self-government) was 'one of the most momentous dates in modern history'" ("The Free World," *Negro History Bulletin* 14, no. 7 [April 1951]: 168).

84. "Ghana as a Model," 43.

85. The *International Bibliography of Political Science* records ten articles on the Sudan published between 1956 and 1958, compared to thirty-four on Ghana. However, this appearance of indifference contrasts sharply with the period 1952–1955, when forty-two articles appeared on the Sudan, as against twenty-five on

size, resources, or strategic location explain the level of outside interest. Compared to the Congo and Nigeria, Ghana was relatively insignificant in respect of size and resources. *U.S. News and World Report* told its readers in 1954 that Ghana was "a country about the size of Oregon, inhabited by tribesmen" ("a small quadrilateral under the lefthand shoulder of Africa," as the British journalist Patrick O'Donovan put it).[86] It was relatively prosperous (mainly from the export of cocoa), but it had no obvious strategic significance.[87]

Ghana's prominence was really a political and ideological phenomenon. Because of its leadership, the promise of political stability and economic development it offered, and the strategies adopted by its first president, Dr. Kwame Nkrumah, it quickly became, for admirers and critics alike, the archetypical "new African state." It was "a model for either good or ill, depending on one's point of view. Above all, it was politically 'advanced.' For those who prized stability founded on a long political tradition, it had that. For those who prized revolution and progress, it had that."[88] Ghana was, specifically, the earliest and most exhaustively discussed case of an African one-party state, with a "charismatic" leader, friends in places the U.S. Department of State did not like, and a soi-disant "socialist" strategy for economic development. It therefore became a universal point of reference in arguments about a range of political, economic, and diplomatic issues of interest to all schools examined here.

The passions that Ghana aroused were so great because of the hopes

---

Ghana. (*International Political Science Abstracts* records eight articles on the Sudan between 1952 and 1958, compared with twenty-six on Ghana.) The reasons for the relative indifference to the Sudan after 1956 are unclear. It was probably due to the flamboyance of Nkrumah, his contacts in the United States, and the controversial character of Nkrumah's actions after independence. But there may also have been a racial factor at work: Ghana was frequently described as the first "new black state," whereas Sudan (quite wrongly) was regarded as really an extension of Arab North Africa because of the strength of Islam in the northern Sudan.

86. "Memo from the Gold Coast," *U.S. News and World Report,* 4 June 1954, 99; O'Donovan, "Ghana—Trial Run in Africa," 11.

87. Donovan remarked in 1961 (when a reaction against the President Nkrumah and his attempts to assume political leadership had set in, at least in the West): "[Ghana] has no strategic significance. Its foreign policy, particularly over the unification of Africa, has hardly left the ground. The Western world could survive without discomfort the loss of its cocoa and ores" ("Ghana—Trial Run in Africa," 11).

88. Wallerstein, "Ghana as a Model," 43.

that it inspired at independence. As the British colony of the Gold Coast, it had undergone what most observers (except those in the Kremlin) agreed was an exemplary process of decolonization. Even such critics of European colonialism as Rev. Michael Scott and George W. Shepherd, Jr., declared that the emancipation of the Gold Coast represented "the best of British tradition" and was "an outstanding example of colonialism at its best."[89] The British, Shepherd noted, were "not being swept out of Ghana on a great tide of violence and revolution": they were withdrawing in an atmosphere of goodwill, after a smooth transfer of power that had established an authoritative constitutional leader and parliamentary institutions. Though some visitors lamented the "essentially British odor" of Gold Coast life (including the odor of British cooking), most admired the territory's political legacy.[90] "People took it for granted," David Reed noted later, "that British-style democracy would flourish in the new country. . . . Looking around, foreigners noted with satisfaction that the Speaker of Parliament and the clerks were garbed in white wigs and black gowns, just like their counterparts in Westminster."[91] Academic students of political development, such as David E. Apter and Henry L. Bretton, differed about the prospects for "the Westminster model." Apter, while cautious about apparent obstacles, concluded: "Parliamentary democracy in the British tradition appears to have excellent prospects."[92] Others thought that it would survive only as long as it served the political and diplomatic interests of Nkrumah and his party (the Convention People's party).[93]

89. Rev. Michael Scott, reported in Jack, "Eyewitness in Ghana," 417; Shepherd, "The Birth of Ghana," 5.

90. "It is hard to believe," Norman Lewis remarked, "that a century of independence will be long enough to expunge the essentially British odor of Gold Coast life—the cooking (brown Windsor soup and steak-and-kidney pie), the class observances, the flannel dances, the tea parties, and the cricketing metaphors" ("A Highlife or Two in Ghana," 134).

91. "Rocky Road to Freedom," 213.

92. "Political Democracy in the Gold Coast," 139. Elsewhere, Apter suggested that the Gold Coast would have "a far easier time developing an accepted unified pattern of parliamentary authority in the near future than Nigeria" ("British West Africa: Patterns of Self-Government," 125).

93. For early skeptical views about the prospects of democracy in Ghana, see (for example) "Birth of a Nation"; Friedenberg, "The Horatio Alger of the Gold Coast"; Bretton, "Current Political Thought and Practice in Ghana"; Love, " 'Saturday's Child' of Ghana," 16. Conservative journals were critical of Nkrumah as

Ghana, however, enjoyed a general reputation as a relaxed, aggressively cheerful society. "The most striking quality of the people," remarked Robert Coughlan, "is their vivacity. . . . Most Africans are marvelously good-natured, but the Ghanaians seem to teeter on the edge of uncontrollable hilarity."[94] Visitors commented with particular frequency on what one termed "the friendly racelessness of modern Ghana."[95] One such visitor was Chester Bowles, an associate of John F. Kennedy: "Nowhere in Africa or Asia, except perhaps in Thailand, have I seen people so gay, relaxed, and unashamedly friendly toward white foreigners as in the Gold Coast. Here Africans have never come face to face with sovereignty on the basis of race, and the difference in their attitude is no less than spectacular."[96] Ghana was emphatically "black man's country"—something that both attracted and intrigued the many African-American visitors after independence. Ghanaians, one group of African-Americans found, "were not possessed with a sense of their blackness. [The visitors] met no Africans there who were caught up in a search for identity."[97]

In addition to its smooth transition to independence, its acceptance of democratic institutions and its apparent lack of racial (and serious ethnic) tensions, Ghana was blessed with a relatively high standard of living. It was, Daniel Friedenberg noted a month after independence, "incredibly rich, . . . the most prosperous British dependency" after Malaya.[98] Some visitors questioned how equitably wealth was spread, but most argued

---

a "megalomaniac" but were significantly sympathetic toward "strong" government, at least until such "strength" was devoted to programs justified in the rhetoric of socialism.

94. "Black Africa," 102. Coughlan found in Accra "a general atmosphere of activity and optimism." David Apter gave a less flattering view of the easy-going nature of Ghanaian society, suggesting that it reflected a leisure ethic, with an accompanying disdain for manual labor: "A high premium value placed upon leisure [he wrote] reduces the motivating aspects of monetary reward as compared with the rewards of leisure. . . . There are . . . few of the prejudices against leisure that exist in the Western world regarding occupational tasks. Few people enjoy social status as a result of hard labor, unless such work is communal or familial" ("Some Economic Factors in the Political Development of the Gold Coast," 415, 416).

95. Russell Warren Howe, "George Padmore," 53. For a similar comment on the lack of racial sentiment in Ghana, see Howe's earlier article "Gold Coast into Ghana," 155.

96. *Africa's Challenge to America,* 68.

97. Stirling, "To Touch the Hand and the Land," 14.

98. "The Horatio Alger of the Gold Coast," 17.

that the territory had the resources to sustain a significant program of economic development.[99]

With all these advantages, Ghana seemed to many foreigners sympathetic to African nationalism to be a territory unusually well placed to realize the hopes and promises of independence. "In spite of all the ills that plague her," the political scientist David Apter wrote, "the Gold Coast remains the most hopeful spot on the map of Africa."[100] If Ghana failed, declared George W. Shepherd, "it would set back the freedom of other African countries by a generation."[101] For African-Americans, even more than for white liberals, it was a crucial symbol of emancipation. As Russell Warren Howe remarked, the events of 6 March 1957 had removed, "better than any other single event, the stigmata on the brow of the Negro."[102]

After 1957, however, Ghana became controversial, initially because of actions restricting political association and other freedoms, and later because of the formal establishment of a one-party state. Liberals were disturbed by the consolidation of a cult of personality around Nkrumah and (after 1961) by the adoption of a socialist development strategy, involving increasingly close links with the Soviet Union and other Eastern bloc countries. Nkrumah himself became increasingly absorbed in diplomatic (and intelligence) activities in pursuit of his wish to establish a

---

99. Several visitors commented critically on the contrast between the newer prestige projects to be seen in cities such as Accra and Kumasi and the conditions in which many ordinary people lived. Leonard S. Kenworthy, for example, wrote: "Near the modern, 600-bed hospital at Kumasi . . . I saw scores of mud-brick houses with their owners living in filth and squalor. Not far from the ultramodern Ambassador Hotel in Accra . . . are the 'tin tops' or shanties of the poor, like the hovels on Capitol Hill in Washington, D.C. In the interior there are thousands of people riddled with yaws, river blindness, and many water-borne diseases, yet there too are some of the finest specimens of humanity that one can find anywhere in the world" ("Ghana: So Young, So Hopeful," 20). For similar comments on the contrast between rich and poor in Ghana, see Hunton, "West Africa Today," 38.

100. "British West Africa: Patterns of Self-Government," 120.

101. "The Birth of Ghana," 5.

102. "Gold Coast into Ghana," 155. In the same vein, *Ebony* magazine remarked in May 1957 that Ghanaian independence day had "marked an abrupt end of a mighty myth"—the myth of African inferiority, current among black as well as among white Americans ("The Ten Biggest Lies about Africa," 58). In 1959, George W. Shepherd noted: "The achievements of Ghana have done more to kindle American Negro confidence in their blood brothers than any other single event" ("Toward a Positive Program in Africa," 26).

"Union Government" for Africa, while mismanagement, falling cocoa prices, and corruption damaged the domestic economy. By early 1966, Ghana—a country which had entered independence with reserves of $560 million—had external debts of approximately $860 million, its reserves were exhausted, and consumers were facing severe shortages in basic commodities. On 24 February 1966, the Ghanaian armed forces seized power and Dr. Nkrumah went into exile in Guinea.

The Congo (Zaire)
From 1960 on, Ghana was overshadowed as an object of American interest by the (ex-Belgian) Congo.[103] The Congo's fame (or notoriety) arose from the political disorder that occurred in the territory after independence, leading to heated argument about the pace and, indeed, propriety of decolonization in Africa.

Even before independence, however, the Congo had vivid associations in American minds familiar with Conrad's *Heart of Darkness* and the excesses of King Leopold of Belgium's rule over the territory. As David Reed remarked, probably correctly, of all African territories the Congo came closest to "the popular notion of what the Dark Continent should look like. . . . It is covered with thick jungle and is literally soaked with water. Torrential downpours are unleashed almost every day . . . Leopoldville [Kinshasa] still has the atmosphere of a 'green hell' about it. . . . Along with king-size cockroaches, there are spiders the size of a man's fist, houseflies as big as bumblebees, beetles that look like walking golf balls, and dragonflies with the wing spans of sparrows. . . . During much of the year, the heat and humidity are so intense that a shirt wilts in a few minutes."[104]

The Congo thus epitomized the stereotypical view of Africa as a mysterious, intimidating concentration of untamed natural forces—a place where the visitor could be overwhelmed by "the sheer force of life itself."[105] As Milton Bracker put it:

103. For reasons of space, I have used material on the Congo more selectively in this work than material on Ghana and Nigeria. While the two latter countries are used to illustrate a range of themes, I inserted specific sections on Katanga in the text to illustrate different approaches to the issue of self-determination and to provide a contrast with Biafra. Given the importance of the Congo (and Zaire), more comprehensive treatment would have enlarged the text excessively. I recognize, however, that the alternative adopted does not do justice to the complexities of the Congo case.
104. "In the Congo's Jungles, a Boom and a Ferment," 93.
105. In 1964, *Time* quoted Conrad as remarking that a visit to the Stanleyville

The Belgian Congo is vivid, beautiful, coveted, and it exerts a kind of frightening spell on all who seek to know it. It is veined with rivers, from mud-brown to a curious brick-pink. One of them, the overwhelming Congo itself, hooks around like a great aorta, carrying the life of the country itself. . . . The dominant impression is one of an interminable forest. There are wrinkled mountainous upsurges, and bare patches of reddish earth; there are lighter green extents of savanna . . . [the forest] is so tightly packed that it suggests a limitless expanse of broccoli. . . . At times, trees seem so close as to form one inseparable mass of foliage, bursting with life, sullen with impenetrability.[106]

Such images of natural primitivism were offset, however, by many admiring reports of social and industrial progress, particularly in the southeastern province of Katanga, where copper and uranium mining had created what some visitors saw as the first industrial revolution in colonial Africa. The excitement that such visitors felt is unmistakable in a passage in an article by John Hughes in the *New Leader*: "In the great copper-smelting works near Elisabethville, I saw an African not far removed from primitive tribal life maneuvering into position with great skill a giant ladle brimming with $50,000 worth of red-hot molten copper."[107]

But—travelers often added—such progress was partial and fragile. Elisabethville (the capital of Katanga) had, Bracker noted, "good roads, fine homes, a splendid air terminal." Yet, he added, "the roads are bordered by great red termite hills, twice as high as a man. . . . A mamba or python is as likely to slither across a road as not."[108]

Even in the mid-sixties, the Congo seemed to outsiders to be two countries, one being "a series of overlapping economic domains . . . controlled by banks, corporations, and individuals living abroad," the other being "the traditional African society, sometimes peaceful and harmonious, sometimes frustrated, violent, and vindictive."[109] Even then—nearly a decade after independence—its political integrity was in doubt. The Congo

---

area was "like travelling back to the earliest beginnings of the world, when vegetation rioted on earth and the big trees were kings" (*Time*, 4 December 1964, 30).

106. "Congo: Pulsing Heart of Africa," 14.
107. "Nationalism in the Congo," 7–8.
108. "Congo: Pulsing Heart of Africa," 107.
109. Gonze, "Tshombe in Wonderland," 5.

remained, in Henry Tanner's words, "what it always was: a huge, virtually ungovernable hunk of Africa, as large as the United States east of the Mississippi, held together by a dozen airports, a network of teleprinter lines, and an improved but still erratic army."[110]

Compared with 6 March 1957 in Ghana, the Congo's independence day was a confused, frightening affair, accompanied by stories of European flight and rumors of African atrocities. It seemed possible that the territory would quickly become completely ungovernable and would break up into its constituent provinces, and possibly into smaller pieces.[111] On 11 July 1960, less than two weeks after the Belgians had formally granted independence, Moise Tshombe, the provincial president of Katanga, proclaimed the secession of his province from the new state. Tshombe's declaration had serious economic as well as political implications for the Congo, since Katanga, through the royalties on its minerals, contributed 40 percent of the national government's revenue.

In declaring independence from the Congo, Tshombe simultaneously asked Belgium to send troops to restore order in the Katangese capital, Elisabethville, and other Katangese towns, following a revolt there and elsewhere in the Congo by the Force Publique, the Congolese army. Meanwhile, in Leopoldville the central government, led by President Joseph Kasavubu and Prime Minister Patrice Lumumba, appealed to the United Nations for assistance. By the end of July, a substantial UN force was in the Congo, gradually replacing troops flown in by Belgium. But, while

---

110. "The Congo Is Still an Active Volcano," 52.

111. Political disaster after independence was predicted by several American journals. The *Nation* commented that the world would be relieved if the Congo turned out "to be merely an ill-mannered or turbulent member." The outlook, it said, was "somber" and the Belgians would be to blame if the territory "plunge[d] into outright anarchy" ("Drums along the Congo," 9 July 1960, 22). John Gunther, the author of *Inside Africa*, remarked that the Congo was "perhaps the most exciting country in Africa except politically." A writer in the *National Review* predicted collapse following Belgian withdrawal: "As the situation stands today, a truly independent Congo wouldn't last more than a few months as a democracy. . . . The Watussis [*sic*] and Bahutus, the Luluas and Balubas would simply massacre each other with that lack of inhibition so typical of central Africa" (Erik von Kuehnelt-Leddihn, "Letter from the Congo," 18 June 1960, 393, 394). The *New Republic*, however, deplored "exaggerated accounts of panic and flight" on the part of the Belgians: "June is always a month of exodus from the Congo, particularly for women and children" ("Summer in the Congo," 20 June 1960, 5).

Dag Hammarskjold, the UN secretary general, eventually arranged (in August 1960) for the substitution of UN for Belgian forces in Katanga, Tshombe continued to reject central government authority. After extended negotiations, the deaths of both Lumumba and Hammarskjold, and three military confrontations between UN and Katangese forces, the secession of Katanga finally came to an end on 15 January 1963.

The Katanga issue (and the whole question of Congolese independence and its aftermath) aroused strong feelings in Africa, Europe, and the United States. In 1962, when Katangese secession was already two years old, David Halberstam of the *New York Times* remarked that it remained "one of the most divisive international issues of the day—a deeply emotional issue and as draining a problem for the West as it [was] a crushing tragedy for the Congolese."[112]

The drama and violence involved in the events of 1960 explain some of the intensity with which the Katanga problem was debated. But the Congo question as a whole was significant in that it brought to the surface, for the first time, the conflicting hopes and fears that outsiders had about self-government and nationalism in Africa. The Congo had, one writer observed, become a "microcosm of the underdeveloped world" for many Americans.[113] At the least, it had crystallized and forced on public attention, as never before (and perhaps never again), some of the basic political and philosophical issues at stake in the establishment of new states in Africa.

The Katanga secession itself involved a new kind of question, about which Americans had never had to think before (at least, since 1865). Previously, the choice had been thought of as one between colonial rule and self-government for colonies. With the emergence of the Katanga problem, a third choice—that of self-government and independence for *parts* of former colonies—appeared. The question became, not whether self-government was desirable, but to whom it should be extended.

Nigeria

A similar problem appeared in Nigeria, though only after seven years of independence, in the form of a secession of its Eastern Region as "the Republic of Biafra." The resulting conflict, known to outsiders as "the

---

112. "Mystery—and Tragedy—of Tshombe," 58.
113. Stolle, "The Congo: A Calculated Confusion," 252. Stolle called the Congo's "the worst story of modern history."

Nigerian civil war," lasted nearly two and a half years and was much more destructive than the Katanga conflict.

Nigeria resembled the Congo in other, more obvious ways. Both countries became independent in 1960. Both were physically huge, had large populations, and were ethnically very diverse. Yet, both before and until well after independence, Nigeria enjoyed a more favorable reputation than the Congo in the United States. Nigeria seemed, in fact, to be the African country for which liberal (and even some conservative) Americans felt the closest affinity (especially as Nkrumah's Ghana fell from favor).[114] Only three months after independence, Harvey Glickman noted: "It is possible to detect an American identification with Nigerians which does not exist with any other peoples in Africa. Perhaps this is because Nigeria, like the United States, is sprawling, varied, bustling, and eager to be successful, and must grapple with many of the same problems we have faced in 'melting' diverse ethnic groups into one nation. Moreover, the federal system adopted to contain these centrifugal forces is not unlike our own."[115]

American sympathy for Nigeria went well beyond the interest that the country's size, her economic significance (and potential), and her diplomatic influence naturally attracted. It arose from a belief that Nigeria was "the epitome of democracy and stability in Africa."[116] It had a federal system (consisting at independence of three regions, each with its own prime minister, and a federal president and prime minister); it had an ostensibly competitive party system; and it had politicians firmly (and often financially) committed to free enterprise.

For many American visitors, the spirit of Nigeria (reminding some of nineteenth-century America) was epitomized in Lagos, the federal capital.[117] Nobody had a bland or neutral reaction to the city. John Oakes remarked that it was "one of the dirtiest, ugliest, noisiest, most crowded

114. Herbert J. Spiro, for example, remarked in 1965 that Nigeria was "one country about which many otherwise pessimistic American students [had] generally been most optimistic" ("Whose Problems?" 3).

115. "Africana Floods the Book Stores," *Africa Report* 6, no. 1 (January 1961): 13.

116. Grundy, "The Congressional Image of Africa," 12.

117. An anonymous contributor to the *Atlantic Monthly* remarked in 1962: "Nigeria in some ways resembles nineteenth-century America, with foreign capitalists rushing in, hoping for quick profits, and with land bloating in value" ("The Atlantic Report—Nigeria and Ghana," November 1962, 16).

—and yet liveliest, gayest, most vibrant—cities of all West Africa. Its open markets glow with color, row after row of bright blue bolts of cloth . . . a ceaseless movement of tall black men in multi-hued robes, handsome women carrying babies on their backs and balancing on their heads immense burdens of vegetables or fruits, furniture, or basketfuls of clucking chickens."[118] Even a writer who described Lagos as "the most crooked city on earth," "the smelliest, ugliest city on the continent," and "the Calcutta of Africa" nevertheless conceded that, "for all its horrors," it was also "one of the most dynamic cities on earth, a boiling ant heap of people."[119]

The country as a whole attracted Americans in the years immediately after independence. By the mid-sixties, some seven thousand Americans were working in Nigeria, among them a large contingent of Peace Corps volunteers.[120] Western, and especially American, scholars showed a corresponding level of interest: between 1960 and 1967, at least two hundred books on Nigeria were published and in 1965–1966 the Social Science Research Council gave seven of its sixteen grants in African Studies for work in Nigeria.[121]

American enthusiasm for Nigeria began to give way to doubt as it became clear that the federal system was essentially unstable and as tensions between politicians in the dominant Northern Region and some of their colleagues in the south became sharper. By 1965, electoral violence and blatant corruption had led to a virtual breakdown of order in the Western Region, which in turn precipitated a military coup in January 1966. When in the summer of 1966 northern politicians organized pogroms against Ibos from the Eastern Region living in the north, a movement toward secession began in the east, led by the then military governor of the region, Lt. Col. Odumegwu Ojukwu. In June 1967, despite attempts at conciliation by the head of the Federal Military Government, Lt. Col. Yakubu Gowon, Ojukwu declared "Biafra" independent of Nigeria.

The ensuing conflict often evoked parallels with the Katanga dispute. In the Biafran (as in the Katangese) case, sharp divisions occurred about

118. Oakes, "Africa—A Continent Afire," 16.
119. Reed, "Rocky Road to Freedom," 215, 216. For an American socialist's reactions to Lagos, see chapter 6.
120. Melbourne, "The American Response to the Nigerian Conflict, 1968," 33.
121. Jenkins, "The Scholars' Paper Nigeria," 48.

what the secession signified and whose side (if any) the United States government should take.

As in the Katangese case, the leaders justified the secession on grounds of the dictatorship of the central government and its insensitivity to local needs. As in the earlier case, both the central and the secessionist governments became significantly involved with Western and Eastern bloc countries in the course of the conflict.

But the Biafran war was plainly different in important respects, though some observers persisted in seeing parallels. First, the secession took place seven years after independence, against a state that was well established, with a sophisticated, if highly unstable, political system. The revolt thus entailed rejection of a society by people who knew it well and had, indeed, been active, even powerful, if ultimately frustrated, political participants in it. In this sense, the Biafran conflict had the special intimacy and horror of a civil war. Moreover, since it occurred within a powerful and well-established African state, nearly a decade after independence, commentary on the war (to the extent that it was tempted into generalization) tended to treat it as symptomatic of failings in African states, rather than of maladies caused directly by colonialism.

Second, while the secessionist leader, Lieutenant Colonel Ojukwu, was accused of exploiting them opportunistically, it is clear that grievances and suspicions between ethnic groups (notably the Ibo of the east and the Hausa-Fulani of the north) were more significant as a direct source (or prominent as an expression) of tension in the Biafran conflict than in the Katangese secession.

Third, the course of the conflict between May 1967 and January 1970 was infinitely bloodier than anything that occurred in Katanga. By some estimates, as many as two million people died as a result of the Biafran war, and the war was notorious for the sufferings of civilians, especially children, from hunger and disease. In its conduct, as in its character, it resembled other civil wars. Bloodshed, and ethnic persecution, also occurred in Katanga, but on a much smaller scale.

Fourth, the international politics of the Biafran war were more complex, and the alignments less predictable, than in the Katangese case. The United States, the United Kingdom, and the Soviet Union actively or tacitly supported the Federal Military Government in Lagos. France, Portugal, the People's Republic of China, Rhodesia, South Africa, and a small but variegated number of black African states more or less openly encouraged or even actively helped Biafra morally, diplomatically, and militarily. Despite frequent allegations about the role of oil and oil companies in the Biafra conflict, the direct influence of foreign economic interests was less apparent, and more divided in its application, in the Nigerian civil war than in Katanga, where the Union Minière du Haut-Katanga became internationally synonymous (fairly or not) with big business at work behind the scenes.

However, there was also a significant difference between the international situation of the United States itself during the Congo dispute and that during the Biafran war. By the time that the Nigerian conflict broke out, Americans were engrossed in the Vietnam War and their interest in Africa had diminished considerably. Their attitudes toward the Nigerian issue were affected by this relative indifference to Africa as a whole, by a tendency to see all foreign issues in the light of the Vietnam issue, and (increasingly) by a more general and growing resistance to all foreign entanglements, especially in the third world.

THREE

Liberalism:

The Safari Honeymoon,

1955–1962

This chapter is concerned, first, with the reactions of writers in American liberal journals to the ending of colonialism in Africa, and, second, with their initial appraisals of the new African states. In both respects, writers in this phase were engaged in an exploration which was cognitive as well as normative in character. It was a time for finding out about broad characteristics of an unfamiliar continent. It was also a time for formulating some general answers to the questions of what liberal Americans should think about the continent, what they should expect from it, what standards they should apply to it, and how they should want their government to deal with it.

Since we are examining a ragged process of discovery and evaluation, it is unrealistic to try to define this phase chronologically. The only realistic measure would be one of intellectual and political evolution—an evolution shaped by individual experience and individual commitments, rather than involving some standard response to a collectively experienced set of external stimuli.

Nevertheless, political changes and changes of intellectual mood among observers do follow roughly parallel courses. In this sense, the years 1955 and 1962 represent very approximate turning points. The first represents the moment when the American media began to interest themselves in the waning of colonialism in Africa: the second, the moment when American liberals began to reexamine and even to abandon some of their initial hopes and expectations regarding African independence.

Africa and Africans

Liberals ran into serious problems as soon as they tried to cope with the basic challenge of conceptualizing African societies and African tradition. Their encounters in Africa led visiting journalists and scholars of broadly liberal sympathies to raise questions, if not about the values of liberalism, then at least about its short-term prospects.

They were troubled, to start with, by the parochialism of African societies (meaning, in fact, the parochialism of individual Africans they talked to). They found (as we noted in the previous chapter) that Africans were suspicious of outsiders. But "parochialism," on closer examination, had a special sense when used by liberals about Africans. It meant (and this was why it was troubling) that those observed or interrogated did not seem to have the specific values (rationality, a belief in progress, and a sense of fellowship with other peoples) that liberals regarded as destined to embrace the world.

The rationality of Africans was, indeed, a particularly troubling—and delicate—issue. It troubled liberals because, like their Enlightenment predecessors, they saw justice and progress as dependent on the triumph of rationality over superstition. This issue also troubled conservatives. But it did so mainly because they feared that liberals were expecting more of Africans than Africans, whether because of their cultural inheritance or their lack of development, could in fact deliver. The result—conservatives feared—would be domestic chaos and international instability.

Early reports about African capacity for rational thought were hopeful, if rather abstract. Salvador de Madariaga—not an American, but assuredly a liberal—wrote in 1953: "No one should entertain the slightest doubt as to their capacity. . . . Intelligent, quick to learn, active, cheerful, charitable and helpful toward each other and toward strangers, the Negroes are sure to make their mark in history as soon as they emerge from the magic-animist stage into a more rational (not necessarily rationalist) form of life."[1] But closer acquaintance raised doubts. Africans, it was agreed, were hospitable and fun to be with ("In the evening Poto-Poto echoes with high-pitched African voices and it rocks in the rhythm of native music").[2] But were they serious about modernization? Some concluded that, regrettably, they were not. "A culture that places a very high

1. "As Africa Comes of Age," 347.
2. Oakes, "Africa—A Continent Afire," 9–13.

value on leisure," one economist remarked, could only be an obstacle to modernization.[3]

The experience of traveling in the bush often caused misgivings. The driving behavior of Africans was particularly apt to set off such misgivings: large generalizations typically followed bad scares. Norman Lewis of the *New Yorker* concluded that one reason for much lunatic driving in Ghana was philosophical or spiritual: "The African tends not to believe in the existence of inanimate matter. Trees and rocks are capable of locomotion, so after an accident a driver, washing his hands of something completely outside his control, may simply say, 'A tree ran into me.'"[4] After a particularly hair-raising trip in Nigeria, Kirk Sale brooded on the implications of various incomprehensible actions and responses he had encountered. In particular, he had been intrigued (not to say endangered) by the behavior of a truck driver who "could see no reason not to park in the middle of a highway, out of sight just over the ridge of a hill, to fix a flat." Such an incident showed, Sale said, that "the gulf between the European and African cultures [was] as vast and unbridgeable as ever." As for the unwitting truck driver: "He is not stupid—not at all; he simply does not happen to be the inheritor of a tradition of culture (in which, for example, romantic love plays a major part he could hardly understand), language and logic that is peculiar to our Greco-Christian world. . . . Logic is not universal, no matter how much the Greeks insisted it was; logic is a cultural phenomenon, and its tenets take different shapes, and its syllogisms different forms, under the tropical sun."[5] Such a commentary, building huge judgments on a brief, if terrifying, incident, may seem preposterous. Would we accept an indictment of Greco-Christian civilization by a Nigerian on the basis of five minutes among Boston drivers in the rush hour? Probably not. Sale's comments, however, exemplify what is probably the process by which many judgments about cultures are made. They certainly illustrate the degree of culture shock, the sheer sense of disorientation which many American observers, liberal and otherwise, experienced in Africa and which led them to grasp for meaning in even the most trivial and transient encounter.

African institutions provided more grist for speculation about "African character." As individuals, Africans might be inscrutable, but their insti-

3. Erasmus H. Kloman, "An African Program for the Africans," 14.
4. "A Highlife or Two in Ghana," 150.
5. "After Colonialism," 27.

tutions were, by definition, public property from which clues about values and views of the world might be gleaned. Institutions—especially political institutions—might, indeed, also yield clues about political issues of concern to liberals. They might be helpful in suggesting the probable nature of and prospects for both nationalism and democracy in Africa. Most nationalisms, after all, claimed legitimacy on the basis of identification with a tradition: African nationalism, therefore, was likely to be shaped to some degree by African tradition. Similarly, democracy elsewhere had been helped or hindered (in the liberal view, mostly hindered) by an institutional and cultural legacy. It made sense, then, to examine African precolonial government in searching for clues about the probable character of postindependence politics.

But there were several obstacles—actual or potential—in the way of this line of enquiry. One was that African nationalists were rather ambivalent about "tradition." Another was that "African traditions" and "African traditional government" were categories containing a great variety of values and institutions. Such diversity should have been an obstacle to generalization: Africa had had kingdoms, empires, more modest chiefdoms, and "stateless societies." Moreover, "tradition" had been overlaid by half a century of colonial government, which had destroyed or distorted both institutions and their sources of legitimacy. But such variety did not dampen the spirit of bold generalization with which outsiders, in this as in other cases, approached Africa. As before, they continued imputing common characteristics to all African societies, while assuming the existence of essential, unchangeable qualities.

The allegedly common characteristics usually involved ways of reaching decisions, attitudes toward opposition, and controls on abuse of authority. In practice, however, observers seemed unable to agree on what these essential features were. They were also divided about how much authority traditional institutions still enjoyed, and indeed about how relevant they were to current political problems.

A further obstacle to speculation about the possible influence of "tradition" and "traditional" institutions on nationalism and democracy was normative. Liberals were reluctant to pursue the question because of a strongly rooted liberal prejudice against tradition and traditionalism. They did, however, show some interest in whether traditionalism could be helpful in promoting modernization and development and in whether traditional government was democratic. Would "tradition" contribute to "political development," and specifically to democracy?

Their instincts told them, however, that the answers would be negative. In general, liberals were quite emphatic about the obstacles that tradition and traditional institutions presented to modernizers. Chiefs were described as "enemies of progress."[6] "Tribalism" was almost universally condemned, either because it was archaic or because it was thought to provide a pseudo-traditional facade for colonial or neocolonial interests hostile to progressive central governments. Judgments on "the tribe" were often unequivocal: "Most of Africa's tribes," wrote the political scientist Henry Bretton, "are too small, too barren of social value to their members, too tradition-bound, to be worth preserving. In most cases, considering its adverse impact on the development of modern economic and political systems, tribalism might well be regarded as a form of subversion."[7] Even the well-respected economist W. Arthur Lewis, otherwise a defender of pluralism, had nothing good to say about ethnicity as a form of political expression.[8]

Such judgments were sometimes clearly inspired by the liberal tradition of opposing aristocracy and monarchy.[9] They also reflected a character-

6. William H. Hessler, "The Agenda for Africa," *Reporter,* 23 June 1960, 35.

7. Bretton, "Congo and Emergent Africa," 242. Modern developments, Bretton added, rendered "the tribe socially valueless to all but the old." In the same vein, Albert L. Guérard commended the Nkrumah government in Ghana for its forthright attitude to ethnic dissent: "It rejects the native cultures, which are tribal. I have seen pictures of a demonstration in Accra, with banners reading 'Down with tribalism!' It is healthy for man to be ashamed of certain features in his past. Tribalism is not a foundation but an obstacle" ("To My African Friends," 62).

8. "The history of any tribe [Lewis declared] . . . is mainly a history of the wars it has fought; the themes are enmity, hatred, and enslavement—hardly suitable material on which to build a national state. Tribalism is associated with conservatism, since the only tribes that can form powerful parties are those governed firmly by aristocratic chiefs" ("The Growing Pains of African Democracy," 35).

The assertion here that the only "tribes" that could form powerful parties were "those governed firmly by aristocratic chiefs" seems very questionable. To take only two examples, the NCNC in eastern Nigeria and KANU in Kenya had roots in ethnic groups (the Ibo and the Kikuyu, respectively) that did not have highly structured chieftaincy structures, and both survived quite well into the postcolonial period. Lewis's comments were all the more significant in view of his extensive experience in West Africa, mainly as an adviser to the government of Ghana.

9. Thus Henry Bretton wrote: "The cruel and cynical exploitation of Europe's masses by the several aristocratic cliques . . . should be kept in mind when we

istically liberal view of the meaning of nationalism. As the historian Hans Kohn put it, nationalism involved "a break with ancient and restrictive traditions, with the immobilities of caste, tribe, and extended family in favor of individuality, social mobility and greater equality."[10]

This view assumed, first, that Western liberals and African nationalists had the same values. Secondly, it assumed that their enemies were the same—that "nation builders" in Africa were facing the same foes as those whom liberal nationalists in Europe had faced. Much liberal writing depicted African leaders as the latest, and most embattled, heroes of modernization—men struggling to build nations in the face of divisive and parochial forces. They were men destined, in Adlai Stevenson's words, to awaken Africans from "the dream of tribal life."[11]

Liberals simply assumed this "destiny." They assumed it because African leaders used the liberal rhetoric of "nation building" when addressing their fellow citizens or when making speeches to bodies like the United Nations or the Council on Foreign Relations. It was not—and at this stage could not be—based on much close observation of what such leaders were actually doing.

Liberals' assumptions about "nation building" actually had some implications that African nationalists could well have found insulting. If they really were nationalists, the dismissive and denigrating remarks of Western liberals about the worthlessness of African tradition and culture would naturally be offensive. Such nationalists might, however, embody some complex mixture of "traditionalist," nationalist, and modernizer. Liberals seemed, however, quite unaware of the problem and of the political danger they were courting. Since, to them, all tradition was self-evidently worthless, they did not bother to qualify their dismissals of African history and African "tradition." On the contrary, several liberal visitors and commentators went out of their way to tell Africans that they were actually rather fortunate to be underdeveloped: "Compared to other emerging continents," Waldemar Nielsen noted, "Africa carried into the modern age a less burdensome baggage of history, of self-pride, of de-

---

examine African chiefs and their 'arrangements' with the illiterates of the bush. . . . The cruelty and brutality, the total disregard of human dignity, associated with political practice in the Dark and Middle Ages in Europe should never be ignored" ("Straight Thinking on Africa," 206).

10. "Changing Africa in a Changing World," 197.

11. "The New Africa: A Guide and a Proposal," 54.

structive ideology and of encrusted social structure to impede progress."[12]
Liberal writers occasionally compared Africa's situation with that of Asia
or Latin America, in order to stress Africa's potential for rapid progress.
But they sometimes did so in a way that seemed almost calculated to give
offense:

> The Africans [wrote William Persen in 1959] do have one tremen-
> dous advantage over the Asiatic peoples—they do not have to divest
> themselves of entrenched cultural obstacles. They have had no an-
> cient greatness with which to mask their present inequality. The
> cultural state of the Africans is so low that they are considerably
> more adaptable to the challenge of Western civilization than the Arab
> or the Indian. They do not have to defend their past. Their past has
> meant only the basic struggle with hunger, disease and the burning
> sun . . . the fact of cultural backwardness can be viewed as an ad-
> vantage in that there are fewer "bad" habits for the African peoples
> to overcome before acquiring the more productive aspects of Western
> civilization.[13]

The point—tactfully made or not—was that Africa was a tabula rasa: in
Adlai Stevenson's phrase, it was a continent "at the threshold of history."[14] It could have a purely modernizing nationalism, because it had
no traditions worth preserving or seriously capable of getting in the way.

Such a dismissive view of Africa's past and its surviving traditional
institutions was not universal. Some liberals did see African nationalism
as embodying continuity with tradition, rather than as signifying its absolute rejection. It is still true, however, that writers who discounted African traditions and African traditional institutions were consistently
applying longstanding beliefs of European and American liberalism, however upsetting their views might be to Africans or to nonliberals.

12. "Africa Is Poised on the Razor's Edge," 62.
13. "Africa in Transition," 3–4. Persen further remarked: "The lack of the
cultural drag of past civilizations means that the African explosion will continue
to move with a speed that no Asian state that has the slightest desire to maintain
humanitarian values can match." As Hans Kohn put it, Africa had "participated
less than any other major part of the globe in the higher manifestations of the
mind, in philosophy, scholarship, [and] great art" ("Changing Africa in a Changing World," 194).
14. "The Issue Is Peace," 9.

Liberals and Colonialism

The same set of principles, flavored by the particular experience of the American Revolution, shaped liberal attitudes toward colonialism, and created some of the ambivalence to be found in them.

Because of the American Revolution, American liberals were instinctive anticolonialists. In the case of European colonialism in Africa, they did indeed find much to condemn. Colonialism had, they claimed, been politically illiberal and had failed to create an atmosphere in which democracy could flourish. It left, wrote Kirk Sale, "no understanding as a legacy, only a regimen; no communication, only the machinery of giving and accepting orders."[15] Colonialism had failed "to educate the African mass." It had exploited Africa economically and had produced "an inequality that beggars description."[16]

Yet liberals (like many Marxists) often added, if grudgingly, that colonialism had served a useful purpose, by destroying feudalism and firing up the engines of modernization. In judging particular colonial systems, they did, in fact, apply the standard of relative modernization: the greater the material advance and the degree of modernization achieved, the more indulgently was the system judged.

The result was some mixed verdicts for everyone except the Portuguese. British colonialism, in liberal eyes, was deficient because of its use of indirect rule, which (Nielsen complained) "had the effect of entrenching and reinforcing ignorance, superstition, stagnation, and separatism."[17] Indirect rule—critics said—had not only preserved outmoded institutions likely to subvert democratic advance, but it had exhibited a streak of racial aloofness on the part of the British, in that it implied that Africans were incapable of making European institutions work. On the other hand, the British were thought to have shown vision and responsibility in accepting the idea of self-government in the colonies earlier than other imperial powers.[18] They had been, one writer suggested, the most successful co-

15. "After Colonialism," 27.
16. Oakes, "Africa's 'Ordeal of Independence,'" Lens, "The Bell Tolls in Africa," 17.
17. "Africa Is Poised on the Razor's Edge," 61.
18. According to Chester Bowles, the British had shown a "high sense of responsibility": in West Africa, they had undertaken "an experiment in self-government which [held] much promise for all of Africa" (*Africa's Challenge to America*, 68).

lonial power in preparing an elite to follow them.[19] Nigeria in particular was seen as, in Stanley Diamond's phrase, "the model of colonial success, an example of how well-intentioned power, sober and lofty design, can create a nation and move a people, with minimum displacement, from a position of tutelage to one of 'independence,' through which the best interests of rulers and ruled are harmoniously united."[20]

About the French, American liberals had equally mixed feelings. But they had such feelings less often, since relatively few American visitors penetrated French West and Equatorial Africa. One such was Daniel Friedenberg, who late in 1953 took a sea journey along the West African coast on a French ship. Friedenberg noted the rough egalitarianism with which the French officers on the boat treated Africans. For example, during a stop at Sassandra in the Ivory Coast, these officers, having openly called the Krou stevedores "monkeys" and "apes," later went down to gossip at length with them. Friedenberg commented: "The French intellectually despise what they call 'inferior' peoples, but are so warm and good-natured by disposition, they end up *practically* embodying a lack of prejudice." This led Friedenberg into some reflections on the hypocrisy of the "Anglo-Saxon liberal" who "believes *theoretically* in the equality of man but actually wants nothing to do with peoples aesthetically displeasing." But Friedenberg had little regard for the political judgment of the French. They were, he thought, likely to be less adroit than the British when it came to handling African demands: "The French, politically speaking, are clumsy louts . . . they still cannot gain enough national wisdom to forfeit the prestige to secure the cash. And so the French, for all their warmth and lack of color prejudice, not the aloof English, will be the first to suffer from West African nationalism."[21]

Belgian colonialism was judged, necessarily, on its record in its one true colony, the Congo. Especially after the collapse and chaos of 1960–1961 in the territory, American liberals were highly critical of Belgium's failure to prepare an African elite to take over at independence. But visitors were invariably struck by the material progress of the colony, and especially by the scale of industrialization and the level of basic social services.[22]

19. Friedenberg, "An African Notebook," 421.
20. "The End of the First Republic," 7. Diamond, it should be said, did not share this view.
21. "An African Notebook," 421.
22. John Hughes, for example, remarked on "the impressive material benefits"

Visitors to Katanga were, as I noted in chapter 2, immensely impressed by the transformation of the province into a bustling center of heavy industry. They found the capital, Elisabethville, "very orderly, business-like and progressive."[23] Even more impressive was the drama of industrialization to be observed in the vicinity of Elisabethville and elsewhere in a territory that a well-known Belgian administrator (and lion tamer) had described as "a million square miles of superstition and disease."[24] On balance, a European writer noted in *Africa Report,* the Belgians could feel "justifiably proud of their economic achievements in the Congo."[25]

The one colonial power that received no such credit for modernization was Portugal. Portuguese Africa, Chester Bowles reported in 1956, was "among the most backward areas in the world and, at the moment, as insulated as any in this modern age could be against the blasts of nationalism."[26] In Angola and Mozambique, other travelers reported, Africans were "held in virtual slavery" and in Angola, especially, " 'civilizing' by forced labor . . . [had] denuded vast areas."[27]

Liberals and the African Revolution

Despite the depressing state of Portuguese Africa and criticisms of colonialism elsewhere, liberals were generally impressed and excited by the scale of change in Africa. A great deal of leaping, bursting, emerging, and straining is depicted in liberal commentary on Africa in the late fifties and early sixties, as well as much metaphorical movement of mighty and irresistible forces.

---

the Belgians had brought to the Congo: they had "constantly plowed back a margin of profit to raise African living standards" and urban Africans "enjoyed good housing,and medical and other social services" ("Nationalism in the Congo," 7).

23. Bracker, "Congo: Pulsing Heart of Africa," 107.

24. The administrator was Jean-Pierre Hallet: his description of the Congo is quoted in a review of his book *Congo-Kitabu.* I have not been able to pinpoint the passage in question in this work and no page reference is given in the review.

25. "Few colonies," Albert P. Disdier concluded, "[had] developed either so far or so quickly; none [had] shown such concern for the native inhabitants' share in the growth" ("The Congo's Economic Crisis," 6).

26. *Africa's Challenge to America,* 28.

27. Persen, "Africa in Transition," 3; Lovell, "Winds of Change in Southern Africa," 231.

Thus Harry Goldberg, writing in the AFL-CIO's journal, saw Africans as making "a leap from a centuries-old darkness into the light."[28] "Many of you," said the historian Albert Guérard in a letter addressed "to my African friends," "jump straight from the jungle trail to the jet plane."[29] John Hughes saw similar personal dramas: "Africans reared in primitive mud-and-dung huts, clustered deep in the shimmering African bush, are today becoming doctors of divinity and medicine."[30]

Liberals were equally enthusiastic about the prospect of African independence. "This march of humanity away from imperialism," wrote Sidney Lens in the *Progressive*, "is the most breath-taking revolutionary wave in all history."[31] Even a philosopher with as deep a historical perspective as Reinhold Niebuhr was moved to declare: "We are obviously witnessing a world-wide historical movement as significant as the disintegration of the traditional European civilization in seventeenth-century England and eighteenth-century France."[32]

Politicians, journalists, and academics reached for suitably elemental metaphors to describe the process. Africa was likened by Grant McConnell to "a vast new volcano risen from the sea before our eyes, flaming, explosive, as yet unshaped but loaded with a meaning for our future which we sense but cannot picture." Chester Bowles portrayed it as "an awakening giant, stretching its limbs and opening its eyes to the first faint prospect of freedom."[33]

African independence, in fact, conjured up an entire complex of me-

28. "Africa: Challenge to World Democracy," 20.

29. "To My African Friends," 62. Goldberg was the AFL-CIO's international representative. "A student in Dakar," remarked Sal Tas, "may be a subscriber to *Le Monde* in Paris, while his father or uncle may still live, half-clad, in a primitive jungle" ("Report on French Africa," *New Leader,* 8 September 1958, 6). "From the Cape to the Sahara" (declared John Oakes), "the peoples of the continent are vaulting in one generation from the neolithic age to the nuclear age" ("Africa—A Continent Afire," 8).

30. "Africa Today," 3: "Even fifty years ago, the wheel was unknown in some parts of sub-Saharan Africa. Now in the Belgian Congo, Africans are working in the uranium plants."

31. "The Birth Pangs of Revolution," 32.

32. "The Negro Dilemma," 13. Niebuhr continued: "The Negro is in the process of validating a common humanity which many white men on all continents have arrogantly and futilely denied."

33. McConnell, "Africa and the Americans," 34–35; Bowles, "Myths about Africa—And the Reality," 8.

teorological and sometimes primeval images: "waves of the future" were whipped by "winds of change" into "rising tides of expectation." Transformation, political and social, was occurring "not at the pace of oxcarts but often at jet speed."[34] However, the determination of Africans "to leap across centuries" inspired fear as well as excitement. Africa, Adlai Stevenson said, was "the most innocent of continents": it now found itself "tremblingly poised on the razor's edge between peace and calamity—between one of the most inspiring possibilities of human liberation and progress in all history and one of the ugliest eventualities of chaos and international danger."[35]

Liberals and Self-Government

As Stevenson's words suggest, liberal enthusiasm about decolonization was tinged with anxiety. Some liberals worried about the results of trying to move territories that had only experienced the autocracy of colonial government into independence under complex democratic constitutions.[36] But for many others, this and other objections to do with "preparation" and "readiness" carried little or no weight, for two broad reasons.

One reason was the characteristically liberal notion of the "irresistible trend."[37] Independence was "the wave of the future." African nationalism

34. Dean, "Democracy East and West," 21.
35. "The New Africa: A Guide and a Proposal," 54.
36. Bowles, for instance, pointed out that, in terms of the educational level and political experience of the successor elite, Africa was less well equipped for independence than the Asian countries had been. The comparison, he concluded, suggested the need for caution: "No responsible government that honestly seeks orderly progress in Africa can advocate the hurly-burly liquidation of colonial rule." Americans, Bowles argued a few pages later, had to gain the trust of colonial subjects, so that they could "help moderate the impatience of those Africans who want more authority than they are yet able to use constructively" (*Africa's Challenge to Democracy*, 118, 127).
37. Kenneth Minogue, in his book *The Liberal Mind*, refers (in a section entitled "How to Make Trends and Influence People") to the importance of "trend-persuasion" as a propaganda tool of modern liberalism. For this tool to work, he notes, it is not essential that trends be "irresistible" (since some of them are identified precisely in the hope that the apathetic will be raised to resist them). But it is important that they be impressive and virtually out of control: "The kind of persuasion by which people may be induced to take an interest in the major trends of the world situation must therefore be teleological, and the persuader

would "inevitably and everywhere triumph in the end"; it was "a tidal movement," "a live volcano."[38] To attempt to resist, deflect, or even quibble at such a tide was simply folly: to do so would simply create resentment on the part of Africans, and that resentment might in turn create an opportunity for communist subversion.

Second, liberals argued, self-government was an inherent right. As such, it was immune to empirical tests of "readiness" or "preparation." Independence was, whether for an individual or a nation, the absolute precondition for real progress and self-fulfillment: without the opportunities and challenges that independence presented, neither an individual nor a people could develop or be judged. The claims of independence not only came before all other claims, but they were absolute.

Or at least they were absolute in principle: caveats tended to find a way in. For example, Woodrow Wilson had said fifty years earlier, in criticizing those who claimed that the Mexicans were not ready for independence: "[When] properly directed, there is no people not fitted for self-government."[39] Similar qualifications tended to creep into liberal declarations about the right of Africans to self-government. Support for independence was sometimes accompanied by explicit injunctions about the need for strong government and by other apparent diminutions of an absolute right of self-determination.[40] The general implication was that, while all peoples had the *right* to self-government, some, for political and cultural reasons beyond their control, needed guidance and perhaps even restraint in exercising that right.

One situation which in liberal eyes justified postponement of independence was that in which power was monopolized by a European minority. Thus James S. Coleman and others argued repeatedly that Americans should not support the granting of independence to territories such as the Central African Federation (and later Rhodesia), Angola, and Mozambique until majority rule was established or at least assured.[41]

---

must cast around for some pressing hopes or fears which can be technically connected with the trend in question" (p. 124).

38. Rudin, "The International Position of Africa Today," 54; Lens, "The Bell Tolls in Africa," 17; Coleman, "America and Africa," 594.

39. Quoted in Pratt, "Anticolonialism in U.S. Policy," 296.

40. Pratt, indeed, points out that Wilson himself had earlier declared in relation to independence for Puerto Rico and the Philippines that "some discipline—it may be prolonged and tedious—must precede self-government and prepare the way for it" (ibid., 297).

41. See, for example, Coleman, "America and Africa," 603, where he sug-

The Katanga Case

The Congo provided the first serious test for liberal ideas about self-determination. Supporters of Katanga's secession argued that since (as liberals admitted) all African states were "artificial," there was no prima facie reason why a province should not seek self-government from the ex-colony of which it happened to be a part. Moreover, they argued, Katanga's claim was particularly strong since it was, both economically and ethnically, different from the rest of the Congo.

Liberals generally opposed Katanga's secession vigorously. They used various kinds of argument—philosophical, legal, economic, political, diplomatic, and strategic—in doing so. Two lines of argument were particularly revealing about the thinking behind liberal support for self-determination. One was that the Katangese claim was false: Katanga was not a nation, and Tshombe did not have popular support for secession. The other was that, even if Tshombe was a legitimate spokesman of Katangese opinion and even if Katanga itself met commonly agreed upon standards for nationhood, the province's claim to independence should nevertheless be rejected, since loss of Katanga's resources would seriously damage the prospects for economic development in the Congo as a whole.

Some opponents of recognition appealed directly to criteria of national self-determination, arguing that (in *Africa Today*'s vivid phrase) Katanga was not a nation, "but simply a series of mining pitheads, high-tension wires, and railroad lines."[42] On these grounds (and others), the Kennedy administration, in the person of Assistant Secretary of State for African Affairs G. Mennen Williams, denied that there was any case for self-determination. The latter, Williams observed, could be "applie[d] only to a recognizable national unit": Katanga was not such a unit.[43] Another

---

gested, concerning the Central African Federation, that the United States should "support the maintenance of Colonial Office control . . . until such time as the African community is strong enough to hold its own."

42. "Katanga," 3.

43. Williams, "Congo Realities and United States Policy," 795. Williams did not indicate what he regarded as relevant criteria of nationhood.

Williams and other diplomats also invoked a legal argument. Tshombe, they pointed out, had, in common with other Congolese leaders, accepted the *loi fondamentale* of 1960 (the provisional constitution establishing the Congolese state) and had participated in the round table discussions of January–February 1960 which had helped to shape the constitution. By these actions, Tshombe had im-

common criterion of nationhood also appeared in Kennedy administration statements, namely, the test of international recognition. Katanga, diplomats pointed out, had not been formally recognized by existing states.[44]

Many political commentators, however, resorted to the more political (or personal) argument that Tshombe was not the legitimate leader of a nationalist movement. The simplest version of this attack was to present him as a puppet of Western economic and political interests—most typically, as a stooge of mining interests and the Belgians generally. This, however, was a view more commonly taken on the left. Many liberals seemed to resist such an easy dismissal of Tshombe's own political interests and skills. Indeed, they were often at pains to stress that Tshombe was as much manipulator as manipulated.[45]

The longer the Katangan secession survived, the more authority and independence outsiders attributed to its leader. Even as early as 1960, Theodore Draper (in a *New Leader* pamphlet on the Congo) questioned the propriety of singling Tshombe out as a "stooge": "Tshombe was charged with being a Belgian puppet, and there is no doubt that he leaned heavily on Belgian support. But he was President of Katanga by virtue of the same election that had made Lumumba Premier of the Central Gov-

plicitly accepted the legitimacy of the Congolese state in its colonial boundaries and had committed Katanga to recognizing the authority of that state (ibid., 795; Cleveland, "The U.N. in the Congo: Three Questions," 22).

In his *New Leader* pamphlet, Theodore Draper questioned the weight put on this argument. Tshombe, he noted, "had always opposed the centralized or unitary state identified with Lumumba and embodied in the provisional constitution." Further, "since the Congolese constitution was purely provisional, a new constitution, reopening the old division was bound to be proposed and debated in the new state" (*Ordeal of the U.N.*, 10).

44. As Harlan Cleveland wrote, "No government anywhere in the world believed that these secessions raised the issue of self-determination. No government anywhere ever recognized the illegal break-away of the Katangan regime" ("The U.N. in the Congo," 22).

45. As Dan Kurtzman put it in an article in the liberal-conservative *Reporter* in November 1961: "The fact is . . . that Katanga is far from being a Belgian colony today. Since independence, the Belgian government itself has had little influence in the territory. It has facilitated the employment in Katanga of military officers, but they, and all other foreigners working for the state, are servants of the government, not its masters. . . . The influence on the government of Belgian businessmen, including officials of the Union Minière du Haut Katanga . . . is also limited" ("Katanga Was Not Crushed," 31).

ernment. By the same token, Lumumba's position could be questioned as that of a Soviet puppet or one which depended heavily on Soviet support." By the same token, observers of Tshombe's relationship with the mining interests tended to emphasize his independence from them—and, indeed, their dependence on him.[46]

Conversely, his critics charged, the evidence of elections undermined Tshombe's claim to a mandate for secession.[47] By some estimates, he was opposed by two-thirds of Katanga's population.[48] Overall, *Africa Today* concluded, Tshombe could not present "a single shred of evidence" that he spoke for "the peoples of Katanga."[49] The fact was (the critics said) that Tshombe's lack of an electoral majority reflected a sharp tribal division between his own Lunda tribesmen and the Baluba who were in a majority in the northern part of Katanga.[50]

Such political geography led U.S. Ambassador Gullion to remark that Tshombe was "a minority leader of a minority part of a province."[51] It

46. Of the main mining company, the Union Minière du Haut-Katanga, Kurzman wrote: "It is more dependent on the good will of the Katanga government than the reverse. The significant question is not how much influence Union Minière exerts on Tshombe but to what extent Tshombe is likely to squeeze Union Minière. . . . In short, the Katangese, who want to see their wealthy territory developed as soon as possible, and the Belgians, who want to continue doing business in Katanga, need each other and are using each other" ("Katanga Was Not Crushed," 32).

47. Tshombe's critics pointed out that in the May 1960 elections to the Congolese Chamber of Deputies, Tshombe's Conakat party had won only eight seats; the opposition Cartel Katangais had won seven. According to Crawford Young, the Cartel actually had "a narrow plurality over the Conakat, 110,000 to 104,000" (*Politics in the Congo*, 502).

Even more significantly, in the Katanga provincial assembly elections of the same date, Conakat had only won twenty-five of sixty seats available: the Cartel had won twenty-three. Moreover, the opposition (dominated by Jason Sendwe's Balubakat) had got a plurality of votes (ibid., 302; Gonze, "Katanga Secession: The New Colonialism," 6). In 1961, *Africa Today* gave Tshombe's provincial assembly support as thirty-eight, with twenty-two for Sendwe's Balubakat ("Business as Usual," 3).

48. In Elisabethville itself, his party had attracted only eight thousand votes, as against twelve thousand for the opposition (Gonze, "Katanga Secession," 6; Cousins, "Report from the Congo," 34; "Business as Usual," 3).

49. "Business as Usual," 3.

50. The Baluba, indeed, made up 55 percent of the population of Elisabethville itself (Young, *Politics in the Congo*, 264).

51. "He [controlled] perhaps 500,000 people in a province of 1.5 million, out

also prompted one academic observer to ask for whom Tshombe was demanding self-determination. Tshombe is, Herbert F. Weiss wrote, "probably as legitimate a leader of his own ethnic group as are other leaders in the Congo. But his own Lunda tribesmen are in the minority in Katanga. Is every ethnic group to have its right of self-determination? Tshombe certainly did not grant it to Katanga's Baluba."[52]

The liberal answer was, of course, that every tribe could not have independence. "Nation building," progress, and economic development depended on keeping and, indeed, strengthening existing states, however artificial they might be. Ironically, then, liberals found themselves opposing uncontrolled self-determination precisely because of the widespread appeal it was likely to enjoy.[53] As Immanuel Wallerstein, at this time a leading liberal "nation builder," put it: "Once the principle of ethnic autonomy is accepted, there will be no end to secession."[54]

---

of a total population in the Congo of some 14 million" (quoted in "Dodd's Private War," 4).

Africa Today remarked: "To this day, two-thirds of that province remains more opposed to Tshombe than the apostles of 'self-determination' care to admit" ("Business as Usual," 3). Tshombe's weakness in northern Katanga did not necessarily lead liberal observers to conclude that he was politically vulnerable, since they believed that the real source of his power was the mineral resources of southern Katanga. As Herbert Weiss put it: "The loss of the north, though a serious setback, does not basically alter Tshombe's strength, since Katanga's mineral wealth is centered in the south" ("The Tshombe Riddle," 5).

Liberal commentators also noted that (in Houser's words) Tshombe had "no real personal strength in any other part of the Congo," except through alliances he made with other politicians opposed to Lumumba and his successors (Houser, "Leopoldville Revisited," 6).

52. "Katanga," 34. Weiss had been criticized by Philip Kay for "conveniently ignor[ing] the key moral issue involved in the Katanga 'secession,'" namely, whether Katanga had the right to self-determination. Kay suggested that it would have been impossible for Tshombe to persist in the secession if he had been supported only by Belgium or by European expatriates: "One must conclude . . . that he has the backing of a vast segment of the African population of that area" (Philip Kay, "Katanga," *New Leader,* 1 October 1962, 32).

53. Even more ironically, Tshombe's own government used the argument that uncontrolled self-determination would lead to chaos in opposing secession by the Baluba from *his* state of Katanga: "Where would one end [asked the Katanga government White Book on the Baluba opposition] if each of the hundreds of tribes inhabiting the former Belgian Congo wanted to erect itself as [an] independent state?" (Weiss, "Katanga," 34).

54. "Congo Confederation," 4.

Even at this point, however, some liberals had doubts about mechanically endorsing the legitimacy of states based on artificial frontiers. They were, as liberals, uneasy about endorsing strong central governments and uneasy also about nationalism in general. They suggested that the Katanga episode had been useful at least in forcing African leaders and their foreign sympathizers "to explicitly repudiate the concept of self-determination except as applied to political entities still under colonial rule." In defending their own governments, African leaders had been compelled to acknowledge their hypocrisy in attacking colonialism and the boundaries it had established. They had demanded self-determination within the artificial boundaries of European colonies, while denying self-determination to domestic secessionists by claiming that these boundaries were legitimate and immutable.[55] But such critics did not necessarily take the next step (as conservatives did) and suggest that African states needed to be broken down into their tribal components.[56]

Such a disintegration—liberals argued—would have undesirable developmental as well as diplomatic effects. In the case of the Congo, successful secession by Katanga would (critics of Tshombe said) have disastrous consequences. Katanga provided some 40 percent of the revenue of the Congo government and produced roughly 50 percent of the country's export earnings. Legally, some observers suggested, Katanga derived any claim it had to the remarkable mineral wealth under its soil through "the Government of the Congo."[57]

But the main objection of liberal commentators was not so much legal as moral and political. It was wrong, they said, for one part of a country to keep to itself wealth which had been developed under colonial government with resources drawn from the entire country: and it was especially wrong when the rest of the country was so lacking in valuable natural resources.[58] The political argument was that to acquiesce in seces-

55. Ferkiss, "Breakdown in the Congo," 326.
56. Reinhold Niebuhr came close to this position, suggesting that not only Katanga, but other provinces unhappy with inherited rule from Leopoldville might indeed be asking the right questions: "Was there any reason why they could not claim to be a nation for themselves? Would they be asked to give an inordinate amount of their wealth to poorer regions? Traditions, habits of loyalty and of justice answer these anxious questions rather than hurriedly written constitutions" ("Imperialism in Perspective," 8).
57. Calder, "Shinkolobwe: Key to the Congo," 165.
58. Katanga, it was often pointed out, had only one-twentieth of the total population of the Congo: it covered only one-twelfth of its total land area.

sion would be to hand a victory to the business interests that were presumed to be manipulating (or at best sustaining) Tshombe.[59] Without Katanga, the *New Republic* believed, the Congo would collapse economically and, quite soon, politically.[60]

Some observers, however, believed that critics of Tshombe were exaggerating Katanga's potential contribution to solving the Congo's problems. Harry Rudin, for instance, pointed out that even if all the revenue accruing from the Union Minière operations were directed to Leopoldville, it would not enable the Congo government to balance its budget.[61]

Nevertheless, such attempts to suggest conditions for the granting (or the successful practice) of self-government always provoked principled liberals. In their eyes, objections were simply presumptuous. They were presumptuous in any form, to any audience: no nation or race had the right to judge the readiness of any other to govern itself.

Such injunctions were—"pure" liberals invariably added—especially presumptuous coming from Europeans. Europeans, the purists continued, had no business preaching to Africans about either peace or democracy: they had started two devastating world wars, and the democratic institutions about which they boasted had (the political scientist Henry Bretton pointed out) "emerged slowly, haltingly, uncertainly from the muck and mud, and the ignorance of times past." Therefore, Bretton (along with many other liberals) concluded, arguments about whether Africans were capable of self-government were "contrived and irrelevant": even ants and bees had successfully organized themselves.[62]

59. Thus *Africa Today* declared: "No group of businessmen can be allowed to dictate the future of a nation; the mercenaries must be removed; Katanga's wealth must help support the entire Congo. . . . The central issue is not the self-determination of Katanga, but the control of a vast capital structure and its revenue" ("Business as Usual," 3).
60. "[A] splitting away of Katanga would throw the rest of the Congo up for grabs. The scramble to pick up the pieces would mean new civil wars between rival leaders, tribes, and ideologies and competition among the big powers for whatever might be salvaged" ("Dodd's Private War," 3).
61. The UMHK paid (to Tshombe's government) roughly $50 million each year: this amount would not go far toward meeting the Congo deficit of approximately $200 million. By 1963, Leopoldville would need over $270 million—an amount equivalent to the value of *total mining output* for one year ("The Republic of the Congo," 336). In 1961, the Congo budget had a deficit of $176 million; in 1962, it was $232 million.
62. "Straight Thinking on Africa," 206. John B. Oakes quoted an African

Liberals and the Analogy of 1776

Liberals argued repeatedly that self-determination not only was a fundamental liberal value, but also was a commitment inherited from the Founding Fathers. All the major political spokesmen of American liberalism referred constantly to the American Revolution when talking about African independence and other third world issues. Chester Bowles, Adlai Stevenson, and G. Mennen Williams, for instance, spoke frequently about the relevance of America's "revolutionary past," "the spirit of '76," and the legacy of anticolonialism passed down from George Washington to Woodrow Wilson and Franklin D. Roosevelt—and, by implication, to them, the friends and advisers of John F. Kennedy.

Stevenson in particular liked to proclaim the significance of the American Revolution for colonial peoples. He liked to present it as both a historical symbol and a continuing movement, invoking for the purpose Jefferson's claim that "the American revolution belongs to all mankind."[63] Since 1776, "the flames of freedom" had spread across the globe. "The domination of [American] national ideals," was, Stevenson believed, especially apparent in the ideals and actions of third world nationalists.[64] Chester Bowles, for his part, was sure that "the independence movement in Africa [had] . . . drawn inspiration from America's revolutionary break with British colonialism, from the words of our Declaration of Independence, and from the historic stand taken by such Americans as Lincoln, Wilson, and Roosevelt, in favor of the self-determination of peoples."[65] Africans, like Americans in 1776, were (in Stevenson's words) standing "at the threshold of history." Their experiences and their dilemmas did not, Henry Bretton agreed, "significantly differ from our own."[66]

politician in Southern Rhodesia as saying: "I admit there aren't enough of us to run a government, but that makes no difference. We'll let the British stay as administrators" ("Africa—A Continent Afire," 8).

63. Between 1776 and 1800, Stevenson declared, "excitement was in the air, for we stood as a nation at the head of a crusade for freedom that was just beginning to unshackle humanity from the servitude of centuries" ("The American Revolution in Our Time," 28).

64. Stevenson specifically claimed that the proceedings of the Bandung Afro-Asian conference in 1955 revealed that "no event in human history [had] said more to the peoples of Asia or Africa, or provided more nourishment for the moral imagination, than what happened in America from 1776 to 1789" ("The Issue Is Peace," 9).

65. *Africa's Challenge to America*, 44.

66. "Straight Thinking on Africa," 206.

Other liberals, however, were not so sure. Some thought that the application of the 1776 analogy to Africa was misconceived. The essentials of the two situations were, they argued, quite different, and the comparison actually had less comforting implications than liberals such as Stevenson and Bowles assumed. Facile use of the analogy ignored particularly the utterly different backgrounds of the two "revolutionary" movements and their consequently different relations with the imperial power. As Grant McConnell put it: "The Americans were in no way like the Africans who are now seeking to cut their ties with Britain. In fact, the Americans were colonists, and if an African analogy is to be sought, that with the Kenya and Rhodesia settlers is in some ways better. Indeed, one of the issues underlying the American Revolution was the ruthless policy which some of the American colonists wished to pursue toward the indigenous Indian population, a policy opposed in England."[67] Not only were the American colonists in a relatively mild "suffering situation" compared to Africans, but, as Vera Micheles Dean noted, their relationship with their supposed overlords lacked the element of racial difference so apparent in both colonialism and anticolonialism in Africa.[68]

This point of historical interpretation in fact exposed a tension within liberal thinking about colonialism. On the one hand, liberals were favorable to the modernization that the European presence had brought. On the other, they sympathized with the Africans who had suffered political subjugation in the process.

The attraction of the 1776 analogy, as used by Stevenson and others, was that it equated African modernizers—the nationalist leadership—with early American modernizers—the New England settlers. In this way, the economic cause of modernization and the political cause of self-

67. "Africa and the Americans," 41. The preference for drawing a parallel between the American colonists and white settlers in the Rhodesias and South Africa was a hallmark of conservative writing on African nationalism. But conservatives generally took a more approving view of both groups than McConnell does here, though some conservatives of an unreconstructed evolutionary or "might-is-right" viewpoint were quite happy to accept that both groups of settlers had treated the natives in a less than liberal way.

68. The American revolution, Dean observed, "was staged by white men against white men, with both rebels and colonial rulers from the same nation and sharing the same culture. Unpalatable as the demands of the British Crown may have seemed to British settlers . . . they could hardly be compared to the relationship established by recent colonial powers with peoples they regarded as inferiors" ("Democracy East and West," 18).

government were made congruent: material progress and liberation could be seen to be in step with each other, at last.

But the equation was vulnerable to competing interpretations both of the American Revolution and of African nationalism. What if the American settlers had actually been collaborators with the colonial power and had themselves been oppressors, whether of black slaves or of American Indians? What, then, was the quality of the modernization they had brought about? How valuable would the American Revolution then be as a precedent and a beacon for nationalists in African colonies? If American liberals had sentimentalized their own revolution, were they likely to recognize or to sympathize with those at whose cost the colonial revolution had been achieved and on whose backs the ensuing "revolution of rising expectations" might be carried? Further, what if American liberals were sentimentalizing or in some other way misunderstanding the nature of African nationalism and the aims and values of those heading it?

As so often, the use of an analogy here captured the essence of an ideological position and at the same point exposed some potential contradictions or weaknesses within it. It also exemplified the general tendency in discussions of foreign affairs, American and otherwise, to evaluate events abroad in terms of apparently analogous domestic precedents or of foreign precedents familiar to domestic audiences.

African Nationalism:
Liberal Orthodoxies, 1955–1962

The independence of African states meant that one liberal value had triumphed, that of self-determination. This political fact shaped liberal discourse about Africa. Henceforth arguments tended to take the form of asking how far independence was contributing to or detracting from the possibility of realizing other important liberal values—notably, those of progress, democracy, individual rights, and international understanding.

The fact of independence complicated liberal discourse in that it was no longer possible to argue as if all choices were open. It no longer made sense (if it ever had) for American liberals to talk as if the future of African societies was a matter of selecting optimal blueprints which would then be realized by a trusted local elite. For better or for worse, African governments were in charge. Such governments, moreover, took very seriously the sovereignty of their countries and insisted that even friends refrain from offering advice or criticism that might infringe on this sovereignty.

The result was an increasingly sophisticated, but also increasingly acrimonious, debate among American liberals about what attitude they should take toward African states. In the first few years, the tone of the debate was earnest, optimistic, and respectful. Independence was seen as a frontier to be explored and occupied, not as a bone to be fought over. The questions preoccupying liberals (and, they assumed, preoccupying Africans) concerned how this frontier should be governed and how it should be developed.

The ensuing debate can be considered as consisting of three, interlocking discourses—one about progress (or, in social science jargon, "modernization"), another about democracy and human rights, and a third about nationalism and self-determination itself.

The first two discourses were thought to be related. The type and level of economic development in African countries would delimit the possibilities for political change in them. Conversely, what kind of government African countries had would determine the extent and the kind of economic development that occurred in them. On this relationship, liberals divided into those who favored a "politicist" approach—one that saw political forms (and interests) as shaping economic development—and those who took an "economistic" view—one that saw economic factors as shaping political institutions and ideologies. On the whole, the "economistic" view prevailed, though it often cohabited uneasily—at least in the "nation-building" school—with a belief in a "strong state."

These questions of domestic development and government were, however, related, if grudgingly, by liberals to the much larger question of African statehood itself. Liberal support for self-government had not been entirely instrumental, but it had been encouraged by an expectation that other good things would flow from the granting of independence. When this expectation was not met, or was only partly met, liberals did not give up supporting independence for territories still under colonial rule. Instead, their disappointment expressed itself in the revival of some old liberal doubts about nationalism itself.

In this section, we shall examine these three discourses in their initial forms. In chapter 4, we shall examine the revisionist arguments which appeared within each fairly soon after independence and the impact of such revisionism on the discourse about self-determination.

Independence and Modernization

The liberal view of African leaders as "modernizers" is crucial to understanding the development of liberal thinking about independent Africa. On the one hand, it explains how liberals were able to suppress in this case—at least temporarily—some well-developed liberal doubts about nationalism as a general phenomenon. On the other hand, it accounts for the rather rapid onset of liberal disenchantment with African nationalism, once liberals became unhappy about the modernizing capacity and commitments of the first generation of African leaders.

Liberals tended to see African nationalist leaders as recruits—the latest recruits—to a global movement directed not just against imperialism, but also against a wide range of archaic institutions and superstitious beliefs. The Africans were thus heirs not only to the American Revolution, but to the entire Enlightenment. They were judged according to how far they honored and carried forward this inheritance (and judged, it might be noted, in cheerful disregard of liberal injunctions about the avoidance of "ethnocentrism").

Liberal attitudes to the "emergent" African elite were, in fact, framed by a severely dichotomous view of development, which in practice (though not in principle) conceded little to cultural idiosyncrasies, or, for that matter, to "self-determination" in its broadest meaning. Liberals tended to see modernization as a battle, a series of global wars, and, indeed, a crusade, to subjugate and destroy various forms of domination subsumed under the terms *tradition* and *traditionalism.*

In the African case, as elsewhere, this propensity led them to be hostile to or suspicious of beliefs and institutions in the countryside. By the same token, it disposed them to sympathize with any leader or elite publicly embracing the goals and values of modernization.

Such sympathy was all the greater since liberals (or at least liberal social scientists) thought that nationalist leaders and their followers had suffered the heaviest social and psychological costs of modernization in colonial territories. They had been hurled into the various maelstroms associated with social change under colonialism. It was they who had suffered the "transitional crisis" (or "transitional pains") involved in moving from the "traditional" to the "modern" sector.[69] African nationalist leaders

69. The "transitional crisis" represented—in James Coleman's words—"an exploitable and highly inflammatory condition marked by a sort of generalized malaise and sense of frustration, an instability of expectations" ("Current Political Movements in Africa," 97).

were, in the cliché of the period, "men of two worlds." Such people were susceptible to any leader or movement that could give them some firm, new identity and a new sense of direction.[70]

According to many liberal observers, African nationalist movements provided such an identity and sense of direction.[71] According to David Apter, a widely quoted early student of African politics, nationalism had a therapeutic value for the uprooted: it served "to refocus their lives, providing acceptable opportunities for whatever gratifications people sought."[72]

Liberals, then, saw nationalist movements as constituting a force for modernization—for achieving progress and propagating rationality. Their leaders had been purged in the fires of social change: they had emerged whole men and dedicated modernizers. They had become intermediaries for carrying Africans into an established and progressive global movement and were founding lodge members of the newly created chapters of the modernization movement in underdeveloped countries.

This view of the sociology of African nationalism helps to explain why American liberals took a more benevolent view of African nationalism than they did (for example) of European nationalism. It protected African nationalists, at least initially, from the suspicion of being the creators of new divisions within humanity—a characterization which previous experiences had led liberals to pin on other nationalists. The notion that African (and other third world) nationalists were modernizers before they were nationalists gained African leaders a large measure of credit with liberals which long outlasted the actual battles for self-determination in the colonies. This credit helped them particularly when they acted and spoke in ways usually offensive to Western liberals. The latter were often prepared to provide active support and earnest justification for authori-

70. As Coleman put it, African nationalists were commonly "the product of the most tortured cultural ambivalences" (ibid., 98).

71. According to the political scientist René Lemarchand, nationalist movements recruited most heavily in what he described (writing about the Belgian Congo) as "shatter-zone" areas—those in which the disruption of "traditional" society had been most severe and where there were very large numbers of rootless (and, apparently, exclusively male) individuals ("How Lumumba Came to Power," 14).

72. "British West Africa: Patterns of Self-Government," 119. According to Apter, recruits for the nationalist parties came from the slums, "where traditional society had loosened its hold."

tarian measures, so long as they were taken in the name of modernization.

Independence and Democracy

Politically, the new African states presented a conceptual challenge to
scholars, as well as an ideological and moral challenge to observers, academic and otherwise. As Gwendolen Carter, a pioneer in academic work
on African politics, put it: "To study Africa is to confront in more elemental and immediate terms issues with which we ourselves should continually wrestle."[73]

Some of these issue were normative, but others were essentially semantic and analytic.[74] Indeed, the assumptions and basic vocabulary of
political science in the United States largely—and necessarily—embodied
American liberal assumptions about how politics worked and what role
government should play. Consequently, arguments about how to describe
politics in Africa often led to, or developed from, arguments about the
desirability of particular institutions or the relevance of particular values.
In this section, we shall examine arguments among liberals about the
nature and relevance of democracy in Africa.

Critics have often claimed that American liberals judged the fortunes
of democracy (indeed, political development as a whole) in Africa in
"ethnocentric" terms. Liberals, the critics claim, insisted that only the
forms of pluralist democracy found in the United States were truly democratic and that the only way to safeguard the substance of democracy
was by maintaining these forms.

A careful reading of what liberals actually said about democracy in
Africa—and they talked about it incessantly—shows that this claim is
only partly true.[75] The real drama of American liberalism in this period

73. "Danger Signs in Africa," 14.

74. "The institutions and policies of the new states," Gwendolen Carter observed later, "do not fit neatly into the categories which political scientists have
painstakingly evolved. In particular, they challenge some of the presumptions
about the differences between democratic and totalitarian regimes" ("The Character of the New States," 13).

75. This point was made in two articles protesting about the "myth" of Western
ethnocentrism published in the early sixties. According to Arnold Rivkin, the idea
that "the West expected to transfer its political institutions and frameworks *en*

lies more in the divisions of opinion that this issue created, and in how these divisions deepened as the sixties wore on. The really interesting story is not that of institutional neocolonialism, but rather that of ideological contradiction—not, in fact, what American liberals did to Africa, so much as what Africa did to American liberals.

American liberals disagreed among themselves about what democracy meant. They also disagreed about what future democracy (however defined) had in Africa. Some—whom I shall call the "institutional nationalists"—insisted on a situational definition: they argued (as did African nationalists) that African countries had to evolve their own institutions. With luck, good leadership, or by popular demand, these institutions might be democratic; but the important point was that Africans, in getting independence, had also got the right to choose their own kind of political institutions. That right was implicit in the broader right to self-determination. What mattered, in this view, was to preserve the essential processes and functions of democracy—those of individual choice and governmental accountability. Some liberal observers believed that the new African one-party states had, in their own ways, provided for these processes and functions.

Other liberals—whom I shall term the "democratic evolutionists"—clung to the hope that democracy, whether in the form that Westerners recognized or in some other form that preserved its essential rights and freedoms, would eventually emerge in Africa. The problem, they thought, was that the preconditions for democracy were absent. Meanwhile, Africans would just have to put up with dictatorships or tribal monarchies or whatever other form was best suited to their current level of development.

An important school (whom I shall call "nation builders") held that the immediate, urgent developmental needs of the continent required, for some years, a more authoritarian kind of government—government of the kind that Richard Sklar has called "developmental dictatorship." Champions of this view usually argued, like the democratic evolutionists, that the preconditions for establishing Western democracies were missing in Africa: they differed markedly from some evolutionists in taking a

---

bloc to the new states" was a straw man ("Principal Elements of U.S. Policy towards Under-Developed Countries," 460). In a subsequent article, Susan and Peter Ritner complained: "No one of any influence today treats the new African systems as 'diseased aberrations' only because they do not fit into any of our already archaic constitutions" ("Africa's Constitutional Malarkey," 18).

positive view of the current—admittedly authoritarian—African alternatives. They typically added that even if democracy was feasible, its result in practice would be to weaken government's ability to take the radical, speedy actions needed to raise living standards. "Nation building" must therefore come first.

Finally, some liberals (whom I shall call the "institutional absolutists") argued that forms of democracy actually were important and that to abandon the forms was ultimately to lose the substance as well. They typically asserted also that democracy was essential for any worthwhile development. So far from obstructing "nation building," it contributed to and, for that matter, was an inseparable part of development in the true sense. It was this group that critics accused of "ethnocentrism."

The "Institutional Nationalists"

According to such writers as Herbert J. Spiro, rejection of Western institutions was a natural, almost obligatory, corollary of self-determination. To experience independence fully, countries had to experience the trials and errors of nation building, rather like an adolescent experimenting with clothes. African states would, therefore, be making "a great mistake by adopting proven Western constitutional forms . . . they should instead evolve their own, suited to their own peculiar conditions."[76] Apart from the fact that Western institutions had caused serious problems in their countries of origin, it was impertinent of Americans and Europeans to expect Africans to adopt them. Spiro, in fact, rejected both the analogy of 1776 and the missionary spirit inspiring its use. "Imagine how our Founding Fathers would have reacted if, in addition to sending economic and military aid to the Thirteen Colonies, the Prussian or French government or scholars had been so arrogant as to send constitutional blueprints to Washington, Madison, Hamilton, and their colleagues."[77] Rather, Americans should leave Africans "to their own imagination and creativeness." Thus liberated, they would "make their own contribution to the constitutional history of mankind."

Henry Bretton, and others, agreed. Westerners, they argued, should be

76. "New Constitutional Forms in Africa," 75. Spiro acknowledged that the United States itself had borrowed, politically and philosophically, from Western Europe. But the success of the American Constitution, he argued, was due not to these borrowings, but rather to "the authors' imaginative creativity" (ibid., 73).

77. "New Constitutional Forms in Africa," 76.

humble and should reserve judgment. It was unfair to judge African coun-tries by ideals "which so-called Western societies have never really at-tained." After all, Bretton concluded, "we have our share of clowns in office."[78]

A common extension of this view was to argue that African states were already showing signs of developing their institutions which, contrary to uninformed foreign critics, actually were democratic in substance. Much alarm about "totalitarianism" in Africa was premature, the political sci-entist Gwendolen M. Carter complained in 1960, and was based on su-perficial knowledge.[79] The reality behind the form of one-party states was, Carter claimed, actually one of open communication and real account-ability.[80]

The "Democratic Evolutionists"

The democratic evolutionists argued that Western liberal or parliamentary democracy had been "a function of an unusual configuration of historical circumstances" that was unlikely to recur.[81]

78. "Straight Thinking on Africa," 206.

79. "Far too little care is being taken to analyze the inner nature of evolving systems, like that of Ghana, before overhasty generalizations are popularized" ("The Character of the New States," 13).

80. "I would maintain that a high proportion of the new African governments have a broad base of mass popular support, that there is a fairly continuous interaction between their political party leaders and the people in the local areas, and that a wide variety of ideas and policies are expressed—and often forcefully so—within the governing political parties. In the light of these facts . . . I find it misleading to call [African one-party states] undemocratic. They represent, in my view, a form of administration and political activity that is distinctively different not only from our own two-party system but also from the one-party systems of either the fascists or the communists" ("The Character of the New States," 13; "The Scholar's Role in Mobile, Perplexing Africa," *Africa Report* 7, no. 8 [August 1962]: 22).

In a similar vein, Melville Herskovits, the dean of American Africanists, sug-gested in 1959 that the emerging forms of African government reflected more traditional, and distinctively African, political values. Herskovits appealed to ob-servers of Africa "to strike beneath the outer forms to deeper meanings; to rec-ognize that power has always entailed responsibility; and to understand that the emergent political forms which may perplex those outside Africa are manifesta-tions of older sanctions" (Summary of the Herskovits report [to the U.S. Senate], *Africa Special Report*, November 1959, 12).

81. Karl de Schweinitz, *Industrialization and Democracy: Economic Necessities and Political Possibilities* (London: Free Press of Glencoe, 1964), 10–11.

Moreover, both African tradition and the legacy of colonial government militated against successful implantation of liberal institutions and principles. Africa, Henry Bretton and others argued, had no experience of democracy.[82] Its tribal structures, Russell Warren Howe asserted, had been "based largely on slavery and caste systems, and what democracy there was existed only at the sort of aristocratic level authorized by Magna Carta."[83] Parliamentary deliberation was therefore an alien notion.[84] Alien, too, was any idea of tolerating opposition. On the contrary, Africans liked strong leadership: chiefs, Russell Warren Howe remarked, "had always been despots, in some degree . . . the African mind [had] been conditioned for centuries to respect a tyrant."[85] Colonial government had, observers believed, reinforced this propensity to authoritarianism. As Martin Kilson pointed out, most of the restrictions on political expression evident in Africa represented "a continuation by African states of a power exercised by colonial governments"—just as colonial governments represented a continuation of traditional authoritarianism.[86]

Even when colonial governments had introduced representative democracy, the character of the institutions concerned was, in the African context, likely to destroy the qualities of trust and compromise necessary to successful democracy. The French system, for example, tended to entrench executive dominance, while the British created a tyranny of the simple majority. Would-be opponents of government were frustrated by the effects of an electoral system based on single-member districts and

82. "Congo and Emergent Africa," 242.

83. "The Second Revolution," *New Leader,* 20 July 1964, 13.

84. "Direct representation in bodies given to formal articulation of issues is not indigenous" (Apter, "Some Economic Factors in the Political Development of the Gold Coast," 423).

85. "These Are the Africans," 12. John Oakes made essentially the same point: "In the ancient tradition of chieftaincy, the people of Africa are prone to follow the leader. That is why in almost every African tribe or rising African state, there is one leader whose word is law. The tendency to create a one-party state and to build it around a single leader is a natural development growing less out of Marxism than out of an Africanism centuries older than Marx" ("Africa—A Continent Afire," 18).

86. "Authoritarian and Single-Party Tendencies in African Politics," 289. "Whatever their other contributions to the non-Western world [Vera Micheles Dean commented], the Western colonial powers acted not as democratic but as authoritarian rulers. . . . In this respect, they continued the traditional authoritarian institutions of non-Western lands" ("Democracy East and West," 18–19).

simple majority balloting. In some cases, it was alleged, colonial governments had actually encouraged the aggrandizement of particular political
parties, in the hope that their strength would ensure stability after independence.[87]

In any case, argued the West Indian economist Arthur Lewis, the Western majoritarian system was positively harmful in societies composed of
ethnic groups divided from each other by language, custom, and religion.
Democracy required "national integration": without it, democracy would,
Henry Bretton believed, result in "the organization of [a] country into
warring camps."[88] In Arthur Lewis's view, the "first-past-the-post" electoral system actually brought such a war closer: it "set one part of the
country against another," creating a dangerous sense of disenfranchise-
ment among voters and groups who lost elections. Conversely, it created
a dangerous temptation to be greedy and exclusive on the part of those
who won.[89]

Lewis favored a modification of liberal democracy to suit African conditions.[90] Many other commentators looked at these conditions and decided that they were unfavorable to any kind of representative democracy.[91] The African electorate, as one observer noted, simply did not have
the necessary level of "political sophistication, civic consciousness, and
general educational achievement" to make democracy work.[92]

87. Carter, "Danger Signs in Africa," 3.
88. By "national integration," Bretton meant "a social structure sufficiently
integrated to provide common perspectives on fundamental aspects of state and
society" ("Congo and Emergent Africa," 242).
89. See W. Arthur Lewis, "The Growing Pains of African Democracy," 38;
"Africa's Officers Take Command," 34–35; and *Politics in West Africa.*
90. The major modification he proposed would require parties to obtain some
votes in all parts of a country ("The Growing Pains of African Democracy," 38).
Such a system was in fact adopted in Nigeria in the late seventies.
91. Thus Reinhold Niebuhr declared: "Western-style democracy is not immediately relevant to non-European cultures. They lack the standards of literacy,
political skill, and social equilibria which would make viable political freedom
as we have come to know it" ("Well-Tempered Evangelism," 11).
92. Reviewing the experiences of the Congo after three years of independence,
James T. Harris, Jr., reported "a gradual realization that at the present levels of
political sophistication, civic consciousness, and general educational achievement,
the Parliamentary system . . . must be replaced by a less cumbersome, more
honest, and more efficient instrument of governance" ("Perspectives on the
Congo," 16). "The electorate," remarked Lawrence McQuade, "lacks the education requisite to intelligent political choice" ("The Showplace of Black Africa,"
228).

Economic development was particularly crucial to democracy. Democracy could only work, declared David Apter, once the overwhelming majority of people in a country were not concerned with "the struggle for basic subsistence."[93] In conditions of poverty, many writers argued, a formal democratic system would, at best, be an instrument by which the wealthy and powerful would legitimize their privileges.

The "Nation Builders"

Soon after independence, African states began to abandon many of the constitutional safeguards on autocratic and arbitrary government imposed by departing colonial powers and started to establish one-party states and other highly centralized institutions. Liberals reacted to this trend either by criticizing it or by defending it: there were substantial numbers on both sides.

Defense of this emerging authoritarianism typically rested on one of two bases. One consisted in admitting the authoritarian trend, but defending it on grounds of the imperatives of accelerated economic development. The other consisted in arguing that the appearance of authoritarianism was superficial or misleading and that the evolving African structures had a significant democratic substance to them (an argument sometimes used by "institutional nationalists," but also by "nation builders").[94]

The "developmental" defense appeared in the early years of independence of almost every African state.[95] The arguments made in defense of

93. "Economic Factors in the Political Development of the Gold Coast," 409. "We must not," urged Sidney Lens, "underestimate the importance of affluence to democracy" ("The Birth Pangs of Revolution," 35).

94. These positions were not completely incompatible. It was possible to argue that the institutions of a country were more authoritarian than Americans would accept at home, while asserting that they nevertheless preserved the basics of democracy. For example, a regime might give voters the right to nominate or reject candidates within the framework of a one-party election.

95. The following passage from a little-quoted article summarizes fairly and succinctly the essence of this approach:

"The emerging states face a wide range of social, economic, and political problems that can be solved only by quick action. Consequently, the Executive assumes the dominating position and the other branches are subordinated to it. . . . For the masses at large, freedom and democracy are mere slogans. They would much rather have a strong government which accom-

Nkrumah's Ghana in the 1960s reappeared, three thousand miles away and twenty-five years later, in the statements of Robert Mugabe and his followers in Zimbabwe. Among Americans, they were presented most frequently and assertively by a sociologist, then of radical but not revolutionary temper, Immanuel Wallerstein.

Wallerstein's argument rested partly on a view of the redundance of Western institutions similar to that of the "democratic evolutionists." Given their unworkability, the one-party state (he thought) represented the only alternative: "The choice," he wrote in 1961, "is not between a one-party system and a multi-party system. The structural prerequisites for the latter do not yet exist to a sufficient degree in Africa. The effective choice for the newly independent states is between a one-party (or one-dominant-party) system . . . and anarchy, which means that power reverts to local princelings and patrons, remote from the intellectual contact and stimulation which infuse the modernizing elite of the national structures."[96]

What Africa needed, then, was "the iron hoop of a strong state."[97] Without order and stability, nothing else would be possible. "It is dangerous," Wallerstein admitted, "to trifle with the protections of human liberty." But: "It is dangerous as well to allow its very basis to be undermined by the breakdown of order within the polity."[98] This preoccupation with "order" and "stability" seldom appeared in the writing of the more revolutionary Wallerstein after 1968.

To Wallerstein and other "nation builders," the Katanga secession was a salutary example of the fragility of African states. Conversely, it confirmed their belief in the necessity for strengthening central governments. Even liberal writers who sympathized with Tshombe's case against the

---

plishes much, than one which indulges in endless debates and accomplishes little. Paradoxical as it may sound, it seems that the chances for democracy look better when a democratic regime is preceded by a strong Executive which has done the necessary spade work" (Karpat, "The Reception of Western Political Institutions in the New Nations," 30).

96. *Africa: The Politics of Independence,* 163.

97. Wallerstein noted that African leaders of all ideological persuasions accepted this need: "Whether clothed in Marxian, liberal or Catholic verbiage . . . the argument is the same" ("A Program for Africa," 13).

98. "An Africanist's Reply," 21. A similar argument was made by Sidney Lens in the *Progressive*: Lens concluded that, faced by incipient disintegration, African governments might "be forced to curtail democratic rights temporarily" ("The Birth Pangs of Revolution," 36).

central government and were skeptical about African nationalists who made claims based on colonial frontiers tended to conclude that Katanga should be reintegrated with the Congo.

Disagreement began over how such reintegration should be effected. Wallerstein (as usual) opposed any weakening of central authority, in this case through adoption of a federal constitution. In his view, Tshombe was "a rebel against the very principle of central government in the Congo and [would] hold out until he [was] crushed."[99] Efforts to compromise with Tshombe and those like him by devising federal constitutions would be worse than useless. Federalism could not provide the sort of strong, mobilizing government that African countries needed: under a federal government, problems would remain unsolved, discontent would increase, and the Congo would eventually provide fertile ground for communism (a fear that, again, would have struck an odd note in the writing of the post-1968 Wallerstein).[100]

Other liberals, more impressed by Tshombe or more skeptical about the prospects for (and, indeed, the merits of) a strong central state in the Congo, suggested that the moral of the Katanga experience was the need for looser constitutional forms, to acknowledge the reality of parochialism. "The Congo," declared the anthropologist Alan P. Merriam, "has never existed as a single unit in the minds of the Congolese, and there is nothing to make one think that a change will be forthcoming in the near future."[101] The British journalist Richard Cox, who applauded Tshombe's willingness to question artificial African frontiers, concluded that the future of Africa probably lay with some form of confederalism: "The next stage after independence is going to be the realignment of frontiers. After the battles of nationalism are over, it may be that the most sensible means

99. "What Next in the Congo?" 5.
100. When the Congolese leaders (including Tshombe) agreed tentatively to adopt a federal constitution at the Tananarive conference of March 1961, Wallerstein commented: "A confederal regime at Leopoldville may, with continued U.N. aid, manage to muddle through for a while. What it will not be able to do is mobilize a modernizing elite and effect significant social change in the Congo." The United States, he believed, should for the time being "attempt to contain the tribalist anarchy of the Congo by supporting the formation of modernizing strong states around it" ("Congo Confederation," 4–5).
101. "The Congo's First Year of Independence," 237. Merriam's best-known work on the Congo was *Congo: Background of Conflict*. His fieldwork was largely conducted in Kasai, the neighboring province to Katanga.

of avoiding civil and tribal warfare will be to follow the pattern of confederation that Tshombe has worked to establish in the Congo."[102]

Nation builders responded that economic development required strong, even authoritarian, central government. Wallerstein warned that the demands of "modernization, nationhood, and international dignity [might] involve the sacrifice of the individual or the minority group."[103] But such sacrifices were acceptable in light of the aspirations of the governing elite, and the urgency with which they wanted to fulfill them.[104]

To the critics of African one-partyism, Wallerstein and others had several kinds of answers. One was to claim that the apparent authoritarianism of such states was fairly mild (even ineffectual) or that it in fact concealed broadly democratic processes at work underneath.[105] Critics, Wallerstein argued, had failed to observe "the real dispersion of power that still exist[ed] in every African country."

Wallerstein's argument had, however, one serious drawback. If economic development and national integration required a strong central government, how much of either would be achieved by governments which, beyond their own offices and outside their own rhetoric, were practically ineffectual? Why, if they were so ineffectual, should anyone take their talk of modernization seriously and defend such autocratic

102. "The Strong Man of Katanga," 24.

103. Robert A. Manners, "Nations Growing up Overnight," 48.

104. "The central government," Wallerstein declared, "usually stands for modernization, universal education, economic development, the possibility for the peasant to express himself and participate in government *for the first time*" ("A Program for Africa," 13; emphasis in original).

105. Wallerstein himself used both elements of this argument: "Although African independent states are not [he wrote] liberal in their practices, they are by no means totalitarian. The citizens do not live in terror of a secret police. Political debate is a commonplace of African life. Opposition to government policies exists, is heard, is even listened to . . . there is an enormous amount of give and take in almost every independent African state" (*Africa: The Politics of Independence*, 159, 161).

Even some travelers, such as the journalist David Hapgood, who did not share Wallerstein's rosy view of African elites, seemed to share his assessment of the actual impact of their rule. Hapgood wrote in 1963: "When you travel through the back country of Guinea and Ghana, you realize that it is nonsense to call these nations 'totalitarian.' The opposition is suppressed, but not with the barbarism of a Hitler or a Stalin. The cult of personality around Kwame Nkrumah of Ghana is distasteful, but it is mild compared to the Stalin cult" ("Africa's New Elites," 47).

behavior as they did exhibit? The justification tended, unfortunately, to undermine the original argument.

A surer—and, to liberals, more appealing—response was to argue, as (we have seen) did the political scientist Gwendolen Carter, that new forms of democracy were being hammered out in Africa. Wallerstein took the same view. Further, he argued that, so far from resembling contemporary totalitarianism, African one-partyism provided a defense against it, and against outside forces that might introduce totalitarianism.[106] Completing the circle, Wallerstein even suggested that the African one-party system was "often a significant step toward the liberal state, not a first step away from it" (a rather surprising justification from the advocate of "the iron hoop").[107] It was such a step because it was establishing the legitimacy and permanence of the national state in the eyes of the citizens. Only when such popular recognition had been achieved could the distinction between the "government" and the "state," essential for liberal democracy, even begin to develop.

Other scholars argued that single-party regimes actually provided the basic requirements of democracy. Ruth Schachter, author of a pioneering study of political parties in French-speaking Africa, claimed, for example, that "single-party systems based on mass parties [were] moving towards democracy."[108] Such parties, in her view, "reinforced the African version of responsibility" and indeed seemed almost impeccably democratic. According to some nation builders, African traditional government provided a democratic foundation for one-partyism, even a guarantee that the latter would remain democratic.[109] Coming from dedicated modernizers, this argument was unexpected. Some commentators, nevertheless, managed to combine, on the one hand, an overall distaste for "tradition" and a dislike for "tribes" ("the embodiment and the fortress of primitivism")

---

106. Writing of events in the ex-Belgian Congo, Wallerstein criticized Washington's failure "to see that a strong central government based on popular support . . . [was] a more effective bulwark, short-run or long-run, against Soviet infiltration than the semi-anarchy which the Congo seem[ed] destined . . . to enjoy for a long while" ("A Program for Africa," 14).

107. *Africa: The Politics of Independence,* 163.

108. "Single-Party Systems in West Africa," 307.

109. John Oakes, visiting Guinea, was struck by Sekou Toure's claim that "the state [was] built on the traditional African community." He noted that the ruling party's hierarchy rested—"at least theoretically—on a popular and traditional base" ("Africa—A Continent Afire," 18).

with, on the other, a favorable view of traditional-cum-tribal government insofar as it provided legitimacy for the party-state.[110]

One-party states, governed by traditional notions of accountability, would, claimed a correspondent in Tanzania, protect what really mattered to the African peasant—"his traditional concepts of dignity and tribal morality." The peasant, John George said, did not mind Africans taking over the privileges of Europeans. In fact, he was proud "to look up from his roadside field and see another African . . . riding to the Government Boma in the large official car of a regional or area commissioner."[111] He would be all too happy if the official waved at him "with the wise friendliness of a politician greeting a voter." Provided that his right to speak out was ensured, the African peasant would accept "a condition of government that people in another culture would regard as unbearable." He would not object if the administration should "become extremely lax and ineffectual by European standards."[112]

Reading such commentary, it sometimes seems as if Western liberals thought that Africans would tolerate just about anything. For example, Herbert Spiro (in a much-criticized passage) suggested that preventive detention was relatively painless for Africans, because "African notions of time and space lend a less unpleasant aspect to arrests than they have to us."[113] (This remark oddly resembled the colonial administrators' theory that Africans enjoyed a stay in jail because they got better food and accommodation there than at home.)

On recalcitrant critics still skeptical of the virtues of one-partyism, Wallerstein and other defenders of nation building used a different, and rougher kind of argument—not so much an *ad hominem* as an *ad patriam* type of defense. They pointed to episodes in American or European politics, recent or remote, which revealed similar degrees of authoritarian-

110. For example, Wallerstein, who described "the forces of tradition" as the main "divisive forces" in Africa, also claimed that "the African tradition of government" valued debate and decision making by consensus: "There is [he wrote] a remarkable similarity between these familiar traditional ways and the formulas that in fact govern the newly independent national governments" ("A Program for Africa," 13; *Africa: The Politics of Independence,* 162).

111. "How Stable Is Tanganyika?" 9.

112. Ibid. In Russell Warren Howe's view, liberals were right about "the African 'liking to know who's boss'—he just wants to choose the boss freely, that's all" ("The Second Revolution," 15).

113. Cited in a review of Spiro's *Politics in Africa* by John Hughes, *Saturday Review,* 2 June 1962, 29.

ism, corruption, incompetence, or whatever vice the critics were currently pinning on African politicians. Their intention was to show that, as Bretton claimed, Westerners had had their "share of clowns in office"—in fact, not only clowns, but tyrants.

The point of such rhetorical aggression was not just to shame "ethnocentric" liberals. It was to soften up critics for the really important follow-up claim, namely, that leaders who had been indisputably neither clowns nor tyrants, but authentic American political heroes, had themselves favored restrictions on freedom as extensive as any practiced in Africa. As usual, the early history of the United States was ransacked—quite successfully—for examples of such restrictions. The United States—defenders of President Nkrumah of Ghana pointed out—had, like Nkrumah's government, adopted Alien and Sedition laws shortly after independence.[114]

Indeed, the Founding Fathers (the historical analogists pointed out) had harbored the same responsible doubts about competitive political parties as those currently troubling African presidents.[115] Moreover, Immanuel Wallerstein cautioned, the adulation given to George Washington himself should make Americans pause before ridiculing hero-worship of African leaders: "It was about this country that a French observer in the 1830s wrote: 'To Washington alone, there are busts, inscriptions, columns; this is because Washington, in America, is not a man but a God.'"[116] According to Waldemar Nielsen, an even more sustained comparison was possible: "In terms of parallels with American history, Africa is in the 1790s. That was the period when we physically drove out of the country and into Canada a good portion of our opposition, tarred-and-feathered some who remained and expropriated (legally and illegally) the property of not a few. We oppressed the native tribes, saw corruption flourish in our new officialdom and denounced the idea of foreign military bases on our soil. We took large quantities of foreign aid and credits, while simultaneously denouncing the greed of those who offered it."[117]

114. See, for example, Kenworthy, "Ghana: So Young, So Hopeful," 22; Oakes, "Africa—A Continent Afire," 16.
115. Indeed, remarked an American diplomat, "the Father of our Country, George Washington, was not sure that this new land should have political parties. . . . He was dead-set against factionalism" (Duggan, "The New African Chiefs," 354).
116. "An Africanist's Reply," 22.
117. "Africa Is Poised on the Razor's Edge," 11.

If that wasn't enough to shame Africa's critics, there was in the early sixties a parallel closer to home that would surely silence all white liberals. If, Kirk Sale remarked in 1965, Americans wanted a prime example of a corrupt, poverty-stricken, petty tyranny, there was "a little foreign country" they could profitably study. It was backward, dependent on agriculture, and like many such states, essentially "unviable." Sale went on: "Also like most of the others, it is run in the familiar form of one-party rule, with dictatorship by a small, corrupt and power-oriented oligarchy, out to perpetuate its rule by keeping the mass of peasants without education, legal rights or a democratic vote."[118] This third world country was Mississippi.

Independence and Nationalism

A common assumption of American liberals was that their values (as reflected in American foreign policy during the Cold War) and those of African nationalism were identical, or at least compatible.

In response to conservatives who charged that African nationalists were communists or anti-American (the two being essentially synonymous), liberals invariably protested that African nationalist leaders were "pragmatic" and "moderate." Their platform rhetoric might suggest the opposite, but many liberal journalists came away from private interviews with African leaders comfortingly convinced that the private leader was the real one. It was therefore necessary to be patient, understanding, and generous—and above all to discourage provocations that might prevent private convictions from becoming public policy. Some senators were also convinced: "These men," declared Hubert H. Humphrey, "are moderate and responsible, moderate in the means they employ, and responsible in their judgments of the international situation. They know what Communism is and what Communism wants."[119] The experts concurred. Most Africans in power, Immanuel Wallerstein insisted, were "sensible, real-

118. "Freedom and/or Progress," 23.
119. Speech to the U.S. Senate, 2 September 1959 (cited in "A Senator Looks at Africa," *Africa Special Report,* September 1959, 7).

istic, competent": they remained "close to Western thought and culture."[120]

This desire to protect "moderate" anticommunist leaders directly affected the attitudes of U.S. policymakers toward issues that might seem domestic African matters. For example, U.S. opposition to the secession of Katanga was based on a concern that if it succeeded, other secessions would follow, causing the breakup of the Congo itself. There was, observed George W. Ball, "no legal case, no political case, and no moral case" for encouraging the Balkanization of central Africa.[121] There was, however, also a pressing diplomatic case for preventing this outcome. "As a practical matter," G. Mennen Williams predicted, "if Katanga seceded, then up to twenty other areas might want to do the same thing. This would have led to chaos and opened the door for Communist and extremist penetration."[122] Ironically, then, Tshombe—a self-proclaimed "friend of the West" and much admired as such by conservatives—was opposed by the U.S. government because his success might help the cause of the Communists.

Meanwhile, liberal Africanists were at pains to stress the essential mod-

120. "Africa out of Joint," 27; "Our Unfriendly African Friends," 11. "Most of the new leaders of the emergent free Africa [declared William Hessler] are sensible, moderate men, with little of the sullen anti-Westernism of Asia and Egypt" ("The Agenda for Africa," 37). Writing about Tom Mboya of Kenya, William Persen warned: "If the United States turns its back on moderate men of his thinking, there is not much probability that the present opportunity to aid and guide the future of the African continent will ever return" ("Africa in Transition," 6).

121. "The government structure which the Belgians left behind . . . is the only political structure the Congo has ever known. Under it, the Congo has evolved from a primitive area to a potentially prosperous power in Africa. . . . To break up this entity into a number of conflicting and competing tribal satrapies could only confirm and render permanent the chaos we have already seen in the Congo" ("American Policy in the Congo," 16).

122. "Congo Realities and United States Policy," 795: "The centrifugal forces of tribalism are such that, if secession ever were successfully maintained, the Congo could break up into dozens of little unviable areas, each subject to extremist infiltration." Norman Cousins also remarked on the possibility that secession would create opportunities for the Soviet Union. Secession, he noted, "inevitably meant nationwide disintegration and this in turn meant that the Congo might be up for grabs in an international free-for-all. The Soviet Union had clearly indicated a prime interest in the Congo. . . . One way or another, a divided and disintegrating Congo might either become a Soviet sphere of influence or repeat the tragic experience of Korea" ("Report from the Congo," 32).

eration of other leaders, such as Kwame Nkrumah, Patrice Lumumba, and Sekou Toure, whom conservatives were belaboring as Kremlin puppets. In defending Lumumba, George M. Houser claimed that not only he, but all of the Congolese leaders at the time of independence were basically pragmatists.[123] In the case of Toure, John Marcum sought out the libeled party himself for reassurance. He found "a large handsome brooding figure in the corner of a large air-conditioned office, pouring over a large pile of papers." Toure explained patiently to his visitor the need for one-partyism in Africa. Marcum's account continues: "Then, pensively chewing on a kola nut, he holds forth on the reasons why the role of religion and religious freedom, the dominance of a communal mentality and the extent of indigenous democratic traditions in Africa are assurance that he and his team are not Communists. . . . He places great stress upon his desire to attach Guinea to the Western world. Even for a future United States of West Africa, he specifically rejects the idea of neutralism."[124] From this and similar pieces of evidence, liberal writers and academics tended to conclude that they had seen the future and that, from the liberal point of view, it would work.

A review of the material cited in this chapter will show few African names being quoted or countries referred to. Even in the years immediately following independence, much liberal argument about colonialism and decolonization took place on a high level of generality and was deductive in character. It derived positions on issues from broad principles, rather than from detailed experience of the continent and its politics. Indeed, despite their view of self-government as an "irresistible tide," foreign liberals tended to take an oddly apolitical view of the future of African societies. They seemed implicitly to regard that future as something to be shaped by the rational application of self-evidently good principles, rather than as a matter of domestic and international pressures and constraints, potentially at the mercy of the political priorities and whims of African leaders and their supporters.

This tendency to argue deductively was to some extent a natural—in fact, unavoidable—reflection of the current state of sheer ignorance con-

---

123. "Ideology [Houser wrote] is not a factor, on the whole, in the positions and alignments which exist" ("Leopoldville Revisited," 6).

124. "Report from Guinea," 5, 6.

cerning Africa. Few American commentators had been there or knew much about the continent. But it was also an expression of a well-established liberal tendency to assume the ubiquitous appeal and relevance of liberal values and institutions. This assumption led to viewing independence as providing an opportunity to practice virtue, not as offering a license to explore alternatives. In this sense, liberals were avid supporters of self-determination but were also potentially among the most demanding critics of its beneficiaries.

As the years passed, and as liberal views became more grounded in the specifics of Africa, so the tensions within liberal doctrine came to the surface in arguments both between American liberals and between liberals and African nationalists. This process involved a direct encounter with actual leaders and real countries, in place of the unreal dialogue with a rather shadowy cast of presumed actors and putative states characteristic of arguments prior to independence.

FOUR

Liberalism and

The African State,

1962–1970

Few American visitors landed at Conakry, the capital of Guinea, in the early sixties, and fewer still got further than the airport. But in 1964 *Africa Report* published an article by an unnamed correspondent who described the desolate state of the Guinean economy. There was, he said, "chaos in every field of economic relations." The country had "an almost worthless inconvertible currency" and the development program desperately needed "an idealism and other human qualities" which, despite Sekou Toure's personal popularity, the regime seemed unable to inspire.[1]

Four years later, Russell Warren Howe reported, following a visit of his own to Conakry, that Guinea was now no more than "an economic corpse dependent for occasional reanimation on the interplay of Western and Eastern aid." Few institutions in the country seemed to work. The only ones that did so "with internationally-accepted efficiency" were such foreign-run enclaves as the bauxite and aluminum complexes and some plantations. Even the phone of the minister of posts and telegraphs had stopped working.[2] All that was left of independence was a few ceremonial trappings: for example, a correspondent remarked, "the band of the Republican Guard . . . still produces at the airport, to greet distinguished visitors, the curious chromaticisms of Keita Fodeba."[3]

1. "Guinea after Five Years," 5, 6.
2. Howe, "A Talk with Sekou Toure," 50.
3. "Guinea after Five Years," 6. Keita Fodeba was a poet and founder and choreographer of the Ballets Africains, the Guinean national dance company. He was also successively minister of the interior, minister of national defense and security, and minister of development, rural economy, and labor. He died in de-

By this time, President Nkrumah of Ghana had been overthrown in a military coup generally greeted in the West as brought on by the corruption and incompetence of his regime. Zaire and Nigeria were also under military rule; but in Nigeria even the iron hand of the military had been unable to stop a descent into a brutal civil war that lasted until January 1970.

The effect of events such as these, and of depressing reports on the state of previously admired countries such as Guinea, was naturally to dampen the hopes and, indeed, the faith of American liberals regarding sub-Saharan Africa. From roughly 1962 onward, commentaries on African politics in liberal journals increasingly exhibited what one writer termed "radical disenchantment" with the continent and its political leaders. Disenchantment was accompanied by indifference: Africa ceased to be a significant arena in the Cold War, and American attention was increasingly taken up with the Vietnam War and with domestic strife associated with opposition to the war and with the civil rights struggle.

Yet the writings in which liberal disenchantment was expressed are of great interest. They provide clues to the larger puzzle of why and how the liberal consensus of the late fifties and early sixties broke up. They reveal not only the fissure lines in this consensus but also some more permanent tensions within the aggregate of assumptions and ideals making up American liberalism.

In this chapter, we shall examine not so much the specific events causing liberal disillusionment as the ways in which the liberal reaction was expressed, the targets at which it was directed, and the lessons that liberals drew from their encounter with African nationalism.

In expressing their disappointment with the political and economic direction of African states, liberals typically concentrated blame on two, fairly obvious targets: themselves and Africans. This choice of targets was not exclusive—responsibility could be, and often was, divided between foolish liberals and faithless Africans. But the choice had serious implications for future liberal attitudes and, indeed, political intentions.

If liberals had been at fault and had fundamentally misunderstood African society and politics, the implication was that they should adjust their expectations of the continent. They should look elsewhere for possible liberal growth areas, or they should adapt their doctrines even fur-

---

tention in May 1969 after being charged with plotting to overthrow President Toure.

ther to fit "African realities." Paradoxically, they could either be true to themselves (and give up on Africa), or they could put Africa first (and give up on some elements of liberalism).

If, however, the problem was not liberalism itself, but the illiberalism or incompetence of African governments, then the moral was to get better leaders, to wait for better times, or even to change American policies, but not to abandon liberal ideals and standards. Liberals simply had to find better ways of realizing liberal values abroad: the problem was essentially tactical, not strategic.

This "choice" was more accurately a recurrent dilemma. *Choice* implies an imperative decision, a commitment of some finality with consequences. American liberal writers did not "choose" in this sense: indeed, they did not need to do so. Rather, they tended toward one view or another, while in Africa and elsewhere in the third world the phenomena troubling them persisted. Consequently, the nature of the liberal dilemma over Africa in the mid-sixties closely resembled that of the dilemma facing President Carter and his liberal colleagues in the late seventies.

Liberal revisionism expressed itself through arguments about specific issues occurring in the discourses about modernization, democracy, and nationalism (each examined below). It also took the form of a more general autocritique of American liberalism, which had intellectual, moral, and sometimes political aspects. Naturally, conservatives, radicals, and African-American nationalists happily supplemented this autocritique with their own—invariably self-justifying—comments on the failings of liberalism.

The intellectual critique consisted in arguing that liberals—academics and journalists alike—had got Africa wrong because they were grossly ignorant about the continent and particularly about its politics. Scholars, the critics said, had failed to get below the superficial rhetoric of African politics. They had, Joseph S. Nye, Jr., remarked, all too often "accepted nationalist slogans at face value"; they had been gullible, as well as superficial, letting themselves be taken in by "such facile phrases as 'rising tides' and 'inevitable forces'."[4] Political scientists had spun out abstract taxonomies, many of which were simplistic and based on little real knowledge of the ways in which African politics actually worked.[5] In 1964, the

4. "Verdict on Rotberg," 9.
5. The fact was, wrote one commentator after the coups of 1965 and 1966, that outsiders still had "a rudimentary grasp of what [was] involved in political development and modernization" (Greene, "Toward Understanding Military Coups," 10).

political theorist Harvey Glickman commented on how little had actually been discovered by his colleagues: "Little is known, for example, about how or to what extent African political arrangements reflect ideas of 'legitimacy' in the minds of ordinary citizens. Nor is much known about the 'effectiveness' of post-colonial machinery. To what extent does 'government' make its presence felt in the village up-country?"[6]

The moral critique consisted in arguing that American liberals had betrayed their own values in coming to terms with African nationalism. As early as 1960, some liberals had raised the question of whether these values were compatible with African nationalist values. Responding to a manifesto issued by the liberal Africa League, Harvey Glickman asked if the authors had really thought through their earnest demands of fellow liberals—especially their demands for sympathy with authoritarian governments.[7]

This challenge was followed by others. Critics attacked what Herbert J. Spiro described as the *"narodniki*-like feeling of inferiority" American liberals displayed toward Africans.[8] Moreover, they claimed, there was an

6. Review of Gwendolen M. Carter, *Five African States: Responses to Diversity* (Ithaca: Cornell University Press, 1964), *Africa Report* 9, no. 10 (November 1964): 34. After "a decade of encouragement to the revision of customary standards of analysis and theory so that we can better comprehend the forces of politics in Africa," Glickman observed, "it is somewhat puzzling to find so few traces of these revisions of standards."

Such ignorance, Glickman commented later, "did not excuse the obvious conceptual inadequacies of the various schemas proposed for understanding political change in Africa: 'the mobilization model,' 'the totalitarian model,' and 'the parliamentary-democratic model' had all been found 'to be conceptually misleading'" ("Dialogues on the Theory of African Political Development," 39).

7. "The question remains whether we fully accept the implications of a wholly independent Africa. Would the Africa League continue to support 'the modern African elite' if that elite did not 'breed large and cohesive interest groups' which can be the sources for nationwide parties? We understand that 'political opposition and national integration often appear to be closely linked,' but must we— shall we—support the deliberate construction of centralized socialist societies? . . . Perhaps the rapid development and integration of African societies along the lines that seem to be forming will permanently preclude private interest groups and competitive democracy" ("Four Critiques of U.S. Policy in Africa," 13). The Africa League pamphlet was written by, among others, David Apter, Ruth Schachter, and Immanuel Wallerstein.

8. "New Constitutional Forms in Africa," 75–76. In 1966, an African-American scholar, Martin L. Kilson, attacked what he termed the "neo-liberal and

implicit condescension, even racism, behind much special pleading and "explanation" of African behavior in liberal journals.

Overall, Afrophiles had (in this view) been guilty of reflexive thinking—leaping indiscriminately to the defense of Africans because they had been victims of colonialism. Unequivocal condemnation of colonialism, as the historian Albert Guérard had pointed out in 1960, too easily became unequivocal approval of anything anti or postcolonial.[9]

But to treat Africans simply as victims of a "suffering situation" was, Russell Warren Howe and others complained, patronizing to them, as well as being a betrayal of liberal values. Howe, a veteran Africa correspondent, had, it may be recalled, earlier applauded Ghana's independence for confirming his belief in "the infinite possibilities of the human being." By 1961, however, he was emphasizing his belief in the finite possibilities of empathy: "Those of us who love Africa must love it, as we love individuals, for what it is, and not for the illusion that it seeks to present to itself and to the outside world."[10]

Honesty, then, was the first duty of friendship, and honesty precluded claiming to believe in things one thought incredible or undesirable.[11] As Guérard remarked: "If we are told that cannibalism, human sacrifices, slavery are part of the aeonial African pattern and therefore should be cherished for the self-respect and mental health of the Africans, we have the right to shrug our shoulders."[12]

The point behind such protests was to reassert the liberal belief in equality and the connection between self-determination and individual responsibility. What was needed, the liberal revisionists (or, perhaps, traditionalists) said, was "a new, more realistic, more genuinely egalitarian approach to underdeveloped man." Anything else, however superficially well intentioned, was at best paternalism and at worst a new kind of

---

neo-radical patronization of black men" pervading liberal writing on Africa ("African Autocracy," 4).

9. Referring to liberal friends of Africa in the West, Guérard had written in 1960: "Because they condemn unequivocally the injustices you [the Africans] have suffered, they commit themselves to whatever action you may take, right or wrong" ("To My African Friends," 60).

10. "These Are the Africans," 13.

11. "One does not show respect for the African by pretending to believe in his rainmakers," a correspondent of *Life* magazine had remarked in 1953 ("Americans and Africa," 178).

12. "To My African Friends," 62.

racism. Conversely, the way to ending racism in all forms led through "according all men the high honor of being their own keepers."[13]

Instead of being honest with Africans and sticking to their own standards, too many American liberals (the critics said) had embraced "spurious liberalism," implicitly consigning "the African" to the demeaning status of a "colored eternal baby." The effect was, Howe declared, to deny Africans full humanity—a denial as culpable as that of any (earlier) imperialist: "Between the derision of early travelers and the flame of the Africanophile, the distinction is one of refinement. The African has gone from Mickey Mouse to Mighty Mouse, but not to Man. . . . Yesterday, all Calibans were grotesque in their wretchedness; this was the so-called 'colonial' attitude. Today they are grotesque in their finery; this is the liberal achievement. The liberal, like the colonial, does not admit the existence, in the African world, of Caesar or Caligula, or even John Doe: there is only one African—Caliban unchained."[14]

The hypocrisy and fawning had, according to revisionists, been particularly bad in relations between American liberals and African politicians. Egged on by liberals, the African politician was in danger of becoming "a new Uncle Tom" who wanted his "humanity" acknowledged, but who also expected to be treated with greater leniency than the rest of the human race.[15] The self-indulgence of African politicians had been further encouraged (an academic suggested) by the opportunism of academic "Africanists" who had persistently curried favor with the politicians by "describing their behavior in unnecessarily laudatory terms."[16]

Revisionists thus set out to be more discriminating about leaders who had been praised too much. One side-effect was that sometimes they also revised their judgments on unpopular leaders. Tshombe was a startling case in point. By the middle of 1961, a number of observers—while still opposed to Katanga's separation—were revealing something close to admiration for Tshombe and the Katangan state. Russell Warren Howe was particularly emphatic about Tshombe's political qualities. Tshombe, Howe

13. "Backward peoples [Howe wrote] are equal in potential, in humanity, in rights, duties and obligations. Just as educated and uneducated criminals are equally guilty, so misgovernment is as reprehensible in Africa as in America or Europe" ("Racism in Africa," 20).

14. Ibid., 19.

15. Ibid.

16. Kilson, "African Autocracy," 4. The effect of such behavior, Kilson argued, was "to whitewash the underside of African politics."

observed, had begun by "being a cat's-paw of the Belgian *Union Minière,*" but he had become much more than that. Indeed, he was "the only dynamic Congolese factor" in the Congo, "the only effective leader the disappointing Congo [had] produced so far."[17] By 1963, Howe (and others) had concluded that this "successful and slippery politician" might have a future in Congolese politics, even though Katanga itself had fallen.[18] David Halberstam was similarly impressed.[19] Like Howe (and equally prophetically), Halberstam was dismayed by the loss of this great political talent to national politics: "One is torn by the thought of what Tshombe might have been, the immense potential of this man. Had he been Prime Minister of a unified Congo, he would probably have been the most popular African ever to visit the United States."[20]

Other African politicians had (according to the critics) been encouraged to escape and, indeed, to refuse responsibility for anything that went wrong. By the mid-sixties, Victor T. LeVine complained, this response

17. "What Is the Congo?" 24, 25. The Union Minière du Haut-Katanga was the dominant mining company in Katanga.

18. "Everybody's Problem Child," 10. In a political epitaph on Tshombe published in 1968, Howe went further, describing Tshombe as "the genuine representative of Katangan nationalism, a sincere but inconvenient phenomenon . . . the only politician to have achieved nation-wide popularity in the Congo" (review of Ian Colvin, *The Rise and Fall of Moise Tshombe, Africa Report* 13, no. 9 [December 1968]: 33–34).

19. "If he is not the most popular African of his time," Halberstam wrote of Tshombe, "he is at least the most controversial; if not the most profound, then certainly one of the most clever and resilient. The son of an African millionaire, he is disdained by his fellow African leaders as a white-man lover. Yet he inspires in the black people of his region a loyalty as fierce as the debate he inspires in the rest of the world" ("Mystery—and Tragedy—of Tshombe," 7).

20. Ibid., 56. Tshombe, other journalists remarked, had "grasped the essentials of strong government" and had understood "the need for continuing economic development." Indeed, he had created an exemplar for other African countries: "Tshombe [the British journalist Richard Cox wrote] need not fear that his army will become uncontrollable at the slightest provocation. He can maintain law and order, and in the Congo today this is a remarkable achievement. . . . There is little doubt that had Katanga always been a separate state, the western nations would be praising Tshombe to the skies" ("The Strong Man of Katanga," 24).

Tshombe was, in fact, appointed prime minister of the Congo on 10 July 1964 and continued in this post until 13 October 1965—six weeks before the military coup that brought President Mobutu to power. For a sympathetic contemporary account of Tshombe's tenure of the premiership, see Clos, "Why the Africans Hate Tshombe."

had become reflexive and universal, an ideological and emotional Band-Aid protecting against all the ills of the continent. In fact, African politicians had completely adopted for their continent (and for themselves) the liberal image of being victims of a "suffering situation." In their view, LeVine noted, everything was "caused by massive neo-colonialist interference"—a convenient assumption, enabling "those who are fearful of the consequences of independence to evade its responsibilities."[21]

The Debate about Modernization

Such critical comment about the ethical maturity of the African leadership was accompanied by growing disenchantment among liberals about its commitment to modernization. Such disenchantment was deep and irretrievable in the same measure as the earlier enchantment had been complete and unqualified.

By the mid-sixties, a number of American liberals were becoming convinced that the African elite was using its power (and abusing their trust) in the worst possible way—namely, to no developmental purpose at all, but merely to enrich itself and to perpetuate its own political control. Given the traditional liberal distaste for government (dormant even in some "New Deal" liberals), this was a particularly damning observation. American defenders of the African leadership retorted that Western liberals were setting a higher standard for African politicians than they set for their own.[22] To this the critics responded that, though this might be

21. "This [idea] has the dual utility of preserving the myth of the political virginity of Africans for those who see the world divided into exploiters and exploited, and of permitting those who are fearful of the consequences of independence to evade its responsibilities. As an explanation, however, it is as demeaning and condescending as that advanced by those who argue the basic political incompetence of Africans. It is clear that the facts support neither explanation" ("Independent Africa in Trouble," 19).

22. Colin Gonze, the editor of *Africa Today*, in fact commented that the degree of Western liberal disenchantment was related to initially excessive expectations. Thus in January 1964 Gonze noted: "The American attitude to Africa as reflected in the press has changed radically in the past few months. Simplistic approval of African independence has been replaced by cynicism or equally simple disapproval" ("First Column," 2).

true, the higher standard was justified by the urgent developmental needs of African societies.

Misgivings about the dedication of African politicians appeared in liberal sources quite early. One theme that became common in the mid-sixties was that African politicians were too interested in converting political power into money. In its simplest form, this meant that they were personally corrupt. In a more abstract and general sense, it meant that they were engaged in realizing the one asset they had—access to government—to transform themselves collectively into a propertied middle class, akin to the bourgeoisie of developed countries, although differently constituted.

As early as 1960, Hugh and Mabel Smythe in fact used the term *new class* to describe the special dependence of the African elite on political, rather than economic, power.[23] This theme was further developed by Martin L. Kilson, Jr., who distinguished the "new" or "political" class from a "true" bourgeoisie.[24] Kilson saw no sign of this elite (or "pseudo-elite") being transformed into "a bona fide modernizing elite": that role had been left to "the foreign capitalist."

In the works of two French-speaking writers, René Dumont and Frantz Fanon, the African elite was subsequently labeled a "political class" (or "bureaucratic bourgeoisie").[25] Both enjoyed wide popularity in the

23. The Smythes commented: "As the new elite stabilizes, it becomes more conservative, preoccupied with maintaining its own power. The zealous young men who . . . made fiery speeches in favor of nationalism and independence are now middle-aged and established leaders with vested interests. . . . There is no question that they intend to maintain their hard-won seats of power and to countenance as little opposition as possible. . . . The top level politicians fear opposition" ("Black Africa's New Power Elite," 14).

24. "Though bourgeois in form and aspiration," Kilson observed, "the black elite in Africa possesses little of the substantive skills or resources (e.g., capital) necessary for them to play a progressive or decisive role in directing the modernization of African societies. The substantive skills and resources are still monopolized by expatriate groups, while the African elite claim little more than political (manipulative) bureaucratic and intellectual skills" ("African Autocracy," 5).

25. The influence of Dumont derived from his extensive field experience as an agronomist in developing countries (and his pungent, occasionally bombastic style, even in the presence of heads of state). Fanon's influence stemmed from his experiences as a black psychiatrist and a supporter of the FLN in Algeria. In retrospect, it seems that perhaps Fanon and Dumont did essentially invert categories and little more. They may have read their own hopes and values into, and even romanticized, the peasants, much as the liberal nation builders cast the nationalist elite in an image of their own making.

---

108 *Liberalism and the African State*

United States, Dumont appealing mainly to disillusioned liberals and socialists, Fanon particularly to black radicals. Their popularity was especially striking since their view of which element in African society offered the best hope for progress was directly contrary to the orthodox liberal view. Where liberals vested their hopes in the "modernizing" (or "nation-building") elite, Dumont and Fanon looked to the peasants (dismissed or at best disdained by liberals, and Marxists, as benighted traditionalists): the urban elite, to them, was the indolent, self-absorbed, consumption-oriented element in African societies. The popularity of an approach so startlingly different from that widely propagated in American journalism and college textbooks clearly reflected a fundamental disenchantment about postindependence Africa. It also, however, appealed to the populist strain in American liberalism—the populism which was ever alert to symbols of "elitism" and ever suspicious of bureaucracy.

By 1965, as military coups became more common and the effects of misgovernment became clearer, a collective schadenfreude began to pervade American commentary on Africa, not least in liberal journals. Writers such as David Hapgood delivered salvo upon salvo of rueful anecdote and sad reproach at the black African elites. According to Hapgood, these elites had "wasted their resources on prestige projects and conspicuous consumption." Moreover, the self-styled "radicals" were just as bad as the rest: "When one observes," Hapgood remarked, "the indifference with which many African 'socialists' view the common spectacle of old women carrying crushing burdens on their heads while young men loaf or frisk about, he realizes what the African revolution was not about. Despite the talk of African socialism, it was not a revolution aimed at greater equality among human beings. It was, rather, a sort of *coup d'état*, a palace revolt in which the elite took over the positions denied them by Europeans."[26] This elite was, in the opinion of many disaffected liberals, one which had succeeded to power too easily and which consequently had no sense of limits.[27] It wanted for itself and the societies it ruled "the material appurtenances of Western upper-class society."[28]

Coming from liberals, this line of attack was rather ironic. For the sin of the postcolonial elite turned out to that of wanting too much—or too

26. "Africa's New Elites," 46.
27. "You want," Eric Sevareid chided African leaders, "a social-welfare state, complete with minimum wages, medical insurance, pensions, before you have created the capital to pay for it" ("Talking back to Africa," 6).
28. Smythe and Smythe, "Black Africa's New Power Elite," 14.

much for itself—what liberals had feared that Africans might not want enough, namely, the appurtenances of modernity. "There are no Bantu Gandhis, enamored of handicrafts and cottage industries. The leaders' eyes are fixed on hydroelectric power and steel mills," declared William Hessler.[29]

But, in American liberal eyes, the real trouble about the African elite's attachment to modernity was not its acquisitiveness but its lack of the appropriate entrepreneurial values and skills. In short, it lacked the dynamism and appetite for risk taking that liberals thought essential to sustained modernization.

Marxists (as we shall see) had similar criticisms of the African elite. But they saw the modernization process in collective and materialist terms: liberals saw it mainly as a revolution in *values,* as a transformation of individual psyches. Modernization, for them, was critically dependent, not on the somewhat impersonal workings of a dialectic, but on the moral and political leadership of "a few good men." If that leadership failed, modernization would fail. And when liberals decided that the African elite was failing to provide an example of energizing, and entrepreneurial leadership, they quickly withdrew as advocates of this elite in its political, and even diplomatic, roles. Hence the surprisingly abrupt descent of liberal opinion from indomitable optimism to inconsolable despair within five to eight years of independence.

The Debate about Democracy

Liberal revisionist commentary on African politics consisted overwhelmingly of an attack on the arguments made by the "nation builders" in defense of African one-party states and authoritarianism generally. This attack questioned both the logic of the nation builders' position and the evidence on which it rested.

First, revisionists—considering cases like Ghana—questioned whether authoritarian regimes had actually achieved anything impressive in the field of economic development—the cause for which, after all, civil and political liberties were being sacrificed. Was there any demonstrable association between the degrees of authoritarianism practiced in particular African states and the success of their economic strategies? Kirk Sale

29. "The Agenda for Africa," 33.

suggested that there was none: indeed, he continued, there was no reason to expect any. Authoritarian measures were aimed, in the first instance, at political opponents. At least in the African case, there was no plausible evidence that opposition activities had been hurting "economic development" and, equally, no evidence that repression had helped it. As Sale put it: "Ghana's Tema harbor could have been built without putting 1,000 political prisoners into jail, and its puppet press is not a necessary concomitant to the Volta Dam."[30] However, if (as others claimed) there was no proof that state control of the economy was "the necessary or the soundest means of achieving even *economic* goals over the long haul," there was a plausible association between authoritarianism and poor economic performance.[31] "Workable economic programs," Sale remarked, "are not helped, and are more often hindered, by a controlled press, an uncritical single-party, a glory-hungry and unheeding leader, and a general fear in the citizenry."[32]

"Nation builders" usually responded that this critique involved too narrow a view, attacking the expression of, rather than the rationale for, "strong central government." Nobody, they complained, had argued that simply locking up the leaders of the opposition would lead to economic growth. Rather, their contention had been that economic development inevitably required certain economic disciplines (such as forced savings and restrictions on consumption) which would inevitably be unpopular and provide material for political opposition. This would be true whatever the philosophy of economic development: liberalism (as advocated by the International Monetary Fund) had its discontents as well as socialism. In both cases, governments would have to resist in defense of their programs: it was the legitimacy of the programs that justified (indeed, required) the authoritarianism of governments.

To this, the revisionists were apt to respond in turn that some nation builders had, indeed, suggested that there was some *direct* benefit for development from one-partyism. Further, they questioned the equation between "strong" government and authoritarianism. A truly "strong" government, in their view, was one enjoying widespread popular approval: the one thing that authoritarianism, as practiced in Africa and elsewhere, did with real efficiency was to destroy a government's authority among citizens.

30. "Freedom and/or Progress," 24.
31. Ritner and Ritner, "Africa's Constitutional Malarkey," 18.
32. "Freedom and/or Progress," 23.

Revisionists suggested, in fact, that the claims of nation builders in respect of "nation building" had been shown to be false. So far from being stable and "integrated," single-party states had turned out to be at least as unstable and fragile as any other states. Indeed, the supposed cure—authoritarianism—had aggravated the disease: regimes that concentrated power in the hands (wealth in the pockets) of a very small number of people inevitably created resentment, which (in Africa) meant instability at the center and/or secessionism on the periphery.[33] The attitude toward opposition characteristic of one-party states simply made matters worse, provoking critics to be more implacable and forcing them to take to violence.[34] For this, the revisionists warned, Western apologists for African authoritarianism were directly, if only partly, to blame. Such "totalitarian liberals" had encouraged "simplistic absolutism" and had also tried to discredit all opposition by branding it as "secessionist."

The indiscriminate association between opposition and secessionism was, in revisionist eyes, a particularly mischievous contribution. For there was no reason to believe that opponents of African governments—even their ethnic opponents—necessarily envisaged breaking up states. Here again an American analogy came in handy: there was, Susan and Peter Ritner remarked, a clear difference "between Jefferson Davis, who tried to secede from the state President Lincoln headed, and McClellan, who opposed Lincoln in the 1864 election."[35] Most African critics were McClellans, at least initially: it was the governments, abetted by their Western "liberal" friends, who turned them into Jefferson Davises.

As with the argument about economic development, revisionists had an alternative—a traditional liberal alternative—to offer. The nation builders, they argued, had fatally reversed the relationship between center and locality in democratic practice. Complexity and interdependence were essential for democracy: it was therefore vital to preserve, not stifle, diversity. The pursuit of "national integration" was therefore dangerous (Aristide Zolberg argued) if it involved attacking "primordial ties"—loyalties to family, clan, and tribe. These ties fostered pluralism and consti-

33. Commenting on the murder of President Olympio of Togo in 1963, Kirk Sale remarked: "In every one of these countries, the national leader . . . has so consolidated his power in his drive for modernization and national unity that he has made the peaceful, constitutional path to change much more difficult to achieve" ("Togo: The Lesson for Africa," 136).
34. Ritner and Ritner, "Africa's Constitutional Malarkey," 19.
35. "Africanism," 26. The Ritners were South Africans by birth.

tuted "a major form of insurance against the growth of totalitarianism by providing a buffer between the individual and the state."[36] Moreover, if diversity was important on the periphery, it was even more important in central government. Democracy depended on "a certain healthy separation of power-centers," if only as "a safety factor."

Applying this traditional liberal standard to African states, revisionists found it absurd to suggest that they were either actually or potentially democratic. It was apparent as early as 1960 that the formal institutions and processes supporting democracy were in decay. Elections were pure sham, and legislative activity was "little more than an elaborate charade."[37]

In these circumstances, the claims of Wallerstein and other nation builders about the existence of "internal party democracy" and respect for consensus in single-party states became crucial. Revisionists suggested that these claims were simply false. They had, Martin Kilson argued, "not been taken very much beyond the realm of assertion."[38] The fact was, Zolberg remarked, that party leaders simply wanted obedience: for them, the ideal citizen was "the enthusiastic, but docile follower of the party." As a result, in many African states, there was "government *for* the people, but not government *by* the people."[39]

36. Zolberg, "One-Party Systems and Government for the People," 6. Zolberg also remarked: "It is not necessarily true that a country in which traditional elements have been weakened is more unified than one in which they co-exist with modern social relationships."

37. In 1960, Henry Bretton reported: "In most of Africa today, elections are a farce, and Western democracies, when they pretend otherwise, do not increase African appreciation of Western ways" ("Congo and Emergent Africa," 242). In 1961, Grant McConnell commented on African legislatures: "It is difficult while watching these supposedly incipient parliaments or chambers in their splendid halls to escape the feeling that what is being witnessed is little more than an elaborate charade" ("Africa and the Americans," 48). Aristide Zolberg declared in 1962: "The crucial function of parliament, that of educating the public politically, is not being performed" ("One-Party Systems and Government for the People," 7).

38. "What kinds of decision, for instance, are influenced by participation and discussion in parties like the PDG, CPP, TANU, and *Union Soudanaise*? How real is the choice of candidates for party and government office given to the masses in these single-party situations? What are the limits of opposition politics in these situations?" ("Authoritarian and Single-Party Tendencies in African Politics," 292).

39. "One-Party Systems and Government for the People," 7 (emphasis in original).

Even if these regimes still had some popular support (Alfred Friendly said in criticizing Gwendolen Carter) and even if they did allow some internal debate, they were still potentially totalitarian.[40] They might not yet have realized this potential, the Ritners declared, but they were already "totalitarianisms as bitter as their state powers permit[ted] them to be."[41]

Given their observations about the failings of African one-party regimes, liberal revisionists were naturally very skeptical about suggestions that such regimes represented a product of African political genius or that they were preparing the way for democracy. One-party rule, Arthur Lewis declared, was just "a cheap import": it would bring as little progress and happiness to Africans as it had to other peoples.[42] Others, including the Ritners, were equally scathing: the arguments in defense of one-partyism were tired and stale, having been used "by innumerable other climbers reaching for power, by innumerable other intellectual and temperamental admirers of simplistic absolutism, of the unwholesome *frisson* of naked force."[43]

Revisionists particularly disliked the blithe—and increasingly dubious —assumption of nation builders that palpably authoritarian institutions could serve democratic purposes and would ultimately give way to liberal democratic institutions. To Wallerstein's claim that the one-party state was "an interim system" and "a significant step toward the liberal state," Kilson retorted that this proposition was "not particularly apparent in the thinking of the leaders of single-party states," and not at all in that of the most radical.[44] An even greater folly—to which intellectuals had always been prone—was the notion "that sturdy libertarians may produce democracy by boring from within a totalitarian state."[45]

40. Letter, *Africa Report* 7, no. 9 (October 1962): 2, 39. Much less, Friendly remarked, did the existence of such support justify the removal of institutions that might obstruct the advance of totalitarianism.

41. "Africa's Constitutional Malarkey," 18. "What real evidence have we," the Ritners demanded, "that the dynamics of party structure ever accommodate practical dissent on matters of substance?"

42. "Africa's Officers Take Command," 34.

43. "Africa's Constitutional Malarkey," 19. "The ordinary American [the Ritners observed] is irked most by the staleness of it all. Everything that can be said in apology or advocacy of the one-party system has been said innumerable times before."

44. "Authoritarian and Single-Party Tendencies," 294.

45. Ritner and Ritner, "Africa's Constitutional Malarkey," 19.

As liberals became more skeptical, both about the commitment of the African elite and about the claims made by this elite and its Western defenders on behalf of postcolonial governments, so they fell back on established American liberal values and institutions, resisting efforts to stretch or change them for the sake of accommodating exotic realities.

In particular, they concluded that they had been too casual about the importance of institutions. Observation of one-party rule suggested to the revisionists that the "institutional absolutists" were right in believing that the institutions of democracy actually were inseparable from the functions of democracy. It was time, the Ritners and others argued, for liberals to be less bashful about asserting that there were principles of good government.[46] If they were true to these principles, they would immediately recognize that there was "next to no chance" that African one-party states could ever meet liberal standards of good government, not least because they had dispensed with the institutions necessary to support these standards.[47]

Other commentators did not go so far. But most of them emphasized procedures that would protect and reinforce pluralism, especially by allowing for greater expression by local interests.[48] Best known were Arthur Lewis's proposals for forms of proportional representation and ethnic coalition so as to avoid both the inequities of Western European parliamentary democracy and the tyrannies of the one-party state. Others suggested greater use of federalism in the case of "large sprawling states with little national cohesion."[49]

46. "What makes governments *good* governments used to be one body of knowledge liberals prized most highly," the Ritners observed, "but no one seems to care any more." Students of Africa, in particular, had, they said, been "singularly reluctant to commit themselves to the desiderata holding for *all* governments," among them protection of individual freedom, rights to dissent, and adequate procedures for succession (ibid., 20).

47. The Ritners concluded: "Whether in Africa or on the moon, individual liberties cannot be maintained in a *modern* state without an independent judiciary, and relatively inviolable constitutional guarantees" (ibid., 19).

48. Gabriel Almond, for example, advocated "a Whig approach to democratization" that involved "a moderate pattern of penetration and centralization in which resisting groups [were] not destroyed, but bargained with, and occasionally conceded to, even at some cost in efficiency" ("Making New Nations Democratic," 23).

49. Rivkin, "The Politics of Nation-Building: Problems and Preconditions," 136.

Nigeria: Revisionists vs. Nation Builders

From the point of view of liberal revisionists, federal Nigeria represented both an example and a consolation. The Nigerians received much applause from them for persisting with a federal constitution and for avoiding the illiberal practices of other African countries.[50] Some commentators thought that it was important to publicize the achievements of what one described as "probably the most misunderstood and unknown of the West African nations."[51]

In fact, her defenders said, Nigeria's success exposed the falsity of many of the claims made about the need for authoritarianism in new African states. "The multi-party nature of Nigerian politics," Russell Warren Howe remarked, made it "possible to express an individualistic political view without excessive risk."[52]

But from 1962 onward tensions between the leaders of the Northern, Eastern, and Western regions began to cast doubt on liberal assertions about Nigerian stability, tolerance, and democratic principles. The troubles which the Federation began to suffer after 1962 naturally cast a shadow on the rather benign image of Nigeria in the United States.[53] The

50. For example, Arnold Rivkin remarked in 1963 that Nigeria was "the only state in Africa to date to come to independence as a single unit with a fully operating federal system, chosen by the democratically elected political leadership of the country and successfully negotiated by them with Great Britain *before* independence" ("Nigeria: A Unique Nation," 329).

51. Several observers commented that the slighting of Nigeria was a result (as Edward K. Weaver put it) of "the romantic rationalizations of some Americans about Ghana and Guinea which, to them, represent[ed] fermenting West Africa" ("What Nigerian Independence Means," 147).

52. "Nigeria in Transition," 12. As "virtually the sole exception to the one-party trend in Africa," Nigeria had (other commentators noted) "survived without deportations, detentions, political restrictions or electoral juggling": she was "one of the very few states in Africa without a preventive detention act" (David J. Eisen, "Apologia for Authoritarianism" [review of Immanuel Wallerstein, *Africa: The Politics of Independence*], *New Republic*, 7 May 1962, 26–27; Rivkin, "Nigeria: A Unique Nation," 333).

53. Doubts about the real stability of Nigeria, as well as about the chances of democracy surviving there, in fact appeared intermittently, but from as early as 1960, in the rather limited commentary on Nigerian politics by American liberals during the first six years of independence. Russell Warren Howe, though impressed by the multiparty system, reported in January 1960 that the country was "very uneasy." Nigeria, he thought, "must begin to concentrate on building a sense of nationhood at home and trying to conquer its own internal divisions" ("Prospects

Action Group crisis of 1962 and the ensuing violence confirmed the suspicions of those nation builders and others who found the continual extolling of "Nigerian democracy" shallow and praise for her "stability" premature.[54] Henry L. Bretton warned against what he called "the new myth of wishful thinking." This myth, Bretton argued, arose from Cold War mental habits and was dangerous in that it led observers to mistake the convenient and agreeable alliance between the conservative political elite of Nigeria and the West "for a valid formula to cope with Nigeria's problems."[55]

---

for Stability in Nigeria," 10).

These divisions, Robert C. Good commented in the *New Leader,* meant that "for the opening years of Africa's post-colonial era, Nigeria's optimism is likely to be disappointed." In particular, she would be too absorbed in trying to solve the tensions inevitable in a country with over two hundred ethnic groups to be able to exercise the influence in international affairs to which her importance entitled her ("Africa's Gulliver," 6).

On the eve of independence, a Nigerian warned that lack of "the necessary human resources" and "the inevitable compromises and jockeying for power that are acutely characteristic of federal politics" were certain to bring disillusionment: "Unless [he concluded] there are new channels of hope, the shadow of a great social upheaval might yet hang over Nigeria" (Williams, "Where Does Nigeria Go from Here?" 4).

54. Two months after the conflict in the Western Region came to the surface, Immanuel Wallerstein noted in the *New Leader*: "There is a widespread belief that of all the newly independent African nations Nigeria is the outstanding example of a fairly stable, relatively pro-Western, liberal democracy. This belief is largely an illusion, nourished on superficial analysis and self-deception" ("Nigeria: Slow Road to Trouble," 15).

The Action Group crisis, Wallerstein said, had "pointed up how far Nigeria really [was] from a stable, democratic government." In particular, competitive party politics existed only at the Federal level (and even there were hampered by the north's permanent majority): each region was effectively a one-party state (ibid., 16). As for the much-vaunted stability of Nigeria, Wallerstein predicted that it was "unlikely to last long": he thought it possible that the army might eventually take over. In any event, Wallerstein was certain that Nigeria had "not yet completed its nationalist revolution" (ibid., 17, 18).

55. *Power and Stability in Nigeria,* 180. In 1964 Kenneth Grundy, reviewing Richard Sklar's book *Nigerian Political Parties,* similarly warned against complacency about the apparent vigor of Nigerian democracy. In his study, Sklar argued that Nigerian democracy had strong local roots: "Communal traditions reinforce the democratic tendencies of a competitive party system based on free elections and constitutional guarantees of civil liberty" (p. 505). Grundy suggested that the first four years of independence justified a less optimistic conclusion: "Events

Yet for some outsiders, the turbulence of Nigerian politics in the pre-coup period reinforced, rather than undermined, confidence in the appropriateness of federalism and multiparty politics. Both (the argument ran) endowed Nigeria with a flexibility essential in a developing country with a number of different regional and ethnic interests. Indeed, the stormier the political weather became, the more impressed such outsiders were with the sturdiness of the vessel.[56] As a British student of Nigeria later remarked: "Observers often clung to an optimism which seems, in retrospect, to have been misplaced. Many were impressed by Nigeria's tradition of brinkmanship in intertribal rivalries . . . such institutional resilience was thought to prove that the elite possessed a capacity for compromise that would always, in the last resort, ensure the triumph of moderation and good sense."[57]

The January 1966 coup put an end to all such hopeful comment and inspired a stream of retrospectively skeptical remarks about the First Republic and its foreign admirers. The coup had shown, Claire Sterling commented, "that Nigeria was never really as promising as it seemed—in fact, it could scarcely have been less so."[58]

------

since independence suggest that Western democratic patterns may not be as deeply ingrained as Professor Sklar indicates. . . . Some politicians in Nigeria are committed to civil liberties and open political competition only to the extent that it applies to their own partisans" ("Power in Nigeria," 14).

56. Thus Arnold Rivkin wrote admiringly in 1963: "The ability of the Federation of Nigeria to evolve institutions and techniques . . . and to undergo basic constitutional development . . . suggests that the Nigerians have found a way to adapt their complicated federal structure to their needs and make their federation responsive to the imperatives of their political and economic development. Thus, for Nigeria, federalism has served as an apt footing for the evolution and operation of a democratic political system. Nigeria's state structure stands out in bold relief in the African context; so too does its political system" ("Nigeria: A Unique Nation," 331).

57. John D. Chick, "The Nigerian Impasse," 292. Every new crisis tended to confirm anew "the theory that Nigeria was a country in which the worst never happened." Thus even during the violence and maneuvering of the 1964 elections, a correspondent in *Africa Report* could comment: "The Nigerian campaign dogfight is demonstrating that Western-style multi-party democracy is not entirely absent from the African political scene" (Astrachan, "A Guide to the Nigerian Elections," 31).

58. "Can Nigeria Catch up with Its Reputation?" 39. In particular, Sterling commented, "the death of the gentle Sir Abubakar [Tafawa Balewa] put an end to the fiction not only of a Westminster-type parliamentary democracy but of

Few observers lamented the First Republic, and a number (such as Colin Legum) argued that Nigeria needed "a completely different kind of constitution."[59] The essential question during the next four years was whether the divisions which had appeared in Nigeria made any kind of constitution making futile, apart from the making of constitutions for entirely new units which represented the "true" nations contained within Nigeria. Nigeria thus faced again the basic questions of nationhood and self-determination that had supposedly been settled at independence.

Independence and Nationalism

Liberal disenchantment with postcolonial governments brought to the surface some latent fears of nationalism which, in liberal minds, struggled with a commitment to self-determination. The problem arose from what Robert Packenham has called the basic liberal axiom that all good things go together.[60] In this instance, liberals assumed that three good things in particular were not just compatible, but mutually reinforcing: self-determination; international harmony; and the triumph of liberal values. They believed firmly in the overriding importance of self-determination as a condition for individuals and nations realizing their potential. They were firm internationalists in the sense of valuing freedom of movement for people, goods, and ideas and in seeing progress as coming about through greater international cooperation. Lastly, they believed passionately in the global relevance and appeal of liberal values.

While in principle these commitments did not have to conflict with each other, in practice they had done so fairly often. In particular, liberal idealism had suffered repeated emotional buffeting from nationalists who, having enjoyed liberal acclaim while fighting for their countries' independence, turned out to be illiberal once in power. Critics of liberalism had enjoyed themselves immensely in the late nineteenth century—and again in the 1930s—ridiculing the chagrin of incorrigibly naive liberals every time a "national liberation" cause they had fostered turned, Fran-

---

nationhood in Nigeria" ("The Self-Defeating Civil War in Nigeria," 24). Sir Abubakar was federal prime minister from 1960 until his murder during the January 1966 coup.

59. Legum, "Africa on the Rebound," 24.

60. See his *Liberal America and the Third World* (Princeton, N.J.: Princeton University Press, 1973).

kenstein-like, into an authoritarian or even fascist government. The central object of scorn was the apparent liberal assumption that because liberals supported self-determination, therefore self-determination would necessarily prepare the way for liberalism.[61] Greece, Italy, Central Europe, and the Balkans had shown that this assumption was extremely flimsy.

Despite its emotional buffeting, however, liberal idealism had clearly suffered no permanent injury (or, its critics would say, learned any lessons). As "third world" territories came to independence, liberals again supported their right to independence (as we have seen) with almost unqualified enthusiasm. Again, they saw "moderation" and a fundamental respect for the liberal West and its values shining from the eyes of nationalist leaders. Again, they suffered disappointment. In Africa, as elsewhere, they found themselves torn between their commitment to self-determination (interpreted to mean the rights of sovereign states to manage their internal affairs as they wished) and a commitment to universal human rights. As Grant McConnell put it rather gently to other American liberals: "Our problem lies in the fact that while we are strongly committed to the same ideal of self-determination which is the core of meaning in the African cry of 'freedom,' that ideal of self-determination may often be found to go with the establishment of arbitrary forms of native rule."[62] In 1962, Rupert Emerson, a distinguished student of nationalist movements, observed that already American sympathy for liberation movements seemed to be waning. Americans, Emerson thought, were having "second thoughts" about "undiscriminating condemnation of colonialism," partly because of the instability and undemocratic ways of some new states.[63]

61. On this theme, see Michael Howard, *War and the Liberal Conscience* (New Brunswick, N.J.: Rutgers University Press, 1978), chapters 4 and 5.

62. It was by just this route, McConnell claimed, that Americans had found themselves supporting dictatorships in Latin America—through indiscriminate liberal support for nationalist, soi-disant democratic leaders, as much as through conservative projects for hemispheric security ("Africa and the Americans," 49).

63. Emerson argued that liberal Americans were beginning to notice a divergence between the ideals of the American Revolution and the direction of the African revolution, especially on questions of human rights, economic development, and foreign policy. (In truth, this left very little to agree about.) They also disliked the use of violence to achieve independence ("American Policy in Africa," 309).

Emerson wrote extensively on political developments in Southeast Asia, the Pacific, and Africa over a thirty-year period, from 1937 to 1967. His African works

Liberal misgivings about African nationalism, in fact, began to appear as early as 1960. A pamphlet issued in that year by the Africa League (and written by a group of—then—impeccably liberal scholars) expressed nervousness about giving a moral blank check to any and all nationalists. The authors declared that it would be simplistic to base American policy toward Africa on blind deference to the principle of self-determination: "The dogma of national sovereignty . . . is not sufficient by itself to guide the United States through the twentieth-century network of relations among nations. . . . Rather than retire behind simple assertions about sovereignty, it is far better that we be aware of the extent to which we are in fact intervening, and therefore [be] conscious of our responsibility for the results of our actions internationally."[64] This was a remarkable statement, coming from a group which, earlier in the same pamphlet, had urged support for Africa's "freedom to develop without outside interference" and had declared that it was neither "right or useful to tell other peoples what kind of government they should have."[65] As a reviewer of the pamphlet noted, it implied that, for liberals, "to raise the problem of sovereignty . . . does not end discussion; it merely inserts a factor to be weighed against others in making decisions."[66]

The Africa League pamphlet did, in fact, accurately represent a well-established liberal view, according to which not just "sovereignty" but nationalism itself had been and could again be a problem. For, while liberals could wholeheartedly support the idea of self-determination, in practice its immediate political effect was divisive. Every new nation-state represented yet another set of boundaries in the world and yet another potential source of belief in unique "national characters" and "national destinies"—both notions that offended the essential internationalism of liberal thinking and could obstruct the spread of liberal ideas and institutions.

To liberals, all forms of exclusive loyalty—tribal, national, or racial—

---

were *Africa and World Order* (1963), *The Political Awakening of Africa* (1965), and *Africa and United States Policy* (1967). Emerson's best-known general book was probably *From Empire to Nation: The Rise to Self-Assertion of Asian and African Peoples* (1960).

64. The Africa League, *A New American Policy toward Africa* (New York, February 1960), 22. The authors of this pamphlet were David Apter, Rupert Emerson, Ruth Schachter (Morgenthau), and Immanuel Wallerstein.

65. Ibid., 16, 20.

66. Glickman, "Four Critiques," 13.

were equally dangerous and equally capable of causing hate and division. Indeed, in the experience of European and American liberals, nationalism had often been a rhetorical vehicle for tyrants, militarists, and demagogues. It had caused wars, had obstructed trade, travel, communication between peoples, and had prevented the rational use of resources.

Some liberal writers did express the fear that nationalism in Africa would show this darker side, creating attitudes and policies that liberals would be forced to condemn. Albert L. Guérard expressed this fear, and set out the reasoning behind it, in his open letter "To My African Friends," published early in 1960. According to Guérard, Africa was vulnerable to three fallacies: the fallacy of "continentalism"; the fallacy of nationalism; and the fallacy of cultural exceptionalism.

"Continentalism" (represented in this case by the slogan "Africa for the Africans") had, Guérard noted, shown itself capable of exercising "a baleful power, even over minds that are not primitive." It was baleful because, Guérard declared, "continents are mere words, conventional historical terms. . . . In judging a man's ability, thought, and character, the continent of his origin is wholly incompetent, irrelevant, and immaterial." For the same reasons, nationalism was as bad—indeed, since it was even more influential, it was probably worse. In a democratic age, it was "an absurdity," representing "the prolonged shadow of monarchy." Men were now returning, Guérard believed, to "the sanity of the eighteenth century—reluctantly, however, to confess their error, their heads still heavy with the fumes of the nationalist intoxication."[67]

More original was Guérard's discussion of his third fallacy. This was the notion—underwritten by some anthropologists, as well as by nationalists everywhere—of nation-states as fixed cultural entities. The theorists and practitioners of "national integration" were actually trying artificially to create such entities. Anthropologists, in Guérard's view, bore a large degree of intellectual responsibility for the problem, since they had refined and reified cultures. As a result, the idea of culture and cultural character had become an active source of intolerance, or at least had provided a rationalization for it. The pursuit of cultural homogeneity, and attempts artificially to maintain it, were likely to lead directly to totali-

67. "To My African Friends," 60–62. "These symbols and metaphors of yesterday," Guérard declared, "do not correspond with either the eternal verities or with the actual condition of our age . . . the strictly national model . . . that unrealistic and unlovely Utopia, is fast losing significance."

tarianism. While nations might be essentially cultural entities, any attempt to create (or preserve) such entities through government policy was
unrealistic, because cultures changed. It was also dangerous, because it
necessarily threatened pluralism, minority rights, and, for that matter,
"the infinite variety of individuals."[68]

Guérard concluded with a frontal attack on the very idea of "culture."
The belief in cultures, he declared, was "a superstition" that was contrary
to "the two essential facts in the study of man": the uniqueness of each
individual, and the universality of "common aspirations."[69] The fact of
uniqueness meant that "a man should think of himself as a human being
and not as a member of a group, determined, without any choice, merit,
or fault of his own, by some chance physical trait."

The existence and claims of "common aspirations" (in the idiom of the
1970s, "human rights") obviously implied skepticism about nationalist
slogans. It also, Guérard thought, implied support for international bodies
such as the UN. Guérard concluded by directly appealing to Africans to
reject nationalism: "Nationalism is not in your normal line of development. You had a shop-soiled, obsolete model foisted upon you." He hoped
that self-determination in the third world would not entail "a secession
from mankind [or] the denial of free universalism." Africa, specifically,
had "the right to transcend its own tribalism without adopting ours."[70]

Guérard's misgivings about nationalism in Africa were shared by a
number of liberal observers in more specific contexts. Many of them saw
nationalism as generally anachronistic: in African conditions, it was positively harmful. More precisely, as *Africa Today* put it, nationalism destroyed one anachronism (tribalism), only to replace it with another.[71]
Africa was poor and needed stability: nationalism would merely lead to
a waste of resources on the costs of maintaining a multitude of sover-
eignties (most of them representing entirely fictitious nations).

Further, it would cause instability by inflaming the petty chauvinism
of insecure states and insecure leaders. Such chauvinism would be exploited by demagogues to deflect discontent about domestic politics

68. Ibid., 63.
69. Ibid.
70. Ibid., 61–63. Guérard discerned in the UN "the germ of a superstate . . .
slowly, haltingly assuming substance and consciousness."
71. Nationalism, the journal commented, "absorbs and erases the archaic and
rigid patterns of tribal societies and . . . creates damaging and quite unnecessary
continental competition and conflict" ("Africa in Curlers," 3).

against fellow Africans who, through the frivolities of colonial map making, found themselves citizens of neighboring "nation-states." It would—as it had done so often elsewhere—be a facade for promoting special interests (especially those of the military) and would lead to various, but uniformly harmful, kinds of economic protectionism. It would probably be used—Kilson and others frequently warned—to expand the domain of the "bureaucratic bourgeoisie" (or "political class"), which would enrich its members through measures ostensibly associated with "state socialism" or "indigenization"—all under the rhetorical umbrella of "national interest" and "economic independence."

Ordinary Africans would thus pay the costs of nationalism, either economically—through higher taxes and prices—or with their own lives—in pointless wars. The cause of African unity would also suffer. To Albert Guérard and those like him, this would not matter, since pan-Africanism was an example of the "continental" fallacy. But most liberals favored pan-Africanism, since it was a step away from a world of microstates toward one of federations and international organizations.

Some liberals doubted whether, in any case, the new African states could survive, especially such microstates such as Togo, The Gambia, and Rwanda (the latter was described by Russell Warren Howe as "a little knot of problems with a population of three million rock farmers").[72] Just because liberals supported self-determination in Africa did not mean, Henry Bretton remarked, that they had to support self-determination within existing boundaries: to do so would be "to invite the notorious troubles of the Balkans."[73] Traditional notions of self-determination should be modified, Bretton argued, to take account of viability. Independence should be granted only to states "able to give at least a minimum of economic security to their subjects." (Bretton, it may be noted, had earlier argued that the idea of imposing conditions for independence and assessing "readiness" was absurd.)[74]

For Bretton and many others, the only worthwhile future for Africa lay in the formation of large, perhaps federal states. Some (such as Adlai Stevenson) even suggested that such states might linked through formal association to "a wider European or Atlantic community."[75] Without

72. "Everybody's Problem Child," 10.
73. "Congo and Emergent Africa," 242.
74. "Straight Thinking on Africa," 206. See chapter 3.
75. "The New Africa: A Guide and a Proposal," 52, 54.

some kind of union, the new states would collapse as a result of poverty, ethnic irredentism, or military conflicts brought on by nationalism.[76]

The behavior of African leaders confirmed the fears of American liberals about the likely effects of nationalism on African unity.[77] In 1961, the *New Republic,* writing about the Congo crisis, complained that most African leaders were "provincial in their view of world problems . . . rash, impatient, inconsiderate of other people's attitudes and ideals and not conversant with the complexities of diplomacy."[78]

But even if pan-Africanism succeeded, might it not (some liberals worried) simply raise nationalism to its very worst form, racialism? Liberals were especially concerned about philosophies claiming, sometimes almost mystically, distinctive racial virtues for black Africans (or, indeed, blacks everywhere).[79] For purposes of fighting white racism in southern Africa, it was important, Adlai Stevenson noted, that black counter-racism not manifest itself in the new African states. If it did, liberals would be forced to condemn both forms of racism, or risk the charge of applying a double standard.[80]

76. Referring to the artificiality of African frontiers, Waldemar Nielsen commented gloomily: "It will require miraculous statesmanship and forbearance on the part of African nations if these fateful markings are rationalized without the fighting of hundreds of battles and the death of thousands of men" ("Africa Is Poised on the Razor's Edge," 61). Henry Bretton expressed similar pessimism: "It is a safe prediction that none of the African states seated in the United Nations in September 1960, with the possible exception of the Malagasy Republic, will survive the next five years in their present shape and form" ("Congo and Emergent Africa," 242).

The African states admitted to the United Nations in September 1960 were Dahomey (subsequently Benin), Cameroon, Central African Republic, Chad, Congo, Gabon, Ivory Coast, Madagascar, Mali, Niger, Senegal, Congo-Leopoldville (Zaire), Togo, and Upper Volta (Burkina Faso). Cameroon and Zaire underwent serious domestic instability after independence, and a civil war developed in Chad well after independence. But all of these states still have the borders inherited at independence: Cameroon, Chad, Congo, Gabon, Ivory Coast, and Senegal have even retained civilian governments.

77. There were, Hessler remarked, "too many prima donnas among the native African leaders to allow any easy, rational consolidation of states" ("The Agenda for Africa," 36).

78. "Straight Thinking on Africa," 206.

79. Harold Isaacs, for example, praised Frantz Fanon specifically for wanting "no part of any kind of counter-racism, no part of *négritude* . . . no part of a 'black culture,' no part of leaning on specious glorifications of the past, no part of adopting the White man's follies as his own" ("Portrait of a Revolutionary," 69).

80. "The New Africa: A Guide and a Proposal," 50.

The treatment of minorities (such as Asians) and ethnic opponents in some new states confirmed the fear of some liberals that (in Howe's words) "the search for an African way [was] essentially a racist urge."[81] One writer even went so far as to remark that there was a threat "to the concept of an interracial society from black Africans."[82] Some liberals thus feared that Africans were doing just what Guérard had accused them of doing in the letter quoted above: "You are seeking an apartheid on your own terms, no less objectionable in principle than that of the Boers."[83]

Further experience with African nationalism in the sixties and seventies led some American liberals to the disenchanted view expressed by the English liberal Henry Richard in 1864, when he wrote: "This idea of nationality is a poor, low, selfish, unchristian idea, at variance with the very principle of an advanced civilization."[84] They remained firmly attached to a belief in the rightness of self-determination as a principle. But they became convinced that African nationalism was much like other nationalisms, rather than being something distinctive and superior.

Liberals and Biafra: Nation Building vs. Self-Determination

Liberal debate about the Nigerian civil war is very interesting for what it reveals about the impact of revisionism on liberal attitudes toward African nationalism. It illustrates the tension between "nation builders" and those who—often disenchanted with postcolonial governments—wanted to see liberals reaffirm a belief in decentralization, and with it self-determination. But the debate was more confused than this summary suggests, because liberals, as noted above, had become wary of the nationalism to which self-determination often seemed to lead.

The Biafran issue is also fascinating as an example of sustained and emotive use of analogies. Both the supporters and the enemies of Biafran secession called on a range of historical analogies to characterize the participants and their conflict for the benefit of bewildered outsiders. Such

81. "Racism in Africa," 20.
82. "Many of them [Grant McConnell said] have taken to heart the apparent lesson that race is the most important aspect of human personality" ("Africa and the Americans," 42).
83. "To My African Friends," 63.
84. Quoted in Howard, *War and the Liberal Conscience*, 50.

metaphorical hand-to-hand combat took place around four familiar historical landmarks: the Holocaust; the American Civil War; the Vietnam War; and the Balkans. As Norman Cousins reported, both sides were apt to exploit analogies with American history in the hope of creating sympathy in the United States: "The power of the American past is in abundant evidence today on both sides of the Nigerian civil war. In Lagos, capital of Nigeria, and in Owerri, provisional capital of Biafra, I had a number of conversations with government leaders, and I couldn't help being impressed by the extent to which major events in American history are points of reference in their thinking about the war."[85]

Pro-Biafran Rhetoric

Sympathizers with Biafra drew upon the analogy of the Holocaust extensively to dramatize their case that the Ibos were an oppressed and deserving minority requiring separate statehood in order to survive. The analogy was persuasive to liberals because of the approving stereotype of the Ibos current among American liberals. Despite their distaste for "archaic" traditional institutions, liberals in fact relied to a surprising extent on tribal imagery in describing the Nigerian civil war (and other conflicts). The war was commonly presented as one between the "energetic," "ambitious" Ibos of the east and the "feudal," "fatalistic," "authoritarian" Hausas of the north.[86] Such a portrayal created a presumptive sympathy for the Ibos in American liberal minds.

85. "What Hope in Nigeria?" 16.

86. See, for example, the references to "the ambitious and often radical Ibo" in Thompson, "Nigeria," 16; to "the industrious and ambitious Ibo" in Good, "Africa's Gulliver," 6.

The Ibos, according to Claire Sterling, were "far more ambitious, adaptable, and fiercely individualistic than their neighbors." The better-known neighbors were the Yoruba ("sophisticated townsmen with a rich and ancient culture") and the Hausa ("Moslems of the most strait-laced medieval kind, semi-nomadic for the most part, dominated by powerful emirs, living in a closed authoritarian society, impermeable to change") ("Can Nigeria Catch up with Its Reputation?" 39–40).

Many writers praised Ibo enthusiasm for education. Norman Cousins, for example, wrote: "No people in black Africa responded more fully to British influence and culture than the Biafrans. Nowhere in black Africa were Shakespeare, Milton, and Shelley better known or loved. Nowhere in black Africa was there more respect for learning, more devotion to books, arts, and sciences" ("The Grisly Aftermath," 22).

The Ibos appeared to such minds a perplexing but distinctly attractive phenomenon—a "modernizing" tribe, a people who "overnight [had] propelled themselves from backwardness into the 20th century," an authentically African manifestation of the Protestant ethic (except that so many of them were in fact Catholic!)[87]

Not very subtly, the general characterization of the Ibos tended to slip into a more specific and tendentious stereotype. "The Ibo spirit," a writer in the *New Leader* remarked, was "loquacious, thrusting, bold ('God never made a shy Ibo,' an Irish priest said), clannish, hard-working and contentious."[88] Such characterization of the Ibos as dynamic, individualistic, democratic, and commercially astute almost inevitably led to depiction of the Ibos as "African Jews."[89] In northern Nigeria, their role and their relations with the majority population had, it was suggested, been tragically similar to those of Jews and other trading minorities elsewhere.[90]

For those sympathetic to the Ibos, it was an easy step from casting the Ibos as "West African Jews" to comparing their treatment by their opponents during the civil war with that of the Jews under Hitler—a com-

87. Lloyd Garrison, "The 'Point of No Return' for the Biafrans," *New York Times Magazine*, 8 September 1968, 91. "Of all Nigeria's tribes," Garrison remarked elsewhere, "the Ibos of the Eastern Region [had] produced the most startling evolution from backwardness to modernity" ("Biafra vs. Nigeria: The Other Dirty Little War," 37).

88. David Robison, "The Price of One Nigeria," 9.

89. Stanley Meisler, indeed, suggested that the Ibos liked "to think of themselves as the Jews of Africa. They are a hard-working, aggressive people, with a thirst for education and its rewards, a willingness to take any job anywhere if it seems to lead to something better and, perhaps most important and most unusual, an avid acceptance of new techniques and ideas" ("Breakup in Nigeria," 335).

90. "Like the Jews of Harlem or the Asians of East Africa or the Chinese of Southeast Asia [Meisler wrote], the Ibos were the prominent outsiders in the economic life of the dominant population and, like the others, they were hated" (ibid., 335). Colin Legum likewise remarked that "like the Jews, the Indians, the Chinese, [the Ibos] have made their homes where they have made their living." Legum further suggested that the brutal reaction of the northerners in 1966 arose partly from the attitudes that the Ibos (as an aggressive, intelligent, and successful minority) had adopted toward the majority: "They looked down upon their Hausa hosts as unenterprising, lazy, backward, and feudal. They were arrogantly self-conscious of their superiority and they showed it. . . . Like all petty traders the world over, they exploited their customers and ignored their resentment. The hatred that grew up around them was dismissed as jealousy fanned by the Northern emirs. They were the sharpest, shrewdest, most successful and most pushful element in a slow-moving society" ("The Tragedy in Nigeria," 23).

parison implicit in the charge of genocide made against Federal Nigerian forces later in the war.[91] Writing in the *New Republic,* David F. Ross remarked that the Ibos had in fact compared themselves to the Israelis since the beginning of the war.[92] But, he thought, the analogy was unfortunately incomplete. Lacking a powerful American lobby of the kind that Israel enjoyed and without a worldwide sense of guilt over their historical persecution, the Ibos were likely to suffer a fate "analogous to that of the Jews, not in Israel, but in the Third Reich."[93] Gowon, Ross acknowledged, was "no Hitler," but his generals were already out of his control and, in the event of a guerrilla war, reprisals "after the fashion of Lidice" were likely to occur.

The political consummation of such rhetoric invariably took the form of a claim that Biafra needed and deserved independence. In making this claim, Biafran representatives themselves sometimes appropriated the standard liberal historical precedent, that of the American Revolution. Thus Norman Cousins found that Biafrans took inspiration "from the heroic achievement of the American people in tearing themselves free from outside rule. They do not feel that secession is an accurate description of their own position today, any more than it would be a fair description of the refusal of the individual American states to give up their autonomy until an acceptable relationship to each other could be worked out."[94] Whether the term was *self-determination* or *secession,* in either case

91. Legum, for example, argued that something like anti-Semitism was apparent in the north. In particular, he commented that anti-Ibo propaganda current in the region during the 1964 elections had "caricatured them in very much the same way as Julius Streicher caricatured the Jews in *Die Stürmer*" ("Tragedy in Nigeria," 23).

92. "Like the Mandingos, who drive sharp bargains farther west along the Guinea coast, the Ibo have frequently been characterized as 'West African Jews.' Unlike the predominantly Moslem Mandingos, they rejoice in the appellation. They are proud of their high level of education and skill, their careful attention to pecuniary values, their tendency to spread out as economically privileged but socially despised minorities among other nationalities" ("Peace Is a Long Way off for Nigeria," 13).

93. Ibid., 14.

94. "What Hope in Nigeria?" 16. Cousins further pointed out that "for four years after the end of the successful American Revolution the states were in a condition of increasing disarray and even open conflict. The political arrangements of 1783 did not fit the existing situation." He did not draw any partisan conclusions from this extended disquisition, but concluded by stressing the need "to begin serious talks" and to avoid catchwords.

liberals looked (as in the Katangan case) for evidence of a democratic mandate. The authenticity and the worthiness of a claim for self-determination depended, for them, on whether it enjoyed popular support (and, second, on whether the entity concerned could survive and prosper on its own).

In the case of Biafra, unlike that of Katanga, many liberals did find evidence of popular support. Indeed, they argued that whereas Tshombe was an opportunist with a very tenuous popular following, Ojukwu was virtually at the mercy of a population determined to protect itself against the brutality it had suffered in 1966.[95] As Lloyd Garrison put it, "Secession was neither the dream nor the act of a single man."[96] He and other supporters of Biafra were particularly anxious to refute the assertion of the Federal government and its supporters that Ojukwu was a megalomaniac dictator who had dragged his unwilling fellow citizens into an unwanted secession. Many liberals—visitors and reporters alike—did in fact decide that Ojukwu was indeed a popular hero and that the population of the eastern region enthusiastically endorsed secession.[97]

---

95. Several commentators asserted that, so far from directing events, Ojukwu was actually hostage to the fears of a frightened population, especially in declaring secession. Ibo fears had been further aggravated by the behavior of Federal forces during the war, so that—quite apart from the positive appeal of a Biafran state—most Biafrans would absolutely resist compromises with the Lagos government lest they be wiped out.

96. "Biafra vs. Nigeria," 39. In this article, Garrison attacked the belief of American embassy officials that Ojukwu was "a 'Black Hitler' darkly manipulating his misguided people in some demonic quest for self-aggrandizement and absolute power. Just get rid of Ojukwu, they say, and all those basically peace-loving, business-minded Ibos will troop back into the Federal fold.

"Even before the fighting began, it was evident that the East's secession was neither the dream nor the act of a single man. And when secession did come, millions of Easterners were clearly resolved to die in the defense of their new homeland, no matter what Lagos said about this being 'Ojukwu's war.' "

In an article in *Africa Today*, George Shepherd argued that experience in the war itself had shown that support for Biafra was not limited to "a small group of power-hungry zealots" ("Biafra—The Issue Is Massacre," 3).

97. As early as January 1967, Jonathan Kwitny informed readers of the *New Leader* that Ojukwu was "the one high office-holder in the country who still exercises effective and unchallenged leadership over his jurisdiction. The people look to him with confidence as he makes each succeeding move in the chess game with the national government" ("Nigeria in Focus," 15).

In the *New Republic,* Ojukwu was described as "the first popular leader Nigeria

However, by this time liberals had, as we noted, become wary of exalted claims by nationalist leaders. Why, they might ask, should they sympathize with yet another nationalist proclaiming heaven on earth in some remote tribal fiefdom? To such skeptics, Biafra's supporters responded that Biafra represented a new kind of nationalism, more authentic than the factitious nationalism of Nigeria and the first generation of African states. Africa, Garrison said (in words that might have pleased some conservatives), "had won the first round for self-determination in gaining independence from colonialism. Now it was facing a second: the demand of Africa's many ethnic groups to shape their own destinies without being bound to the colonial-imposed concept of 'territorial integrity.' "[98] Biafra, in this view, represented "something unique in Africa"—"the first truly black African republic," "a nation . . . conceived in violence, hardened in war, united in suffering."[99]

The other acid test of nationhood in liberal minds (and one that bothered scholars such as Bretton) was that of economic viability. Biafra, sympathizers insisted, had all the human and material resources necessary to survive and prosper as an independent state. Indeed, many pointed out, it had substantially more resources than a number of existing African states.[100] Even with its oil terminals blockaded, Biafra still had

---

has produced since independence" (cited in Howe, "One Nation, Divisible," 15). In the *Saturday Review,* Charles Miller applauded him as "a determined and resourceful" leader. "If Ojukwu accomplished nothing else during the two and a half years of Biafran secession, he showed himself to be one of the more capable and honorable leaders in a country where, to use his own words, 'squabbles for parochial and commercial patronage' far too often take the place of "purposeful coordinated service of the people" (review of C. Odumegwu Ojukwu, *Biafra, Saturday Review,* 31 January 1970, 32).

98. "Biafra vs. Nigeria," 37.

99. "While other African states have gained their independence through a gratuitous stroke of the colonial master's pen, Biafra, whatever becomes of it, has dared to fight and die for its freedom. In victory, history could well enshrine Biafra as the first truly black African republic, with Ojukwu its most prominent symbol" (Garrison, "Odumegwu Ojukwu *Is* Biafra," 9).

100. As early as May 1966, Claire Sterling had noted the relative advantages of the east in the event of Nigeria breaking up: "Separately, only Iboland might come close to self-sufficiency; although too small to grow all its own food, it lies on a sizable bed of coal and a good portion of an underground petroleum sea that may eventually make this country the fourth largest oil producer in the world" ("Can Nigeria Catch up with Its Reputation?" 42). In a further article, in August 1967, Sterling remarked that "an autonomous East would be sitting pretty" ("The Self-Defeating Civil War in Nigeria," 30).

considerable mineral resources and (two economists suggested) "could eventually make a go of it alone": it had a gross domestic product "larger than that of a dozen or more independent states" and would be among the ten most populated countries in Africa.[101]

Even with such evidence of a potential for independence, however, liberal sympathizers with Biafra did not necessarily argue that she would be better off separated from Nigeria.[102] They wanted recognition of Biafran grievances and a negotiated, rather than a military, solution to the conflict. Such an approach would involve recognition of the heterogeneity of Nigeria, which was an artificial entity, without any historical, cultural, or geographic sense to it.[103] Nigeria, Biafra's supporters repeatedly declared, was "little more than a geographical expression": it had "never been a nation."[104]

101. Rake and Farrell, "Nigeria's Economy: No Longer a Model," 20. Moreover, Biafra contained, George T. Orick pointed out, "an aggressive human core"—a remarkable concentration of trained and able people, many of them refugees from the other regions ("Nigeria: A Study in Hypocrisy," 11). Stanley Meisler asserted that "Biafra, had it gone on without war, might have emerged as the strongest economic unit in Africa" ("Nigeria and Biafra," 26).

102. Several commentators suggested that a confederal solution might be appropriate—what the *New Republic* called "a Nigerian commonwealth of independent states" ("Arming the Nigerians," 8). As late as October 1969, Stanley Meisler argued that such a solution might still be acceptable to the Biafrans: "The most plausible compromise is a weak union or confederation of Nigeria in which Biafra has a special autonomous status, including the right to maintain its own army. Biafra might accept this now, though it is doubtful that the federal government of Nigeria would . . . it would represent a solution that both sides could have had in 1967 without any fighting at all" ("Nigeria and Biafra," 29).

In October 1967, Meisler had, indeed, proposed an essentially similar solution: "In the event of negotiation, a settlement can come only if the federal government accepts a confederation in which it would have little more power than that of representing the various regions in the United Nations. In exchange for this, Biafra likely would have to agree to participate in an economic union, which distributed a share of Biafra's ample oil revenues to the rest of the confederation" ("Breakup in Nigeria," 336).

103. "The question at issue," Claire Sterling wrote, "is whether a Federation of historically incompatible tribes, thrown together by a British colonial administrator, should or can be forcibly preserved when its inhabitants are literally incapable of living together any longer" ("The Self-Defeating Civil War in Nigeria," 23). Russell Warren Howe suggested: "To expect that these artificial entities will all survive the withdrawal of colonial force is unreasonable—nor, apparently, is any reason ever produced why anything more than economic integration is required" ("Nigeria's Civil War," 16).

104. "Nigeria," Claire Sterling wrote, "should presumably be a viable nation,

Biafra's supporters were therefore particularly critical of the analogies from American history used by the Lagos government and its supporters, especially that of the American Civil War (discussed below). Appeals to "unity" and "patriotism" made no sense, they argued, since Nigeria, unlike the United States in the 1860s, was not a nation in the hearts and minds of its citizens.[105] Nor, Russell Warren Howe complained, was the American Revolution suitable as a precedent to prove the feasibility of large federations: "The thirteen American colonies were monolingual and monoreligious; more important, they had just been united by the adversity and idealism of war against a common enemy."[106]

Moreover, even if the Nigerian state had some plausible claim to legitimacy, its government did not. As the *New Republic* commented in June 1968: "The Nigerians have been talking as if they were Northerners fighting the American Civil War all over again, and secession was unthinkable. In fact, Colonel Ojukwu has about as much (or as little) claim to legitimacy as General Gowon, who owes his current ascendancy to a series of obscurely motivated military coups."[107]

Biafra's supporters also had to cope with analogies with the Vietnam War.[108] Sometimes they used such an analogy for their own purposes,

---

and economically it is. Politically and sociologically, however, it is little more than a geographical expression" ("Can Nigeria Catch up with Its Reputation?" 39). In the same vein, Stanley Meisler wrote in October 1967: "Nigeria has never been a nation; it exists only because some white men, in an almost playful mood, sat down at the turn of the century and drew some lines on a vague map" ("Breakup in Nigeria," 336). Yet, Meisler remarked bitterly a year after the war began, perhaps a hundred thousand people had already died ("Pomp or Carnage," 132).

105. Claire Sterling, for example, noted that the Lagos government likened itself to the Unionists fighting the Confederates. But, she objected, "the American Civil War was fought by people sharing a common language and culture. Nigeria's breakaway Eastern Region and its ten million Ibos have almost nothing in common with their fellow countrymen except hideous memories" ("The Self-Defeating Civil War in Nigeria," 23).

106. "Nigeria's Civil War," 16.

107. "Arming the Nigerians," 8.

108. The Vietnam analogy was applied to U.S. policy toward the Nigerian conflict as well as to depict the struggle itself. For example, a liberal Democratic senator who had visited Biafra remarked on his return: "The gulf between ideals and practice in Biafra is grimly reminiscent of the crisis of conscience that has plagued us in Vietnam. In both places, we have had the most estimable intentions; but in both places, we seemed powerless to avert wholesale human tragedies" (Charles E. Goodell, "Biafra and the American Conscience," 24).

comparing Ojukwu and his followers to the apparently indestructible Vietcong.[109] But they also had to counter their opponents' application of the then-fashionable domino theory to Biafra. To allow one secession, Lagos and its supporters argued, would encourage a string of further secessions, ending with the collapse of a viable state system in West Africa—in effect, the old "Balkanization" analogy rendered dynamic and contemporary.

According to Garrison and others, the analogy was inept, since each African country was sui generis.[110] No other group had either "the grievances . . . or the capacities of the Ibos" and every crisis was unique. Therefore, "the domino theory work[ed] no better in Africa than in Asia."[111]

Federal Rhetoric

Sympathizers with the Federal government both turned historical analogies favored by Biafra's supporters to their own account and invoked others they felt would persuade Americans and outsiders generally to support Lagos.

A favorite rhetorical weapon of Federal sympathizers (and, indeed, Federal officials) was (as noted above) the analogy of the American Civil

109. In May 1968, for instance, the *Reporter* commented skeptically on the Federal government's chances of establishing its authority over the eastern region: "Whatever happens to Biafra as an organized national state, there is as little chance of Lagos establishing effective government over the Ibo as there is that the Vietcong would willingly submit to the present Saigon government, and for the same reasons: they don't have to, and they think they know what would happen if they did" ("Divorce, Nigerian Style," 8).

110. Garrison wrote: "There is much hand-wringing over 'Balkanization' which is really a bogus issue. There are more than 600 major tribal entities in Africa, many as different from one another as the Italians are from the Swedes, or the Arabs from the Israelis" ("Biafra vs. Nigeria," 44). Movements such as that in Biafra were, he added, "part of a natural sorting-out process" made inevitable by the artificiality of inherited frontiers.

111. "Each potential trouble spot," David Robison said, "is in a class by itself, dominated by local factors and power struggles. If other secessions do eventually occur, the Biafran example will have been neither the cause nor the restraint" ("The Price of One Nigeria," 9). In May 1969, Sen. Eugene McCarthy, an advocate of American recognition of Biafra, reportedly declared that "the balkanization argument . . . was the same domino theory discredited in the Vietnam debate" (*Africa Today* 16, no. 2 [April–May 1969]: 14).

War. This analogy could, in fact, be used quite neutrally and vaguely to convey a broad sympathy with the problems facing developing countries.[112] But (as Norman Cousins pointed out) it was a highly significant precedent for Nigerians committed to the Federal cause:

> On the Nigerian side, the American Civil War is more than a source of illumination; it is a stern historical prescription. Abraham Lincoln's conviction about the need to preserve the Union, despite all tragedy and travail, has become a mandate for leaders of the Nigerian government. Theirs is a struggle, as they see it, against dismemberment or fragmentation. They take heart from Lincoln's steadfastness in facing up to the issue of secession, and from his ultimate success in holding the nation together. Indeed, when Nigerians attempt to explain to Americans the central issue of their war, they speak about America's conflict over the cause of national unity more than a century ago.[113]

Nigerian officials in the United States in fact often invoked the precedent of the American civil war in answering the assertions of Biafra's supporters. Thus a Nigerian information officer responded in *Harper's* to the novelist Herbert Gold (who had visited Biafra with a delegation of the Committee for Biafran Artists and Writers): "In 1861, when the United States had to fight a bloody civil war, the Confederate States had claimed to be fighting for their survival. True enough you can't lose such a war. The victory of the Union ensured the survival of America as a nation which included advocates of the Confederacy."[114]

112. Sen. Edward Muskie used the parallel in such a way on a visit to Nigeria in 1971. In a speech delivered in Lagos on 7 March 1971, Muskie declared: "We should not be surprised that colonialism has not ended easily, and we should not be surprised that independence has not made nation-building an easy task. America won her independence through a revolution which did not produce a stable government until eleven years had passed. Seventy-one years after the inauguration of our first president the country was torn apart in a civil war. Our early growth was largely dependent on capital resources from Europe. Today, after two hundred years, we are still struggling with deep and divisive questions about freedom, equality, opportunity and justice" (cited in *Issue* [African Studies Association] 1 [Fall 1971]: 29).

113. "What Hope in Nigeria?" 16.

114. Letter from M. O. Ihonde, information officer, Permanent Mission of Nigeria to the United Nations, *Harper's*, January 1970, 6. What the official meant by saying "True enough you can't lose such a war" is unclear and reference to

Foreign critics of Biafra, rather more daringly—and ingeniously—took the purported similarity between the Ibos and the Jews and turned it upside down. Norman Uphoff and Harold Ottemoeller, for example, argued that the war could "be better understood and its aftermath better assessed by thinking of the Ibos more as Nigeria's Germans than as its Jews. . . . Biafran secession and civil war turned more on issues of Lebensraum and Anschluss than pogrom and genocide."[115] Recalling the early phase of the war, when the Biafran army had invaded the Mid-West Region en route for Lagos, Uphoff and Ottemoeller likened Ojukwu's strategy and his control of non-Ibo minorities within Biafra to Hitler's treatment of Western Europe in 1940.[116] Biafra had, in their view, been intent on setting up "a Vichy-type government" of Yorubas in Lagos.

The totalitarian character of this analogy was useful in reinforcing the main critique of Biafra directed at her foreign liberal supporters. The critique claimed that, so far from being enthusiastically supported by the population of the former Eastern Region, secession had been conceived by a minority and imposed, often brutally, upon the non-Ibo populations in the east, as well as on Ibo opponents of Ojukwu. Naive outsiders (Uphoff and Ottemoeller complained) never recognized "the 'master race' aspects of Ibo rule"—the detention of opponents and the subjugation of the roughly 40 percent of the region's population who were non-Ibo.[117] Regarding the domestic opponents of Ojukwu, one Federal sympathizer compared their plight directly to that of the Germans who had plotted to overthrow Hitler: "The Biafrans who are opposed to Ojukwu's "Bavarian redoubt" policy are mainly well-educated, responsible, professional and middle-class people. They are the same kind of people who endeavored to kill Hitler in the Rastenburg plot of July 1944, to save Germany from

---

Gold's article does not make it any clearer. (See Herbert Gold, "My Summer Vacation in Biafra"; for his reply to Ihonde, see *Harper's*, January 1970, 6.)

115. Uphoff and Ottemoeller, "After the Nigerian Civil War: With Malice toward Whom?" 1.

116. "The *casus belli*," Uphoff and Ottemoeller wrote, "has usually been seen as Biafra's secession, but the immediate and compelling cause was the occupation of non-Ibo territories by the Biafran army once secession was declared. Nigeria's ignoring Ijaw, Efik, Ogoja and others' interests would have been like the world's ignoring those of Germany's occupied neighbors some thirty years ago" (ibid., 2).

117. The authors strengthened the parallel with foreign admirers of Nazism by stressing such admirers' praise for "the discipline and technical virtuosity" of the Biafrans (ibid., 3).

the final, most devastating phase of a war already lost."[118] The non-Ibos had not been consulted and their leaders had been detained when they criticized Ojukwu.[119] James O'Connell, a political scientist with considerable experience of Nigerian politics, claimed that the secession was really the work of the Ibo elite, which had favored separation partly as a form of ethnic self-protection but also as a way of achieving a power denied to them in Nigeria.[120]

The achievement of Biafran propaganda, O'Connell and others argued, had been to persuade outsiders that only the self-determination of the Ibos mattered and that only their self-determination was threatened. This propaganda victory had concealed the true Nigerian revolution—the creation by Gowon of a new, twelve-state system that had effectively freed the minorities throughout Nigeria from domination by the Hausa, Ibo, and Yoruba.[121] Fidelity to liberal principles of self-determination, such writers said, demanded concern for these minorities, if necessary at the cost of withdrawing support from Biafra.[122]

118. Kenneth Lindsay, "Can There Be a Peace Settlement in Nigeria?" 15. Lindsay added that "conditions [were] still a little more flexible in Biafra. . . . It is just possible that those who favor a peace settlement may yet carry the day without recourse to such expedients."

119. According to Uphoff and Ottemoeller: "The non-Ibo people of the East, who bore no love for the Ibos because of decades of manipulation and neglect, were not consulted on secession. . . . Non-Ibos were not to be given the same right claimed by the Ibos for themselves—self-determination and separation from 'hostile' Nigerian neighbors" ("After the Nigerian Civil War," 1). A Nigerian, Monday Efiong Noah, remarked similarly that "Biafran secession without proper consultation with the minorities was a fatal assumption and a wilful neglect of minority problems" ("The Nigerian Civil War and the Gullibles," 6).

120. "The Scope of the Tragedy," 10. O'Connell noted at another point: "Whatever redress was likely [for Ibos] was made impossible by the refusal of the Ibo leadership after August to accept conciliation within any agreement that would keep the federation in being" (ibid., 11).

121. As a Nigerian writer remarked in *Africa Today*, the minorities in Eastern Nigeria "did not favor secession. They wanted their own state within the Nigerian Federation. They had never fared well under the Ibo-dominated Eastern Regional Government even at a time when the Federal Government served as a check and could never have been expected to entrust their destiny to a 'Biafran' regime" (Monday Efiong Noah, "The Nigerian Civil War and the Gullibles," 6).

122. The failure of Biafra, an anonymous contributor to the *South Atlantic Quarterly* suggested, was due to the fact that the Ibo had gambled on being able to carry the minorities with them, but had failed to do so. These and other minorities realized that they "needed the larger framework of protection which a united

Sympathizers with the Federal government also argued that support for African self-determination implied respect for African sovereignty. Liberals such as Senators McCarthy and Kennedy who spoke dismissively of such "petty political considerations" as Nigerian sovereignty in urging dispatch of aid to Biafra were, in the eyes of Federal sympathizers, both untrue to their own ideals of self-determination and "enormously condescending" to Africans.[123] Moreover, to suggest, as Biafra's supporters did, that Nigeria did not deserve such respect because it was "artificial" was to overlook the fact that Biafra was equally artificial.[124]

In the view of critics of Biafra, the essential political questions had been buried by the emotion generated by the horrors that had occurred during the war (and by the skillful Biafran exploitation of this emotion). Among these questions, they agreed, were real issues of self-determination. But by a cruel irony, the wave of Western humanitarian sympathy for Biafra had helped the Biafran regime to suppress discussion of its own

---

Nigeria alone could provide. . . . Not only were the Ibos unable to carry their minorities but they chose the very moment to try when the minorities throughout Nigeria had come to power at the center as the result of the *coup* of July 1966" ("Nigeria's Civil War," 144–45).

123. As one writer asked rhetorically: "How would Kennedy regard Cuban relief flights to Mississippi? We have never taken our sovereignty lightly, but it seems that in Africa boundaries don't count. Beneath much humane energy lies the conviction that Africans can't take care of themselves" (Steven Jervis, "Biafra Has Oil as Well as Starving Children," 9).

In a speech in January 1969, Sen. Edward Kennedy, in calling for various measures to end the war, had reportedly "rejected the suggestion that efforts to impose a solution would be internal neo-colonial interference [and had] repeated his long-held opinion that relief flights did not need Nigerian approval; they overrode such 'petty political considerations.' . . . 'The essence of international law [Kennedy said] is humanitarianism. It springs from divine law, from natural law'" (*Baltimore Sun*, 9 January 1969, cited in Roy M. Melbourne, "The American Response to the Nigerian Conflict," 40).

124. As Steven Jervis noted: "The borders of the old Eastern Region were determined by the British for administrative reasons, and like Nigeria it is a multitribal area" ("Biafra Has Oil as Well as Starving Children," 9). Moreover, to talk of Biafra as an "independent" state was nonsense, the British journalist John Mander complained: "This is a strange argument indeed: for the Federals run their show (with British and Soviet material support, but not manpower), and Biafra relied for its foreign support on South Africa, Rhodesia, Portugal, Israel and possibly (through Tanzania) on China. Moreover, its chief supplier—through Gabon and the Ivory Coast—was France" ("Britain's Vietnam," 6).

role in denying self-determination to nearly half of the population of Eastern Nigeria.

Suppression of this issue, the critics claimed, did allow supporters of Biafra to evade or deny the issue of fragmentation raised by those who tried to apply the analogy of the domino theory to Africa. But, in fact, the Biafra issue also posed, unavoidably and in an acute manner, the deeper dilemma of Western liberals identified earlier by the Africa League pamphleteers—how to show respect for the sovereignty entailed by self-determination while remaining true to values held by liberals to be universal.

A central theme of liberal writing about Africa in the sixties was, as Vernon McKay put it, that Africans were "not inferior, but only different."[125] Yet when revisionism had done its work on the illusions and misunderstandings to be found in early liberal writing on Africa, a central conundrum remained for liberals, as for all believers hoping to gather converts globally: how much diversity can a philosophy absorb without losing its integrity?

Clearly, the message of revisionism was that liberals had tried to stretch their beliefs too far. They should, in future, be true to themselves. But true to themselves in what? Where did integrity end, and "ethnocentrism" begin? These were difficult questions for American liberals: the difficulty came from the fact that they believed in both the uniqueness *and* the essential similarity of peoples throughout the world. They rejected what they saw as divisive in cultures, while applauding them as expressions of individuality. They yearned for wider acceptance of liberal ideas, values, and institutions, yet acknowledged the right of others to be different.

Revisionism identified and illuminated such problems, while applying a corrective to the empirical and conceptual looseness of much liberal writing about Africa. But it could not solve the dilemmas it brought to the surface, since these dilemmas reflected some confused commitments and loyalties in American liberalism itself. In all three discourses examined, the central questions were questions of value, and in all there was some conflict between liberal values—in particular between the value of self-determination, on the one hand, and other values which liberals

125. "A United States Policy for the New Africa," 2.

held should transcend barriers of race and nation. Resolving this conflict was rather harder because, as an expression of their commitment to the self-determination of others, liberals practiced self-denial in making "value judgments," except insofar as they were based on a supposedly universal value of "rationality." In principle, liberals shunned value judgments. Self-determination, in their view, was a right, and this right implied an entitlement to be different in ways other than just having a different name and a different flag. They therefore set their faces against those who equated a difference in values with a difference in civilization (which, as we shall see, conservatives quite happily did).

But this was actually a very superficial response. It dealt with the cruder expressions of racial superiority without actually providing an answer to the more profound question of how there could be values without value judgments, and how diversity could be "confronted fairly"— that is, without either crude moral imperialism or unnecessary self-deprecation. Liberalism, in this respect, provided some good working rules for tourists, but no clear formulae for politicians and diplomats.

FIVE

The American

Left and Africa

I n the late sixties and early seventies, both liberal and conservative writers on Africa found themselves being challenged by "critiques" produced by writers of the resurgent left. Such critiquing was both intellectual and political. In general terms, it usually claimed that writing about international affairs ignored the role of capitalism in creating and maintaining existing patterns of inequality, both between countries and within them. It argued that theories of development and democracy which American and Western European intellectuals used in studying and evaluating events in the third world embodied capitalist and "ethnocentric" assumptions.

Positively, writers on the left called for the adoption of concepts which would illuminate the dynamics of inequality and oppression and which would explain, as a British scholar put it, "the unequal appropriation of resources in society . . . the unequal appropriation of resources throughout the world, and the social relationships which flow from, or are presupposed by this unequal appropriation of resources."[1] Such an intellectual revolution was particularly important to socialists since, although they regarded historical change as essentially a product of material forces (rather than ideas), they also saw vigorous analysis and careful choice of strategy as crucial to *praxis*. Moreover, just as political and economic structures were mutually influential, so intellectual and political functions were intertwined. Therefore, intellectuals responsible for glamorizing or whitewashing imperialism could be treated as at least accomplices in its crimes.[2]

1. Gavin Williams, paper entitled "Sociological Explanation and Neo-Colonialism." Quoted in Waterman, "Radicalism in African Studies," 266.
2. Thus Herbert Aptheker, the communist historian, wrote: "To justify a system whose birth was fertilized with human flesh watered with children's tears

The Left and African History

Socialists approached the subject of African traditional institutions with many of the same assumptions and values as liberals. They typically had little time for nostalgia about precolonial societies and had few doubts about the benefits of modernization. They were just as hostile as liberals to "feudal elements" and if anything were even more earnest about the golden future to be built by the application of reason to social institutions.

Yet socialists and liberals differed in one crucial respect. While liberals tended to be indiscriminately enthusiastic about capitalism and industrialization, socialists saw these processes as involving alienation. Capitalism, they argued, had destroyed the equality and interdependence characteristic of agrarian communities, had turned common property into commodities and had separated men from the products and fruits of their labor. Socialism could be conceived as a way of restoring the form and sentiment of community prevalent before capitalist accumulation began.

Socialist writing about Africa in fact contains a significant and surprising element of nostalgia about precolonial societies. Under imperial rule, wrote the well-known British Africanist Basil Davidson, huge numbers of Africans had been wrenched from "the relative security and mental peace of their traditional ethos into a hurricane of moral and social disintegration."[3] Before this disaster (an African contributor to *Political Affairs* claimed), Africans had enjoyed "a simple natural culture which enabled them to build their homes and dance away their sorrows amid an atmosphere of communal fellowship."[4]

In earlier times, however, socialists had, while recognizing the tragedy of those dispossessed by enclosure in Europe, nevertheless acknowledged the historical logic propelling it. In the same way, socialists looking at recent African history could respect the values of precolonial communities while insisting that there was (*pace* Western conservatives and some "African socialists") no way back. Socialism and communal values had to be established by mastering the forces and prevailing in the conflicts set off by capitalism and its overseas offspring, imperialism. Historical context defined both what was progressive and what was possible (in

---

has required special ingenuity. The exercise of such ingenuity developed a special breed of thinker, of scholar, of intellectual" ("Africa and Imperialist Intellectuals," 32).

3. "Difficulties, Not Disillusionment," 27.
4. Mokwugo Okoye, "Communism and African Perspectives," 48.

both cases, "objectively"): it also defined what was redundant and what was reactionary.

In Africa, village communities belonged historically to an age before primitive accumulation. Chieftaincy, however, either belonged to a more feudal phase or had been perverted by imperial rule. Whether feudalism had existed or had been significant was a matter of dispute. Soviet Africanists, such as Ponomarov and Potekhin, tended to regard feudalism as a necessary historical phase and to identify "feudal elements" as the immediate foe of African revolutionaries.[5] Western radical Africanists were more cautious about applying such received labels. The noted French Marxist scholar Jean Suret-Canale remarked: "The feudal elements or their remnants do not form a socially important force. Before colonization, such feudal elements only existed in certain regions, and their importance varied greatly."[6] In the view of radical scholars, the more typical situation was one in which colonialism destroyed the legitimacy of chiefs ruling communities of a broadly egalitarian character, making them into petty autocrats, and clients of imperial administrations. The position of such chiefs was anomalous: except in regions such as northern Nigeria, northern Cameroon, Ruanda, and Burundi, they did not represent a distinct mode of production with an associated and archaic social structure.

The Left and Colonialism

Compared to conservatives and even liberals, radicals and socialists could not see any benign element in imperialism, nor (as some liberals did) did they see it as a temporary and essentially European aberration from Western ideals. In Marxist theory, imperialism might have some objectively

5. Thus B. Ponomarov wrote in *Political Affairs*: "Imperialism has an ally in the colonial countries first of all in the feudal top group, which seeks to preserve the remnants of medievalism which fetter the development of productive forces. . . . To sweep out feudalism and the remnants of medievalism is one of the important tasks of the revolution. That is why it is an anti-feudal revolution" ("On National Democracy (Part II)," 47).

Similarly, Potekhin, while considering federalism appropriate for Ghana in the late fifties, had no doubt that Ashanti nationalism was "rooted in the interests of 'the feudal rulers'"; see Bird, "A Soviet Ethnographer Visits Ghana."

6. "Colonialism's Impact on Africa," 35.

progressive effects (such as the building of railways in India or East Africa), but it was as exploitative as any other capitalist enterprise.

Regarding the origins and nature of colonialism, few American radicals dissented from the conventional Leninist view that the role of colonies had been "to supply raw materials to the industries of the industrial metropolis, and to serve as an outlet for the manufactured goods of the metropolitan industries."[7] Under capitalism, this relationship created new (and usually captive) markets for industrial producers, who were facing a crisis of underconsumption and falling rates of profit at home. It also enabled such producers to survive, by giving them access to cheap raw materials and cheap labor abroad. The profits thus generated were exported to the metropolitan country, denying even the benefits of capitalist reproduction (originally envisaged by Marx) to the colonies. Industrialization was therefore unlikely to occur in third world colonies. It would be difficult to achieve even after independence because of the draining of surplus by metropolitan monopolies, whose interests were allowed to dominate the economies of European colonies.

As restated in the fifties and sixties by the American Marxists Paul Baran and Paul Sweezy, socialist theory stressed the inequality of relations between developed capitalist and underdeveloped countries, notably in commercial relations, but also in political relations. According to Baran and Sweezy, the dominant classes in developed countries had "the power of initiative" and the behavior of other classes (including the dominant class in developing countries) was "primarily reactive."[8]

Writers in American socialist journals could see nothing especially beneficial resulting from the subordination of African countries.[9] "British imperial rule of Nigeria," declared a Soviet writer in *Political Affairs,* "brought the people of Nigeria poverty, starvation, and disease."[10] The black American socialist Alphaeus W. Hunton had a similarly poor impression of Nigeria when he visited Lagos in 1959. In the suburbs, he found "new residences of extraordinary sumptuousness in which senior officials and other members of the African upper strata dwell." In the

---

7. Ibid., 30.

8. "Notes on the Theory of Imperialism," 17.

9. The British Communist Joan Bellamy referred to the "systematic dismantling of the African continent carried through by the monopolies," a process that had "condemned the people to poverty, hunger, illiteracy, ill health" ("A Valuable Study of Neo-Colonialism," 60).

10. M. Gostev, "Nigeria: The Problems of Independence," 91.

street, Hunton wrote, the visitor would see "a chauffeur-driven limousine contesting the right of way with a two-wheeled cart piled high with wooden crates and being pushed by four or five black men."[11]

In contrast to the cautiously approving verdicts on Belgian colonialism pronounced in liberal and conservative journals, the judgements of radicals on the state of the Congo at independence were generally critical. One visitor reported that there were 280,000 lepers and 100,000 victims of tuberculosis in the colony, and that malaria was "undermining the health of the whole population."[12] Such, it was suggested, were the "benefits" of colonialism. "Three-quarters of a century of imperialist rule," wrote the editor of *Political Affairs*, "have left the Congo woefully backward, with no industrial development, with much of its natural resources untapped and with millions of acres of highly fertile land unused, while its people live in the most abysmal poverty."[13]

Yet socialists did respond to the industrialism in Katanga. After a visit to the region in 1955, Basil Davidson, a British socialist and historian of Africa, remarked: "Here at last, in these expanding Congo industries, the white man's contact with Africa has acquired a fertilizing form that can stimulate and sponsor an African culture and civilization genuinely in step with the modern world."[14] "At last" here obviously implied that overall the experience and the impact of imperialism had been exploit-

11. "West Africa Today," 39.

12. Roger Clain, "The Congo Freedom-Struggle," 57.

13. Hyman Lumer, "U.S. Imperialism in the Congo," 10. However, Basil Davidson came away from a trip to Katanga in 1955 with a more positive view. He found no color bar in industry there and concluded that race relations in the region were generally good. In particular, Davidson (like so many other visitors) was excited by the vision of an industrialized Africa that he glimpsed in the Congo. Watching "a team stamping out steel bars in the Jadotville foundry," he commented: "It was difficult not to feel that one was looking straight into the future—at an industrialized Africa no longer *necessarily* inferior to the rest of the world" ("Enlightened Colonialism: The Belgian Congo," 35).

14. "Enlightened Colonialism: The Belgian Congo," 39. Katanga's uranium resources added further to its impact on visitors. Noting the secrecy surrounding the Shinkolobwe mine, Davidson commented: "It was out of the silence and obscurity of Shinkolobwe, lost in the semidesert scrub of middle Africa, that the raw material for Hiroshima's bomb was taken" (ibid., 34). Ritchie Calder, a British scientist and radical, wrote in the *Nation*: "Shinkolobwe is a gray ulcer on the landscape near Jadotville, eighty-seven miles northwest of Elisabethville. It is, however, one of the most important mines in the world. History of the most portentous kind was dug from it" ("Shinkolobwe: Key to the Congo," 163).

ative, and any benefits it might have had were purely incidental. To the left, imperialism was a universal phenomenon, rooted in the imperatives of Western capitalism, not (as some liberal anticolonialists seemed to think) just a romantic enterprise run by dotty missionaries and ambitious subalterns. If, however improbably, it led to industrialization, this would be an objectively progressive outcome: for only through industrialization could the proletariat develop that would force socialism upon the world.

The Left and Decolonization

Robustly simple though this view was, it made decolonization apparently difficult to explain. Since such large material interests were involved in colonial empires, were profiting so handsomely from it, and were so instrumental in determining the policies of colonial governments, the withdrawal of imperial control presented a major analytic and political challenge to socialists. Given the left's materialist view of capitalism, explanations based on supposed ideals of "self-determination" could not make any sense: nor could purely political or strategic explanations. The essential point of reference had to be the interests of capitalism: the question had to be, How were such interests expressed in the phenomenon of decolonization?

The usual answer was that decolonization was essentially a tactical retreat. In each territory, decolonization involved a deal between imperial governments (representing metropolitan capital) and the African middle class. Under this deal, Africans would take formal political control, in return for a guarantee that capitalist interests (notably those represented by trade and investment) would be left intact and allowed to operate, in all essentials, freely.

According to the radical anthropologist Stanley Diamond, such a "neo-colonial formula" was appealing because "classic colonialism" was "no longer profitable or prestigious."[15] By granting formal political independence, imperial countries could put a stop to some of the criticism aimed at them by third world (and American) politicians. Moreover (according to Paul Sweezy), in the eyes of imperial governments and their African collaborators, such a strategy had the merit of "heading off the development of genuine revolutionary movements among the oppressed peoples

---

15. "Modern Africa: The Pains of Birth," 169.

of the colonies."[16] The successor elites had, Immanuel Wallerstein argued, implicitly accepted the job of "internal policing . . . of . . . potentially radical peasants and workers."[17]

This line of analysis obviously raised some awkward questions about how socialists should deal with African nationalists and the regimes they headed. Some socialists also felt that it was important to account for the role of American capitalism in decolonization. Radicals conceded that the United States had applied its diplomatic influence to force European states to decolonize, but (they argued) the diplomatic campaign had been inspired by the needs of American capitalism. The real significance of decolonization was that it provided a means for American capitalism to replace its decaying, uncompetitive European rival. The rhetoric of "self-determination" and American "anticolonialism" simply masked this transfer of control: it provided a set of superficial slogans to adorn the reality of one imperialism busy installing itself in place of another.

Some radicals saw a particularly clear line of American imperial succession in the Congo and Angola—both territories ruled by weak and marginal colonial powers. They saw U.S. policy in the Congo after the collapse of Belgian rule as designed to enable the supplanting of Belgian by American capital and, with some ingenuity, argued that American opposition to the Katanga secession had similar roots.

Angola and the other Portuguese territories represented a different situation—one in which (according to Minter, Mittelman, Saul, O'Brien, and others) "the neocolonialist alternative" was not practical. Portugal, they pointed out, was itself a backward country lacking "the kind of industrial, economic and colonial infrastructure . . . necessary to maintain economic domination once political control is relinquished."[18] The colonial country had therefore been unable to create "a significant dependent bourgeoisie" in its colonies: even the leadership of the nationalist movements was largely drawn from the small academic and clerical elite. The 1974 coup in Lisbon might have been an attempt to impose a neocolonial solution, but it had failed. The liberation movements in Angola,

16. "Modern Capitalism," 8.
17. The metropolitan powers had made concessions "in order to separate the nationalist leadership from these strata and prevent a more coherent and conscious degree of radical political activity" ("Looking back at African Independence Ten Years Later," 3).
18. O'Brien, "Portugal and Africa: A Dying Colonialism," 35.

Mozambique, and Guina-Bissau had then stepped into the vacuum created by the collapse of Portuguese authority.[19]

This collapse, however, had (the radicals argued) led to a defeat for American capitalism. The United States had long since superseded Portugal as the main trading partner and source of capital for the Portuguese African colonies. This being the case, Portugal's persistence in fighting for her colonies seemed irrational (indeed, her empire seemed to have lacked any easily identifiable economic rationale at any time). Her capitulation made complete sense. Much less than 20 percent of Portugal's trade was with her African colonies, and many Portuguese businessmen saw their interests as lying overwhelmingly in the European Community. According to the radical thesis, Portuguese capital (such as it was) had decided to abandon the colonies in order to obtain membership of the EC. But the normal sequel—establishment of American dominance—had been aborted in the Portuguese colonies. Nationalist movements with genuine socialist credentials had come to power—the impeccability of their credentials being confirmed by the relentless hostility that American administrations showed toward the governments of Angola and Mozambique.

In most other cases, however, decolonization had been essentially an imperial strategy, executed according to the imperialists' timetable. Socialists were bound to be wary of the African governments that had come to power as a result of such a process. Objectively, their accession to power might be a progressive step, opening the way to more radical decolonization. But—radicals claimed—it was typically not as large or progressive a step as the nationalist movements themselves claimed. Socialists consequently insisted on assessing African nationalism according to socialist standards.

The Left and the Analogy of 1776

If the rhetoric of African nationalism was suspect, what of the rhetoric of American liberalism? Did socialists find anything useful in liberal attempts to draw on the mythology of the American Revolution?

Predictably, the answer was typically negative. The Constitution of the United States (declared a writer in *Monthly Review*) was *"par excellence* the document and servitor of the eighteenth century bourgeois revolution

19. Mittelman, "Some Reflections on Portugal's Counter-Revolution," 59–60.

and thus, as Lenin's *State and Revolution* teaches, totally unsuitable for making a new world."[20]

The democratic socialist Sidney Lens argued in *Liberation* that while the American and African revolutions resembled each other in rejecting European rule, their aspirations differed sharply. African nationalism, Lens thought, "in its own confused way . . . [aspired] to a socialist future, rather than to capitalism." In fact, it resembled the Russian Revolution in that it was striving "to destroy feudalism, tribalism, and other out-moded social forms." But, then again, it was neither a "proletarian rev-olution," nor a "revolution of the peasantry and proletariat."[21]

Interestingly, it was a Soviet writer who provided one of the more his-torically sophisticated Marxist analyses of the American Revolution. Writ-ing in 1976 in the Soviet journal *International Affairs,* Y. Melnikov commented: "The War of Independence . . . was largely inspired by what in those days were progressive principles and slogans. It therefore pro-duced many examples of staunchness and heroism, had the support of progressive circles and leaders abroad and laid the foundations for dem-ocratic tendencies in the development of American society."[22] However, Melnikov continued, although the American revolution was "in fact the first anti-colonial war of liberation in history," it was also "limited as regards national and social relations." Its leaders had allowed slavery and the expropriation of American Indian lands to continue.[23] Yet, while con-cluding that the American Revolution had "consolidated power in the hands of America's well-to-do elite," Melnikov stressed that indepen-dence had been "won chiefly by the masses" and had left a "progressive heritage," albeit one subsequently betrayed, abused, and perverted by the American ruling class.

While skeptical about parallels with 1776, socialists generally reserved judgment on the class character and "progressive heritage" of the "Af-rican revolution," unsure about how far *it* had been won by the masses and limited *it* would prove in terms of "national and social relations."

20. H. W. Edwards, "The Colonial War at Home: A Comment," 448.
21. "The Revolution in Africa," 8. The term "revolution of the peasantry and proletariat" was given currency by Lenin in 1905.
22. "U.S. Foreign Policy: Traditions and Present Trends," 88.
23. In these and other respects, "while demanding freedom and sovereignty, the young American bourgeoisie leading the war [had] made private property sacrosanct" (ibid., 89).

The Left and Self-Determination

The problems posed by decolonization recurred in all radical discussions of third world nationalism. The agreed premise for such discussions was that class struggle provided both the essential dynamic of history and the ultimate touchstone of political loyalty. Socialists must therefore evaluate nationalism in the light of its relationship—actual or potential—to the class struggle.

In coming to terms with African nationalism, they had to ask themselves some fundamental and familiar questions. Was nationalism really or invariably a mask for bourgeois interests—a potent and dangerous ideological distraction from issues vital to the working class? Should socialists give tactical support to movements (and regimes) in the third world led by nationalists or social democrats? In what circumstances were nationalist movements "objectively progressive"? Who, for that matter, should speak for socialism, given the widening gap between Moscow and Beijing?

Radicals had to ask such questions not just because of the priority of class analysis in most socialist theory, but also because of the fundamental internationalism of all socialist thought. In form at least, this internationalism resembled that of the liberals, and it led to similar doubts about nationalism. It was also basic to socialist strategy. The hope of the left (a contributor to *Monthly Review* declared) should be for an ever-intensifying, ever more global revolutionary movement. As this movement established itself, so "the whole notion and reality of exclusive 'national' boundaries [would] begin to fade into relative insignificance."[24]

Support for nationalism (and self-determination, and any other proximate political goal) had, then, to be conditional on nationalism having, or being associated with, elements conducive to eventual movement toward socialism. For socialists (as for many liberals), nationalism was as

24. J. Michael Dawn, "Toward an International Strategy," 40. The editors of *Monthly Review,* indeed, exhorted their readers to "think of themselves as members of an immense international movement capable of embracing an overwhelming majority of mankind" ("Tell the Truth," 3). The first issue of the magazine in fact suggested a rather different orientation: "We shall follow the development of socialism all over the world [the editors declared], but we want to emphasize that our major concern is less with socialism abroad than with socialism at home" ("Where We Stand," 1). On the politics of this journal, see Clecak, "*Monthly Review*: An Assessment."

nationalism did. Judgments had to be made continually about the objective value and potential of specific movements and leaders, just as they had to be made about specific issues of self-determination.

The Left and Katanga

The Katanga secession seemed to American socialists to be the perfect case of imperialist and capitalist interests manipulating the symbols of self-determination. Tshombe was clearly a puppet of Western economic and political interests—a stooge of the Union Minière and the Belgians generally. He was "the Belgian Quisling in Katanga," "the Belgian lackey," or (more elaborately) "a businessman grown fat off the leavings from the imperialist table."[25] According to writers in such journals as the *Nation* and *Africa Today*, the Union Minière and its related financial interests had from the start been (and continued to be) the underwriters of Katangan "independence."[26]

Interestingly, as Tshombe held on to power, a revised and more nuanced view began to appear. Perhaps as a way of dealing with the problem of American opposition to the Katangese secession, radical observers began to suggest that Tshombe was more his own man than he had at first seemed to be. By late 1962, even an observer of fundamentally radical sympathies such as Herbert Weiss was questioning the degree to which foreign interests were calling the tune in Katanga: "Belgium, and in a sense also the Union Minière, have become the whipping boys of the Katanga problem. Actually, they are no longer in a position to change the basic power balance. As things now stand, the Union Minière, rather than controlling the Katanga President, is clearly the prisoner."[27] Indeed, by

25. "Up the U.N.!" 22; editorial, *Monthly Review* 12, no. 11 (March 1961): 548, 551.

26. "Never," declared the editors of *Africa Today*, "has there been so clear an example of neo-colonialism at work." The United Nations had, they said, had "to fight a company war in a company province. . . . The prime movers were the mining companies. They financed, equipped, and organized secession" ("Like Father Like Son").

For similar views, see Calder, "Shinkolobwe: Key to the Congo," 165; "Congo Drums Again," 339.

27. "The Tshombe Riddle," 6. "It would be a mistake [Weiss wrote] . . . to assume that Moise Tshombe is simply a tool of foreign interests. His own economic and political self-interests are also involved." David Halberstam came to a similar conclusion during his visit to Katanga in the summer of 1962: "No matter

1964 Colin Gonze, editor of *Africa Today,* had concluded that Tshombe was "not a stooge for anyone." He was, rather, primarily a tribalist politician and an opportunist whose personal ambitions made it "profitable for him to cooperate with the Belgians for the time being."[28]

Whatever Tshombe was or was not, Katanga seemed to socialists (as to some liberals) to be a clear warning about the worm in the bud of nationalism, whether in Africa or elsewhere. Katanga, one observer remarked, should alert the left to the dangers of following every nationalist bandwagon, in the hope that something politically useful might fall off the back. According to the editor of *Africa Today,* radicals should learn from the example of Katanga the lesson "that the catch-all word 'independence' is not the end to all equations in African politics."[29]

The issue of how to treat nationalism did in fact go on causing disagreements between writers in American socialist journals. Some commentators worried about what they felt was insensitivity on the part of socialists toward the grievances and aspirations firing third world nationalists. Critics such as Stephen Torgoff charged that American socialists had shown an arrogance and lack of imagination in this regard: they had, he complained, failed utterly "to understand the importance of the national question."[30] Solidarity with the third world (according to a writer

what Tshombe may have been before, he is no one's puppet today. (For many observers, he now has as much leverage over the Union Minière in Katanga as this Belgian mining company has over him.) Tshombe makes his own basic political decisions and although each may eye the other a bit suspiciously, each benefits the other immensely" ("Mystery—and Tragedy—of Tshombe," 56).

28. "Tshombe in Wonderland," 5. Although *Africa Today*'s editorial view was that the "Katanga secession was only secondarily motivated by African tribal dynamics," the editor himself argued in a signed article that Tshombe's political alliance with his minister of the interior, Godefroid Munongo, "was, in effect, an attempt to reconstitute the old Bayeke-Lunda empire." See "Like Father Like Son," 3; and Gonze, "Katanga Secession: The New Colonialism," 4.

29. Gonze, "Katanga Secession: The New Colonialism," 4. The editor was not, however, hopeful that the lesson would be learned. Many Americans, he feared, were still "prepared to accept political independence as a praiseworthy goal, [and would] continue to be confused by the turn of events in Africa" (ibid.).

30. "Some Thoughts on Earl Ofari's 'Marxism, Nationalism, and Black Liberation,'" 80. In the same vein, Stanley Diamond—an anthropologist by profession—warned against "moral colonialism," exemplified by attempts to apply Western standards to such phenomena as corruption. Moral colonialism, in Diamond's definition, was "a curious piece of psycho-political business which gives us the chance to evade our own history by adopting fantastic expectations of carefully chosen others" ("Modern Africa: The Pains of Birth," 177).

in *Liberation*) implied and required nonintervention: "By all the principles of self-determination and non-interference we extol . . . those people directly on the scene should have the right to settle their own problems."[31]

To other socialists, however, such an approach smacked of political abdication. Nationalism, they argued, might have been progressive in the nineteenth century and earlier, when it enabled the bourgeoisie to break the power of the European monarchs. But since 1917 (a South African Communist suggested), the relevant standard for judging nationalism was how far it helped or hindered the spread of socialism. The phenomenon was to be judged "from the point of view of the development of the world proletarian revolution." Socialists had a duty to apply this standard every time a movement for national self-determination sought their help.[32] Such movements might have to make tactical compromises with capitalism. Socialists should be understanding about such compromises, and should accept that social and economic circumstances might not allow an easy or rapid transition to socialism. Nevertheless, given the existence of the socialist camp, there was no longer any real need for bourgeois nationalism: "The nations emerging today, in the period when the bourgeoisie had [*sic*] outlived its usefulness, can achieve their destiny under the banner of socialism."[33]

The Case of Ghana

Not only did socialists disagree about the right posture to take toward nationalism, but the official line—which in some instances meant the Moscow line—changed. While Stalin had been very suspicious of anticolonial movements, Khrushchev encouraged a much more pragmatic approach. Attitudes toward particular movements and leaders could change quite dramatically, sometimes because of changes in their own postures, sometimes because of changes in party doctrine.

In the fifties, for example, Kwame Nkrumah and the Convention People's party in Ghana got a distinctly lukewarm press in both Soviet and Western socialist journals. Until Stalin's death (as John Hatch has pointed out), "Kwame Nkrumah was described as a spokesman for the Ghanaian bourgeoisie, Nnamdi Azikiwe of Nigeria as an African Gandhi."[34] Simi-

31. Ann Morrissett, "Cold War in the Congo," 9.
32. Zanzolo, "The Struggle for Nigerian Unity," 8.
33. Ibid., 9.
34. "Africa between East and West," 21.

larly, when the veteran black socialist Alphaeus W. Hunton visited Accra in 1959, he compared both the city and the government in power there rather unfavorably with what he had seen earlier in Guinea.[35] Again, in 1960 a writer in *Dissent* (by no means a CP or Trotskyite journal) actually described Nkrumah as something of a neocolonialist: "Kwame Nkrumah of Ghana, though he parades himself as the first modern Negro premier in Africa, in a most subtle way—unknown even to himself—is a British stooge; for Lever Bros., Ltd. can say more, and with greater authority, through a black than a white mouth on the Gold Coast."[36]

By 1962, however, Ghana (or at least Nkrumah) had turned sharply in the "correct" direction, embracing Soviet ideas and applying them both to its domestic programs and to its foreign relations. "All around," Shirley Graham wrote lyrically from Accra in the fall of 1960, "one witnesses the renaissance of the ancient glories of Africa giving flower to the loftiest reaches of Socialism."[37] By 1964, all of the squalor that Alphaeus Hunton had observed had apparently disappeared from the Accra metropolitan area. At least, it had done so when Herbert Aptheker was in town: "In Ghana," Aptheker reported, "there are no beggars, the people are without sores and eye diseases, the children have solid frames and clear eyes and are unafraid. And the people are inspired and excited for they not only have accomplished a national-liberating revolution; they are also consciously moving towards socialism and are consciously seeking to help create a united, free Africa—*integrated with socialism.*"[38]

However, Aptheker also saw Ghana as a warning to socialists about the dangers of African nationalism, as preached by Nkrumah's friend and adviser, George Padmore. Padmore, a West Indian and sometime CP activist, had become an associate of Nkrumah in the fifties. According to Henry Winston, a black American Marxist, Padmore, having embraced "bourgeois nationalism," used his influence to draw Nkrumah away from

35. Hunton commented disapprovingly on the luxurious conditions at the (then new) Ambassador Hotel, remarking that he had found "little such modernization as yet under way in the housing of the city's poorer workers or upcountry" ("West Africa Today," 38).

36. Daniel M. Friedenberg, "An Economic View of Negro Independence," 191. Lever Brothers (Unilever) owned the United Africa Company and a number of affiliates in French-speaking African countries, all of which controlled a substantial part of the import and export trade of the territories concerned.

37. "The African Personality," 17.

38. "Present Thinking in Socialist Countries," 49; emphasis in original.

"an orientation based consistently on a scientific socialist direction internally."[39] Prominent among Padmore's sins (at least as enumerated by Winston) were his support for "an anti-Communist color strategy" and his (alleged) belief that imperialism was not an inherent stage in the development of capitalism, but a "policy" that corporate capital could turn on or off at will.[40] The CP's bitterness at Padmore was naturally all the deeper because of his earlier communism and perhaps also because of the strategic and symbolic importance of Ghana, both to socialists and to African nationalists.[41]

The Problem of Black American Nationalism

The timing of Winston's attack on Padmore was significant, since in the early seventies the American left was in fact having to deal with two kinds of black nationalism, one African, the other Afro-American.

Some American socialists (certainly the CPUSA) were strenuously opposed to theories linking the black American experience to that of African colonies. Black Americans had not, they argued, been "colonized" as Africans had. By the same token, they opposed anything resembling a nationalist "color strategy" (in Winston's phrase) for the emancipation of black Americans. Instead, Claude Lightfoot declared, "the advocates of a black nation must identify themselves with all that [was] required to set up a socialist America . . . black people alone could never destroy capitalism."[42]

In fact, the CP was critical of both black nationalists and civil rights organizations, such as the NAACP. Its leaders saw integration, pursued through civil rights activism, as an inadequate strategy. Pursued as an exclusive goal, it would (they argued) simply facilitate the cooptation of blacks into capitalist America, and the main effect of such a strategy

39. "Padmore, the 'Father' of Neo-Pan-Africanism," 16.

40. Ibid., 14, 3. Padmore's best-known work was his *Pan-Africanism or Communism? The Coming Struggle for Africa* (New York: Ray, 1956).

41. Winston, indeed, concluded that Padmore had given joy to the trusts and the imperialist states and, domestically, had "strengthened the bourgeois forces in Nkrumah's C.P.P. . . . But for the influence of Padmore's anti-Communist perversion of Pan-Africanism, Ghana would now probably have been advancing towards socialism—an inspiration to all Africa as Cuba is to all Latin America" ("Padmore," 14).

42. "The Right of Black America to Create a Nation," 11.

would be to strengthen the black bourgeoisie. Only "a thorough-going social revolution" could bring about true integration.[43]

In relation to black America and to Africa, the left thus regarded nationalism as a means, not as a sufficient ideological end. Generally, they supported African and black American claims—to independence in one case, to civil rights in the other. Socialists (like liberals) were anxious not to prejudge or alienate African national movements and African governments. They accepted the "noncapitalist path" as a possible road to development, though not to the point of identifying it with true socialism. Nevertheless, here as elsewhere, socialists reserved the right to judge claims to national self-determination on their ideological merits and by appropriate strategic standards.

The Left and Postindependence Africa

For socialists, any analysis of domestic politics (and external policy) presupposed analysis of social dynamics, and particularly the dynamics of class formation and conflict. In the fifties and sixties, they had to decide, specifically, on an appropriate analytic language for African and other third world societies that seemed to have a mixed, transitional character. Was—for example—the language of class analysis appropriate to societies that had experienced neither feudalism nor capitalism in its industrial form?

The Problem of "Tribalism"

In the African case, socialists went about answering such questions partly by confronting the standard vocabulary used in depicting African societies. In particular, they criticized the use of concepts of "tribalism" in journalistic writing, attacking the tendency (encouraged by conservatives) to explain all African political behavior by reference to this term. Writers on the left insisted that "tribalism" was not simply a rooted indigenous atavism, a "natural" phenomenon seeking expression at all levels in African society. Rather, they argued, it was typically a facade for the expres-

43. As *Monthly Review* put it, "The hope of any meaningful form of integration within the framework of this exploitative and thoroughly corrupt society is illusory" ("Socialism and the Negro Movement," *Monthly Review* 15, no. 5 [September 1963]: 231).

sion of conflicts and interests of a more contemporary kind. As Daniel Schechter, a leader of the radical Africa Research Group, put it: "Whenever a tribal name appears like 'Ibo' or 'Kikuyu,' readers must ask themselves: 'What is the class position of the ethnic group vis-a-vis the neocolonial economy?' This way one can avoid the tautology constructed by the ideologists of colonization which sees tribalism as the *cause* rather than the *result* of underdevelopment."[44]

Writing on the Congo, Nigeria, and Ghana provides many examples of this approach. The Congo was in the eyes of socialists a notorious case of the exploitation of allegedly "tribal" divisions by capitalism in order to protect "clearly reactionary policies." Editorializing on the Congo conflict, a writer in *Political Affairs* declared in 1961: "Contrary to the picture painted by the spokesmen of imperialism, the conflict in the Congo is no struggle between rival factions, hostile tribes or 'pro-Communist' and 'anti-Communist' leaders. It is a struggle of the Congolese people for the realization of freedom."[45] If conflict expressed itself in ethnic terms, an American writer remarked, it was because the colonial system in the Belgian Congo had tended "to accentuate ethnic and regional cleavages."[46]

Similarly, radicals strenuously attacked the tendency to interpret the Nigerian civil war in simplistic and tendentious "tribal" terms. The animosity between the Ibos and other groups was, Stanley Diamond suggested, best explained by referring to the colonial history of Nigeria. Of all groups in Nigeria, the Ibos had responded most eagerly to the opportunities for trade and self-improvement created by colonial government. They had emigrated from their poor and overcrowded homeland: everywhere they settled, they had been "in the forefront of the modernization forces."[47] Other Nigerians had become envious, and such envy found expression in the idiom of tribalism.

But "tribalism" should never be taken at face value. "It would be inaccurate to claim that the basic conflicts that convulsed Nigeria were tribal," Diamond warned. At least in the Ibos' view, "their rivalry with other groups has been, primarily, ideological, not tribalistic."[48] Others saw

44. "From a Closed Filing Cabinet: The Life and Times of the Africa Research Group," 46.
45. "Notes of the Month," March 1961, 17.
46. Weissman, *American Foreign Policy in the Congo, 1960–1964*, 15.
47. Diamond, "The End of the First Republic," 8.
48. Ibid.

alleged "tribal" difficulties in Nigeria as due to "the trouble-making potential of world imperialism," exploiting and enlarging minor differences so as "to retain economic and strategic advantage."[49]

The main trouble with such an approach was that, for all its boldness, it avoided the issue of whether "ethnicity" or "tribalism" (or the groups to which they referred) was at any level a reality. The writers cited above did not on the whole deny that the phenomenon existed: rather, they saw ethnic sentiment as aggravated and exploited by the surrounding forces of imperialism. To the extent that (like Schechter) they did want a direct substitution of the language of class for the language of ethnicity, they still had to face up to several questions.

First, what exactly was the correspondence between ethnic and class identity? Second, if class conflict was the "basic" reality and "tribalism" merely a projection of it, why did such conflict so universally assume an ethnic form? Why was it, even instrumentally, so convenient and appealing to have it take this form? It is hard to imagine answers to these questions that would not, even implicitly, attribute some kind of independent reality to ethnicity, as well as some degree of cultural specificity to Africa.

Indeed, as the sixties advanced, some of the more sophisticated socialist writers on Africa suggested that the reality of ethnicity should be recognized. Thus Roger Murray, writing in the British *New Left Review* of the Nkrumah period in Ghana, argued that more attention should be paid to "vertical stratification." It was not enough, he argued, to look at the "horizontal stratification" represented by class. At least in Ghana, class structure was "diffused . . . 'politics' is a complex, criss-crossing interaction of *horizontal* (class, status group, economic group) and *vertical* (regional, 'ethnic') allegiances and interests."[50] Immanuel Wallerstein, in elaborating his world-system model, made the same point more abstractly: "Nor is class consciousness the only form of consciousness. Empirically, it is obvious that within a capitalist world-economy ethno-national consciousness is a far more frequent phenomenon than class consciousness. Furthermore, the interrelationship between class consciousness and ethno-national consciousness is not the same in states located in the periphery as against the core of the world economy."[51]

49. Zanzolo, "Struggle for Nigerian Unity," 1.
50. Murray, "The Ghanaian Road," 68.
51. Wallerstein, "Class and Class Conflict in Africa," 37.

Such a statement was a real advance on the crude, mechanical formulations of Marxist orthodoxy found in *Political Affairs* and *World Marxist Review.* It allowed for the possibility that Africa might be different (though it left the difference to be clarified). Moreover, it reflected a general uneasiness about the adequacy of "the Moscow line" for understanding developments in the third world. This line was marked, one commentator complained, "by dogmatism, Eurocentrism, and political pragmatism," producing interpretations apparently intended "to simply illustrate a preexisting theoretical or political position."[52] Given the integrated and comprehensive nature of Marxist theory, such revisionism affected attitudes on a number of other issues, notably the relationship of imperialism to decolonization and the prospects for socialism in African states.

The Problem of Democracy

Just as nationalism did not, in socialist eyes, merit "universal and unconditional support," neither did particular constitutional and political arrangements. A reference to "wistful parliamentary cretinism" in a *Monthly Review* article on Angola accurately conveys the tone of much socialist discussion of democracy in the third world. According to the conventional socialist critique of liberal democracy, formal, individual freedoms had to be related (and, if necessary, subordinated) to collective needs: "positive" freedoms (such as freedom from hunger) must have priority over "negative" freedoms (such as freedom from arbitrary arrest).

In many places (and especially in the third world), "bourgeois democracy" was (radicals argued) an alien institution, and a redundant—even obstructive—one in the struggle to achieve the positive freedoms offered by socialism. Thus in 1959 the *Monthly Review* proclaimed its editors' view of the world's political future, when bourgeois democracy would collapse, along with the capitalist structure it protected and embodied. "In its place will be a planned, coordinated world community producing goods and services according to capacity and distributing them according to need. . . . The Chinese commune, under the general leadership of the Communist party, will prove to be one of the norms of the new socialist world."[53]

The journey toward the establishment of such a community might be

52. Waterman, "Radicalism in African Studies," 270, 264.
53. "Bourgeois Democracy in Eclipse," 408.

hard and painful, but, a Nigerian writer declared, "the conquest of the Promised Land, not the consolation of laggards and stragglers, is the main thing: regimentation is bad, it is true, but vegetation is worse and it is salutary that the collective will of the community shall prevail over the egomania of the few."[54]

The left was in fact particularly irritated by the way in which liberal democrats held up Nigeria as a beacon of democracy and freedom, in contrast to radical states such as Ghana and Guinea. It had, Stanley Diamond complained, been "the standard against which we invidiously compared developments that we neither understood, nor had compassion for, in other African states."[55] Despite all the violence and corruption that had marred the first years of independence, Western liberals had insistently lavished praise on the Federation just because it had the appearance of a multiparty constitutional democracy.

In reality, socialists claimed bitterly but with satisfaction after the 1966 coup, Nigeria had been the beneficiary of a "successful public relations hoax."[56] In fact, the country had been choked by corruption and capitalism of a rather unproductive kind. Thus, Steven Jervis noted in *Dissent*, "the popular Western version of Nigeria—a showplace of democracy in black Africa—was a thinly-disguised fraud. The vaunted multi-party system masked corrosive disunity, not creative opposition. Racked by corruption and violence, the country had been unable to hold an honest election since its independence was proclaimed in 1960."[57] So far from being "the model of colonial success," as alleged by liberals, Nigeria was, Diamond declared, "the model of a colonial failure. . . . Nigeria's 'moderation,' the vaunted 'conservatism' of Northern leaders, the well-publicized 'democratic character' of the coalition, have all been political myths, sanctioned by legal and constitutional documents."[58]

54. Okoye, "Communism and African Perspectives," 50. The writer supported his statement with the following, exceptionally obscure reference to Nigerian folk wisdom: "We have a saying in Nigeria that one does not consult a diviner to become a widow when one's husband dies and the forest that obscures baskets should not grow mushrooms."
55. "The End of the First Republic," 7. The British writer Victor Allen remarked similarly: "Social democrats in Britain wanted a measure against which to condemn Ghana with its one-party state. The mere bones of a democratic constitution in Nigeria were enough for that. . . . Nothing was accepted which stained the model of political democracy" ("Nigeria: Coup on a Tightrope," 143).
56. Ibid.
57. Steven A. Jervis, "A Letter from Nigeria," *Dissent*, July–August 1966, 418.
58. "The End of the First Republic," 7. Nigeria, Diamond concluded, was "a

The collapse of supposed democracies such as Nigeria strengthened the conviction of socialists that programs should come before procedures. If elections threatened to allow individualistic egomania to run wild, as had been the case in Nigeria, they should be postponed or abandoned. They should not be allowed to blunt the long-term historical thrust of a socialist revolution.

Paul Sweezy actually applied this standard to the situation in Portugal in 1975, arguing that the Armed Forces Movement's preference for postponing elections was "a sign of [its] growing maturity . . . as a serious revolutionary force."[59] In the event, elections did take place. Two-thirds of the votes went to "quintessentially bourgeois parties" (liberals, social democrats, and democratic socialists), prompting Sweezy to remark that "it might have been better to postpone the elections for an indefinite period."[60]

As with self-determination, victory in the class struggle must be, socialist writers argued, the acid test by which parties and constitutions should be judged. Generally, this test favored single parties and centralizing constitutions. In the case of the new African states, socialists agreed that strong central government was required: their arguments for such government resembled at many points those used by liberals of the "nation building" school.

Socialism, after all, was defined, at least by the old left, as "public ownership of the decisive sectors of the economy," permitting comprehensive planning. None of this could happen without centralized government.[61] Decentralization and federalism—whatever liberal political theorists said—tended simply to reinforce the power of local oligarchies, enabling them to resist progressive change.

Developments after independence reinforced the left's preference for centralized government, and its corresponding suspicion of most kinds of

---

prime example of [Western] denial of African realities." For all the talk about liberal democracy, "the majority of Nigerians did not participate effectively in their government."

59. "Class Struggles in Portugal," 12.

60. "The significance of the elections," Sweezy wrote, "was minimal. They had no effect on the underlying class struggle" (ibid., 13).

61. In its first issue, *Monthly Review* stated: "By 'socialism' we mean a system of society with two fundamental characteristics: first, public ownership of the decisive sectors of the economy, and second, comprehensive planning of production for the benefit of the producers themselves."

federalism. The dramatic collapse of government in the Congo immediately after independence was due (according to many socialist—and liberal—observers) to the failure of the Belgians to put a strong, authoritative government in place before their departure. Following the same instincts, socialists were invariably against schemes for federalism in the Congo broached between 1960 and 1963. Although they found many other culprits for the chaos following independence, they saw federalism as simply a recipe for continuing and aggravating the chaos. They also made clear their suspicion that those backing federalism were doing so precisely to benefit politically from the weakness it would cause.

For example, in March 1961 both *Monthly Review* and *Political Affairs* attacked the plan for federal government sponsored by President Kasavubu and supported by the Kennedy administration. According to *Political Affairs,* Kasavubu's plan was "a thinly-concealed device for giving the Tshombes a free hand."[62] *Monthly Review* likewise claimed that "the formation of such a government would be the greatest victory for the colonialists and their stooges."[63] The argument between centralizers and federalists in the Congo was, the journal warned, "no mere academic debate. . . . It is a struggle between those who want an independent Congo, and . . . those who want to keep the Congo a weak, divided, and permanently exploitable colony of giant Belgian and American mining and financial corporations."[64] Such interests, the left argued, had backed Katangese secessionism and had worked flat out to discredit and destroy Lumumba, and the unitary state he wanted. By backing federalism, Kasavubu and the U.S. government had given these interests what they wanted. It followed that, to ensure true independence and to allow progressive forces to prevail, a unitary state with a strongly centralized government was an overriding priority.

The rather simple axiomatic logic at work here ran into trouble—logically, if not politically—during the next few years. It could not, for example, really account for the emergence of strong American support for the ending of secession of Katanga. Also, taken at face value, it seemed to make no distinction between types of centralized regime. In this sense, the left should have been content when Mobutu took power in 1965 and established an undeniably strong, indeed authoritarian, government in

62. "Notes of the Month," March 1961, 17.
63. "New Labels for Old Products," 551.
64. Ibid., 550–51.

the Congo. But, given the character of the regime, centralization as such had nothing to recommend it to the left in this case—quite the contrary.

Radicals were naturally also dubious about Nigerian federalism. Some even suggested a parallel between its conservative character in the United States and its impact in Nigeria. "Just as federalism protected the Southern whites in the United States," remarked *Africa Today*, "so it protected Northern Emirs and their Southern allies in Nigeria."[65] In 1963 Stanley Diamond defended Ghana against enthusiasts for Nigerian federalism: "In Africa the proponents of central governments are almost always more ideologically democratic and responsive to local communal traditions than are those who insist on intranational regional autonomy."[66]

Westerners, Diamond thought, were too fearful of totalitarianism. Such fear was understandable in view of experiences in industrialized countries, but it was excessive and damaging when related to the problems of Africa, which required for their solution political unity.[67] This, of course, was the standard liberal nation-building view. Socialists merely added to it a concern with the *content* of development.

But did the connection between centralization and progressive change mean that socialists should always support centralized, even authoritarian rule? The answer was clearly as conditional as that to pleas for support of nationalist movements. Everything depended on the socialist quality of programs and the direction of change. But even with governments of an undeniably socialist orientation, were there unacceptable levels of authoritarianism?

For Marxists at least, political and human rights issues could not be treated in absolute terms or as individual cases isolated from the class struggle. For them, the real question about, for example, one-partyism was whose interests the party represented and how far it was, or could be, an instrument of socialism.

But some democratic socialists became increasingly worried by authoritarian trends in Africa in the 1960s. An interesting case is the British

65. "Nigeria: Toward Democracy," 3.
66. "The Weight of the North," 4.
67. "The principle of radical decentralization [Diamond wrote], which many social democrats in industrialized countries understandably support, simply does not apply to ex-colonial territories, where the people at large must grope towards union across a great many artificially erected, and a few authentic, barriers, while attempting the most difficult feats of national development" ("Modern Africa: The Pains of Birth," 174).

writer Rita Hinden, editor of the Fabian journal *Socialist Commentary*. In 1963, Hinden argued for the familiar nation-building distinction between constitutional forms and political values. In principle, such values (in this case the values intrinsic to democracy) could, Hinden said, be sustained in different institutional settings. The absence of an organized opposition should not be cause to label a country "undemocratic," as long as three conditions obtained: "the functioning of a representative assembly, the maintenance of civil liberties, and respect for the rule of law."[68] To label countries in which these conditions were met as "undemocratic" would, Hinden claimed, simply "drive a wedge between ourselves and almost the whole of Africa."

Yet even in 1963, Hinden was clearly worried by the nature of one-partyism in Ghana—the case around which most discussion turned. She concluded that Ghana had already "advanced far on the totalitarian road."[69] By April 1964, her concern had deepened. Nkrumah, she had decided, was "no democrat . . . [but] something of a megalomaniac": he would "stop at nothing to get his way." The open fraud and intimidation practiced in the one-party state referendum of 1964 had deprived Ghana of "the last vestige of international respect. . . . Infinite damage has been done to the cause of African nationalism."[70]

Interestingly, this pessimism accompanied a change in Hinden's overall view of democracy. In 1963, she had been criticized by a Fabian colleague for ignoring "the problem of power." "Intraparty democracy," her critic remarked, was no substitute for "an effective, orderly, and popularly operated sanction."[71] By 1964, Hinden had apparently come to agree with this point of view: there were, she remarked in an article on Ghana, "certain institutions" that could not be destroyed without a country "ending in an outright tyranny."[72]

Like many liberals at this time, Hinden was also becoming uneasy about the risk of applying a double standard arising as a result of efforts to make allowance for Africa's special problems: "We make it harder for

68. "Emerging Africa: Is Democracy Possible?" 38.
69. Ibid., 36.
70. "Is It Time to Denounce the Dictators?" 6.
71. Jay Blumler, "Is 'Vanguardism' Enough?" 41.
72. Hinden continued: "Do away with the opposition and the independent associations, then the loss of civil liberties follows; do away with an independent judiciary and that is the end of the rule of law" ("Is It Time to Denounce the Dictators?" 7).

these people when we justify *everything* their rulers do in the name of unity, or economic development. We make it easier when we recognize that an African prisoner suffers just as much as a European prisoner."[73]

One widely quoted writer on African single-party states—Immanuel Wallerstein—also became less sanguine about them. Interestingly, in Wallerstein's case, this disenchantment occurred in the late sixties as he moved leftward. Writing in 1971 about his 1961 book *Africa: The Politics of Independence*, Wallerstein remarked that he still felt that the one-party system was "more viable and more beneficial to Africa and to the world than any present alternative."[74] However, he admitted that in retrospect his picture of one-partyism (and of "charismatic leaders") had been "somewhat rosy" . . . "I did not stress the degree to which the single-party system, in most cases, was, in Fanon's phrase, a dictatorship of the bourgeoisie."[75] This apologia, and its use of the verb *stress*, was quite disingenuous. The truth was that phrases such as "the dictatorship of the bourgeoisie" were not even in Wallerstein's public vocabulary in 1961. At that time, he had wholeheartedly—and, more to the point, quite indiscriminately—endorsed the authoritarianism of African one-party regimes, on the grounds that they were "nation builders" who would bring "order" and "stability." Was it that the governments in question had changed since 1961? Or was it, rather, that Wallerstein himself had undergone a Saul-like conversion somewhere in the vicinity of Columbia University in the heady year 1968? In any event, the really engrossing aspect of this conversion was Wallerstein's ability to maintain his commitment to authoritarian government, despite a 180-degree change in the direction from which he justified it.

The Problem of Class Struggle

Behind this rather strange realignment lay a broader debate about the nature not only of "the bourgeoisie," but of classes and the class struggle in Africa. The most fundamental argument here was that dividing the Marxists from "African Socialists." The latter claimed that Africa presented unique circumstances which, while not invalidating the broad rel-

73. Ibid., 8.
74. "Looking back at African Independence," 5.
75. Ibid., 4. The party in many African countries had become, Wallerstein concluded, "a ceremonial institution subordinate to the state."

evance of socialist values, required a radically different social analysis and new conceptions of socialist strategy.

Writers in journals such as the *African Communist* and *Political Affairs* relentlessly attacked "airy and ill-defined talk of 'Africanism,' " with the "vague generalities" and "mystical notions" accompanying it.[76] In particular, they disliked the persistent tendency of some "African socialists" to deny the relevance of class and class conflict as concepts usable in understanding African politics (and to criticize Marxists using them). "It is not the communists," declared a contributor to *Political Affairs*, "but the inevitable march of history which divides nations and peoples along class lines."[77]

But, even if the existence of classes was acknowledged, their nature and roles were matters of dispute. The disenchantment with African nationalism current in the mid-sixties encouraged scrutiny of the struggles for power and the ideological battles going on behind the curtains of nationalism.

For, if socialists had ever in fact been tempted to assume that self-government would erase or soften oppression and inequality, by 1966 they were thoroughly immune to any such illusions. "For most Nigerians," the British Communist Victor Allen remarked, independence had meant "a transfer from a white minority to a black minority, a substitution of black capitalists for white ones. It has removed little of the exploitation of the colonialist days; just added another dimension to it."[78] True independence, socialist commentators concluded, and particularly economic independence had eluded African states. These states had, Wallerstein remarked, failed to develop "national economies" and had remained "geared into a larger world economic complex."[79]

Although for many socialists the true "ruling class" in Africa lived in Europe, they nevertheless focused their bitterness on the African elites themselves. In 1964, Keith Buchanan wrote in the *Monthly Review* of "the jackal-like quality of many of the African elite groups" (a reference to

76. Winston, "Padmore," 17; "Africa in Revolution," *Political Affairs*, December 1960, 12.
77. Rather than "blaming the communists for the inevitable process of history," he concluded, such critics "would do better to study concretely the nature and role of the various classes that exist in Africa" (N. Numada, "Marxism and African Liberation," 60).
78. "Nigeria: Coup on a Tightrope," 144.
79. "African Unity Reassessed," 44.

the Kikuyu proverb, "When hyenas go away, jackals rejoice").[80] Some of the most actively committed outsiders were the most disappointed: "The disease of reckless egotism has overcome the elites," declared Basil Davidson in 1967. ". . . Corruption, irresponsibility, contempt for ordinary folks: these are the stigmata of a political failure which has already driven several African governments behind the protection of military rulers."[81] The African revolution had failed, Stanley Diamond believed: "The national leadership is basically elitist . . . [presiding over] a form of internal colonialism in which the ultimate commands still come from abroad."[82]

But what kind of elite was it? Clearly, as liberal commentators had pointed out, it was not an entrepreneurial, much less an industrial bourgeoisie; rather, it was a "national bourgeoisie." In the Soviet view, this group had "taken part in the struggle against colonialism, trying to weaken the grip of foreign monopolies," but it had also kept contact with "the imperialist powers."[83] The "national bourgeoisie" was often useful to liberation movements. Its members had helped to provide offices "and all the other things for which money is required."[84]

However, after independence setting up offices seemed to be the bourgeoisie's main activity. To socialists, such as James Petras, who looked to a revolution brought about by "an alliance of the working class and the peasantry," this class had emerged as "a source of exploitation and underdevelopment, certainly neither 'progressive' nor an ally of those concerned with development, social equality, and freedom."[85]

To others, less attracted to Maoist notions of revolutionary spontaneity, such rejection of leadership smacked of romanticism and even anti-intellectualism. It was romantic to think away the state, suggested Paul Beckett in a critique of Fanon. Socialists could not dispense so easily with "political elites, administrators and technicians of the state apparatus. . . . As the experience of socialist countries elsewhere has shown, such groups are as necessary as the state itself (for they *are* the state).

80. "When Hyenas Go Away," 309.
81. "Difficulties, Not Disillusionment," 27.
82. "The Biafran Possibility," 16.
83. Ponomarov, "On National Democracy," 48.
84. "Many Africans from a capitalist background," Numada remarked, "have been and still are loyal and true sons of Africa" ("Marxism and African Liberation," 61).
85. "The Roots of Underdevelopment," 53.

And it is the state, in turn, which is necessarily the guardian of the socialist revolution."[86]

Such administrators were drawn from the intelligentsia—a group about whose revolutionary potential socialist writers were rather undecided. African intellectuals, at least, were the target for some caustic remarks.[87] Various writers commented on the "intellectual character" of many African Marxist groups, despite their supposedly proletarian basis.[88]

But Marxism, stressing the need for sound theory, necessarily assigned a significant role to intellectuals. The proletariat was, of course, to be the central revolutionary force, but the intelligentsia could, as a vanguard, help to provide leadership. In the African setting, given the weakness of the proletariat, it seemed that such leadership would be especially important.

The proletariat was weak not just because it was numerically small, but also because (at least in the eyes of some socialists) it was a privileged group. Workers employed by multinational corporations often enjoyed decent wages and fringe benefits, job security, and good working conditions. Many others were employed by the state and were able to use strikes and even direct political action to get their way.

To neo-Marxists such as Giovanni Arrighi and John Saul, the urban working class represented a "labor aristocracy" that shared in the extraction of a surplus from the truly oppressed group—in this case, the small farmers.[89] In Tanzania, remarked Richard Stren, urban wage earners clearly were a privileged minority that would have to be educated to accept austerity.[90]

Such comments challenged directly orthodox Marxist assumptions about class struggle, as determined by "the general laws of capitalism." Writers in *Political Affairs* and elsewhere did recognize this problem. They

86. "Frantz Fanon and Sub-Saharan Africa: Notes on the Contemporary Significance of His Thought," 67.

87. The British Marxist Pat Sloan, for example, concluded that the Ghanaian intelligentsia was "almost to a man petty bourgeois, self-seeking, 'get-rich-quick'" ("Ghana without Illusions," 28).

88. The PAI of Senegal, for instance, was known in Dakar as "the proletarian party without proletarians."

89. "Socialism and Economic Development in Tropical Africa," 13.

90. Stren remarked that "an implicit power struggle" was under way in Tanzania "between a rurally oriented socialist party state and an urban elite" (review of William H. Friedland, *Vuta Kamba: The Development of Trade Unions in Tanganyika*, *Africa Report* 15, no. 2 [February 1970]: 40).

admitted that economic development and class formation had "not taken exactly the same shape in Africa as it [had] in the classic countries of capitalism."[91] Concerning the period just before and after independence, they quoted Lenin regarding countries on the periphery of capitalism: "The preponderance of precapitalist relationships is still the main determining feature in these countries, so there can be no question of a purely proletarian movement in them. There is practically no industrial proletariat in these countries."[92]

Yet orthodox Marxists found the idea of the peasants replacing the proletariat as a revolutionary group (as suggested by Fanon and others) quite unacceptable. John Pittman, for example, attacked Fanon's works because of their author's "underestimation of the revolutionary potential and role of both the African and the European working classes, without which the prospects of Africa's liberation would be bleak indeed."[93] It might be necessary, Joan Bellamy thought, to wait until the working class had grown "in experience and numbers."[94] The proletariat would certainly need to be "organized and trained in . . . modern and advanced principles of social science" and it would also need the leadership of a party informed by the principles of scientific socialism. Over time the basis for a revolution would be formed, Bellamy suggested, as the growing and maturing working class began "to attract to itself the genuinely nationalist sections of the petty bourgeoisie, farmers, intellectuals and traders, to throw off the economic domination of the monopolies."[95]

Such a process obviously did not amount to the supplanting of the proletariat by the peasantry. As one South African Communist remarked, the peasantry might be "the basis of the great army of African liberation—the soul of the regeneration of Africa." But it would provide troops, not officers. "In the nature of things, we cannot often hope or expect to find the leadership of the African revolution emerging from the heartlands

91. Numada, "Marxism and African Liberation," 61.

92. Cited in Rogers, "The African Liberation Movement," 36.

93. "Toward Eradication of Colonialism," 97. He also criticized Fanon for giving "no indication of acquaintance with Lenin's works," for failing to appreciate the example and help provided by the socialist countries to those in which the working class had been "stunted by colonialism," and for dabbling in "psychoanalytical and idealist concepts."

94. "A Valuable Study of Neo-Colonialism," 64.

95. Ibid.

of tribal society. They look for awakening, for enlightenment and leadership, to the towns."[96]

For those who looked to China rather than to the Soviet Union for ideas about revolutionary strategy, such declarations simply proved the rigidity of Soviet and Western communist thinking. Much communist writing on Africa, Peter Waterman noted, was apparently meant just to "illustrate a preexisting theoretical or political position": it was marked by "dogmatism, Eurocentrism, and political pragmatism." To get away from Eurocentrism, radicals should approach third world societies without "the debased axioms of textbook Marxism."[97] As it was, Buchanan complained, "Western socialists [showed] precious little real understanding of the struggle of the 'damned of the earth,' the tropical peasantries, to assert their stature as full men—and of the relevance of this to the future of world socialism."[98] The peasantry was "the great unknown" and any revolution in Africa would depend, Diamond said, on "first bringing about a revolution in agrarian life and production."[99] The "state-based establishment" could not create the ideology or institutions necessary to bring about such a revolution.

Perhaps, as Lewis Coser suggested in *Dissent*, the African peasantry was, like its European counterpart, doomed in the long run. Yet its destruction would be a prolonged process, and meanwhile the peasantry might well (possibly with the help of dissident intellectuals) "create large revolutionary movements."[100]

Some radicals thought that such movements might appear in Nigeria. "Nigeria," a Nigerian writer declared in *Africa Today* in 1964, "is on the threshold of a socialist revolution—the revolution will certainly come."[101] "The Nigerian revolution has begun," exclaimed the editors of *Africa Today*

96. Numada, "Marxism and African Liberation," 61.

97. "Radicalism in African Studies," 264, 270, 271–72.

98. "When Hyenas Go Away," 314. In Africa especially, another writer argued, progressive social thought had been "misled . . . by the ideological imperialism of the Western left, with their focus on urban working classes and their attempt to fight Western class battles on the field of Africa" (Beckett, "Frantz Fanon and Sub-Saharan Africa," 67).

99. "The End of the First Republic," 9.

100. Africa, Coser concluded, might yet see "a repeat performance of Europe's peasant revolts before it enters the new world of modernity. For quite some time to come, the new rulers of the African nations will be faced by the specter of peasant uprising and disaffections" ("The Myth of Peasant Revolt," 303).

101. Akintunde Emiola, "Diamond Was Prophetic," 6.

in 1965, as the crisis in the Western Region began to destroy the First Republic.[102]

In view of the country's size and importance, such a prospect was certainly appealing. But interestingly it was the north rather than the more developed south that was the focus of some revolutionary hopes. As early as 1963, Stanley Diamond suggested that the founding of a Communist party in northern Nigeria showed "the critical significance of the region for the whole of West Africa." Northern Nigeria, he concluded, "must be viewed as the most potentially explosive area in West Africa."[103] By the late sixties, however, the most haunting specter was not that of peasant revolt, but that of military intervention. At first, socialists saw such intervention hopefully. The Nigerian army, Victor Allen predicted, would be a force for change. The workers' representatives had welcomed the first coup: the army was "a rational body, based on strict disciplinary lines and with little or no opportunity for corruption."[104]

The military was not, however, a natural ally for socialists—the colonially trained African military least of all. Many radicals, while welcoming the overthrow of decadent and elitist governments, were strongly skeptical about the likelihood of military rule proving any better. Wallerstein was particularly unimpressed. Military governments, he thought, were "unlikely to succeed in channeling political energy more effectively than the one-party systems they replaced. Indeed, they are more likely to become way stations on the road to avowedly oligarchic, anti-revolutionary regimes."[105]

However accurate Wallerstein's prophecy might have proved, the overall impression left by the predictions quoted here is one of desperation. Quite

102. "Armies in Rebellion," *Africa Today* 12, no. 10 (December 1965): 3.
103. "The Weight of the North," 15. In another assessment, Diamond suggested that "post-colonial Nigerian youth, seeking a *national* unity on the left, finding their brothers in all four regions, [might] well be the next protagonists in the drama" ("The Trial of Awolowo," 27).
104. "Nigeria: Coup on a Tightrope," 145. Even Basil Davidson found the spate of coups "a sign of evolution [and] an evidence of progress." It reflected the undercurrent of discontent with neocolonialism and waste ("Difficulties, Not Disillusionment," 28).
105. "African Unity Reassessed," 44. In the case of Nigeria, Stanley Diamond believed that the 1966 coup would not solve the country's problems. It simply marked "the sad end of the beginning of the struggle for a unified and, within the limits of the contemporary world, an autonomous nation" ("End of the First Republic," 9).

simply, the left did not know where to find a group which both ought to—and did seem to—have revolutionary potential.

Biafra: Unity or Autonomy?

Military intervention in Nigeria certainly did not lead to greater stability, and the four years following the 1966 coup posed some difficult choices for foreign radicals. Their problems over the Nigerian civil war illustrate some of the larger dilemmas facing socialists at this point.

In assessing the war, the left found itself torn between ingrained loyalties. On the one hand, their general preference was for large units with centralized governments, on the assumption that rational and efficient planning could best be carried out within such units by governments with the authority and resources of a large state. Experience (including the Katanga experience) also made them wary of supporting insurgent movements if such movements adopted the idiom of national self-determination used in expelling European colonial powers. In the Nigerian case, these preferences and suspicions were encouraged by the decision of the Soviet government to support the Federal government.[106]

On the other hand, socialists had long seen federal Nigeria as a symbol of all that was most corrupt and regressive in postcolonial Africa. Even the most hard-boiled Moscow loyalists in the CPUSA admitted that support of the federal government did not "imply support of individual reactionaries in the federal government or the ruling groups who stand behind it."[107] The Ironsi and Gowon military governments had not lived up to the initial hopes that socialists had placed in them.

So, in a period of growing disenchantment in Africa and a time of revolutionary activism elsewhere, some radicals were tempted to sym-

106. On Soviet attitudes and policies toward Nigeria, see, for example, Sonnenfeldt, "Nigeria as Seen from Moscow"; Klinghoffer, "Why the Soviets Chose Sides"; Stent, "The Soviet Union and the Nigerian Civil War: A Triumph of Realism"; Ogunbadejo, "Ideology and Pragmatism: The Soviet Role in Nigeria, 1960–1975."

107. Zanzolo, "Struggle for Nigerian Unity," 12. Nigeria, Zanzolo admitted, was a country which could not claim to be on a "non-capitalist" path. Interestingly, Zanzolo (a South African Communist) similarly argued (five years *before* the fall of Emperor Haile Selassie) that while the Eritrean movement for independence from Ethiopia was "progressive," socialists should not support it, since secessionism had "weakened the general struggle for a new democracy and modern Ethiopia" (ibid., 11).

pathize with Biafra, seeing in it a rejection of the corruption and neo-colonialism characteristic of the first generation of postcolonial governments in Africa. As an English student of Nigerian politics observed, Biafra acquired the aura of "a revolutionary society which would be the inspiration of a regenerate Africa. In a year of protest against the status quo, such a view exercised a wide appeal, although it seems to have been based on rather flimsy evidence."[108] The resulting alignments on Biafra were sometimes confusing, justifying the rather disarming comment of a *Political Affairs* contributor that "even among progressives [there was] utter confusion as to the attitude that should be adopted on this issue."[109]

Those on the left who came out in support of the Federal government did so because of concern about the effects of fragmentation rather than out of any apparent admiration for the policies and achievements of those currently in power in Lagos. In the main article on the war to appear in *Political Affairs*, A. Zanzolo (a South African Communist) admitted that for progressives "there [was] very little choice between Ojukwu's group [and] that around Gowon."[110] Reasons of domestic and international political strategy dictated the preference for backing Lagos. Domestically, Zanzolo argued, the progressive cause needed the Ibos.[111] Whatever wrongs they had suffered, the requirements of proletarian internationalism had to come before the demands of ethnic nationalism: "Tribal divisions, ethnic disputes, boundary and territorial claims cannot be to the advantage of the common people of the world."[112]

Balkanization could only weaken the leverage that Africans could exercise in dealing with Western imperialism. Biafra's boundaries were just as artificial as Nigeria's, and there was no evidence that the Ojukwu regime was either particularly progressive or overwhelmingly popular. Ojukwu's government, Steven Jervis noted, laid claim "to ideas of progress" and the people of the region had certainly every reason to fear and dislike the Federal government.[113] Yet, while the case for Biafra was "sim-

108. John D. Chick, "The Nigerian Impasse," 296.
109. Zanzolo, "Struggle for Nigerian Unity," 1.
110. Ibid., 8.
111. "The effects on Nigeria of the departure of the Ibos," Zanzolo wrote, "would be serious, especially for the progressive and working-class movement, which would lose some of its best contingents" (ibid., 12).
112. Ibid., 9–10.
113. Jervis noted that the Federal government had not attempted to apologize to the Ibos for the treatment they had received within the Federation: "What right has the federal government to compound its sins by violent opposition to the secession which it has made inevitable?" ("Nigeria and Biafra," 16).

ple and compelling," in reality the secession was "animated by the most regressive kind of tribal chauvinism."[114] Those leading it had managed to deceive some romantics in Europe and the United States, misled by Ojukwu's attempt to sound—and look—like Fidel Castro.[115]

Moreover, the critics charged, even as an ethnic entity, Biafra was no less artificial or divided than Nigeria. Since nearly a half of the population was non-Ibo, the secessionist state was in fact "as vulnerable as Nigeria to the logic of Balkanization."[116]

The pro-Biafran view was mainly put by Stanley Diamond, who argued that the Ibos had once been—and now again were—the truest nationalists in Nigeria. They had "an authentic sense of national mission" and were "the basic national revolutionary group in West Africa."[117] For them, the old Nigerian federation had been an instrument of northern power and that federation in any case was completely artificial—"a British colonial convenience, a ghost of a polity conjured out of company trading."[118] Now Biafra, according to Diamond, had become "the emerging hope of the African revolution. . . . It had the potential to become the first viable state in Black Africa and the crystallizing center around which a modern Africa could build itself."[119] Therefore Western radicals "should be for Biafra, because Biafra could well be the first move in a more unified West African thrust toward freedom and economic development."[120]

But Diamond (and radicals like him) did not necessarily want Biafra

114. Ibid., 17.

115. "Ojukwu [Jervis wrote] has a flimsy reputation for radicalism, no older than the Castroish beard he began last July [1967]. . . . The bourgeois establishment with which he has surrounded himself is unlikely to encourage revolutionary spirit ("Nigeria and Biafra," 17).

116. Ibid. "Secessionist arguments depended [Jervis continued] upon a unanimity within Biafra which does not exist. . . . There has not been true debate in Biafra since long before secession" (ibid., 16). Jervis reported that several newspapers had been banned and the Consultative Assembly had been packed with "discredited politicians without local support." Dissidents had left or had been arrested: "Streets and offices were festooned with injunctions to 'report any strange faces to the police,' and inevitably some familiar faces were reported too. If there was opposition to Ojukwu's secessionist course—and there was—it could hardly be made public in the increasingly repressive atmosphere of pre-independence Biafra" (ibid., 17).

117. "The Biafra Secession," 2; "The Biafran Possibility," 16.

118. "The Biafra Secession," 2.

119. "The Biafra Secession," 1; "The Biafran Possibility," 16.

120. "The Biafra Secession," 2. For other comments by Diamond on the Ibo role in Nigeria, see "The End of the First Republic," 8–9.

to stay detached from Nigeria. Rather, they seemed to regard Biafra as an example, and as the core around which an entirely new Nigerian entity might be built—perhaps on confederal lines.[121]

Richard Sklar, a respected student of Nigerian politics, went rather further. While skeptical about some of the charges made by supporters of Biafra, Sklar had by March 1969 decided that the region's secession did enjoy popular support.[122] The solution he envisaged was based on a more general redrawing of African boundaries, since no solution was possible within existing frontiers. "The way out is *via* a truly pan-African solution—one that would transcend both the parochial nationalism of Nigeria and the parochial nationalism of Biafra. . . . From the pan-African perspective, Biafran nationalism and Nigerian nationalism are equally parochial and inadequate."[123]

The interesting feature of both pro- and anti-Biafran positions on the left was that neither depended on invoking a right to self-determination. Polemically, both used liberal criteria for independence (such as the criterion of representativeness); but, as might be expected, the main standard was the interests of the progressive or socialist cause. As Zanzolo summed up the orthodoxy: "Marxist-Leninists do not support all national movements or all attempts of nations to secede or separate from a larger unit. The proletarian movement supports national movements of oppressed peoples, and their right to secede from oppressor nations. And, in every case, the interests of the proletarian struggle as a whole take precedence over the parts."[124]

The Katangan, Biafran, and Angolan experiences illustrate the quandary socialists faced when dealing with movements for national self-determination. But their dilemma was no different from, or worse than, that

121. "The idea of a unified Nigeria with a strong Central Government, fair distribution of resources and no dominance by parochial regional interests, is still a valid one" ("The Biafra Secession," 2).

122. The destruction in Biafra had, Sklar argued, gone well beyond anything justifiable to preserve "the unity of a recently inherited state. . . . What cannot be doubted now is the desire of the Ibo-speaking people to secede from Nigeria. Few peoples or nations in modern times have been as resolute and united in the face of death as have the Ibos" ("Nigeria/Biafra," 3).

123. Ibid.

124. "Struggle for Nigerian Unity," 9–10.

facing any group, domestic or foreign, for which nationalism and independence were insufficient ends in themselves.

For liberals and socialists, there were values higher than those asserted by nationalism. Both were intrinsically cosmopolitan and internationalist in their commitments. Socialists, at least, took as their text Marx's declaration in *The Communist Manifesto*: "The working men have no country. We cannot take from them what they have not got." Their difficulties arose when working men (or their leaders) came to believe that having their own country was essential to securing their collective interests.

When this happened, socialists had to revise either their theory or their practice. They wanted to believe that the causes of self-determination and socialism were compatible. (Engels, indeed, had written in the 1892 preface to the *Manifesto*: "Without restoring autonomy and unity to each nation, it will be impossible to achieve the international union of the proletariats."[125]) Yet the tension remained, and many experiences, both in Europe and in the third world, added to the inner reservations socialists had about endorsing nationalism and strengthened the instinct clearly expressed, for example, in a letter written to *Africa Today* a propos of the Angolan conflict of 1974–1976: "Nationalism and claims to self-determination do *not* merit universal and *unconditional* support. On the contrary, they must be seen as thoroughly subordinate to internationalist revolutionary socialism."[126]

The problem, however, was to identify situations that suggested a potential for such socialism to emerge. By the early seventies, some earlier prospects (such as Nkrumah's Ghana) had evaporated. Immanuel Wallerstein had occasionally issued a short list of countries "harboring unfulfilled nationalist revolutions" which at different times included Nigeria, Zaire, Algeria, and South Africa.[127]

125. Cited in Berki, "On Marxian Thought and the Problem of International Relations."

126. Letter from John Ehrenreich, *Monthly Review* 27, no. 1 (May 1975): 58. The writer cited in his support Lenin's defense of the rejection by Marx and Engels of the claims of small nationalities within the Austro-Hungarian Empire for self-determination. Lenin had written: "The right of self-determination is one of the demands of democracy which must naturally be subordinated to the general interests of democracy." How he had decided that this statement sustained his argument is unclear.

127. According to Wallerstein, these were all countries which were "candidates for [the establishment of] . . . a state which would cut off all its economic links

But dissection of failed socialisms, such as that in Ghana, brought to the surface disagreement about the meaning of socialism itself. "Instant socialism" would be undesirable, critics remarked, if it was conceived simply and narrowly as a program of redistribution.[128] Wallerstein, for example, ridiculed the idea of "a socialist commonwealth with equal sharing of non-existent goods," while Paul Beckett criticized the intellectual sloppiness of African leaders who ("uninterested in the technicalities of the argument") talked at large about socialism and mouthed Lenin's views on imperialism, without facing the tough question of what socialism meant and how it could be achieved in poor, dependent countries.[129] Beckett was disappointed by the lack of independent, original thought about the relevance and content of socialism in Africa, as well as by a general fuzziness about feasible strategies. There was, he concluded succinctly, a "disturbing tension between an objective situation which is morally unacceptable contrasted with a moral position which is objectively impossible."[130]

Self-deception also prevailed, still other critics said, concerning that great axiom of socialist belief, proletarian internationalism. Workers in industrialized countries—Arghiri Emmanuel and others claimed—had benefited from colonialism and were therefore indifferent to the condition of workers in colonial and ex-colonial countries.[131] To the CP editorialists

---

with the capitalist world" ("Looking back at African Independence," 5). In 1966, Wallerstein's list included Nigeria, Zaire, and South Africa: an update issued in 1971 identified Algeria along with the other three (see "African Unity Reassessed," 46).

128. As early as 1960, Sidney Lens remarked about "the African revolution" that "its techniques are insular . . . one seldom hears ideological discussions, so dear to the Western left. . . . There is little thinking on the questions of capital formation, on the virtues of a mixed versus a nationalized economy, on the theories of 'administered' socialism versus Titoist 'self-management'" ("The Revolution in Africa," 8).

129. Wallerstein, "What Is Revolutionary Action in Africa Today?" 5; Beckett, "Frantz Fanon and Sub-Saharan Africa," 65. Beckett complained that Frantz Fanon's writing was afflicted by this same vague, moralistic approach: "The objective fact that, divided equally, the GNP of Algeria is sufficient to provide some $220 per capita is not brought into consideration" (ibid.).

130. Ibid.

131. In a *Monthly Review* article entitled "The Delusions of Internationalism," Emmanuel argued that national integration (and presumably domestic political peace) had "been made possible in the big industrial countries at the cost of international disintegration of the proletariat" (p. 18).

in *Political Affairs*, such disparagement of the proletariat in industrial countries was, of course, outrageous.[132]

Arguments, indeed, arose on the left wherever there was any kind of stratification—racial, national, ethnic, or communal—different from that predicated by class struggle. Alternative forms of stratification (and the sentiments and ideologies associated with them) had in Marxist theory to be either secondary, derived phenomena or vehicles for class domination.

However, theoretical injunctions aside, socialist analysis and prescription continued to be complicated by the existence of national boundaries and national governments, by claims to national self-determination, and by the distinct identities and interests stimulated by nationalism. Socialists continued to argue about how to deal with national movements, ethnicity, separatism, and civil rights questions, and these debates shaped arguments about strategies for realizing socialist development programs in Africa.

Socialists had to ask themselves: Could nation-states provide a foundation on which to build socialist societies in an unfriendly capitalist world? Or was such autarky doomed? At what level were the values of self-determination compatible with and supportive of those central to the socialist tradition? Or—the most dangerous possibility of all—had nationalism obtained so complete a cultural and intellectual hegemony as to threaten the integrity, the universality of socialism itself?

From the point of view of socialist writers in Western Europe and North America (not to mention those in the Kremlin), this possibility—lurking in notions of "African socialism" and "third world" solidarity—threatened the essentially internationalist (or supranationalist or "post-nationalist") vision of Marx. Taken to an extreme, nationalism—in Africa and elsewhere—could pose a radical cognitive and analytic challenge to socialism. Even in its more moderate, accommodating forms, it was a source of continual distraction and argument for socialists engaged in trying to construe the meaning of their philosophy in the "third world," and trying to devise programs and strategies for moving third world societies in a socialist direction.

132. For the polemics between CP commentators and "Maoists" such as Paul Baran and Paul Sweezy, see (for example) Perlo, "The Baran Memorial Volume," 64; Pittman, "The October Revolution and National Liberation," 35.

SIX

African-Americans

and Africa

At least until the late fifties, African-American periodicals often reflected both a low level of interest in Africa and a rather disdainful attitude toward its inhabitants. Such distancing of African-Americans from Africa can be traced back, as we noted earlier, to the nineteenth century when, at least among the elite, it was commonly believed that it was the duty of those in the diaspora to go to Africa as missionaries. Otherwise, African-Americans seemed to want to turn their backs on the continent and anything that associated them with it.

This situation persisted until the 1950s, at least among those African-Americans for whom acceptance into the American mainstream was a priority. Even then, expressions of support for self-government were sometimes accompanied by approving remarks about the distance that Africans had traveled from primitivism.

Moreover, negative comment on colonialism sometimes appeared in African-American journals alongside quite unself-consciously patronizing anecdotes about "the African" and his ways. For example, in 1951, a writer in *Ebony* described the work of an African-American physician, Aaron McMillan, in Angola ("one of the worst pest-holes of the world"). The writer reported McMillan's reflections on his problems in training African assistants: "He laughingly admits that all of them, probably because of their recent savage ancestry, love to operate or 'cut' at the slightest provocation or without any at all. He is forced to keep knives and other edged instruments locked up for fear they will 'experiment' on some hapless native while he is not there. . . . 'They are just lovable but mischievous children,' he says of them, 'who like a different kind of fun than we do.' "[1]

Even writers clearly sympathetic to African demands, such as Hugh

---

1. Chrisman, "Jungle Doctor," 48.

Smythe and Martin Kilson, tended to take an unflattering view of the level of awareness among ordinary Africans and to criticize them in ways that would have become completely unacceptable by the mid-sixties.[2]

Rejection of Africa was intimately linked with a rejection of blackness in America. As James Baldwin recalled, "At the time that I was growing up, Negroes in this country were taught to be ashamed of Africa. They were taught it bluntly by being told, for example, that Africa had never contributed 'anything' to civilization. Or one was taught the same lesson more obliquely, and even more effectively, by watching nearly naked, dancing, comic-opera cannibalistic savages in the movies. They were nearly always all bad, sometimes funny, sometimes both."[3] Roger Wilkins, son of the NAACP leader Roy Wilkins, had similar memories of the climate in which he grew up. Because of the pervasive rejection of blackness, he remarked, "to identify with the black clods of Tarzan's Africa never entered my mind."[4] To Countee Cullen's question "What is Africa to me?" the answer for Wilkins' generation—those born in the thirties and adults by the fifties—was therefore "nothing except a reminder of shame; irrelevant except for our need to repress and forget it in our drive for assimilation here in America."[5]

2. In a book review published in the NAACP's journal *Crisis* in 1954, Smythe, while approving the author's call for whites to give up their "attitude of patriarchal superiority" toward Africans also noted: "He constructively advises the black man to recognize that there can be 'little hope of genuine partnership until the Africans learn something about the nature of civilization'" (review of Vernon Bartlett, *Struggle for Africa, Crisis,* May 1954, 310–11). Kilson, then a senior at Lincoln University, wrote in the same journal in 1953: "With the help of the educated few who live among the ignorant masses of the colonial areas, the people [of Africa] have become aware of the fact that squalor and destitution [were] not destined for them" (note in *Crisis* 60, no. 3 [March 1953]: 142).

3. As Baldwin remarked, an assault on the physical characteristics of blackness accompanied rejection of its supposed cultural characteristics: "One's hair was always being attacked with hard brushes and combs and vaseline; it was shameful to have 'nappy' hair. One's legs and arms and face were always being greased, so that one would not look 'ashy' in the wintertime. One was always being mercilessly scrubbed" ("Africa's Effect on the U.S. Negro," 6; abstracted from "A Negro Assays the Negro Mood," *New York Times Magazine,* 12 March 1961]).

4. "One had to look as white as possible, to adopt as many white standards as possible, and to reject as much blackness as possible. To call someone black was an insult of a high order. In order to achieve, one had to distinguish oneself from blacker and poorer Americans" ("What Africa Means to Blacks," 134).

5. Ibid., 130.

The fact that white racialists so often asserted that African-Americans were "really" Africans (and therefore had no claim to full emancipation in America) reinforced the wish to forget Africa. Only in the fifties did the idea that Africa, African history, and African origins might be a source of pride begin to gain ground outside of a small circle of African-American scholars and writers.

African-Americans and Precolonial Africa

The reevaluation of Africa that began in this period naturally raised questions about the reasons for the existing disparagement of African history and institutions in the United States. Some critics blamed it on systematic prejudice among white scholars and journalists. The latter, Charles P. Howard and others claimed, had been unwilling to accept evidence that challenged their notions of racial superiority or that might expose the degree of destruction and exploitation entailed by colonialism.

Africa, Howard claimed, had been the victim of a "campaign of falsification . . . since the early days of the slave trade." This campaign, he said, had continued under colonial governments, which "had found it desirable to black out the real truth about those areas and their inhabitants so that they might continue to exploit without competition."[6] The opportunity to discover and propagate "the real truth" was, indeed, what excited Shirley Graham about the opening of the national archives in Ghana. The new archives would provide an opportunity for researchers to expose the myths put about by "disgruntled and iniquitous writers whose prime aim was to sabotage Africa."[7]

Several notable African-American scholars had, in fact, been engaged in such research for several decades. Reacting against current assumptions about African primitivism, Carter G. Woodson and William Leo Hansberry set out to identify and publicize the technological and cultural innovations of precolonial Africa. The result was to invert the conventional view of Africa's place in history. Instead of being seen as the most backward continent—the last to receive the benefits of Western civilization—Africa (the revisionist view implied) should be respected as the continent

6. "How the Western Press Defames Africa," 362, 363.
7. "Nation Building in Ghana," 373. Shirley Graham was the wife of W. E. B. DuBois: after independence, when DuBois moved to Ghana, Shirley Graham became director of the Ghanaian government's public television service.

from which several elements of that culture and, indeed, humanity itself had sprung.[8]

The general theme of an African "golden age" gave rise to specific claims about known historic entities, particularly precolonial kingdoms such as Ghana and Mali. The use of their names by two newly independent states brought the causes of intellectual and political nationalism together, the existence of each adding a symbolic element to debate about the other. Large claims were made, for example, about the achievements of precolonial Ghana (which was in fact historically located hundreds of miles to the northwest of the boundaries of the present coastal state). Murals commissioned from an African-American artist, Earl Sweeting, by the new Ghanaian government depicted Africans teaching the alphabet and shorthand to the ancient Greeks and showed basic research in chemistry and medicine under way in precolonial Ghana and Mali.[9]

The revisionists commonly projected the achievements of African societies sufficiently far into the past to make it possible to claim that Europe had learned from Africa, rather than vice versa.[10] For example, Shirley Graham, in a characteristically euphoric article about Nkrumah's Ghana, referred to the president's speech opening the National Assembly in 1962 as being spoken "in a language which was old when Homer wrote" and went on to assert that the *kente* robes of the assembly members were "worn draped in the style copied by the senators of Rome."[11] Following a lead set by Carter G. Woodson, African-American writers sometimes

8. Thus in 1961 the president of the Association for the Study of Negro Life and History argued that it was important to establish that Africa had a history of its own and, moreover, had "a definite historical claim to be the cradle of civilization" (Charles H. Wesley, "Resurgence in Africa's Historical Tradition and the American Reaction," 85).

9. The new state of Ghana, noted *Ebony* in the month of its independence, was directly descended from a "black civilization that [had] flourished ten centuries ago, before there was an England" ("Birth of an African Nation," 17). Skeptical comment on the Sweeting murals appeared in an article entitled "If You Have No History, Invent One," in *Newsweek,* 31 October 1960, 45.

10. Europe, John Henrik Clarke wrote in *Freedomways,* had been "languishing in her dark ages at a time when Western Africa was enjoying a Golden Age" ("Africa: New Approaches to an Old Continent," 300). Clarke also observed: "Civilization did not start in European countries and the rest of the world did not wait in darkness for the Europeans to bring the light. . . . When the light of culture came for the first time to the people who would later call themselves Europeans, it came from Africa and Middle Eastern Asia" (ibid., 298).

11. "The African Personality," 365. See also Graham's "The African Personality."

attributed both technical innovation and extensive trading to the savannah kingdoms.[12] Thus in a 1962 issue of the *Crisis,* a contributor claimed that "the Mandingoes of the Mali and Songhay Empires, and possibly other Africans, crossed the Atlantic to carry on a trade with the Western Hemisphere and further succeeded in establishing colonies throughout the Americas."[13] Predictably, such claims were ridiculed by more conservative writers. Even some African-American critics remarked that they involved a romanticization of Africa and arose from a crudely reflexive reaction to white stereotypes.

On the subject of African tradition and precolonial institutions, African-American writers displayed a variety of attitudes, corresponding broadly to their ideological affinities. Integrationists tended to value institutions such as chieftaincy more as cultural symbols than as institutions having any contemporary political relevance. They found such institutions significant as evidence that, contrary to the assertions of disparaging white—and some African-American—writers, Africa had created societies of a complexity comparable to those of Europe and North America.

But what really caught the imagination of the African-American elite was the emergence of a "modernizing" middle class in Africa. Moreover, when the goals of this class conflicted with "tradition" and its representatives, African-Americans rarely showed much sympathy for the latter. Indeed, some African-American writers, such as the socialist Alphaeus Hunton, were actively hostile to chieftaincy.[14] *Ebony,* whose writers enthused about the modernization of Africa, on one occasion referred to the emir of Kano in northern Nigeria as typifying the "outdated feudal system that hamper[ed] the region's progress."[15]

Other African-American writers did, however, regard chieftaincy as both a valuable symbol of tradition and a basis upon which an African

12. Carter Woodson had argued that the use of iron had been learnt by the Greeks, albeit indirectly, from the people of Timbuctoo.

13. Lawrence, "African Explorers of the New World," 322. The writer also referred to evidence of African colonies in New Mexico and possibly even in Peru. For black Americans, such an idea might be particularly appealing, insofar as it wiped out the historical stereotype of blacks as passive, coerced immigrants.

14. When the government of Guinea abolished chieftaincy, Hunton praised it for "eliminating a feudal barrier to the development of political democracy" ("Guinea Strides Forward," 24).

15. "Nigeria Unshackled," 28.

form of democracy might grow. Interestingly, Shirley Graham and George Padmore, both individuals associated at one time or another with the left, emerged as defenders of chieftaincy in Ghana. Graham combined a close affinity to Marxism in America with a rather misty-eyed, at times almost mystical, attraction to "the African personality" and other cultural nationalist phenomena generally treated with scorn by Western socialists. Thus, unlike Hunton, Graham valued "the basic African rhythm built on the tradition of the chiefs" and welcomed the incorporation of chiefs into the Ghanaian constitution.[16]

Padmore's conversion to nationalism was even more unambiguous. He was anxious that chiefs should be preserved as part of the tradition upon which nationalism anywhere depended. Having attended an assembly of chiefs in 1952, he wrote that "it would be a regrettable loss to the Gold Coast should the institution of chieftainship be liquidated."[17]

To admirers of chieftaincy, its loss would also destroy a tradition of accountability that would help to nurture democracy in the new states.[18] Yet, as among white liberals, some African-American writers were dubious about such claims on behalf of Africans. "Their tribal past," remarked Franklin Parker in the *Negro History Bulletin*, "has usually been characterized by autocratic rule. Can they be expected to learn quickly the difficult art of constitutional self-government?"[19]

African-Americans and Colonialism

African-American commentary on colonialism and decolonization was distinctive in several respects from commentary in the white-dominated liberal, conservative, and socialist journals. First, its overall assessment fluctuated according to how African-Americans regarded indigenous African cultures. Second, African-American commentary tended to be concerned with an issue that was never encountered in predominantly white journals, namely, whether colonialism existed in America and whether

16. "Nation Building in Ghana," 371.
17. "Bloodless Revolution in the Gold Coast," 175.
18. As Chancellor Williams put it: "There are so many truly democratic principles in African customary law that we must conclude that the development of cooperative democracies by Africans will be quite in line with their own traditions" ("African Democracy and the Leadership Principle," 830).
19. "The Republic of the Congo," 61.

African-Americans specifically could be considered "colonized" like their brothers and sisters in Africa. This section of the chapter therefore follows a slightly different course than its predecessors, dealing in turn with the issues of colonialism in Africa and "internal colonialism" in the United States.

Colonialism in Africa

African-American writers on Africa in the late forties and early fifties did not necessarily challenge assumptions made in much European and white American writing about European colonialism. In particular, they did not necessarily question the meaning and propriety of "civilization" as a goal both for colonial administrations and for Africans themselves ("civilization" meaning the values and institutions respected in Western Europe and the United States).

Accordingly, these writers' criticism of colonial governments concerned more their failure to provide conditions in which Africans could successfully emulate Europeans than their failure to respect the distinctiveness of African culture. The miracle of Africa for such writers was not its traditions, but its transformation. The drama of Africa, as a writer in *Ebony* put it, was one of extreme contrasts: "While witch doctors still rattle bones over cholera victims and stick thorns in images of people they do not like too well, scientifically-trained doctors answer phones and make night calls in autos."[20] The good news was the emergence of Africa's "talented tenth"; the bad news was that the other nine-tenths were still under the sway of superstition and apathy.[21] From the point of view of *Ebony*'s editorialists, therefore, it was up to Africans to use opportunities, however meager, to advance themselves. If they failed to do so, they could properly be criticized.[22]

Even settler governments occasionally came in for sympathetic com-

20. "Africa's Quiet Revolution," 100.

21. The average African, remarked *Ebony,* still had "no more than he had three centuries ago: a dirt-floored hut, two imported pots, a spear for throwing, and sometimes a wife or two" (ibid., 94).

22. Thus in 1951 a writer in *Negro Digest,* reviewing educational progress in Kenya, concluded: "The astonishing background to all this is the dark backdrop of a continent of people confined in a prison of their own making from almost the dawn of time until about 60 years ago. . . . Channels of contact had been open for hundreds of years. But the Africans had no use for progress of any kind" (John Allan May, "Little Red School House in the Jungle," 8).

ment, at least in the fifties and early sixties and at least in journals such as *Ebony* and the *Crisis*. For example, in the summer 1962 issue of the *Crisis,* a reviewer of Gann and Duignan's book *White Settlers in Tropical Africa,* after criticizing the treatment of Africans in Rhodesia, went on to remark: "The white settlers do, however, have a case. . . . And it is obvious that former subject peoples cannot dismiss or rid themselves of the basic cultural contributions of their former masters."[23]

Throughout the colonial period, however, African-American writers were consistently critical of colonial government and its treatment of Africans. While approving of modernization as a goal, the critics often claimed that conditions of life for Africans had actually deteriorated under colonial rule. For example, the *Liberator* declared in 1961 that Ghana was struggling "to overcome the impoverishment and disruption resulting from years of British colonial exploitation."[24] When Christine Johnson, national president of the African American Heritage Association, returned from a visit to Ghana for the opening of the Volta Dam in 1966, she commented that the Nkrumah government had started cultivation of such crops as groundnuts, palm oil, coffee, vegetables, fruit, tubers, and rice. "None of this," she remarked, "was there under British rule and the rule of the chiefs. Most of the food was imported, especially beef" (a clear misrepresentation of the facts, except where beef was concerned).[25]

Nigeria drew even more uncomplimentary remarks. According to *Ebony,* the country suffered from "shockingly inadequate educational and public health facilities."[26] About health, *Ebony* was particularly emphatic: Nigeria, it said, suffered from "an appalling state of public health, a legacy inherited from the British administration." Under that administration,

23. *Crisis,* June–July 1962, 369. Two years earlier, a writer in the *Negro History Bulletin,* having similarly deplored the restrictions and pressure on Africans in Rhodesia, concluded: "One can also understand the white government's concern to want the Negro to work for his own advancement and for the prosperity of the country" (Franklin Parker, "Pass Carrying Requirements for African Negroes in Southern Rhodesia," 153).

24. "Ghana: How U.S., British Press Fabricate and Distort News," 2.

25. "Letter on the Ghana Coup," 152.

26. "Nigeria Unshackled," 27. The reference to education here contrasted oddly with a statement by the same journal's Era Bell Thompson in its December 1960 issue. According to Ms. Thompson, "More than any other country, Nigeria was ready for independence. . . . Nearly 20,000 Nigerians have had British university training and nearly a thousand more now attend schools there and elsewhere" ("Freedom Comes to 83 Million Africans," 151).

there had been only one doctor for every fifty-four thousand people: "Consequently, Nigeria in the past has been easy prey for epidemics of rampant tropical diseases. . . . Nigeria's leaders are agreed on the necessity for wiping out *these effects of colonialism*."[27] Readers were thus left to conclude that before colonialism the doctor-to-patient ratio and the incidence of "tropical diseases," such as smallpox and malaria, had been much lower.

French colonial administration drew similar criticism. Writing about Guinea, Alphaeus Hunton remarked that there as elsewhere, African governments had to cope with "the colonial legacy of poverty, disease, and illiteracy."[28] Another French territory, the Congo, and its capital, Brazzaville, got an equally poor report. A reviewer in the *Crisis* in 1958 referred to "the ambient stench of disease and death which haunts the colony. Poverty, ignorance, superstition, and exploitation are everywhere."[29]

But the streets of Leopoldville (Kinshasa) and cities in the Belgian Congo left a rather different impression on African-American visitors (much as they did on their white counterparts). Although Homer Jack found more political freedom in the French colony across the river, he was impressed by the labor laws, social services, and general prosperity prevailing in the Congo in 1953. Marguerite Cartwright, after a visit in 1954, came back struck not only by the value of the colony's uranium for the United States, but also by the size and level of skills of the African labor force: "It is the native who operates the cranes, bulldozers, steam shovels and huge trucks. All locomotive engineers are natives, all policemen, all soldiers. . . . There is no unemployment or underemployment. The native has the best economic status in Africa. . . . A greater proportion of the natives can write than in any other part of Central Africa."[30]

Portuguese administration in the neighboring territory of Angola was for African-American observers (again, as for many of their white colleagues) an unqualified calamity. Portugal, according to the *Crisis*, was

27. "Nigeria Unshackled," 27; emphasis added.
28. "You can see in the streets of Conakry as elsewhere the effects of criminal waste and degradation of human life" ("Guinea Strides Forward," 25).
29. *Crisis*, February 1958, 124.
30. "Progress in the Congo," 126. Cartwright, like other visitors to the Congo, did qualify such observations by noting that the Belgians had made little effort to provide educational or political opportunities for an African elite.

"the most ruthless exploiter of Africans among the European colonial powers": the African worker in Angola was "little better than a slave."[31]

Up to this point, much commentary in African-American journals was similar to that in mainly white journals. A distinctive tone appeared when African-American writers recognized something in an African situation that recalled their own experiences. This typically happened when they wrote about territories with significant communities of white settlers such as Kenya, the Rhodesias, and South Africa.

In the fifties, during the Mau Mau emergency, Kenya was of particular interest to African-American writers.[32] Their reactions were especially interesting because they exemplified a difference of view between the integrationists of the NAACP and black nationalists such as Stokely Carmichael and Malcolm X. The NAACP, as a nonviolent organization, deplored the brutality of Mau Mau, though it also criticized the British administration very sharply. In 1953 the organization issued a resolution that said in part: "We view with alarm the terrorist methods of the Mau Mau in Kenya. We condemn the terrorist methods used against the Mau Mau and others who fight to abolish colonialism and racism."[33] To NAACP leaders and their sympathizers, Mau Mau was a symptom of the failures of colonialism. In a slightly patronizing comment (characteristic of much African-American commentary on Africa in the fifties), *Ebony* remarked that such failure was the reason "why the American Negro, nearing the end of the same emancipatory period that his African brother is now entering, is in full sympathy with the Mau Mau's cause, although he may deplore its methods."[34] The problem, according to *Ebony*'s writer, was lack

31. "Rising Tide of Color," 307; "Portuguese Colonialism," 99. At the time of the 1961 uprising, the editors of the *Crisis* noted that the colony was still controlled by "an organized apparatus of terror, forced labor, and enslavement" ("Portuguese Colonialism," 99). In August 1961, the *Liberator* published a letter allegedly sent by an African deserter from the Portuguese army who denounced "the most terrifying barbarism" committed by the Portuguese forces. The letter concluded: "The U.S.A. must send forces to occupy in Angola the little southern village of Terica de Exce; when [sic] I will unhide myself" (*Liberator*, August 1961, 1).

32. As Robert Weisbord has noted, "No single post-war independence struggle in Africa caught the imagination of the American public to quite the same degree as Kenya's Mau Mau (1952–1960) . . . both its nature and the fruits of Kenyan sovereignty which it yielded earned a special place for Mau Mau in the hearts of black Americans, particularly black nationalists" (*Ebony Kinship*, 185).

33. Reported in *Crisis*, August–September 1953, 443.

34. "How to Stop the Mau Mau," 88.

of political participation by Africans and the fact that there was "no N.A.A.C.P. to fight their cause." Stokely Carmichael and Malcolm X, by contrast, spoke admiringly (albeit later) of Mau Mau (and hinted at the possibility of something similar closer to home).

Direct use of a geographical analogy was the most reliable sign that an African-American had recognized an African situation which evoked in him or her a parallel with African-American experience. Such analogies might take the form of an implicit parallel between the norths and souths of the two continents. Homer Jack, for example, referred to "the fluid Mason and Dixon line known as the Congo River." To its north, in the French Congo, Jack found that "the Africans seem to be recipients of a relatively humane colonial administration."[35]

To the south of this line, whether in Nyasaland (Malawi), in Katanga, or in the white-controlled territories of southern Africa, writers frequently discerned parallels with the American South.[36] Rhodesia and South Africa naturally evoked the strongest parallels. Rhodesia was "worse than Mississippi," an African-American woman living there told John Oakes of the *New York Times* in 1960: "The worst thing of all is being called 'Nanny,' and hearing my husband called 'boy' by any clerk or shopgirl who happens to be white."[37] An African-American visitor to South Africa in 1976 found an Alabama Trio playing in the Alabama lounge at a Holiday Inn in Johannesburg. Here and elsewhere, he felt that he had "stepped back into the pre-1954 'separate but equal' Alabama of his childhood"—as the title of his article put it, "An Afrikaner Dixieland."[38]

Such analogies, while tempting and perhaps inevitable, could be perilous. The casual or figurative use of an analogy could too easily lead to the assumption that an exact parallel existed. Several African-American writers did recognize the danger of invoking American parallels when dealing with southern Africa.[39] Later in the sixties, reference to the civil

35. "Tale of Two Cities," 253, 217.

36. "Blantyre [the capital of Malawi] reminds me of our colonial South," wrote Era Bell Thompson ("Progress, Africa's Untold Story," 80). In the Congo, the Katanga secession seemed to one writer "somewhat like the secession of the southern states from the Union" (Parker, "The Republic of the Congo," 61).

37. "Africa—A Continent Afire," 8.

38. Charles Morgan, Jr., "Afrikaner Dixieland," 466. Morgan went on to stay in the town of Alice, a community, he noted, "a fraction of the size of Plains, Georgia" (the home town of the then newly elected president, Jimmy Carter).

39. Even in Rhodesia, Franklin Parker commented in 1960, "the four-way

rights experience in the United States became much more common, though critics continued to point out the large historical and political differences between the United States, on the one hand, and Rhodesia and South Africa, on the other.

African and "Internal Colonialism"

The nature of such differences was crucial to the broader debate about links between African-Americans and Africans. To what extent were the interests and experiences of the two groups really similar? Were their situations and problems really the same? Were objectives and strategies pursued in one context relevant in another? What rights and obligations did one group have with respect to the other? Was there, in fact, the basis for a black nationalism or pan-Africanism joining African-Americans and Africans?

The specific issue raised that is relevant to this chapter was the question of whether African-Americans, like Africans, had undergone a "colonial experience." If they had, then that shared experience would be one more plank for a black nationalist platform, one more piece of evidence that their interests had been shaped by the same forces and that therefore their goals and values might indeed coincide.

The usual form of the argument was a claim that African-Americans had suffered "domestic colonialism" at the hands of white Americans. African-American nationalists, wrote John Henrik Clarke in *Freedomways*, "feel that the Afro-American constitutes what is tantamount to an exploited colony within a sovereign nation."[40] Prejudice, another *Freedomways* contributor claimed, was "essentially a colonialist policy, which can be compared to the experience of the Congolese and Guineans."[41]

Harold Cruse, the author of a major book on African-American writers and black nationalism, accepted the analogy with colonialism, although with some modifications: "From the nationalist viewpoint, the nature of economic, cultural and political exploitation common to Negro experience in the United States differs from pure colonialism only in that the Negro maintains a formal kind of halfway citizenship within the nation's

---

racial situation is much more complicated than is the race problem in our own country" ("Pass Carrying Requirements for African Negroes in Southern Rhodesia," 153).

40. "The New Afro-American Nationalism," 295.

41. J. H. O'Dell, "A Special Variety of Colonialism," 9.

geographical boundaries." Cruse was thus able to conclude that "Negro nationalism in the U.S. [had] its roots in the same kind of soil as the nationalism of the African colonies proper."[42] The political implication was quite clear. If, a contributor to *Freedomways* declared, "black Americans accepted the idea that they were "U.S. colonials," then their struggle would have to be "one against all forms of colonialism . . . [African-Americans] will have an anti-colonial struggle."[43]

Not all writers did, however, accept the idea. The critics had two kinds of objection. The first was that the analogy with colonialism in Africa was loosely drawn: the second was that it was simply irrelevant. Colonial rule, in the classical sense (critics argued), involved an alien minority ruling over a native majority: the colony itself was a territorial entity. Decolonization, consequently, involved the expulsion of the ruling minority, which typically returned to its homeland.

Where, then, in the United States was the "exploited colony" to which Clarke referred? Although African-Americans were especially numerous in some rural counties in southern states and in urban ghettos in the North and West, they were nonetheless dispersed across the country. Even in states such as Alabama, Mississippi, and South Carolina, there were relatively few counties or cities in which they represented a majority, much less the overwhelming majorities to be found in African colonies such as Nigeria or Tanzania.[44] Short of enormous migrations reminiscent of the partition of India, it was impossible to identify physically a black colony for the independence of which the "anti-colonial struggle" might be waged.

If, however, the "anti-colonial struggle" took the entire United States as its arena, then it could have only one of three aims. The first might be the subjugation or removal of the white majority; the second, the achievement of equal citizenship (the aim of the integrationists and one derided by black nationalists); the third, the establishment of a plural society made up of stable and competing ethnic groups. Harold Cruse seems to have preferred the latter course, believing that the special problem of the African-American was that "he [could not] sever his ties with

42. "Negro Nationalism's New Wave," 16. Cruse's book was entitled *The Crisis of the Negro Intellectual.*

43. J. E. Campbell, "Struggle: The Highest Form of Education," 412.

44. This point was made by, among others, Theodore Draper in *The Rediscovery of Black Nationalism,* 141–47. See also Draper's article "The Fantasy of Black Nationalism."

his rulers and go his own way." Cruse did not seem to see that this observation destroyed much of the point of the analogy with colonial Africa, and much of the value of imitating African nationalist tactics.[45]

According to Cruse and other black nationalists, African-Americans had suffered from a "mechanism of exploitation" that had placed them in "a kind of 'underdevelopment' similar in essence (though perhaps somewhat less severe in degree) to that suffered by other peoples in Africa, Asia and Latin America."[46] But the "mechanism" was never carefully defined. According to O'Dell, the situation of African-Americans was like that of American Indians or Mexicans and was "the result of a long established policy of depriving [blacks] of equal opportunity to acquire certain skills and professional training."[47] But lack of opportunity as such hardly constituted a working criterion of colonialism at work. Also, references to a common experience of "exploitation" hardly distinguished African-Americans, or indeed colonial peoples, from millions of others in the world.

Moreover, retorted critics in such socialist journals as *Monthly Review,* the "underdevelopment" of black America was such only relative to the "overdevelopment" of white America.[48] African-American living standards were (it was argued) substantially better than those of Africans.[49] Moreover, suggested the economist Robert S. Browne, there was likely to be an actual conflict of economic interest between the two groups in

45. Cruse, "Negro Nationalism's New Wave," 17. See also Cruse, *The Crisis of the Negro Intellectual,* 433, where he remarks that "the American Negro was also a subject of a special kind of North American domestic colonialism. . . . It was not until 1962 that even the new AfroAmerican Nationalists began to see the domestic colonialist nature of the Negro's position in the United States. It is only when such factors are grasped that it is possible to get to the bottom of many misconceptions the African, Afro-American, and West Indian share about each other."

46. O'Dell, "A Special Variety of Colonialism," 9.

47. Ibid.

48. As a contributor to *Monthly Review* put it: "Afro-America actually lives a dual existence: while it is indeed the exploited 'sub-proletariat' of the United States on a world scale at the same time, a large portion of it definitely thus far benefits (even if to a lesser degree than whites) from international United States color exploitation" (H. W. Edwards, "The Colonial War at Home: A Comment," 449).

49. Edwards cited census figures published in 1959 showing that "at least half of the Afro-American community [was] thirteen or more times better off than the highest paid African worker south of the Sahara."

future: "Unpalatable as it may be to admit it, every black American enjoys direct material benefits from the exploitation which has taken place in the third world. . . . Whether we like it or not, we are a part of the vicious system; we benefit from it, and we must share the blame for its consequences."[50]

The Communist party also attacked the colonial analogy as applied to African-Americans.[51] The Communists' position (as the African-American Communist Henry Winston expressed it in his pamphlet *Strategy for a Black Agenda*) was that to depict, notably, the Black Belt in the South as "a colony of the United States" was to use "artificially construed analogies." Certainly, Winston said, "national oppression" had the same character there as in third world countries and it was particularly severe there. But, he concluded, "the Black Belt is not in itself, either economically or politically, such a united whole as to warrant its being called a special colony of the United States."[52] Monteiro and other CP tacticians concluded that the really fatal error in the "colonial theory" was that it was "totally blind to the class struggle, and particularly its multi-racial, multi-national character in the United States."[53]

50. Browne (at one time an advocate of black separatism) argued specifically that the expansion of low-wage employment in third world countries might occur at the cost of jobs for poor blacks in the American South, while improved commodity prices for developing countries would inevitably mean "higher prices for black housewives at the A & P and at Sears" ("The Black Stake in Global Interdependence," 418).

51. "We cannot agree," wrote Tony Monteiro in *Political Affairs*, "that the substance of Afro-American oppression is colonial" ("James Forman's Pseudo-Marxism," 87). This article was an attack on Forman's book, *The Making of Black Revolutionaries*.

52. Cited in Monteiro, "James Forman's Pseudo-Marxism," 87.

53. The CP position was challenged by Maoists, who argued that American blacks did indeed belong, by both experience and interest, to the third world. As Keith Buchanan put it in *Monthly Review*: "The Negro problem in the United States is a problem of underdevelopment; the relationship between the Afro-American and the dominant culture of the United States is the relationship of a depressed and exploited colonized group to its colonial overlord." American blacks thus formed "part of an international colored majority." American socialists—Buchanan charged—had failed to take account of the special problems of blacks: they therefore had only themselves to blame if blacks rejected their leadership. ("The Negro Problem—An Outsider's View," 239).

For a somewhat similar view, see Carl Manzani, "Reflections on an American Foreign Policy," *Monthly Review* 12, no. 9 (January 1961): 487.

Whatever position was taken on the question of how African-American experience compared to that of Africans, the issue clearly had serious implications for political strategy. If black America was indeed a colony like other colonies, two strategies might be suitable, both of them involving separation from white America. One was a strategy of self-determination—the constitution of sovereign African-American entities, whether in the form of autonomous localities in urban areas or in that of a separate state or states within the United States. The other was emigration to Africa, in the expectation that, given the observed similarities of history and culture, African-Americans could easily settle in Africa and would be welcome there. If black America was not in fact a colony, nationalist strategies similar to those used by African nationalists were irrelevant.

African-Americans and Decolonization

Whatever differences African-American writers might have about the "colonial" status of their community, all were wholeheartedly enthusiastic about decolonization in Africa. Their response to the emergence of independent African states was marked by a warm, almost intimate, pride in the achievements of people whose goals and sufferings many African-Americans felt they had shared.

To less nationalistic African-Americans, the coming of independence represented the achievement of assimilation by Africans, the attainment of equal citizenship in the world community. Attitudes toward Africa on the part of African-Americans seem to have changed initially not because of a resurgence of black nationalism in the United States, but rather because middle-class African-Americans realized that there was now an African middle-class elite with tastes and ambitions similar to their own. The emergence of this African elite, rather than some sudden reappraisal of African tradition, sparked an interest in Africa among readers of journals like *Ebony* and the *Crisis*. As *Ebony* put it (in words that would have made the radicals of the sixties shudder): "The emergence of Nkrumah and other pipe-smoking, cultivated African leaders who wear Bond Street tweeds and carry brief cases is gradually changing U.S. Negro opinions of Africa."[54] A vivid and moving example of the pride that the success of

54. "Africa's Quiet Revolution," 100.

leaders like Nkrumah stirred in African-Americans can be found in an eyewitness account of the meeting in Monrovia between Nkrumah and President Tubman of Liberia in 1953. Writing in a church journal, Rena Karefa-Smart described her own reaction thus: "In one blinding clear moment of Revelation, I, an American Negro in Africa, knew that God was letting the past, present, and future merge before my eyes that I might know for once and all that black people everywhere do have a place in this world second to none. That we shall some day know our full history, the meaning of the sufferings, strength and humiliation.[55] Established leaders, such as Emperor Haile Selassie of Ethiopia and Tubman himself, also came in for lavish and sometimes slightly incongruous praise. For example, an *Ebony* reader wrote to the editor in 1954 expressing his feelings about the emperor in the following admiring terms: "I know greatness when I see it. There is no white man on earth who is a 33rd degree Mason or who lives so close to God . . . I wish we had such a man."[56]

African-Americans and 1776

The independence of Ghana in 1957 had special significance, however, since it represented the creation of an entirely new, modern state from a European colony. African-American leaders attended the independence celebrations, and many African-American writers (like Rena Karefa-Smart earlier) saw in Ghana a symbol of hope for blacks everywhere.

However, they also tended, like white Americans, to draw parallels between African independence movements and the American Revolution. Nkrumah's slogan "Freedom Now" was, remarked a speaker at the NAACP convention in 1960, merely "the present-day application of the ideas of men like Thomas Jefferson and Patrick Henry."[57] Nkrumah's associate George Padmore likened him to George Washington and predicted that Nkrumah's autobiography would "do for Negro liberation what Tom Paine's *Common Sense* did for the Americans."[58] When, in 1958, Nkrumah

55. "Africa Asks Questions of the West," 48–49.

56. Letter to the Editor, *Ebony,* August 1954, 48.

57. Phaon Goldman, "The Significance of African Freedom for the Negro American," 2. This article was a reprint of a speech delivered by the writer on behalf of the NAACP Political Action Committee.

58. "The Press Campaign Against Ghana," 612; Padmore, "The Birth of a Nation," *Crisis,* April 1957, 197. In the autobiography, Nkrumah himself recalled

and Sekou Toure of Guinea announced a union between their countries, the official announcement began (a correspondent reported) "with a reference to the happy example of the thirteen American colonies which ultimately developed into the United States."[59]

Even stringent critics of American foreign policy, such as Shirley Graham, were apt to reveal an attachment to the idea of an American liberal mission abroad. "We rejoice," Graham wrote about the celebration of the Fourth of July in 1961, "that our revolutionary brothers created this timely Independence Day. . . . We are filled with pride that our American revolution was the first in modern times. . . . The seeds of our Declaration of Independence scattered far and wide and this July, 1961, they are flowering in many parts of the earth."[60] Even eleven years later, after all the turmoil of the sixties and the appearance of radical black nationalism, an African-American writer could declare that "an Afro-American perspective or an Afro-American ideal policy towards Africa would be based upon ideals expressed in the Declaration of Independence."[61]

But among African-Americans, as in other groups, there were skeptics concerning what one called the "liberal mythology of American national development." In colonial America, J. H. O'Dell remarked, "it was the Africans and the American Indians who were the colonized people," and they remained so after the white Americans got their independence.[62] The prominent African-American writer John Oliver Killens remarked that both Washington and Jefferson were slaveowners on a large scale.[63]

---

how, on leaving the United States after ten years, he had looked at the Statue of Liberty and vowed that he would strive to carry its message to Africa (*Ghana: The Autobiography of Kwame Nkrumah,* 40).

59. Reported in *America,* 13 December 1958, 331.

60. "The World We Live In," 115. Graham did, however, go on to note that blacks and Communists were being excluded from enjoying the freedoms guaranteed by the Revolution.

61. Black Americans, the writer said, were striving for achievement of these values and they represented "the rights that Afro-Americans feel Africans in Africa ought to enjoy" (Badi G. Foster, "United States Foreign Policy toward Africa: An Afro-American Perspective," 49).

62. "Colonialism and the Negro American Experience," 300. O'Dell concluded: "The de-colonization of the American mainland achieved by the Revolution of 1776, which at the same time left the institution of slavery intact, meant, in effect, that the African population in America remained a colonized people."

63. Jefferson (Killens noted) had made many speeches attacking slavery, yet "he was never able to convince himself to the extent of manumitting his own slaves during his own lifetime" ("Explanation of the 'Black Psyche,'" 38).

Radical black nationalists argued that black nationalism could have nothing in common with the kind of liberal nationalism symbolized by 1776. According to the Revolutionary Action Movement's 1964 manifesto, black nationalism was revolutionary and dedicated to liberation, while white nationalism was "capitalist," reactionary, and exploitative.[64] For Malcolm X, the moral of the American Revolution was that nationalism needed land to secure independence and that violence was usually necessary to get land: "How was [the Revolution] carried out? Bloodshed. Number one, it was based on land, the basis of independence. And the only way they could get it was bloodshed."[65]

Such apparent advocacy of violence disturbed more liberal or conservative African-American writers. Some of these writers were also unhappy about the lack of preparation for independence in certain colonies, notably the Belgian Congo. Others (such as Carl Rowan) were alarmed at what they saw as the demagogy of African nationalism.[66]

Yet nearly all African-Americans would have shared the pleasure that the Rhodesian nationalist Joshua Nkomo expressed to Marguerite Cartwright when in 1960 Lord Listowel, the departing governor-general, entered his plane on leaving Ghana. As the plane's door closed, Nkomo remarked: "That is the sound I enjoy most, the slamming of the door on the last symbols of imperialism."[67]

Most African-Americans, too, would have appreciated the poignancy of an incident Cartwright observed later in 1960, at the Nigerian independence celebrations, when another British governor-general left, this time by sea. While other guests went out on the balcony of the Federal Palace Hotel in Lagos to watch Sir James Robertson's ship sail out of the lagoon, Cartwright noticed one elderly guest looking firmly the other way: "Indifferent to the pageantry that transpired outside, the old fighter sat erect facing in the opposite direction. He had given his back to this last remnant of colonialism."[68] The "old fighter" was W. E. B. DuBois, who

64. Quoted in *Monthly Review* 16, no. 1 (May 1964): 7.

65. Quoted in Draper, *Rediscovery of Black Nationalism*, 90.

66. The great danger in Africa, Rowan warned, was no longer "the hungry lion or the wounded rhinoceros but the glib-tongued orator in the city slums, exhorting the people to hopes and dreams that seemed so far beyond their reach" ("How the U.S. Looks at Africa," 117).

67. Cartwright, "Travel Diary," 35. Although independent, Ghana only became a republic in 1960: until that year, it had a governor-general answerable to Queen Elizabeth as head of the Commonwealth.

68. "Zik Becomes Governor General," 106.

as early as 1925 had written: "Black British West Africa is out for self-rule and in our day it is going to get it."[69]

African-Americans and African Nationalism

African-Americans, then, took great pleasure in the ending of colonialism and the rise of independent African states. How far, however, was their view of African nationalism original and distinctive?

To some extent, the answer must be "not very far." Once the unifying theme of blackness in America was removed, philosophical differences among African-American intellectuals showed themselves in a range of attitudes and judgments resembling those among white writers of contending persuasions. In ideological terms, the resemblance was admittedly very partial: African-American writers were overwhelmingly to be found in the "liberal" and "socialist" categories, although there were African-American writers (such as George Schuyler and his daughter) who published in conservative journals.

In the broadest terms, most African-American writers claimed that the experiences and interests of African-Americans and Africans were essentially the same. This claim to shared identity had both positive and negative elements. Positively, African-American writers stressed the fact of belonging to the same historical stock, with whatever cultural affinities that implied. Negatively, they emphasized that, in the words of the Revolutionary Action Movement's manifesto, "black people of the world (darker races, black, yellow, brown, red, oppressed peoples) [were] all enslaved by the same forces."[70] Consequently, the veteran black radical Richard B. Moore declared, the interests of Africans and African-Americans were essentially identical.[71] Like DuBois, Moore argued that Africans and African-Americans should support each others' struggles, since

69. Quoted in McKinley, *The Lure of Africa,* 198.

70. Cited in *Monthly Review* 16, no. 1 (May 1964): 7.

71. Moore observed: "No conflict really or properly exists between vital interest in our African heritage and the liberation of the African peoples and deep and active devotion to the cause of human rights and equal citizenship status here in the U.S.A. For the same social forces which spawned colonialist subjugation in Africa and other areas are the identical forces responsible for brutal enslavement and racist oppression in the Americas and elsewhere" ("Africa Conscious Harlem," 333).

they were fighting a common oppressor. For the Africans, the struggle was one to achieve independence: for African-Americans, it was one to achieve integration.

But specifying the goals in this way does reveal some difference in objectives. It also prompts some basic questions. Was exploitation at the hands of a common oppressor sufficient basis for a common strategy? Did it actually shape the two groups' interests identically? There was a tight fit here between conceptual and strategic questions. How observers saw the African and African-American pasts directly affected their ideas about what kinds of goals were worth pursuing and what kinds of strategies were likely to work.

African-American writers differed radically in the ways they approached the conceptual issue and in their ideas about political strategy. The simplest approach was a straightforwardly racial or genetic one, asserting that ''blood brotherhood'' was the basis for black nationalism (or pan-Africanism)—a nationalism that would transcend all boundaries and all differences of historical experience. In reality, however, African-American writers rarely took this approach, perhaps because it was so evocative of white racialism, perhaps because it failed to give sufficiently specific answers to the problems facing a group very well aware of its peculiar history and circumstances.

The more important choice was that between an essentially integrationist approach and a nationalist or pan-Africanist one. While they differed on much else, the NAACP and the CP agreed in sharing an integrationist vision of the future of African-Americans. The NAACP envisaged a strategy of nonviolent pressure involving, if possible, members of both races and aimed at ensuring the extension to African-Americans of the individual, constitutional rights enjoyed by whites. The CP and other socialist movements, for their part, envisaged an incorporation of African-American and the African-American struggle into a wider proletarian movement for the overthrow of capitalism in the United States.[72]

Despite an obvious, and profound, ideological difference between them, the two strategies shared an explicit rejection of black separatism,

---

72. As James Jackson, the principal black theoretician of the CPUSA, put it: ''The mass of Negroes who are poor and working-class have no choice but to seek to effect alliances with the comparably disadvantaged whites who are exploited by the ruling class of monopolist interests which dominate the society'' (''The Meaning of 'Black Power,'" 4). See also Jackson's ''National Pride—Not Nationalism'' and ''Separatism—A Bourgeois-Nationalist Trap.''

whether pursued domestically within the United States or through a "back-to-Africa" movement.[73] This common ground made it possible (though not necessarily easy) for DuBois to be involved both in the NAACP and in white-dominated socialist organizations.[74]

Black nationalists, such as Malcolm X and Harold Cruse, were skeptical about integrationism and suspicious of integrated movements. They identified themselves with a distinct black nationalist tradition, traced back through earlier leaders such as Martin Delaney, Bishop Henry Turner, and Marcus Garvey. The heart of this tradition was a belief in an irreducible identity of interests among black people, whether located in Nairobi, New Orleans, or Newark, New Jersey. Such a belief might or might not inspire a wish to migrate to Africa. But those holding it felt that African-Americans might as well go back, so dismal were their chances of ever achieving equality in the United States. It expressed itself, for example, in the defiance of a correspondent in *Liberator* who wrote: "I . . . would rather be a full citizen in Balubaland in the second century B.C. than a second-class citizen in Oxford, Mississippi; Montgomery, Alabama; or even Scarsdale, New York."[75]

73. The CP had, however, advocated "black belt separatism" in the South in the interwar period. The NAACP was relentlessly hostile toward the CP and intensely critical of the involvement of black intellectuals such as DuBois and Hunton in communist or communist-affiliated bodies. In a typical attack, the *Crisis* in 1952 commented that "it was evident to Negroes that a foreign ideology, propounded mainly by people they regarded as declassed, could hold out no hopes for racial salvation. . . . It was Communist ignorance of Negro psychology and history that defeated them. The American Negro is not a revolutionary. He is an oldline American whose roots go back to the founding of the country" (Review of William A. Nolan, *Communism versus the Negro, Crisis*, January 1952, 59). Blacks, the anonymous reviewer remarked, suspected that a Soviet America "would be run by white commissars."

As regards DuBois, a reviewer of his book *In Battle for Peace* asked, "How did this great warrior ever get himself tied up with the American Communists in the first place?" (*Crisis*, December 1952, 673). Alphaeus Hunton's book *Decision in Africa* was described by James W. Ivy of the NAACP (and editor of the *Crisis*) as "a Communist tract" (*Crisis*, December 1957, 641).

For other aspects of the relationship between black Americans and the CP, see Wilson Record, *The Negro and the Communist Party*.

74. It also, in Harold Cruse's view, explained the converse tendency for white socialists to get involved in ostensibly black radical bodies: see *The Crisis of the Negro Intellectual*, 147ff.

75. W. Ofuatey-Kudjoe, "My Unwilling Brother," 10. The text of the letter indicates that the writer was, in fact, an African living in the United States.

Often, however, such utterances actually involved Africa only abstractly and even negatively. Africa was a postulated, symbolic alternative to the United States, and to the indignities experienced by blacks living there. Statements of this kind did not necessarily mean that the writer had any personal experience of Africa or, indeed, any wish to visit it. The Black Panthers, for example, regarded "cultural nationalism" and talk of a return to Africa as a distraction from their main task of liberating the "black colony" within the United States.[76] Yet they saw themselves as black nationalists and believed (in the words of their leader, Huey Newton) that it was important for blacks "to recognize [their] origins and identify with the revolutionary Black people of Africa and people of color throughout the world."[77]

Indeed, "pan-Africanism," in the minds of some American exponents, was far removed from the diplomatic and political meaning it had in the minds of Africans. It was essentially an ideological concept, an existential principle, or just a state of mind.[78] To John Henrik Clarke, pan-Africanism was "actually an Afro-American creation."[79] Malcolm X himself took a quite instrumental view of pan-Africanism, regarding it as one way of mobilizing friends abroad to help black *Americans* and to spread the American civil rights movement to other countries. Malcolm X's strategic vision was remarkable for its assumptions about where the world's obligations lay: "Once the civil rights movement is expanded to a human rights movement, our African brothers and our Asian brothers and our Latin American brothers can place it on the agenda at the General Assembly. . . . And we have friends outside the U.N.—700,000,000 Chinese who are ready to die for human rights."[80]

Such expectations of help from others did not necessarily mean that black nationalists were attracted to socialist internationalism. In fact,

76. As one of Huey Newton's associates put it, cultural nationalism was "a bourgeois, capitalist scheme, to confuse the masses of people so that they will not assault the city halls, the bank tellers, and managers, or seize control of community schools" (cited in Draper, "The Fantasy of Black Nationalism," 44).

77. Ibid., 43.

78. "The international black man [wrote a correspondent in *Ebony*] must seek and *be* black world unity" (Don L. Lee, "African Liberation Day," 46).

79. "The New Afro-American Nationalism," 295. In Clarke's view, pan-Africanism was to be seen "not only as an instrument for the unification of Africa, but as a broader means for the unification of all people of African descent the world over."

80. Spellman, "Interview with Malcolm X," 19.

some, including Malcolm X, explicitly rejected it: "There can be no worker solidarity until there's first some black solidarity. . . . I think one of the mistakes Negroes make is this worker solidarity thing. There is no such thing—it didn't even work in Russia. Right now it was supposedly solved in Russia, but as soon as they got their problems solved they fell out with China."[81] It was really foolish (a writer in *Liberation* asserted) to flirt with "the notion that there exists an international revolutionary [movement] regardless of race. . . . History has taught us that there are two different causes of classes in a given society—unequal wealth distribution and racism. Marxists are only equipped to solve the first." Therefore, the writer concluded, it was up to black nationalists to deal with the racial problem at home and abroad by themselves.[82]

Black nationalists and pan-Africanists in the United States, on the whole, had little to say about particular African issues, whether these issues were political, economic, or diplomatic. They tended to regard the continent as a cultural symbol, and its inhabitants as potential allies of African-Americans in their struggle for civil rights.

Many African-Americans did, however, travel to the continent and some made homes and careers in African countries. Integrationists were dubious both about pan-Africanism (in its Afro-American, philosophical form) and about schemes for returning African-Americans to their African "homeland." The leaders of the civil rights movement were wholeheartedly enthusiastic about African independence and did encourage African-Americans to visit Africa and take pride in their African cultural heritage. But they were unanimously opposed to any pan-Africanist strategy that distracted African-Americans from pursuing achievement of full citizenship in the United States.[83] Rev. James Robinson, for example, encouraged both black and white Americans to visit Africa through his Crossroads Africa organization, but he was expressly opposed to schemes

81. Quoted in ibid., 24.

82. Wanyandey Songha, "Marxism and the Black Revolution," 17: "The solution to Black problems must come from a pure Black approach . . . we had better achieve our maximum unity first as a group before we begin to dilly-dally with ideologies."

83. For example, Bayard Rustin (head of the A. Philip Randolph Institute) complained that it was "unrealistic to divert the attention of young Negroes at this time either to the idea of a separate state in the United States or to go back to Africa" (quoted in Edeani, "Realities of Mass Emigration to Africa," 41).

for large-scale repatriation.[84] It was this struggle for equality, Ralph Bunche argued, that distinguished the African-American movement from its counterpart in colonial Africa: "The American Negro is seeking the full stature of American citizenship; the African . . . is seeking release from colonial rule and the attainment of independence. The African is motivated by nationalism, while the American Negro seeks only equality, his constitutional birthright in the society he has helped to build."[85] It was easy enough, remarked John Morsell (a leading member of the NAACP), to sympathize with the impulse to escape from American racism. But the African experience of decolonization was a singularly inappropriate model for African-Americans wanting to develop a stronger sense of their own worth and of being in control of their destinies: "Fixing on Africa as the chief symbol of Negro militancy is something of a paradox: it really implies acceptance of a derogatory stereotype of the American Negro as submissive and dependent, the passive beneficiary of a freedom bestowed upon him. . . . Africa's new states won their independence, not on the field of battle, but by the relinquishing of sovereignty through negotiation and under the pressure of world opinion."[86]

The left was as suspicious of philosophical pan-Africanism as of other forms of nationalism, black and white. It might, in the view of socialist spokesmen, distract African-Americans from following their best interests (represented by the workers' movement), might cause them to keep bad company, and might cause them (just as importantly) to neglect their political friends.[87]

---

84. Noting that there was no effective African lobby in the United States, Robinson commented: "Negroes should stay here and mount that lobby, fight their problems, and get our equality as Americans" (quoted in Edeani, "Realities of Mass Emigration to Africa," 41).

85. Quoted in Morrison, "His Toughest Assignment," 36.

86. "The Meaning of Black Nationalism," 70–71. Instead of adulating possibly unworthy African leaders, in ignorance and from a distance, black Americans should, Morsell said, honor "heroes and heroines from the American Negro's too little-known record of slave revolts, escapes, resistance to captors, abolitionist crusading, and valiant combat" (ibid., 71).

87. Pan-Africanists, according to Henry Winston, were misleading both African and black Americans. James E. Jackson, the leading black theorist in the CPUSA argued that black nationalism and "black power" slogans were largely irrelevant: "Black Power of itself is not," he wrote, "and cannot be sufficient to overcome the tyranny of the power of the monopoly capitalists" ("The Meaning of 'Black Power,' " 4).

Moreover, the left criticized African-Americans who thought the world was waiting for a chance to help them. It was naive, H. W. Edwards warned, to assume that "the world black revolution [would] automatically come to the aid of Afro-Americans once they start their bloody holocaust in the name of self-defense." Instead, the African-American community should adopt socialist goals so as to bring it "into political harmony with its 'natural' allies."[88]

African-Americans and Postindependence Politics

With independence, a phenomenon appeared that was unique to African-Americans—that of individual citizens (as distinct from journalists and academics) making trips to Africa. The reason for such trips was not, in the narrowest sense, "political." Those undertaking them were trying in the first instance to relate Africa and African independence to their own experiences and problems.

For many such visitors, the first reaction was one of surprise at the degree of material development in Africa. Martin Luther King, for example, remarked that "Accra was less primitive than he had been led to expect." At least one boy from New York said that he had expected that on landing in Ghana he would have to buy a gun to protect himself from "the natives."[89] Often such initial apprehensiveness gave way to a sense of release at finding oneself no longer in a racial minority but rather a relatively anonymous black face in a "great sea of black faces." As one visitor put it: "It gave me a sort of joy. . . . On the streets, the billboards with black faces, and most of all, that great sea of black faces the day I went to the [Accra] stadium."[90]

In turn, this sense of relief was commonly followed by experiences which revealed, as a correspondent in *Liberator* put it, that "Africa is not

88. "The Colonial War At Home," 448, 449. Only such a strategy, Edwards concluded, could "evoke that outside all-out support indispensable to the Black Revolt's own success."

89. Jack, "Eyewitness in Ghana," 4,461. Stanley Meisler quotes a teenager as saying: "When I got off the plane, I thought I'd have to buy a gun. I mean I didn't think there were any towns in Africa. I mean I knew there were some towns, like Accra, but I thought elephants and lions came in, and that's why I'd need a gun" ("New York's African Summer," 9).

90. Quoted in Isaacs, "The American Negro in Africa," 8.

exactly what you had in mind."[91] Class and ethnicity divided Africans, as did nationalism itself.[92] Some visitors responded by asserting that, whatever the minor differences they had observed, Africans and African-Americans were nevertheless one people. Thus a writer in the *Negro History Bulletin* reported on her trip to Africa that "the Senegalese were no different from the African people we met in Zanzibar, Ghana, Lagos, nor were they noticeably different from us."[93] However, deeper acquaintance often led to a different view. "All native-born Africans," remarked a correspondent in *Liberator,* "do not think that they have the same culture, just as all native-born Europeans do not claim that they have the same culture . . . an Ethiopian officer who participated in the attempt to end the conflict in the Congo said that he almost lost his life when he approached a Congolese with the attitude that because they were the same color and born in Africa they had something in common."[94]

Yet when African-American writers dealt directly with African problems, the sense of racial solidarity reasserted itself in the form of a defensive, even protective, attitude toward the new states and their governments. Whether the threat to African regimes was internal or external, the reaction in African-American journals was one of almost instinctive legitimism. Deeply influenced by the experience of being a racial minority, African-Americans tended to see their first line of duty as that of defending states and governments with which they shared a racial affinity against the large and dominant white countries, led by the United States.

This protective instinct had been apparent earlier in the cases of Ethiopia and Liberia. It was stimulated again by the Congo crisis in 1960–1961. In this episode, the "cause of Africa" became identical with that of Patrice Lumumba, especially after his murder in 1961. The *Liberator* claimed, for instance, that "no single event in the history of the world [had been] met with such immediate militant and unanimous response as the death of Patrice Lumumba."[95] According to William Strickland in *Freedomways,* in the "squalid welter of greed and treachery and incompetence" that was Congolese politics, "only Lumumba [was] heroic."[96]

91. Pete Haraty, "Futile Revolution," *Liberator,* April 1969, 16.

92. As Richard Gibson remarked, "A black skin is no substitute for a valid passport in this continent" ("African Unity and Afro-Americans," 18).

93. Mildred C. Fierce, "Africa—Some Views and Previews," 79.

94. De Courcy Edwards, letter, *Liberator,* August 1969, 22.

95. Editorial, *Liberator,* March 1961, 1.

96. "Documenting Congo Betrayal," *Freedomways* 7, no. 3 (Summer 1967): 251.

His murder, John Henrik Clarke declared, was seen by protesters who disrupted a session of the UN as "the international lynching of a black man on the altar of colonialism and racial supremacy."[97]

While the cause of nationalism and of nationalist heroes such as Lumumba received enthusiastic and uncritical support, their opponents received endless abuse. President Kasavubu (who removed Lumumba from the premiership in September 1960) was described as "a monster" who was "going to devour his own country.", Tshombe, for his part, was likened to a black collaborator with the Confederate forces during the Civil War.[98] Indeed, the black journalist Carl Rowan described American supporters of Katanga as "avowed defenders of racial segregation."[99]

Similar analogies and reactions appeared in African-American writing about the Nigerian civil war. The strength and unity of African-American opinion on this question, involving Africa's most populous country, was due, as Roy Melbourne has pointed out, to the connection made by many observers with "the domestic situation of Blacks in America. . . . Blacks were thoroughly aware that Nigeria was the most important Black African country. That it should succeed was their sincere hope, for it was also an overseas symbol of their aspirations for America. They keenly wanted their African cultural roots to prove capable and vigorous and, in the case of Nigeria, to constitute the essence of a country on which they could look with pride. If Nigeria were fragmented, it might (in terms of their analogy) be a setback to the struggle of Blacks in America."[100] Consequently, many African-American commentators put great emphasis on unity where African states were concerned, and especially so in the case of a country as politically and symbolically important as Nigeria. The *Crisis* summarized this response fairly and succinctly in February 1970, after the civil war had ended: "Even though appalled by the misery endured by the progressive Ibos and other tribes of the late Biafran republic, most black Americans supported the Federal government because we fervently want a strong African nation, and a united Nigeria affords the best

97. "The New Afro-American Nationalism," 285.

98. Howard, "What Price Kasavubu?" 231; Parker, "Republic of the Congo," 61.

99. They were, he said, the same people as "those who want to destroy the Supreme Court, largely because of its ruling on school desegregation, and so forth" (quoted in *National Review*, 28 July 1964, 639; and in Howe and Trott, *The Power Peddlers*, 180).

100. "The American Response to the Nigerian Conflict, 1968," 39.

opportunity for realization of that dream."[101] What Africa needed, the *Crisis* believed, was "not fragmentation of existing nations, but, rather, consolidation of smaller countries into strong federations."[102]

The activities and statements of African-American leaders during the civil war were consistent with this view of the conflict. Several delegations of civil rights leaders traveled to Nigeria and to the capitals in which the Organization of African Unity was meeting during the war to urge a mediated solution to the problem. As early as March 1967, Roy Wilkins, Martin Luther King, and Whitney M. Young—all members of the American Negro Leadership Conference on Africa—cabled Gowon and each of the regional military governors, expressing the pride of African-Americans in Nigerian independence and their fear of "the breakup of Nigeria and the prospect of bloody civil war."[103] In this and subsequent communications and missions, African-American representatives "carefully refrained from taking sides in the conflict."[104]

However, the bulk of commentary by both African-American politicians and journalists revealed a clear sympathy for the Federal cause and a suspicion of the motives of those supporting Biafra. In 1968, Edward Brooke, an African-American senator for Massachusetts, challenged the assertions of both conservatives such as Richard Nixon and liberals such as Eugene McCarthy and Edward Kennedy about the nature of the conflict and the proper direction of United States policy. In a letter to the *New York Times* on 19 September 1968, Brooke objected to a call by presidential

101. "Long Live Nigeria," 42. According to the journal, the civil war had been "a monstrous mistake which could have been avoided if both the Federal government and the rebellious Eastern region had agreed upon a compromise which would have affirmed the primacy of the Republic of Nigeria while protecting the rights of minorities" (ibid., 41).

102. "Long Live Nigeria," 41. The magazine dismissed the charge of genocide against the Nigerian government as an "international canard": "evidence [had] mounted steadily that there was no sanctioned abuse of either military or civilian personnel."

103. "The American Negro Community and the Nigerian Civil War," 20–21. Their message concluded: "We ask our brothers in Nigeria to mediate their differences for the sake of us all." For other reports on mediation efforts by black American leaders during the war, see the *Crisis*, October 1968, 291–92; and June–July 1969, 296–97.

104. "The American Negro Community and the Nigerian Civil War," 21. This neutrality was emphasized by Roy Wilkins in the fall of 1967 when denying a claim by Radio Biafra that he and other civil rights leaders had attacked "Nigeria's aggression against Biafra."

candidate Richard Nixon for the use of American power to ensure the delivery of larger relief supplies to Biafra.[105]

In Congressional hearings on the Biafra issue (chaired by Sen. Eugene McCarthy) in October 1968, Brooke argued that the United States should direct any aid to the Federal government and should back the OAU's efforts to mediate in the conflict.[106] Brooke was supported at the hearings by the civil rights activist James H. Meredith. Meredith said that he had seen no evidence of genocide in Nigeria during his several visits and urged American support for the Federal government. United States policy, he declared, should not "be dragged along on the wave of racist and imperialistic intervention by forces at home or abroad."[107]

In the African-American press, supporters of the Federal government and, indeed, the Federal government itself appealed for support by claiming that "the evil manipulations" of European powers were at the root of the war. The white racists, it was said, were exploiting the war as part of their "relentless efforts to perpetuate enslave Black people."[108] A Nigerian correspondent in the *Liberator* wrote: "The racist coalition is vigorously trying to weaken Nigeria, the only country in Africa which, because of its enormous manpower and resources, can threaten and destroy the white power structure and all forms of neo-colonialism in Africa."[109] When *Ebony* published an article describing the war as "an

105. Letter cited in Melbourne, "The American Response to the Nigerian Conflict," 37. In a letter published in the *New York Times* on 10 September 1968, Nixon had remarked: "While America is not the world's policeman, let us at least act as the world's conscience." In response, Brooke advocated a "noninterventionist stance in this very complex matter." He specifically criticized those who alleged that Nigeria was pursuing a policy of genocide, remarking that on a recent trip to Nigeria he "had found 38,000 Ibos living in Lagos and 'no evidence of genocide.'"

106. "To do otherwise [he declared] is to intrude more deeply than is wise or necessary, a role which we have already found creates both distrust abroad and dissension at home" (cited in Melbourne, "The American Response to the Nigerian Conflict," 39).

107. Meredith concluded that the answer to the relief question was "for those people who want to help to stop giving aid and comfort to the rebels so that the war can be ended and all the suffering can stop" (quoted in ibid., 39).

108. Ayorinde, "The Racists' Role in the Nigerian Crisis," *Liberator,* September 1968, 16. One writer even claimed that at bottom the war was one of "white versus non-white interests" (Lindsay Barrett, "A Message to Black Activists on the Nigerian Crisis," 212).

109. Ayorinde, "The Racists' Role in the Nigerian Crisis," 16. Nigerians, the

embarrassment to the OAU and a threat to African unity" (and describing the expulsion of "highly advanced Ibos" from the north), the Nigerian consul-general complained about the details of the story and concluded: "If America fought a Civil War not only to free the black slaves but also to save the Union, I think those who have had a similar experience should rally to Nigeria's cause without prevarication."[110]

An African-American who had previously worked for the Eastern Region government in Nigeria wrote an analysis of the conflict for *Freedomways* which claimed that foreign powers and "international economic interests" had effectively controlled Nigerian politics since independence. Since 1966, he said, they had worked to play regional leaders off against each other, "finding and supporting any internal movement that might promote division": Ojukwu had chosen to follow them rather than reach a reconciliation with the Federal government and had got "their unqualified support."[111]

The state Ojukwu had set up (wrote a correspondent in *Freedomways*) was itself based on oppression of minorities (the non-Ibo peoples of the former Eastern Region). "Biafra," concluded the writer, was just "a fraud masking Col. Ojukwu's Hitlerian attempt to establish the rule of the Ibo 'master race.'"[112] Since it was also a vehicle for the designs of white reactionaries on African independence, blacks everywhere had a duty to oppose the secessionist state. Lindsay Barrett told African-Americans: "Reality and reason demand that those of us who are Africans born outside of Africa should now address all our efforts and selves to supporting Nigeria's cause, the unity of blackness and the dignity of man, wherever we are, whenever we can."[113]

But African-American writers were not blindly loyal or completely un-

---

author claimed, were "sick and tired of being told by the racist world what their differences and problems" were. As for the Biafrans, they were using white mercenaries and were exploiting their own people's starvation as a political weapon.

110. Letter from Nigerian consul-general, *Ebony,* September 1969, 18 (in response to Era Bell Thompson, "Africa's Problems: The Other Side of the Story," *Ebony,* July 1969, 121). In an earlier article, Thompson had said that the Nigerian civil war was "the unhappy instrument keeping alive the myth of heathenism" in Africa: the world, she complained, ignored what was happening in Czechoslovakia, Vietnam, and the Middle East to concentrate on condemning Africa for what was happening in Nigeria ("Progress, Africa's Untold Story," 74).

111. Barrett, "A Message to Black Activists," 212–16.

112. Solomon M. Landers, letter, *Liberator,* June 1969, 22.

113. "A Message to Black Activists," 220.

critical of African politicians and their governments. African leaders, even the most favored such as Nkrumah, did not enjoy a completely free ride in the African-American press.

Indeed, not all African-American writers agreed with Lindsay Barrett that solidarity, "reality and reason" implied uncritical support for the Nigerian Federal government. Biafran supporters argued that African-Americans should resist their instinct to back automatically any government which happened to be filled with African faces. If—Biafra's supporters said—African-Americans really believed in minority rights, self-determination, revolution, democracy, and "the black personality," might not commitment to these values be found more on the Biafran side than on the side of a conservative, military government? After all—they pointed out—the Federal government was firmly supported by the United States and Great Britain, two archetypical imperialist states. Moreover, so far from helping black liberation, the Lagos government had (argued a Biafran supporter in *Liberator*) "perpetuated the enslavement of millions of Black people in Zimbabwe, South Africa, Angola and Mozambique."[114]

On other issues, writers less influenced by black nationalism (that is, NAACP integrationists), some black nationalists less concerned with Africa, and writers of a socialist, revolutionary disposition, tended to be the most independent-minded. By 1970, the experience of a decade had led African-American observers toward a more differentiated view of the continent that allowed them to be more discriminating about leaders and regimes.

As the Biafran supporters' arguments show, such a shift did not involve any basic change of values, nor did it need to do so. It simply meant recognizing conflicts within African countries, accepting the need for political choices, and then trying to make sense of some basic but very generalized commitments in relation to such conflicts and choices.

To the extent that African-Americans concerned themselves with Africa, then, they were forced to specify more closely the meaning of some initially very broad assumptions derived from American racial politics. There were only two alternatives to making such an effort. One was to abandon judgment—to give a blanket endorsement to any and all positions adopted by African governments as long as they were couched in

114. African unity, the writer concluded, was important; but not "unity imposed by arms, and designed to further the interests of imperialist powers and foreign monopolies" (Nehe Nwankwo, "The Nigeria-Biafra War," 17).

the right kind of rhetoric. The dangers of this approach could readily be seen by considering cases such as Bokassa's Central African Empire and Amin's Uganda. In the case of Uganda, conservative critics enjoyed themselves at the expense of, for example, Andrew Young, who, while acknowledging that there had been "massive violations of human rights and destruction of people," went on to suggest that some of it seemed to be just the result of "an imminent kind of chaos" and that the Ugandan problem was caused by "the excesses of colonialism and neocolonialism."[115] Equally remarkable, if less noticed, was a 1973 interview with Roy Innis, leader of the Congress of Racial Equality. When asked what he thought of Amin's alleged approval of Hitler's treatment of the Jews, Innis commented: "As black people, we have no records to prove if Hitler was a friend or an enemy of black people."[116]

The other, related, and equally hard to defend, alternative was to apply a double standard, condoning behavior in African governments which would have been unacceptable if it had occurred in white Western countries. In fact, during the late sixties and early seventies, African-American writers began to argue with increasing frequency that the time had come to give up special pleading and to adopt a more sophisticated and independent-minded attitude toward Africa and its governments.

This change was accompanied by some trenchant self-criticism. In fact, signs of impatience with the cult of all things African began earlier. In 1962 a black actor and dancer from the Caribbean, Geoffrey Holder, published an article entitled "The Awful Afro Trend," which lampooned the advent, in both black and white liberal circles, of what he called "Love Thy African Neighbor Time."[117] The more self-critical mood of the late sixties challenged a range of assumptions and activities. African-Americans, Richard Gibson said, tended to have a superficial view of Africa: "They prefer to sink into easy fantasies about the homeland of their ancestors. In the fantasies of those who have never touched its soil, Africa is a continent peopled with Mau Mau generals, steel-nerved freedom fighters and militant Black masses marching against Whitey. This never-never world, of course, does not exist, and the fact that it does not correspond with the complex reality is certainly not the fault of the Afri-

115. Quoted in Gershman, "The World According to Andrew Young," 20.
116. Canada, "Pan-Africanism and Black Nationalism Are One," 35.
117. *Show,* March 1962; reprinted as "It's All Africa This Year!" 41.

cans."[118] Instead of exploring the complexities of Africa's domestic politics and foreign policies (said another writer in *Liberator*), African-Americans abroad had been content to evaluate each African leader solely according to "his posture on international issues and his pronouncements on the plight of the Black American." They had, he thought, no business making judgments on such a basis.[119] Too often, the *Crisis* complained, "vocal and ostentatious advocates of Africanism" ignored the sensibilities of Africans and showed themselves to be "concerned only with the superficialities of African life."[120]

Just as African-Americans visiting Africa were criticized for making facile judgments, so African-American writers were criticized for being naive and sentimental in their treatments of the continent. African history, the critics said, had been romanticized and perhaps was in any case irrelevant.[121] Several writers were particularly concerned about the low standard of work produced on African history in response to the growth of black and Afro-American studies programs. In 1972, the *Negro History Bulletin* complained about "inferior materials" and the "creation of false heroes and heroines to promote black pride."[122] Black studies (said Richard A. Long, director of the Center for African and African-American Studies at Atlanta University) had become "a major software industry,"

118. Gibson suggested that color was largely an irrelevant issue, at least in the independent African-ruled states: "class and ethnic origin and education are vastly more significant to Africans" ("African Unity and Afro-Americans," 16).

119. "We have not elected him, he must first nurture the support of the majority at home" (A. T. Young, review of Kwame Nkrumah, *Neo-Colonialism, Liberator,* May 1966, 11).

120. "The Courteous Africans," 272. In the same vein, an observer of the sixth Pan-African congress (held in Dar-es-Salaam in 1974) complained about the "loud bickering" among the two hundred black Americans who comprised the "largest, loudest and best-dressed" delegation (Alma Robinson, "Africa and Afro-America," 9).

121. Thus Dan Aldridge wrote in 1969: "If we attempt to hold on to concepts, ideas, and styles of living of past generations . . . we are guilty of a most self-restricting form of chauvinism. We must not allow any group of people to halt the march of history: not even ourselves" ("Politics in Command of Economics: Black Economic Development," 19).

122. "Black Studies and History Week," *Negro History Bulletin* 35, no. 2 (February 1972): 29. The trouble was, John Henrik Clarke commented in 1971 in a review of some recent books on black history, that "a large number of unprepared people [had] rushed into the field and hurriedly produced books that [were] a disservice to the subject" ("Africa: New Approaches," 303).

a pandering to fashion, enabling black Americans to indulge in comfortable myths and to avoid both serious thought and hard choices.[123] Long observed: "The present passionate desire on the part of many young Black people to proclaim their identification with Africa would please me greatly if a tiny portion of the time and energy expended in this pursuit were devoted to learning a little about the Africa of their fathers. . . . It is easier to *be* Black than to *learn* Black; easier to shout than to study; easier to thump than to think."[124]

African-American writers who were critical of their colleagues and friends were often also critical of African governments. Their criticism did not usually imply a political or cultural dissociation from Africa, although some African-Americans did conclude from travel in the continent that there were real and deep differences of attitude and interest between them and the Africans they met. More commonly, criticism indicated a growing ability to distinguish between the particular—and transient—interests and postures of governments and the more permanent interests of citizens.

The specific charges made by African-American critics in fact closely resembled in tone and content those uttered by white radicals. African leaders, they claimed, had proven corrupt and had done "little to change the abject poverty in the life of the man in the streets or the bush"; they had wasted money on expensive prestige projects and gimmicks and had done little for the rural majority in their countries.[125]

Moreover, the critics argued, experience had shown that postindependence politics was controlled (as Barrett remarked of Nigeria) "not by the desires of the masses but by the manipulation of foreign power politics and international economic interests."[126] An African-American visitor to the World Festival of Negro Arts in Dakar in 1966 commented similarly on the extent of French dominance in Senegal: "The French are in full economic control of this African nation . . . one has only to walk down the streets of Dakar, to look at her restaurants, beaches and private clubs to get the message that this is a country whose real independence is yet

123. "The Black Studies Boondoggle," 6; "Race and Scholarship," 6. "At this time in our history," Long remarked, "there is a tendency . . . to use Africa alternately as a crutch and as a club to resolve externally complexes which we, each of us, need to resolve internally" ("Race and Scholarship," 5).
124. "Race and Scholarship," 6, 7.
125. Young, review, *Liberator,* May 1966.
126. Barrett, "A Message to Black Activists," 212.

to come."[127] But such comments expressed disappointment with the ways in which the ideals of independence and self-determination had been realized, not disillusionment with the ideals themselves. African-American writers and politicians continued to cherish these ideals, demanding especially that they be realized for Africans under white minority rule in southern Africa. Indeed, the passion with which these ideals were declared suggested that the passage of time since independence had not broken the connection that African-Americans felt with Africans south of the Sahara.

127. William Greaves, "The First World Festival of Negro Arts: An Afro-American View," 313.

SEVEN

American

Conservatives

and Africa

I n 1962, William F. Buckley, Jr., stood on a river bank in Mozambique, observing the "spirit of easy-going chaos" that presided over the operation of a pontoon ferry. It occurred to him that, with an hour's work and "without the use of a single tool unknown to the Stone Age," he could have reduced the ferry's journey time substantially. The fact was, Buckley reported to *National Review* readers, that Africans "simply do not use their minds and do not change their ways."[1]

To American conservatives, the conservatism of Africans (and their apparent reliance on instinct rather than intellect) was quite appealing. Unlike liberals, they found African traditionalism intriguing. Nevertheless, "African ways" and "the African mind" were as mysterious to conservatives as to liberals.[2] Stewart Alsop, for example, found himself wondering "what these people are really like, what really goes on in their heads, behind the big white smiles with which they greet the strangers from a far-off land."[3] Attempts at communication sometimes only increased the puzzlement of strangers, as happened with Erik von Kuehnelt-Leddihn when he fell into some "fascinating conversation" with various Congolese in 1961. Africans, he found, "were curiously unable

1. "Must We Hate Portugal?" 468.
2. "The black man's mentality," Thomas Molnar remarked, "is an enigma to whites." The drama of colonialism, he argued, had been a record of "the white man's curiosity, his stubbornness in the face of [this] enigma" ("An Outsider Speaks," 149).
3. "All together the Africans are most likable people. Yet there are barriers imposed by culture and language" ("Africa: The Riddle without an Answer," 84).

214

to think in the abstract, to reason about causes and ends . . . reason has not yet replaced the effervescence of sentiment with all its unpredictable oscillations.''[4] Such "effervescent sentiment" not only encompassed a belief in magic (exemplified for subscribers to *Reader's Digest* by the bewitching of soccer balls in Kenya), but might also (a contributor to the same magazine warned Americans in 1961) produce some strange foreign policy behavior on the part of new states: "What goes on in the African mind," Robert Coughlan declared, "is an important matter, and we must realize that it may not be the product of logical reasoning as it is understood in the West. . . . In our relations with the nations of Black Africa we may often find ourselves dealing at first-hand with the forces of superstition. We had better face that fact—and keep our fingers crossed.''[5]

Colonialism and Modernization

Given the evident cultural distance between Europeans and Africans (conservatives argued), it was clear that forcing the pace of "modernization" (or even modernization itself) would be unwise and probably disastrous. The long-ingrained values of Africans could not be uprooted casually by outsiders. Even if the effort were made, African values would reassert themselves once the white man had gone, mocking all he had done or thought he had done.

The best-known and most frequent spokesman of this point of view was the English writer Elspeth Huxley, who had spent much of her life in Africa (especially East Africa) and had published extensively on African problems for some thirty years. Huxley argued in particular that the institution of the tribe, so far from being archaic and retrograde (as lib-

4. "Letter from the Congo," 394. In a later article, von Kuehnelt-Leddihn wrote that Africans suffered from "a lack of that rational objective realism that distinguishes Western civilization" ("The Afro-Asian Inferiority Complex," 836).

5. "Black Magic: Vital Force in Africa's New Nations," *Reader's Digest*, September 1961, 156, 160. In January 1973, subscribers to the *Reader's Digest* were informed that a Kenyan soccer team had "paid $3000 to witch doctors to get forecasts of results. Before important matches, guards are hired to ensure that no one bewitches the ball" (Reed, "The Rocky Road to Freedom," 228).

erals claimed), actually provided Africans with physical, emotional, and spiritual security.[6]

Yet conservatives were torn between a respect for African tradition and an equally strong belief in the values and achievements of Western societies—a belief which often propelled American conservatives toward a more hierarchical view of societies. To the extent that tribal loyalties, respect for tradition, and religiosity corresponded to values they admired, conservatives felt some sympathy for them (as well as a great deal of sympathy for Africans in their plight at the hands of liberals).

But such sympathy was framed by a strong sense of what was appropriate for Africans and what was appropriate for Europeans. "Tradition" and "community," conservatives held, were valuable anywhere; but this did not mean that their forms in Africa and the West were necessarily of equivalent worth, much less interchangeable. Indeed, an emphasis on the nobility and permanent value of African tradition was commonly the obverse of a belief that Africans were, ipso facto, culturally disqualified from appreciating and absorbing Western culture. As a writer in *National Review* put it, "The forms of Occidental life merely distress and demoralize the members of races to whom the spiritual essence of Occidental culture must forever remain incomprehensible."[7]

Conservative reactions to claims for African history illustrate this tendency to place societies in a cultural hierarchy. American conservatives unanimously shared the Oxford historian Hugh Trevor-Roper's description of third world history as "the unrewarding gyrations of barbarous tribes in picturesque but irrelevant corners of the globe." Africans, a senior official of the Eisenhower administration was reported to have said, had "no history, no literature, no continent-wide religion of their own,

---

6. Tribalism, Huxley wrote, was "like the big striped umbrellas held over chiefs who parade in ceremonies. . . . Everyone can shelter there. No tribesman is ever alone. Every fellow-tribesman is bound by sacred rules to give him shelter, food and comfort whenever he needs it—a perfect welfare state, based on blood relationship. It has inspired all of Africa's arts—its vigorous dances, its rich legends, the carvings, masks, decorative bead and basket work, songs and music. Despite its crudity, it is a spiritual force as well as a remarkably successful way of living in society. . . . It is the African's guarantee of immortality. It gives him his mother-tongue and the pride that lifts him above the status of rootless person" ("Africa's First Loyalty," 14, 110).

7. R. P. Oliver, review of Prince Modupe, *I Was a Savage*, *National Review*, 17 May 1958, 476.

no traditions of the past apart from the sounds of the jungle."[8] Before colonialism, conservatives said, there had been little or nothing of significance in Africa.[9] African nationalists might like to pretend that there had been sophisticated, literate civilization in precolonial Africa, but—declared Nathaniel Weyl—"if there were Ghanaian Roger Bacons, Abelards and Chaucers, they sank, like the lost continent of Atlantis, without trace."[10] Thus in conservative eyes Africa might have had societies, but they had not had a civilization.

Indeed, (conservatives argued) the societies that existed in the continent were in decay and tearing each other apart when the European colonial powers arrived. The Europeans had thus (conservatives such as Gann and Duignan claimed) brought peace and security to Africa.[11] If they were interlopers, they were interlopers whose impact had been overwhelmingly beneficial. Indeed, the argument continued, in some parts of Africa, Europeans were not interlopers at all: they had settled there before the supposed "natives."[12]

Conservatives further asserted that differences in the degree of progress achieved in different African territories were directly—and proportionately—due to the size of the European presence. Thus progress had been

8. The deputy director of the United States International Communications Agency, quoted in Wesley, "Resurgence in Africa's Historical Tradition and the American Reaction," 82.

9. "The marks of historical man," wrote James Burnham, "are only scattered dots on the huge blank surface" ("The View from the Outside," 128).

10. "New Mythology of the Negro Past," 1,022. See also the exchange between Anthony Harrigan and Lewis Gann about the origins of Zimbabwe, in the *National Review,* 12 October 1973, 126; and "Letters," *National Review,* 23 November 1973, 1,274.

11. Colonialism had, in fact, put a stop to "a state of affairs in which tribes massacred each other and villagers could not leave the vicinity of their huts alone without exposing themselves to kidnapping, rape, or armed attack by men of the neighboring village" (Molnar, "An Outsider Speaks," 133). Peter Duignan and L. H. Gann, similarly, remarked that "the coming of a rule of law [had] ended tribal warfare and the slave trade. It limited the arbitrary rule of chiefs and the practice of witchcraft. Ritual murder and the killing of twins were forbidden" ("The Case for the White Man," 20).

12. Such claims were usually made on behalf on behalf of whites in South Africa and Angola. For example, Ronald Waring ("Angola: Terrorists on the Run," 190) states that the Portuguese were in Angola "before the present Bantu population, which invaded the country from the North sometime after the Portuguese settlement."

greatest in South Africa, Rhodesia, Kenya, and other settler colonies, and much less in, for example, West African territories. Even within West Africa (the English conservative Peter Bauer claimed), territories differed significantly in their levels of development according to the impact of European settlement and control.[13]

Conservatives (like many liberals) were particularly impressed by the achievements of the Belgians in the Congo. In the fifties, more popular journals such as *Time* and *U.S. News and World Report* consistently praised Belgian colonial administration. In 1955, for example, *Time* declared: "The Belgian way is working. The Congo, under hard-working capitalism, has become a tropical cornucopia in the heart of a poverty-stricken continent. . . . Nowhere in Africa is the Bantu so well fed and housed, so productive and so content as he is in the Belgian Congo . . . the Belgians have injected twenty centuries of Western mechanical progress into a Stone Age wilderness . . . in forests where fifty years ago there were no roads . . . no schools . . . no peace . . . the sons of cannibals now mine the raw materials of the Atomic Age."[14]

Given such achievements, Bauer and others argued, it was absurd to suggest that African colonies had been neglected, had "experienced no material progress," and were "caught in a vicious circle of poverty and

13. There was, Bauer argued, a striking difference between, on the one hand, such ex-colonies as Ghana and Nigeria and, on the other, a country such as Liberia which had not worn (in Elspeth Huxley's phrase) "the velvet-lined colonial yoke" ("Motes in the Eye of Africa," 854). Contrary to the assertions of anti-colonialists, Bauer continued, "the colonial status of [Ghana and Nigeria] does not seem to have retarded their progress. Rather the reverse, as it promoted the inflow of administrative, commercial, and technical skill as well as capital changes in West Africa" ("African Political Economy," 50).

14. *Time*, 16 May 1955, 32. In a later issue, the magazine noted: "Nowhere in Africa is there such a solid, well-paid class of native technicians" (23 December 1957, 22).

U.S. News was equally admiring, especially of the Belgians' success in keeping communism at bay. In an article entitled "Where Reds Are No Problem," the magazine reassured troubled readers: "If you're wondering whether there is any place in the world where the white man can hold his own against Communism and anti-Western agitation, you should come to the Belgian Congo. . . . Here, you see no signs of organized agitation or Communism. . . . The Belgians work harder than any other colonial power in Africa to keep Communism out of their domain. There is paternalistic but thoroughgoing control of the native here. Agitation of any kind is nipped before it ever gets started. . . . The Belgian Congo looks like one of the West's safest, as well as richest, bets" (23 July 1954, 35).

stagnation."[15] In fact, poverty had been Africa's original condition and, so far from being caused or aggravated by outsiders, poverty had survived in its most desperate forms where contact with the outside world had been least.

To appreciate the benefits of such contact, it was only necessary (a contributor to *Reader's Digest* declared) to fly south from Ethiopia—which had "enjoyed" independence for so long—and then take a train ride from Nairobi: "A rail journey is a delight: a spotless train, sleeping compartments equal to our best, good food, and from the windows a view of fields of coffee, tea, pyrethrum, sisal, corn, being cultivated under justice and peace. One cannot help realizing that this is what British colonialism has brought to a country that without it would still be a primitive wilderness."[16]

But had not the pleasures of such a train trip been purchased in the blood and sweat of ordinary Africans? Were colonial "peace and justice" in fact worth the suffering and lack of freedom that accompanied them?

Conservatives certainly did not deny that colonialism—and capitalism—entailed costs. Self-interest had undoubtedly played a part (indeed, many conservatives would have been nervous and skeptical about any movement in which it did not). In fact, however, Erik von Kuehnelt-Leddihn claimed, many colonies had been "a tremendous loss . . . from a purely economic point of view."[17]

In any case, even if altruism had not been the main motive for colonization, private vices did have public benefits. Certainly, compared to the draconian regimentation and "deliberate under-consumption" of communist societies, the essential process of primitive accumulation had been relatively painless in colonized countries, even in those of southern Africa. Admittedly, Duignan and Gann observed, European settlement and economic development had "brought enormous social problems to Africa"; but, they added, "so has industrialization wherever it has occurred."[18]

15. Bauer, "African Political Economy," 50.
16. Drake, "Don't Decry Colonialism," 66.
17. Kuehnelt-Leddihn wrote: "Nationalism, pride, love of adventure, a sense of mission, religious zeal, military considerations and fear of a loss of prestige preserved the colonial empires—not economics, though certain individuals and certain companies reaped profits" ("What about Katanga?" 266).
18. "A Different View of United States Policy in Africa," 919. The main price for Africans, the authors thought, had been acceptance of "certain economic,

The tone of these comments is surprising, in light of the sympathy that conservatives generally showed toward traditional societies and their concern about destruction of these societies by "modernization." The apparent enthusiasm of the authors for industrial progress is reminiscent of liberal writing on modernization, and it reveals the tension in conservative thinking between the "libertarian" school and the "traditionalists."

The "libertarians," like many old-school liberals, believed in individualism and the progress it could bring about. They were "conservative" in wanting to defend this tradition and were hostile to the collectivism of both African traditional institutions and contemporary statism (Kuehnelt-Leddihn actually referred to socialism as "a self-defeating mammoth tribalism favoring backwardness").[19] From this point of view, the sooner Africans were assimilated into European culture, the better.

The "traditionalists" felt that the cultural gap between Europeans and Africans was so large that assimilation was an unrealistic aim, at least in the short term. Conservatives such as Elspeth Huxley—in a sense, conservatives in the most literal sense—felt that Africans were better off left as they were, in a milieu in which they were comfortable and in which they could be whole and dignified human beings. They emphasized the contribution that interdependence and shared values made to the welfare and sense of integrity of individuals. As a corollary, they were skeptical of capitalist development in that it undermined existing and well-established communities.

The same tension appears, naturally, in discussions about the character and sources of African economic behavior. Was "the African" *homo economicus*? Was he, that is, if not a natural liberal, at least a potential entrepreneur? Conservatives of the more traditionalist bent thought that (happily) he was not. "The African," they believed, was impervious to the rationality (and the selfish acquisitiveness) that motivated Europeans and Americans. For better or for worse, the collectivism of the extended family and the tribe worked against risk taking.[20] The fact was, Molnar

---

social and political privileges for the white minority" ("The Case for the White Man," 17).

19. "Africa in Perspective," 424.

20. Duignan and Gann noted: "Tribal society, even at its most advanced level, implied poverty; the 'web of kinship' discouraged individual enterprise; communal tenure inhibited experimentation and advances in agricultural techniques" ("The Case for the White Man," 16).

declared, that "African mentality and inventiveness, culture and customs" were "realities in their own right." It was also a fact, he said, that these realities would not please earnest modernizers: "The black Africans lack many of the qualities which go into the building of modern, efficient, well-administered societies. . . . Tenacity, drive, persistence, reliability, and individualistic spirit . . . are disturbingly absent."[21]

Traditionalists did not, of course, find such characteristics "disturbing," whereas libertarians did. Conversely, traditionalists were disturbed by the idea of forcing Africans to change attitudes and institutions, fearing that modernization had taken place too rapidly and had already gone too far. It had, they claimed, already produced "rootless people." "History," Robert Coughlan observed, had "simply moved too fast": African towns were thronged with "detribalized . . . semi-literates" who had lost "the ballast of tribal custom without really understanding the values of modern society." Africa was suffering from a trauma of forced modernization. It was "lurching onto the world scene trailing anachronisms."[22] The individual victims of such a trauma would inevitably be confused, and their confusion might well cause instability and even violence in domestic politics (as well as some erratic behavior in international relations).

This description of the psychological effects of modernization resembled quite closely that of liberal students of African nationalism who wrote about the "transitional crisis." Conservative observers diverged from liberals in their assessments of the costs, benefits, and future of modernization in Africa or elsewhere. The sin of liberals, in the eyes of many conservatives, was to enthuse about modernization and to urge it on,

---

21. Molnar, "An Outsider Speaks," 151. Critics of the conservatives frequently suggested that much commentary of this kind on the alleged characteristics of "the African" was at best tendentious and at worst thinly veiled racial prejudice, no matter whether it was phrased approvingly (as in the case of "traditionalists") or in what might be called the plantation-owner idiom of impatient modernizers.
A good example of the latter idiom occurs in an article on Angola printed in 1956, in which the author justified the use of forced labor by referring to "the ordinary African's" lack of economic motivation: "No-one [wrote Irene S. Van Dongen] who has lived side by side with the ordinary African fails to realize that the incentive of larger material gains for more work does not operate in his natural milieu with the same force that it does for the worker in temperate climes, whose attitude has been influenced by a long industrial experience" ("Angola," 6).
Time magazine referred, in its issue of 26 October 1959, to the Lulua of the Belgian Congo as "a tribe of warriors who hated work in any form."
22. "Black Africa Surges to Independence," 102, 100.

without recognizing its costs to others. Liberals were therefore always taken by surprise when third world peoples rejected modernism, taking up instead with ideas and movements which to liberals seemed reactionary or downright primitive.

The liberal reaction, Peter L. Berger argued, reflected a failure of imagination and cultural insight. Liberals did not understand that while modernization had, in certain respects, a great appeal to third world peoples, it was also seen by them "as a threat to long-cherished institutions, values, and identities." Liberals, dazzled by utopian ideas of transforming the third world and largely insensitive to the cultural dimension of life, were unable to appreciate the real spiritual and emotional dislocations that change often entailed. They were therefore invariably bewildered by the apparent inconsistency, irrationality, and even plain ingratitude of third world leaders and their followers regarding "the gifts of modernity and . . . the bearers of these gifts."[23] Conservatives, on the other hand, had to put up with the same mindless (and, worse, soulless) modernizers at home. They could therefore easily sympathize with the reactions of their victims abroad.

Nontraditionalists, such as the economist Elliot Berg, took the view that Africans were not so much victims of modernization as unrecognized, albeit confused, maximizers. Specifically, Berg denied that there was any ingrained antipathy to gain among Africans. The problem, he argued, was not whether Africans "would . . . like more money income," but whether they were "willing to make the changes in ways of life that [would be] required to get more income."[24]

Berg, Bauer, and other "market-oriented" conservatives were in fact confident about the power of material incentives to overcome "culture" and "tradition," supporting their belief by pointing to the growth of peasant cash-crop agriculture in territories such as Ghana and the Ivory Coast.[25] Such cases, Bauer remarked, exposed as myths the beliefs that

23. "The Third World as a Religious Idea," 185.
24. "Socialism and Economic Development in Tropical Africa," 564. Conservatives often asserted *both* that Africans were lazy and indifferent to incentives *and* that they were uncontrollably greedy and indiscriminately covetous of Western material goods. "The native [Kuehnelt-Leddihn wrote] usually understands nothing but European money, newer and better cars, neater and nicer homes, better paid jobs, prettier women 'with long hair'" ("Letter from the Congo," 394).
25. Berg, "Socialism and Economic Development in Tropical Africa," 564, 563. According to Berg, "The African peasant . . . cannot easily be pushed into

Africans would not respond to economic incentives, could not produce competitively for world markets, were "invariably unenterprising," and were children of nature,"living for the present" and unable to "take a long view."[26]

Conservatives and Decolonization

How conservative writers saw modernization naturally affected their views not only about colonialism but also about the prospects for Africa after independence. Free-enterprise conservatives such as Bauer and Berg tended to be concerned about a range of threats to individual enterprise, some of which issued from traditional societies, others from colonial government itself, and others again from collectivists among the African nationalists. The issue for them was the advancement of individualism, and that issue arose in different contexts.

The libertarians did not therefore see decolonization as melodramatically as other conservatives, for whom it represented a showdown between two strong and mutually exclusive cultures, one "civilized" (or secular), the other "primitive" (or traditional). Those who did see decolonization in this way generally argued that the impact of modernization had been superficial.[27] The educated elite, they stressed, was tiny, and a huge gulf separated it from the "enormous native mass." The villages in which this mass lived still looked "for the most part precisely as they must have looked before the first European set foot on African soil."[28]

This group disagreed about whether the impact of modernization,

---

the market. He must be pulled into it, encouraged, enticed by positive inducements, among which the most effective is no doubt that most banal of incentives—the possibility of higher real income" (p. 565). Cf. P. T. Bauer, "Capitalism and Economic Development," *National Review,* 29 June 1965, 542–45; and "African Political Economy," 55–57.

26. "African Political Economy," 56, 57.

27. "European manners and mannerisms [wrote Kuehnelt-Leddihn] characterize only small minorities; they do not penetrate the village, still less into the bush, and under stress even the 'Europeanized' leaders yield to tribal traditions and feelings" ("Will Africa Make the Transition?" 1,114).

28. Alsop, "Africa: The Riddle without an Answer," 83. "The cultural level of most of the population [James Burnham reported] is incredibly low: for the most part, the natives are—and, who knows, may perhaps long be, perhaps prefer to be—at the stage of primitive, pre-civilized barbarism" ("What Is Ahead for Black Africa?" 240).

slight or not, had been beneficial. Those who thought it had been beneficial saw decolonization in cataclysmic terms. James Burnham, for example, lamented the collapse of Western imperialism as an apocalypse comparable to the fall of the Roman and other great empires. History, he declared, would depict the West "fleeing as the defeated fled before Genghis, Alexander, Pompey, Caesar: fleeing in thousands, in tens and hundreds of thousands, our weapons spiked and abandoned, our homes looted, our property smashed or stolen, our women raped, our children brutalized. . . . Our giant warships turn and flee from the harbors; our superb warplanes flee from the great fields built by our talents and wealth; our intricate guns are pulled from their emplacements; our soldiers get their command: Retreat!"[29]

Civilization, conservatives warned, would quickly and irretrievably disappear under a resurgence of "African ways." Faced with this prospect, Sen. Barry Goldwater declared, Europeans (and their American sympathizers) had a duty to recognize the propriety of the task they had undertaken, to understand the dangers likely to result from forcing change faster than desirable, and to resist the threats and criticisms of white liberals and black nationalists alike. As Goldwater put it in 1961: "We know that the privilege of being born in the West carries with it the responsibility of extending our good fortune to others. We are the bearers of Western civilization, the most noble product of the heart and mind of man. . . . We must recognize the difficult but necessary task of elevating Africans to the point, culturally, economically, and politically, where they are capable of responsible self-government."[30]

Conservatives believed, almost unanimously and usually with some passion, that this point of readiness had not been reached in the late fifties, when Western liberals began surrendering to the demands of African nationalists for independence. The Congo represented, in conservative eyes, the ultimate proof of the catastrophe resulting from liberal cowardice and African unreadiness—an "independent" country "created *ex nihilo* out of Wilsonian abstractions by Belgian funk."[31]

---

29. "The African Shambles," 45. Other writers, equally pessimistic in tone, wondered (like Thomas Molnar) whether progress could be maintained "or whether occult influence [would] prevail and the temptation of indolence prove stronger than the efforts needed for civilizing work" ("An Outsider Speaks," 133–34).

30. "A Foreign Policy for America," 180.

31. "Whose Drums on the Congo?" 7.

While for liberals decolonization was both a victory for one principle and a prelude to the realization of some others, for conservatives it was a calamity, a prelude to disaster, and therefore a problem to be explained. The problem, for believers in Western civilization and its mission in Africa, was to understand how Western governments could have behaved so recklessly, abandoning their responsibilities almost without a fight.[32] How could such folly, with such appalling consequences, have come about? Why had the West retreated when it so clearly had overwhelming military strength, economic resources, and—not least—moral superiority? Why, James Burnham asked, had the West displayed the same "moral funk and mental stupor" that had led it "to be pushed so humiliatingly out of most of Asia"?[33]

For conservatives, decolonization was a gratuitous surrender, not a defeat at the hands of an overwhelmingly strong opposition. Consequently, the real culprits were to be found at home. The usual liberal suspects were duly arraigned. It was liberals and socialists, declared conservative Congressmen Joe Waggoner in 1966, who, following earlier acts of political abdication, were preparing the way for the expulsion of Western influence in Rhodesia and its replacement by communism.[34] The activities of the left, Burnham and others argued, had helped to cause the collapse. "Several generations of Marxian agitation and activity," both in the West and in Africa, had (according to Burnham) undermined support for the imperial enterprise.[35]

32. The tragedy of Africa was, Frank S. Meyer remarked, a "tragedy of impatience" due to a "decay of belief, failure of nerve and confidence, an immoral casting aside of burdens" ("The Prickly Dilemmas," 14; Meyer, "Abdication of Responsibility," 218).

33. "Eurafrica or Afro-Asia?" 388. Likening the whites of Africa to the Jews, Burnham commented that at least the Israelis had enjoyed the support of Jews throughout the world: the whites of Africa had been "denounced, rejected, condemned and even actively fought by most of the Christian, Western whites of the world" ("The Loneliest Men," 164).

34. "Now that the white man has led [the natives] out of savagery [Waggoner declared], the Socialist, left-wing camp is up in arms to turn the country back to them. This is, of course, a not too subtle way of building a Socialist bridge from democracy to Communism" (quoted in Lake, The "Tar Baby" Option, 118). Waggoner began by remarking: "Three generations ago, a group of resourceful white men went into the jungle of what is now Rhodesia and carved a civilized land by sheer force of their brains and management ability."

35. Burnham, "The United States, the United Nations, and Africa," 243–44.

The State Department was another culprit. It had convinced itself that truckling to African nationalists would make the new African states friendly to the United States and that supporting "non-Communist revolutions" would win friends in the Cold War.[36] But the State Department and those it persuaded were deceiving themselves. As Anthony Harrigan argued, "What's good for Ghana isn't necessarily good for Uncle Sam."[37]

Burnham, however, warned against taking a simple and comfortingly conspiratorial view of American policy toward decolonization. The truth was, he said, that American policy—in his view, a crucial factor in undermining European colonialism—had enjoyed the support of the American people. On this, as on many other issues at this time, conservatism faced the dilemma of any minority in a democracy. What or who was at fault? Was it the electorate, which was uninformed or ignorant of its real interests? Was it the American political system, which had failed to reflect accurately the electorate's views? Or was it the conservative cause itself, which had failed to win over voters?

Naturally, the most reassuring answer for conservatives was that the system was at fault. In that case, all that would be required would be some reform. Burnham, however, refused such a comforting answer, at least on the question of decolonization. Conservatives, he said, had to face the fact that "the anti-imperialist posture" of the U.S. government had been "in accord with prevailing public opinion."[38] Further, conservatives should avoid the temptation (to which liberals invariably yielded in attacking conservative programs) of ascribing popular anti-imperialism to material and selfish interests. However much conservatives might dislike them, the injunctions of popular liberalism were in fact "moral imperatives, telling Americans what is 'right,' not what is expedient . . . Americans, however deficient may be their understanding of the conditions of freedom and prosperity, do really wish that other nations and

36. Von Kuehnelt-Leddihn, "Africa in Perspective," 426.

37. State Department liberals, Harrigan argued, suffered from the false assumption that "alteration of old patterns of life and political order [was] automatically to the advantage of the United States." Liberals in the State Department and elsewhere had too easily assumed that "proclamations of independence and democracy in faraway countries immediately created a community of interest with the United States" ("America Needs a Realistic Foreign Policy," 13, 12).

38. "Anti-imperialism [Burnham wrote] and its accompanying proposals for the universal self-determination of nations and peoples are among the axioms of popular thinking and have long been felt to be part of the tradition incorporated in American history" ("The United States, the United Nations, and Africa," 244).

people should be free and prosperous. They are ready to give something from their own plenty to realize that wish, and within the policy of their government both the wish and the readiness have been reflected."[39]

That said, however, the policy was still wrong, and the electorate's understanding of the world was deficient. No doubt, it did sincerely believe that decolonization would bring peace to the world and make friends for the United States. But in foreign affairs, sincerity was not enough: sincerity and good intentions were no substitute for realism and clear thinking about interests. Tedious and unpopular though it might be, the job of conservatives was to educate sincerity in self-interest.

In pursuit of this education, conservatives concentrated on destroying some of the central myths of liberalism. One particularly harmful myth was the assumption that history consisted of "tides" and "irreversible trends." Once nationalism and decolonization became firmly identified in popular minds as "tides" and "irreversible trends," all serious attempt to control or direct them had stopped. They somehow became, in the public's mind, presumptively virtuous. They acquired the unearned but nevertheless unbeatable claim of "invincible forces," as well as the endorsement of that rather elusive authority, "world opinion," which itself was supposed to foreshadow and embody "the Verdict of History."[40]

Applying labels such as "historic" and "unbeatable" in this way (conservatives complained) had the effect of paralyzing and silencing all who might otherwise wonder aloud about the benefits the forces in question might bring, the costs their victory might entail, and the motives of the people behind them. Such verbal canonization of nationalism alone accounted, in the conservative view, for the most damaging feature of liberal policy toward decolonization, namely, its surrender of judgment and control over the timing of self-government. If a trend was inevitable, liberals seemed to say, then the sooner it had its way, the better.[41]

Just as harmfully, liberals had systematically denigrated the idea of political responsibility, cheaply equating it with elitism and authoritarianism. Fearing to take responsibility, they had surrendered control over

39. Ibid., 245, 249.

40. Lejeune, "Can Britain Stop Rhodesia?" 22.

41. Liberals, Lejeune (a British conservative) remarked, could not "believe that there could be another point of view or that 'the movement of the times' might be checked. . . . They talk as though the European retreat from Africa were not merely desirable but predestined; and they abdicate all responsibility for its consequences" ("Cult of the Messiah," 330).

decolonization and had undermined those who believed in continuing to exercise such control. As a result, the colonial powers had, in Elspeth Huxley's words, "been hustled off the scene like cattle driven to the roundup."[42]

Moreover, conservatives suggested, a deeper cultural failure lay behind such "shameful" events as the Belgian abandonment of the Congo. Moral abdication had preceded political and physical abandonment: Western nations had lost "their older sense of a positive civilizing mission," replacing it with an "abstract humanitarian sentiment."[43]

Liberals, in the conservative view, were also guilty of "soft thinking" about the probable results of surrendering Africa. In particular, they suffered from a number of "comforting illusions" about the probable attitudes and behavior of African nationalists. All such illusions, Lejeune claimed, were rooted in one basic, major delusion (in fact, the cardinal fallacy of liberalism)—the belief that "the whole world is populated by natural liberals who are simply waiting for the chance to put their lofty ideals into practice."[44]

Even as late as 1961, some conservatives (including Barry Goldwater) still thought that it might be possible to slow down the decolonization of Africa. What was necessary, Goldwater and others declared, was the establishment of a joint Western protectorate over Africa—an umbrella held by a number of powers, including the United States, which would exclude communist influence and foster a more deliberate movement toward self-government. Under such a protectorate, Africans would be prepared for independence "in an atmosphere conducive to the triumph of Western concepts of justice and freedom."[45]

Such schemes assumed that American and Western European interests in Africa were compatible. According to conservatives, the trouble was that American liberals either denied that such compatibility existed or, where it did exist, they regarded it as having sinister consequences. Given the dominance of liberalism in the United States, schemes for extending

42. "Disengagement in Africa," 94–95.
43. Meyer, "Abdication of Responsibility," 218; Burnham, "The United States, the United Nations, and Africa," 244.
44. "The Day Lumumba Died," 182.
45. Goldwater, "A Foreign Policy for America," 180. Others suggested that control should be exercised for a defined period by an international consortium of investing nations which "would be committed before the world to prepare the Africans for self-rule according to plan and to withdraw completely at the end of the time specified" (Weigle, "How to Deal with Africa," 346).

colonial rule were therefore unlikely to work. For them even to be considered would require, Harrigan noted, "a complete reversal of policy." Even when they were sponsored by such prestigious scholars as Hans J. Morgenthau, plans to bring decolonization under responsible political control had little chance of succeeding.[46]

Yet without such a planned reversal of decolonization, conservatives said, Africa was likely to suffer "total disaster at the hands of anticivilization forces."[47] For that, and for succeeding disasters, the widespread but ill-conceived assumptions of liberalism would be to blame. Liberalism had not (Burnham and others admitted) been exclusively responsible for the Western retreat from Africa. But, as projected through American global power, liberalism played a central (and disastrous) role in easing the withdrawal, making it seem both inevitable and right: "It has," Burnham argued, "been the ideology that has sanctioned it, supplying the comforting slogans that have allowed men to interpret every failure as a success, and every surrender as a victory. . . . Liberalism has contributed . . . a shout of victory each time we have willingly put the knife to our veins and let out some more of our life's blood."[48]

Conservatives and the Analogy of 1776

American history had, of course, provided many of the "comforting slogans" that liberals had supplied to third world nationalists. Conservatives particularly disliked the use made by liberals of the American Revolution in their efforts to glorify anticolonialism. Liberals, they felt, had distorted this piece of American history quite irresponsibly in putting it forward as a model for the third world. The scorn of conservatives for the proselytizing of Bowles, Stevenson, and others was inexhaustible:

We have been rampaging through the world [remarked a *National Review* contributor] sowing revolution among people little able to grasp the spirit of '76. Behind us lie the wrecks of empires, whose fragments are patiently gathered up by the Soviet Union, the only long-run beneficiary of an American policy based upon misunderstanding and misapplication of the principles which inspired our revolutionary statesmen . . . we who have misunderstood our own

46. See Morgenthau, "United States Policy toward Africa," 324–25.
47. Harrigan, "America Needs a Realistic Foreign Policy," 12.
48. Paraphrased in Frankel, "A Conservative Autopsy," 6.

history are now committed to encouragement of virtually all "independence" movements everywhere.[49]

In replaying American history, liberals had (according to conservative critics) fatally miscast the actors. They had concentrated on the relationship between the British and the colonists: the more relevant relationship for purposes of comparison with Africa was (as liberal skeptics had, indeed, noted) that between the colonists and the American Indians.[50] If liberals would only explore the implications of using this second relationship as an analogy, they would (Burnham suggested) be less facile in their condemnation of colonialism and more guarded in their optimism about African independence.

If we seek our parallels not in the relation between the North American settlers and the English but in the relation between the Indians and the settlers, or if we merely note how the American West was actually brought under the sovereignty of the government established by the Philadelphia constitution, we will not find it so easy to separate heroes from villains in the Asian and especially the African dramas of this postwar epoch. . . . Where are the warring, primitive tribes that *our* ancestors found in this land? What will be our vote in the U.N. when delegations from the Iroquois and Sioux demand rule over the country we stole from them?[51]

African nationalist leaders might have British ideas and principles, remarked Nathaniel Peffer, but they had another, much more powerful inheritance which was illiberal, not to say irrational.[52] The true heirs of the American colonists were, conservatives argued, to be found, not among the nationalist leaders of Africa—the black Jeffersons and black Wash-

49. J. D. Futch, "The Day of the Let's Pretends," 328. It should be pointed out that not all conservatives were as skeptical about the parallel. John Foster Dulles, for example, said in 1954: "We ourselves are the first colony in modern times to have won independence. We have a natural sympathy with those everywhere who would follow our example" (quoted in Pratt, "Anticolonialism in U.S. Policy," 291).

50. "The men of 1776," Nathaniel Peffer remarked, "had inherited British ideas, principles, traditions, conceptions of government" ("Colonialism: New Problems for Old," 73).

51. Burnham, "The United States, the United Nations, and Africa," 245; "Image in What Mirror?" 15.

52. "Colonialism: New Problems for Old?" 73.

ingtons of the liberal imagination—but among the colonial officials and white settlers whose life work the liberals were trying so hard, so self-righteously, and so successfully to destroy.

Burnham and others hoped that once events exposed the irrelevance of liberal comparisons, Americans would see Africa quite differently. They would be far more sympathetic to the true spiritual heirs of the American pioneers, such as the settlers who had built up Rhodesia. They would become as incredulous as was Anthony Lejeune about the liberal campaign to destroy the work of the European frontiersmen in Central Africa, and they would wonder, with him, "what the second generation frontier families of the last century would have said if they had been asked to hand over political control to the Apaches and Sioux."[53]

Conservatives and Self-Determination

Conservative suspicions of decolonization were not surprising, given the esteem in which they held the colonizers as bearers of a civilizing mission. But why should conservatives have been so suspicious of African nationalism? After all, they were (unlike most liberals) unashamed nationalists, scornful of "one-worlders": they were passionate believers in cultural idiosyncrasies, and strong defenders of sovereignty. Logically, how could Americans who believed so strongly in the right of the United States to be left alone deny the same right to other peoples?

And if, as American conservatives asserted, the world was populated

53. "No Surrender in Rhodesia," 282. Lejeune remarked that the atmosphere of Salisbury (the pre-independence name of Harare) reminded him of that of "a town in the American Middle West."

An equally critical view of American liberal misuse of the 1776 parallel appeared in the *Reader's Digest* in 1960, when Vivian Drake commented that liberals seemed "to forget that the men who wrote our Declaration were among the most idealistic, educated and politically enlightened men of their day, and that our new citizens had brought with them the best of the civilization of the Old World. In contrast, the vast majority of Africans today are uneducated and uncivilized. The struggle is to find enough of them, in any country, capable of self-government, and to educate enough of the voters to resist witch doctors and extremists" ("Don't Decry Colonialism," 66). This version was, it might be noted, more flattering to the American colonists than Burnham's "realist" version, which acknowledged the fact of conquest and the use of force in American history and which scorned the liberal view (essentially like Drake's) as sentimental.

not by liberals, but by the tough and the self-interested, why would they be troubled by the prospect of like-minded, self-regarding nationalists taking charge in Africa? Clearly, there might initially be more conflict if the world was ruled by self-interested nationalists. But, according to conservative realists, such a world was likely in the long run to be a more stable world than one in which evangelistic liberals were forever launching misguided campaigns of interference in their neighbors' business.

The objections raised to decolonization did not in principle supply reasons for opposing self-determination. These objections mainly concerned the abandonment of responsibility by Western countries, encouraged or blackmailed by the United States. In fact, American conservatives did sometimes say that they were not in fact opposed in principle to self-determination.

Admittedly, they had doubts. Some conservative writers, such as Graham Weigle, regarded self-determination as a dangerous abstraction. If followed consistently, Weigle said, self-determination would dissolve every community.[54] William F. Buckley, Jr., was also reluctant to endorse a universal right to self-government: *"National Review,"* he told a critic, "denies it is the 'unalienable right' of every people to govern themselves, under any circumstances."[55]

However, Buckley went on to say (with reference to Kenya) that it was necessary to "recognize the reality of nationalist aspirations, and their essential legitimacy."[56] In the same vein, Thomas Molnar remarked that the trouble with whites in Angola and South Africa was that they could not grasp "the crucial fact that the natives want to be independent, because at a certain stage of development people want to look after their own business." The fact was, he concluded, that the pressure for independence in Africa was "not an artificially created agitation, but a genuine idea."[57]

Interestingly, Molnar did not here invoke an objection sometimes used by opponents of nationalist movements, namely, that they only repre-

54. "All decent social organization above the level of the family would disappear. . . . Its invariable consequence is anarchy, usually followed by tyranny" ("How to Deal with Africa," 345). According to Weigle, self-determination was "the soil that nourished Hitler, Castro, Nasser and today, jungle law in Africa."
55. *National Review,* 25 April 1959, 29.
56. "Uhuru-Ushuru," 38.
57. "An Outsider Speaks," 138, 139. Vivian Drake (the writer who had so much enjoyed the amenities of colonialism in Kenya) declared in 1960: "Self-rule is right . . . it is inevitable" ("Don't Decry Colonialism," 70).

sented minorities. After all, not only were American conservatives themselves in a minority in the 1960s, but they often asserted that right principles had nothing to do with electoral majorities.[58]

Some conservatives did, then, recognize the applicability of the conservative principle that any nation had a right to be superior or inferior in its own way (as distinct from the liberal principle that it had a right to be free as long as it exercised its freedom liberally). But this principle was often hedged with two conditions, one apparently semantic, the other political. The semantic condition—obvious enough—was that national self-determination could only be claimed by nations. The political condition—an even more restrictive one—was that the right to self-determination entailed a duty to respect the national interests of other states (in this instance, mainly those of the United States). The effect of these conditions was that while conservatives were sympathetic to nationalism in principle, they were skeptical about its relevance to and its consequences in Africa, as well as its probable implications for American interests in that part of the world.

Their skepticism was certainly to some extent a corollary of their respect for colonialism. Reflexively perhaps, but logically, they were suspicious of any movement overtly hostile to and critical of colonial governments. They were also highly critical (as we shall see) of the qualities and values of the leaders of nationalist movements. By association, some of this disapproval undoubtedly influenced their attitude to the issue of self-determination itself.

However, conservatives had a more fundamental reason for doubting the credentials of nationalism in Africa. It arose from their assumption that Africans were "naturally" tribal in loyalty. Since such "tribalism" was deeply rooted, it would make more sense to accept it and to create institutions that corresponded to the "reality of tribalism" than to try—vainly—to destroy it. Most conservatives shared the sentiment expressed by a *New York Times* journalist in the course of a visit to the Congo: "Africans have a strong sense of community but nationalism is not natural to them; nationalism is a European invention; it can appeal to a heterogeneous collection of clans and tribes on the basis of ethnic solidarity but it cannot heal the innate fragmentation of their own social system."[59]

58. Molnar, in fact, explicitly embraced this position: "Decolonization and independence are in the consciousness of a minority; but movements in history are always propelled by minorities" ("An Outsider Speaks," 139).

59. Edward R. F. Sheehan, "It's Still the Heart of Darkness," 83–84. A writer

Instability and civil war would inevitably result from attempts to force national institutions (as understood by Europeans) on Africa. By extension, schemes for African unity were hopelessly far-fetched, doomed to remain forever "the dreams of a few men." Conservatives therefore generally favored an increase, not a decrease, in the number of political units in Africa. When a domestic crisis occurred in an African country, their instinct was to attribute it to over-hasty modernization and the unreality of "national" governments. Their solution was to recommend the creation of smaller units, based on the "reality" of tribalism. In practice, this would mean either a multiplication of states or, at least, a loose federal structure for existing states.

On this issue, liberals and conservatives were fundamentally opposed. Liberals, as we have seen, recognized the existence of tribal loyalties, but deplored them and regarded them as passé. In their view, the best way to deal with tribalism was to pursue "national integration"—to create strong national institutions (including a strong national government) which would draw popular loyalties away from more local communities. Liberals felt sure that such a strategy was both desirable and practicable. Parochialism was historically doomed and it would therefore be easy (and right) to persuade those under its sway to abandon their emotional ties to the tribe and similar parochial forms.

The usual liberal response to crisis and instability was therefore exactly the reverse of the conservative response. Liberals typically argued that the crisis showed the need to accelerate modernization, to strengthen national governments, and even, indeed, to abolish them in favor of regional or continental super-states.

In short, while conservatives usually thought that African states were "unviable" because they were too large, liberals thought that they were unviable because they were too small. For conservatives, the problem of independent Africa (if there had to be such an Africa) was how to scale down the state's framework to correspond to the entities that enjoyed popular loyalty—the tribe or ethnic group.

This position did not really involve a retreat from the normal conservative attitude of supporting nationalism and respecting nationality. It

---

in *Atlantic* reached similar conclusions: "The tribe remains a powerful unit which resists the best leaders' determination to replace old loyalties with new. . . . The crux of the continent's dilemma is not just Africa for the Africans, but what Africa, for which Africans?" (Margaret C. Hubbard, "The Threat of African Tribalism," 45).

merely called for adapting the principle to African conditions and African culture, both of which conservatives regarded as extremely resistant to change, if not actually rooted in "nature." The conservative view thus emphasized the crucial importance of culture and, by implication, the extreme difficulty of bridging cultures—a difficulty likely, in the conservative view, to undermine the entire liberal agenda and associated liberal campaigns for "progress" and "human rights."

A key analogy in the American (and European) debate about statehood in Africa was that of the Balkans between the two world wars. In liberal eyes, Africa was "Balkanized," by which they meant that it had been broken up into too many small, "artificial" units. To them, the implication of the analogy was not (as it certainly seemed to be at first sight) that both Africa and Eastern Europe would have been better off had the empires in question survived. It was that Africa needed larger states which would be more "viable" for the purposes of contemporary statehood than those inherited from colonialism. But why would creating fewer, larger states overcome the problem of artificiality? Liberals usually did not seem to notice this problem, presumably because for them statehood was important mainly as a step toward modernity. Just as self-determination was justified as a condition for progress, so the requirements of modernization shaped their attitude toward the constitution of states. States were as states did: and their degree of artificiality was ultimately less important than their potential for fostering development.

Conservatives read the Balkans analogy rather differently. For them, the significance of the Balkans experience was that it showed the folly of assuming that self-determination for nations would somehow lead to freedom for their citizens. History provided, they said, no basis for such an optimistic assumption, and the Balkan case pointed in exactly the opposite direction. In that instance, as Duignan and Gann pointed out, "what emerged was, except for Czechoslovakia with its relatively developed middle class, a series of thinly disguised dictatorships, possessed of a most unfortunate knack of persecuting their minorities, and characterized, moreover, by a marked inability to defend themselves when challenged from without."[60]

Conservatives expected just such a pattern to emerge in Africa, and quite possibly something worse. They expected little but trouble from African nationalism, at least as long as it tried to emulate its European

60. "A Different View of United States Policy in Africa," 919–20.

counterpart. Also, given their assumptions about the "natural" constitution of African states, they were automatically suspicious of African
politicians claiming leadership of nationalist movements in Africa. Since
in their eyes most such movements did not and could not represent
true nations, the credentials of such politicians were, by definition,
bogus.[61]

The Case of Katanga

But some African politicians, including some leaders of independence
movements, did attract conservative support, the best-known case being
that of Moise Tshombe and Katanga. Why were conservatives so enthusiastic about Katangan self-determination, when they were generally so
skeptical about independence movements in Africa?

American conservatives certainly were early enthusiasts for Tshombe
and the Katanga cause.[62] By 1961, this enthusiasm was taking an actively

61. The only exceptions might be territories such as Lesotho, Swaziland,
Rwanda, and Burundi in which colonial boundaries roughly coincided with the
boundaries of precolonial kingdoms.

62. As early as October 1958, *Time* magazine was reporting the formation of
the Union Katangaise, an organization set up by Europeans in Katanga to press
for confederation in the Congo, with each province directly responsible to Brus-
sels, rather than to Leopoldville (*Time,* 27 October 1958, 29).

In April 1959, David Reed reported at length in *U.S. News and World Report* on
this movement: "Leaders among these settlers are pressing now for a decentralization of the Congo Government, so as to make the Katanga at least partly
independent of Leopoldville and the Bakongo tribe. . . . As a trump card, they
say they might try eventually to break away from the rest of the Congo, to become
either a separate state or to federate with the Rhodesias. If it ever came to a settler
rebellion, it's felt that no African government would be powerful enough to stop
it" ("In the Congo's Jungles, A Boom and a Ferment," 100).

Twelve days before independence, Kuehnelt-Leddihn predicted the disintegration of the new state. Some parts, he thought, would be annexed by neighboring
states, while others "would seek to preserve certain ties with Belgium." Specifically, he forecast that "the very rich Katanga, sick of centralist but disorderly
Leopoldville, might follow a more conservative policy. . . . As the situation stands
today [Kuehnelt-Leddihn observed] a truly independent Congo wouldn't last
more than a few months as a democracy" ("Letter from the Congo," 393). In a
visit to the Congo earlier in the year, Kuehnelt-Leddihn had found that both
Europeans and Africans in Katanga regarded the prospect of Katanga's absorp-
tion into a Leopoldville-dominated regime "with reluctance and dismay" ("Katanga's Case," 77).

political form in Congress, largely through a number of senators sympathetic to Katanga.[63] Following fighting between U.N. and Katangese forces in December 1961, an organization entitled the American Committee for Aid to Katanga Freedom Fighters (ACAKFF) was established, headed by some well-established conservative luminaries.[64]

63. Congressmen frequently identified as sympathizers with the Katangese cause included senators Everett Dirksen, Thomas J. Dodd, James O. Eastland, Thruston B. Morton, Richard B. Russell, and Strom Thurmond. Dodd, in particular, associated himself publicly with the secessionists. In his capacity as a member of the Senate Foreign Affairs subcommittee and chairman of the Senate Internal Security subcommittee, he visited Katanga in 1961. While Dodd claimed later that he had never favored an independent Katanga, he did argue that the province had "a moral right" to secede (Krosney, "Senator Dodd: Portrait in Contrasts," 551). Dodd also became a vocal congressional critic of the role of the United Nations in Katanga, claiming that UN policies, "if pursued to their logical conclusion, [would] turn the Congo over to Communist imperialism" ("Dodd's Private War," 4).

64. On 30 December 1961, *National Review* reported the formation of ACAKFF. The inaugural meetings of the ACAKFF took place on 9 and 10 December: the fighting in Katanga began on 5 December and lasted for ten days. (The United Nations action was also attacked by ex–Vice President Richard M. Nixon in a syndicated column.)

The chairman of the new committee was Max Yergan, and its members included several of the editors of *National Review,* as well as Marvin Liebman (of the Committee of One Million, a body dedicated to opposing the Chinese communist government), George S. Schuyler, Clarence Manion, and Gen. Albert C. Wedemeyer. Schuyler was editor of the *Pittsburgh Courier*; Manion was an ex-dean of the Notre Dame Law School, a member of the national council of the John Birch Society, and a member of the national advisory board of Young Americans for Freedom; Wedemeyer was a member of the editorial advisory committee of *American Opinion* (the major organ of the John Birch Society) and of the national advisory board of Young Americans for Freedom. Other members included Tom Anderson (the publisher of *Farm and Ranch* magazine, an advocate of impeaching the Supreme Court over its decision on school desegregation, and a contributor to the radical right journal *American Mercury*); John Crichton (a Texas millionaire); and Charles Edison (an ex-governor of New Jersey).

On the establishment of ACAKFF and its subsequent activities, see "Katanga, the Committee, the U.N."; "Next Phase Coming Up"; "How to Cure the Congo"; and references in the *National Review,* 16 January 1962, 7; 13 February 1962, 80; 13 March 1962, 154; and 31 July 1962, 49.

ACAKFF drew strenuous and sarcastic criticism from what the *National Review* described as "the fever swamps of the Left." See, for example, "Dodd's Private War," 3–4; Krosney, "Senator Dodd: Portrait in Contrasts," 547–53; "Those Katanga Freedom Fighters"; and Howard, "Katanga and the Congo Betrayal."

Conservatives' reasons for supporting Katangese secession had to do with Tshombe's politics, with the nature of Katangese society, and with the giddy chaos that lay beyond the province's boundaries. Conservatives supported Katanga's secession partly because it represented the opposite of what in their view were the more destructive aspects of African nationalism, and because of its leadership's ostensible attachment to unfashionable, Western values. In particular, they admired Moise Tshombe as an independent—not at all the "puppet" of Western capitalism depicted by his liberal and socialist enemies.[65] Indeed, they said, he was radically independent in a way that few of his African contemporaries dared to be—someone who dared to defy the hypocrisies and falsehoods of international liberalism and its African proteges.[66]

To start with, conservatives claimed that Tshombe, unlike other African nationalist leaders, was not a racist. He was, said *Time* magazine, "that rarest of Africans who seems to have no complexes about being black."[67] He dared to believe that there could be cooperation between the races.[68]

65. Conservatives repeatedly protested, whatever his detractors might say, that Tshombe "was not simply a tool of European financial or political interests, as [had] been alleged by communist and neutralist leaders. He was the astute leader of a combination of local and external forces, which he both served and used in his turbulent struggle" (Ernest Lefever, review of Jules Gérard-Libois, *Katanga Secession,* [Madison: University of Wisconsin Press, 1966], *Africa Report* 12, no. 4 [April 1967]: 52). Nor was the Union Minière in any way controlling Tshombe, as radical critics believed. Rather, remarked Ernest Van den Haag (in company with several liberal commentators), it was the UMHK that was the prisoner, having no choice but to pay Tshombe ("The U.N. War in Kantanga," 202).

66. The common view in conservative journals was that, as the *National Review* put it, Tshombe was "a man more sinned against than sinning." Senator Dodd, for example, described him as "one of the most impressive men I have ever met and one of the most maligned." Tshombe was typically seen as a multiple victim. He was, Philippa Schuyler asserted, a victim of "the fiction that the Congo [was] a nation" ("Behind the Congo Crisis," 76). In general (others asserted), he was being victimized because "he refused to develop an ideology that would satisfy the domestic and international intelligentsia" (Burnham, review of Tshombe, *My Fifteen Months in Government,* 817).

67. *Time,* 4 December 1964, 32. In *Time*'s judgment, Tshombe was also "canny, unscrupulous, candid and pragmatic."

68. As a contributor to the *American Legion Magazine* put it, Tshombe was "the only prominent Congolese who believed that Africans and Europeans could live and work together" (Peter D. Bolter, "The Congo . . . Seven Bloody Years"). According to the *National Review,* Tshombe was "convinced that the progress of his country and of Africa could be achieved only through the cooperation of black

In embracing multiracialism, Tshombe (according to Philippa Schuyler) exposed one of African nationalism's dirty secrets, namely, that Africans often had more in common with the ex-colonizers than with each other: "Belgians liked Congolese more than Congolese liked each other. Belgian direction was the unifying force that kept tribal warfare down. Congolese of different tribes hated each other actively and intensely. Belgians did not always respect Congolese, but they seldom hated them."[69]

Tshombe's honest readiness to accept Western help had, conservatives claimed, enabled Katanga to realize the potential that so many observers had noted before independence. Katangans, declared the *National Review*, were "an orderly, industrious people—the most promising, in many respects, in Africa."[70] Compared to the nightmares encountered elsewhere in the Congo, Katanga was an island of order, sanity, and kindliness—a kind of Congolese Lake Woebegone. As Erik von Kuehnelt-Leddihn reported enthusiastically: "I found people in Elisabethville well-dressed, friendly, cooperative. The (former) native quarter was attractive and clean, the children charming, the schools frequented almost equally by girls and boys. All the natives I met were convinced that, for a long time to come, they needed European advice, European aid, European industrial and commercial relations. I have never met more level-headed people anywhere in Africa."[71]

After a further visit, Kuehnelt-Leddihn developed a rather elaborate theory of Katangan exceptionalism. Katanga, he said, had become, partly

---

with white and the aid of white expertise and capital" ("Moise Tshombe, R.I.P.," 685). The *National Review* also pointed out that Tshombe was "a believing, unapologetic Christian."

69. *Who Killed the Congo?* 93.

70. "Operation Smash, Phase III," 12. Erik von Kuehnelt-Leddihn reported that Katangan society "showed more sanity, balance of judgment and intellectual maturity than any other place in the Congo" ("Katanga's Case," 77).

71. "What about Katanga?" 266. The Congo north and west of Katanga was, by contrast, "a genuinely primitive, tribal society, living partly in the jungle," partly in city suburbs "where unemployment and demagoguery ruled supreme" (ibid.).

Not all conservative visitors were as impressed by Elisabethville. The English writer Anthony Lejeune commented in March 1961 that it reminded him of "a small seaside town—out of season. Nothing works properly any more. Tshombe money looks like soap coupons and is worth about as much. . . . Everything is calm but there is an undercurrent of nerve-tearing tension. A little way to the north are the hostile Balubas: and the Balubas, not to put too fine a point on it, eat people" ("The Day Lumumba Died," 182).

because of industrialization, "a logical society dominated by thrift and hard work, by good education and well-organized social services."[72] Kuehnelt-Leddihn thought that a new type of African, which one might call a "Katangese man," might be emerging, thanks to the social services provided under colonial government and, in this case, by the Union Minière. These services had "led . . . to the creation of a new 'biological' type of second and even third generation workers who had grown up with the right vitamins, the right infant training, the right mental disposition."[73]

In the case of their leader, this mental disposition led to an unfashionable and commendable concern with Western interests. Therefore, argued the *National Review* (after reviewing the chaos and bloodshed taking place elsewhere under the auspices of "Lumumba's mountebanks"), Western countries should recover their nerve and stand by "the one Congo position that [had] held out, so far, against the tidal disintegration."[74] If the Katangese redoubt could be held (Buckley declared), it "would transform central Africa into a great bastion of Western strength, instead of the frightful vacuum into which it is now being turned."[75]

Having thus identified Tshombe and Katanga as an ideological ally, conservatives were not seriously bothered by the idea of supporting secession. If, as liberals protested, Katanga was not a nation, the Congo was hardly more so. Like most African countries, it was a tribal mosaic—a nation only by benefit of diplomatic courtesy. "The present map of the Congo," one writer noted, "is not a map of the land of one people, but a map of the drainage area of this second-largest of the world's rivers."[76]

72. The typical Katangan was, von Kuehnelt-Leddihn observed, an industrial worker who thought rationally and "realize[d] that an intricate plant cannot be run by the inspirations of medicine-men" ("What About Katanga?" 266).

73. Ibid. The phrase *Katangese man* is the author's, not Kuehnelt-Leddihn's.

74. Buckley, "Will the Jungle Take Over?" 30 July 1960, 39. Surveying the Congolese scene in December 1961, the *National Review* remarked gloomily: "The jungle and the ways of the jungle are beginning to recover those regions of the Congo . . . from which they had so precariously been beaten back . . . the Katanga region has been the lone Congolese rampart against the jungle's advance" ("Jungle Taking Over," 366).

75. "If," Buckley continued, "there were among the leaders of the West today a bold strategist of historical dimension, we believe that he would move at once to recognize Katanga's independence and to see that adequate force and aid were immediately sent to hold its structure together. The Katanga base could then become the attractive magnet around which a reconstituted civil order could be constructed" ("Will the Jungle Take Over?" 39).

76. Boulter, "The Congo . . . Seven Bloody Years," 8.

For conservatives, the implication was that, since the Congo was so artificial, each region could and should be free to pursue its interests as its leaders saw them, while the West should feel free to support those leaders who shared its values and its view of international politics. Buckley declared that the province had "at least as much formal right to independence as the Congo in general." Indeed, he thought, it was quite viable as a separate state. It had rail connections eastwards and could develop not only a federation with other dissidents in Kivu and Kasai provinces, but a "close and mutually profitable linkage with the Rhodesians to the east."[77]

Why, conservatives wondered, was the world "so dead set against letting Katanga decide what kind of regime and government" it wanted? Other countries had been allowed to break into two or more parts or, for that matter, to unite—all without much argument in liberal circles "over what kind of internal regime develop[ed]."[78] Moreover, other parts of the Congo were actually in a state of de facto secession (again, without being subject to much adverse comment from liberals). While the African and Western liberal press was full of earnest debate about ending Katanga's "neocolonialist" secession, nobody said anything about the effective secession of Orientale province, where (Kuehnelt-Leddihn pointed out) Antoine Gizenga was "doing pretty much as he please[d]."[79] In fact (some conservative commentators remarked), Tshombe was actually much more amenable to arguments for a federal Congo and much less of a principled (or unprincipled) secessionist than his critics alleged.[80]

77. "Will the Jungle Take Over?" 39.

78. "How to Cure the Congo," 88. The editors referred to the case of the ex-Belgian Trust Territory of Ruanda-Urundi which at independence had divided into two sovereign republics, Rwanda and Burundi.

79. "What about Katanga?" 266. The United Nations, Ernest Van den Haag complained, seemed quite willing to tolerate Gizenga's and Orientale's independence, arguing that, with patience and diplomacy, they would eventually come back into the Congo: "Why did the U.N. not feel that similar patience would have healed the breach between Katanga and the Central Government? Patience with Stanleyville was maintained in the face of many murders and atrocities. Those regions of Katanga in which the U.N. attack took place were calm. Patience toward Katanga would have spared the population much unnecessary suffering. Yet the U.N. was patient only in relation to Stanleyville, where intervention could have saved the Congolese people from unbelievably savage acts" ("The U.N. War in Katanga," 200).

80. Conservatives sometimes argued that Tshombe did not want a permanent separation from the Congo and that he had only led secession because (as Van

While arguing that Katanga was better governed and more orderly than the rest of the Congo, conservatives did not accept that the province's economic contribution was essential to the survival of the larger state. Other regions of the Congo had, a correspondent in *National Review* suggested, adequate mineral and natural resources of their own. It was therefore unnecessary to crush "Katanga's unique effort among the Congo people to achieve a peaceful and prosperous economy."[81]

Apart from claiming that Katanga was essential to Congolese economic development, liberals also claimed that Tshombe was not a legitimate political leader. This point was not usually challenged directly in organs such as the *National Review.* Conservative writers hardly ever broached the question of Tshombe's electoral mandate, or lack of it, which was so much an issue with liberals. They were evidently more concerned with the *quality* of Tshombe's government, the "civilized" quality of the society over which he presided, and the (in their eyes) admirable qualities of his foreign policies. Who had voted for whom was apparently a secondary consideration, especially given conservative skepticism about democracy in Africa and, indeed, elsewhere.

Occasionally, they did refer to the leftism of the Cartel katangais opposition, and after the ending of the secession the *National Review* reported several times on how popular Tshombe still was in Katanga.[82] But his

---

den Haag put it) "a dictatorial pro-Communist and lawless government of gangsters seemed to prevail under Lumumba" ("The U.N. War in Katanga," 199). Tshombe, in this view, wanted some kind of federalism and the right to negotiate with the other Africans in the Congo about the form that such federalism might take.

81. Rev. John Morrison, letter, 22 May 1962, 383. Kuehnelt-Leddihn, however, said that, without Katanga, the rest of the Congo " would be a bankrupt mass of jungles, swamps and rivers" ("Katanga's Case," 77). According to him, the Katangans disliked "the loud-mouthed politicians" in Leopoldville and did not want to have their resources used for such parasites and "for the benefit of distant, lazy and backward tribes with whom they had nothing in common" ("What about Katanga?" 266).

82. In April 1963, for example, the *National Review* reported that Tshombe had been touring Katanga, campaigning for a new federal constitution and that he was being "enthusiastically welcomed" everywhere ("Beats of the Heart of Darkness," 268). In August 1960, Philippa Schuyler wrote that the Cartel opposition in Katanga was largely "composed . . . of immigrant workers led by leftist officials of the Elisabethville University" and that it had helped to give power in Leopoldville to leftist parties, such as Lumumba's MNC ("Behind the Congo Crisis," 76).

popularity, they suggested, was that of a man of the people, not that of a slick-suited city politician. Tshombe, a reviewer of his autobiography remarked, was "Africa's most realistic and genuinely African leader," who "never forgot that the real Africa was 'the Africa of the peasants,' no matter how high-sounding the great discourse of Westerners on the problems of development."[83]

Interestingly, from arguing that Tshombe was a down-to-earth leader, conservatives did not usually take the further step of claiming that realism had led him (as it should in conservative philosophy) to construct a state on ethnic lines. Their defense of Katanga rested more on a negative proposition about the political unworkability of the Congo than on a positive identification of Katanga as a "proper" (that is, a tribally based) African state. They did refer to Tshombe's African credentials as a descendant of a ruling family, but they preferred to stress his "modern" qualifications (as a merchant and a politically astute leader of a wealthy territory).

To argue that Katanga was an "authentically African state" (one based on tribal identity) would, in fact, have been risky. As liberals pointed out, Katanga was (to put it politely) a multi-ethnic province; in the eyes of Tshombe's critics, his was a Lunda-dominated tribal tyranny, which was oppressing the members of the rival Baluba tribe.[84]

Conservatives denied that this was the case. Nevertheless, they generally defended Katanga's right to self-determination, negatively, by referring to the chaos and hopelessness of the rest of the Congo and, positively, by pointing to Tshombe's qualities as (in the *National Review*'s words) "a believer in orderly government, in a continuing alliance with the West, and in freedom of commerce."[85] It was therefore as much a duty as a right of Western conservatives to insist that their governments resist the blustering of third world countries in the UN and support leaders such as Tshombe who had the courage to be *truly* independent.

83. J. Bernard Burnham, review of Tshombe, *My Fifteen Months in Government*, 817.
84. The Lunda and Bayeke were, with the Baluba, the major ethnic groups in Katanga. Tshombe was a son-in-law of the Lunda paramount chief, the *Mwata Yamvo* Ditende Yawa Nawezi III (who supported Tshombe's CONAKAT party and whose subjects lived in Zambia and Angola as well as Katanga). Godefroid Munongo, his minister of the interior, was a grandson of Msiri, the Bayeke warrior who had established a complex kingdom in Katanga in the late nineteenth century, and a brother of the current Bayeke paramount chief.
85. "We're on Their Side," 403.

Conservatives and African Nationalism

If "African nationalists" were not—and could not be—real nationalists, what were they? What did "nationalist" leaders and movements actually stand for? Skeptical conservatives regularly suggested three possibilities, three alternative "isms" to nationalism—racism, communism, and opportunism.

Conservative critics frequently took the first choice. African nationalism, they claimed, signified the replacement of one essentially racial ideology by another.[86] This ideology involved great ambivalence about modernization (as, conservatives warned, liberals would discover to their chagrin in due course). It had all the capacity for erratic, violent, and petty behavior that such ambivalence created. Africa, declared Elspeth Huxley, was in fact sick—stricken by "the virus of black nationalism"— a virus spawned by envy. "To the African," wrote Kuehnelt-Leddihn, "the white man is still a fabulous creature who can do the most startling things anywhere and at any time. The African is like a child who marvels at the unexpected antics of grown-ups and who unthinkingly adopts their way of life and ideas."[87] Behind their rhetoric, James Burnham declared, what African "nationalists" really wanted was "to destroy the power and privileges of the white men; to take over their property, or most of it; and to permit white men to remain only as servants and handmaids."[88] Even

86. "The independence movement," Nathaniel Weyl declared, "is largely one of racial resentment against real and imaginary wrongs" ("The Ordeal of Negro Africa," 445). Patrice Lumumba, according to Sen. Thomas J. Dodd (a prominent congressional sympathizer with Tshombe), had at the time of the Congolese Force publique mutiny "fanned the flames and incited his people with demagogic appeals to black racism" ("Congo: The Untold Story," 137).

87. "The Afro-Asian Inferiority Complex," 836. "The black man [Molnar wrote] has a deep-seated admiration for the white man . . . independence, freedom, the amenities of modern life are associated in the average black man's mind with the white man's qualities, with whiteness" ("An Outsider Speaks," 134).

88. "The Loneliest Men," 164. Burnham considered that for Africans terms like *nationalism* and *self-determination* were "just ritual words, without substantial content" (ibid.). African nationalists, Anthony Lejeune asserted, were essentially dogmatic and destructive: "Every vestige of European control and restraint is to be swept away. There must be no compromises, no slow development, no 'fancy constitutions'" ("No Comfort for the West," 586). The *National Review* remarked in March 1959 on "savage eruptions of what the Liberal ideologues primly term 'African nationalism' . . . inflamed by the sorcerers' apprentices who beckon them on, the mobs work consequences which are purely destructive" (editorial, 28 March 1959, 604).

when the inner motives of African politicians were neither acquisitive nor destructive (Frank Meyer remarked), the results of their taking power would be disastrous. Neither African nationalism nor pan-Africanism would be "conducive to the technological progress so ardently proclaimed by the nationalist leaders as their goal."[89] Both would discourage the investment of foreign capital and use of foreigners' skills. Both would cause waste and instability, since the claims and ambitions of nationalist politicians would inevitably lead to tribal wars or to attempts at continental domination. Altogether, claimed the British writer Anthony Lejeune, African nationalism was merely an adopted term lending respectability to the most visceral racialist feelings.[90]

Communism—whether as provocateur or as ultimate beneficiary—was, in conservative eyes, the second most probable accomplice or source of inspiration of African "nationalism." Conservatives frequently alleged that leading nationalist leaders were Communists or communist agents. John Foster Dulles, for example, claimed that the colonial territories had been "marked out by International Communism as special prey." Once the nationalists had got rid of the colonial powers, he predicted, the Communists would "move in to 'amalgamate' the newly independent peoples into the Communist bloc."[91]

Individual leaders sometimes acquired almost demonic stature in conservative eyes. Patrice Lumumba of the Congo was variously described in the *National Review* as a "bold, psychotic adventurer," "a small-time megalomaniac crook," and "Moscow's Man."[92] The *National Review* and other conservative journals applauded his removal by Mobutu in the autumn

89. "The Prickly Dilemmas," 14.

90. "The black man's envy and resentment [Lejeune wrote] now go very deep. . . . Racial vanity has become the touchstone of all his affairs" ("Africa without Fear and Favor," 833).

91. Quoted in Satterthwaite, "The Challenge of the Hour," 11.

92. "Grand Guignol," *National Review*, 27 August 1960, 102; Lejeune, "The Day Lumumba Died," 182; James Burnham, "At the Crack of Khrushchev's Whip," 272.

Tshombe, on the other hand, was described as "the most dazzling politician in the Congo" (*Time*, 3 December 1965, 34). Two months earlier, *Time* had described Tshombe as "the Congo's most popular politician" (22 October 1965, 45). In its issue for the same week, *Newsweek* reported that Tshombe was "indisputably the most powerful single figure in the Congo" (25 October 1965, 48). Whatever Tshombe's popularity might have been, events in the succeeding month showed that Mobutu was the more powerful of the two.

of 1960 as a blow to communist designs on the Congo (designs which, they alleged, were being abetted by the United Nations). Lumumba's murder in February 1961 called forth, not the grief and anger apparent in the left and liberal press, but rather expressions of relief.[93]

Burnham, for his part, noted the occurrence in Central Africa of "wild rioting in which Communist agents invariably play[ed] their part." In West Africa, he reported, observers had seen "Communist agents, money and arms pour from Communist ships into Communist-trained Sekou Toure's Guinea."[94] Everywhere "Communist-trained operatives" were doing their bit to turn Africa into a "bloodily boiling cauldron."[95]

One conservative view thus had Communists directly involved in fomenting and organizing anticolonial nationalism. Another saw them as residual legatees of the chaos and tribal conflict that such movements would inevitably produce. This view was popular among Republican politicians who were unwilling to condemn nationalism as Communist-led, but who worried about the possibility that independence would prove (as Dulles put it) "but a brief interlude between the rule of colonialism and the harsh dictatorship of International Communism."[96]

Such an outcome was all the more likely, many conservatives believed, given the unscrupulous opportunism and demagoguery of nationalist politicians, and the unimaginable gullibility of their followers.[97] Elspeth Huxley found that people in the bush were often "unable to resist the

93. On this occasion, the *National Review* observed: "What is surprising is not that Patrice Lumumba was killed, but that he stayed alive so long, once he had been taken captive. . . . We cannot mourn his death, any more than we would mourn the death of any other treacherous, deadly foe slain in a continuing, ferocious war" ("All the King's Horses," 102). According to another *National Review* contributor, "The tragic end of Patrice Lumumba . . . illustrated the dangers of associating national movements of liberation with sorcery, witch doctors and fetishism" (Gilbert Comte, "Are There Any Conservative Africans?" 491). The writer—an ex-French colonial administrator—did not enlarge on this statement.

94. "Watch out for That Back Door!" 11.

95. Burnham, "What Kind of War?" 228.

96. Quoted in Satterthwaite, "The Challenge of the Hour," 11. Stephen Weissman has noted that moderate Republicans "emphasized the wildness and instability of the new states and their consequent openness to external adversaries" (Stephen R. Weissman, *American Foreign Policy in the Congo, 1960–1964* [Ithaca, NY: Cornell University Press, 1974], 257).

97. "Native politicians," commented a writer in *Reader's Digest*, "inflame men of unbelievable ignorance and Communist agents wait hopefully to take over from the politicians" (Drake, "Don't Decry Colonialism," 65).

blandishments of demagogues." Such people, she noted, were typically "only one generation removed from tribalism, still fearful of magic and ancestral spirits," overwhelmingly "illiterate and ignorant of the larger world." Even in urban areas, Molnar commented, migrants were "an easy prey to demagogues."[98]

Abandoned by their colonial mentors to the mercy of such rapacious and cynical leaders, Africans could (conservative observers unanimously believed) only look forward to corruption and collapse after independence. The result of the abdication encouraged by liberals would be a collapse of effective and responsible government in most parts of Africa, the disappearance of whatever measure of democracy and self-determination had ever been achieved, and probably the actual disintegration of a number of nominal "nation-states" into tribal kingdoms or empires. Events in the ex-Belgian Congo (James Burnham wrote in October 1960) were but "a mild prelude to what is coming . . . the expectation must be of a crackup of the new African structure even before it is formally completed. As tribal savagery blasts the cobweb framework from the bottom, aspiring local gauleiters . . . backed by Moscow, London, Washington, Paris, will strike out for the crown of a black Alexander." Given the artificiality of the new states, the depth of tribal loyalties, and the "incredibly low" cultural level of the population, the problem of Africa's future could not be solved, Burnham warned, "according to the dreams of Western liberalism. . . . It can be solved as it was for many centuries, by suspension in a primitive, pre-civilized, static tribal frame . . . the greater part of Black Africa cannot rule itself except in a condition of savagery; and even if immensely better endowed, could not, granted the hodgepodge of the new political structure."[99]

Conservatives and Independent Africa

For American conservatives, the course of postindependence politics was to be a mournful vindication of their warnings about premature decolonization. For them, it would also be a continuing demonstration of the spiritual, intellectual, and political bankruptcy of the liberal creed applied to foreign affairs.

98. Huxley, "Two Revolutions That Are Changing Africa," 69. Molnar, "Rhodesia at the Crossroads," 972.
99. "What Is Ahead for Black Africa?" 240.

As a result of the chaos after independence in the Congo, the more pessimistic forecasts tended to become apocalyptic in tone—all the more so because of the high regard that conservative commentators had for the Belgians.[100] Many, indeed, drew specifically on images of the Congo—both physical and political—to illustrate their premonitions about the future of the continent. For example, one writer likened Africans' facile expectations about independence to "that tropical plant called the water hyacinth which floats with similar aplomb down the long course of the Congo River, only to be dashed to bits when it reaches the rapids at the lower end."[101] One month after the Congo became independent, the *National Review* quoted the South African writer Stuart Cloete on the imminent disappearance of civilization in the area: "The jungle is a living force that will close over houses in a matter of weeks and trees will grow through roofs. In a few days machinery lying untended is ruined. . . . Communications, always precarious, will soon cease to exist. Floods and landslides and normal jungle growth will close the roads. . . . The Leopard men and Crocodile men will reappear, cannibalism be resumed and the great Congo basin return to sleep."[102] One year after the Congo became independent, the editor of *National Review* endorsed this view. The moral of the terrible first year, Buckley declared, was that black Africans, "with some but insufficient exceptions," could not handle their own political and economic affairs.[103] The implication was that to implement self-government elsewhere would "turn one after another additional area of Africa into Congos."

As the rebellion against the Portuguese got under way further south, conservative writers had similar dire visions of the future of Angola. After talking to some unpersuasive guerrillas, Thomas Molnar recalled: "In my mind's eye, I saw the lights of Luanda go out under careless city management, grass grow again in the streets as it does in Leopoldville, and

100. Frequent *National Review* contributors such as Elspeth Huxley and Erik von Kuehnelt-Leddihn spoke warmly of Belgian achievements. The Belgians, Huxley remarked, had "gone all out for the health, wealth, and material happiness of their fourteen million Congolese" ("The Nationalist Tide Sweeps Africa," 30). They had, Kuehnelt-Leddihn wrote, "protected the natives against tyrannical chiefs and against overbearing tribes" ("Letter from the Congo," 393).

101. Mildred Adams, "Key Pieces in the African Puzzle," 75.

102. "Will the Jungle Take Over?" 39.

103. "They tend [Buckley said] to revert to savagery against both whites and their own civilized minority, and in their own mode of existence" ("Rx Africa: The Kennedy Doctrine," 170).

insecurity with its twin, demagogy, take control."[104] Elspeth Huxley had
a much more detailed picture of the decade to come. She prophesied that
by 1969 the continent's population would have risen to three hundred
million, 75 percent of whom would be under independent governments:
"Democracy, as we understand it, will be dead or dying. . . . Government
will be in the hands of small cliques of power-wielders supported by
parties prepared to stamp out ruthlessly any challenge . . . at the end of
the decade Nkrumah (discounting accidents) may be the most powerful
man in Africa. Thanks to Nkrumah's campaign [for African unity], the
newly independent African states may be linked into two or three loose
confederations."[105] The one-party state, the conflicts in the Congo, Nigeria, Rhodesia, and Angola, the advent of military government—all were
seen as vindications of conservative warnings about the dangers of decolonization—and of unheeded conservative warnings about the follies
of liberalism at large in the world.

Independence and Democracy

Of all the hollow claims made by liberals, the worst in conservative eyes
were those to do with the future of democracy in Africa and the imputed
benevolence of her new rulers. Conservatives were especially scathing
about liberal expectations of democracy in Africa. They were also utterly
skeptical about liberal claims on behalf of single-party states, whether as
a form of indigenous democracy or as a framework for economic development.

To conservatives, decolonization had completely different political implications from those discerned by liberals, who apparently expected an
African replay of the American Revolution. Conservatives ridiculed such
expectations: "Voters who cross themselves beneath the image of a rhinoceros, or of an elephant sitting on a triangle, do not necessarily institute
governments as envisaged by Thomas Jefferson, Rousseau or Mazzini."[106]
In their view, liberals were only able to maintain their preposterous hopes
for democracy south of the Sahara because they clung to two, almost
willful, pieces of misunderstanding—a misunderstanding of the African

104. "The Truth about Angola," 280.
105. "The Nationalist Tide Sweeps Africa," 35.
106. Von Kuehnelt-Leddihn, "How Europe Sees Foreign Aid," 484.

political environment, and a misunderstanding of African nationalism and its leaders.

The problem about the environment was, as Burnham put it, that "the social premises" for democracy did not exist. Trying to sell liberal democracy to Africans was, Elspeth Huxley said, like selling "television sets before there is any electricity."[107] The depth and persistence of tribalism meant (as, indeed, many liberals acknowledged) that there was an insufficient sense of common interest, of shared citizenship among the population in African countries. Once "the focus of unity" provided by anticolonialism had gone, "the disruptive, centrifugal forces of tribalism" would destroy any basis for effective stable democracy (and perhaps any basis for effective national government).[108] The truth was, Huxley argued, that democracy and tribalism were incompatible: "You cannot combine a democratic system with a tribal setup. The old warfare of spear and assegai simply gets translated into a warfare of votes and parties."[109]

Like Immanuel Wallerstein and other liberal "nation builders," conservatives tended to argue that the only alternative to disintegration was authoritarian central government. Unlike the nation builders, however, conservatives usually had little expectation that authoritarianism would help economic development. Some (including Elspeth Huxley) did argue that authoritarian government might be not only necessary but constructive. More typically, though, conservatives took a firmly pessimistic view of the emerging authoritarianism. Dictatorships would arise, they said, because the divisions of plural societies created opportunities for dictatorships or because Africans were naturally or culturally disposed to authoritarianism.[110] The accompanying rhetoric about "nation building" was, in their view, just that, and those who took it seriously were heading for serious disappointment.

107. Huxley, "Two Revolutions That Are Changing Africa," 69. Burnham, "The Explosion of Africa," 140.

108. Huxley, "A Confusion of Colonels," 467. "The normal, preferred relation between tribe X and tribe Y [Burnham wrote] is, often enough, hostility: a hostility that may express itself in torture, killing, cannibalism. The white man's law, religion, power blocked the outward expression, but did not have time to dry up the inward source" ("What Is Ahead for Black Africa?" 240).

109. "Africa's First Loyalty," 110.

110. Commenting on the stability brought to Zaire by Mobutu, the *National Review* remarked in 1970: "Left to their own, most of the successful newly independent states in Africa have evolved authoritarian one-party governments that seem, the more's the pity, to fit their needs" (Editorial, 14 July 1970, 713).

Liberals (conservatives believed) had misunderstood nationalist leaders because they had failed to appreciate how opportunistically these leaders had behaved before independence. In particular, they had allowed themselves to be manipulated by leaders skilled in telling foreign liberals what they wanted to hear—that Africans, leaders and led, were "good liberals too, moderate, eager to compromise, full of childlike faith in the sanctity of agreements and the virtues of the ballot box."[111]

If this was what they believed, then (conservatives warned) liberals were "due for some nasty shocks." African political tradition showed little concern for democracy, dissent, or, indeed, individual rights in any form.[112] Indeed, so powerful was the authority of chief and elders in African custom that before colonial rule there had been no need for police or prisons.[113] The resulting, almost mystical deference to authority was likely to carry over into postcolonial politics, inhibiting the development of a democratic outlook.[114] Indeed, being unused to choice, Africans were also unused to compromise and negotiation: "When Africans approach the point at which they must choose, differences often become violent. Thus far Africans do not easily discipline themselves to the technique of quiet elections. They seem happier in a state of clamor: long tribal habits divide them into a great number of small groups preferring to beat drums and shout for local leaders rather than to develop national political skill."[115] Given both their respect for power ("Africans respect a winner," in *Time*'s phrase) and their shrill partisanship, Africans were unlikely to

111. Lejeune, "Cult of the Messiah," 330. The language of African leaders, Nathaniel Peffer remarked, "was convincing to Western liberals, especially American liberals who wanted to believe and did" ("Colonialism: New Problems for Old?" 72–73).

112. In precolonial society, Robert Coughlan observed, "the prevailing method of rule was authoritarian, often at the point of a spear" ("Black Africa Surges to Independence," 102).

113. As Elspeth Huxley wrote: "Not even the most hardened criminal challenged the authority of the chief or the council of elders who sat in judgment, because behind their verdict lay all the sanctions of the supernatural world" ("Africa's First Loyalty," 24).

114. This emphasis on the authoritarianism of precolonial societies was not, of course, limited to conservative writings, as some of the quotations in chapter 3 make clear. For example, Mildred Adams wrote in the *New York Times*: "An African brought up under the rigid discipline of the tribe may find it hard to adjust his habits, his ways of thought and his sense of personal responsibility to the complexities of democracy" ("Key Pieces in the African Puzzle," 75).

115. Ibid.

take to the milder, duller, and more egalitarian practices of democracy. Their history and culture disposed them, Thomas Molnar thought, to be intolerant of deviation: "The tribe has been everything, the individual nothing; innovators have been denounced, intimidated, put to death by neighbors, elders, witch doctors. Even today, the individual's efforts are thwarted, absorbed by tribal obligations, parasitism, and palavering."[116] Nor, as liberals fondly believed, were Africans especially peaceful. "Their history," noted Elspeth Huxley, "is one long record of warfare, bloodshed, conquest, and strife, just like the record of other peoples."[117]

Now, Huxley and others saw much to admire in African tribal organization and belief (for example, the rather humane African attitude to war).[118] Indeed, the strong sense of community in African societies appealed to them (as it did to some socialists). Nor, in fact, did a lack of democracy necessarily bother them. Much more troubling, indeed, to conservatives was the inanity of what one writer called "the doctrine of egalitarian numerical intuitivism" (the notion that a process in which authority was based on a majority of equally weighted votes would produce good government).[119]

The general point that conservatives wanted to make was that, their own beliefs and assessments of tribal life aside, Africa offered no hope of realizing even the most qualified liberal expectations of democracy. Such expectations were foolish because they were based on shallow analysis which disregarded African tradition and culture. The Congo experience had been salutary, conservatives thought, in destroying "the dreamy illusion that took such a terrible toll in money and blood—that the Congo and other African states could make a leap from colonial dependency to full-fledged democracy overnight."[120]

Liberals (as we have see) did regard "tradition" and "culture" as phenomena that were derivative and malleable, while for conservatives they

116. "African Paradox," 826. Erik von Kuehnelt-Leddihn similarly declared: "Tribalism is . . . an anti-personal collectivist force" ("Africa in Perspective," 424).
117. "Disengagement in Africa," 96.
118. "Africans are in many ways more civilized than Europeans or Americans. By comparison with our wars, tribal wars in Africa are rather genteel: bloodletting is usually kept to a minimum by tacit mutual agreement" (Alsop, "Africa: The Riddle without an Answer," 84).
119. Kuehnelt-Leddihn, "The Mozambique Story," 232.
120. Editorial, *National Review,* 14 July 1970, 713.

were fundamental and determinative. In this instance, conservatives held that the political attitudes and institutions of postcolonial Africa, so far from transcending or supplanting precolonial institutions and values, actually embodied and perpetuated them. The one-party state was thus a new expression of the organic instincts of precolonial society. Similarly, the "charismatic leader," beloved of modernization theorists like David Apter, actually incorporated the mystical authority of chieftaincy.

Moreover, conservatives believed that, to the extent that the conditions of political life had changed, they had actually become less favorable to democracy. The immense gap between leaders and led weakened accountability, and modernization created seemingly insatiable material appetites in some politicians. In this respect, conservatives tended to share the disillusioned liberals' view of African politicians (the difference being, of course, that the conservatives never held any other view). African politicians, according to Chester A. Crocker and William H. Lewis, were not the earnest developmentalists of liberal imagining: "Except at the rhetorical level, development is not the only goal of African leaders or even the principal one of most. Like politicians everywhere, they are concerned first with acquiring and retaining office. Any other assumption smacks of romanticism."[121] The power-hunger and venality of the postcolonial political class had been foreshadowed in earthier terms in an exchange which Elspeth Huxley had with an African minister in 1957: "The spirit of the English Puritans, he said, acclimatized in North America, doesn't thrive in Africa. 'It needs a cold winter,' he smiled. 'You never find it in the sunny countries—Spain, Italy, South America.' He waved his cigar in an expansive gesture. 'It may be,' he added, 'that we shall revert to more *human* standards.'"[122]

In subsequent years, conservative journals assiduously documented what Lejeune called "the indolence, incompetence and petty dishonesty of postcolonial Africa," as well an array of alleged instances of primitive and superstitious practices.[123] In particular, they frequently compared the

121. "Missing Opportunities in Africa," 156.
122. "Two Revolutions That Are Changing Africa," 69–70; emphasis in original.
123. "Africa without Fear or Favor," 833. At different times, the *National Review* referred (with obvious relish) to such alleged instances of primitivism as a ban on the export to the Congo of cans with labels picturing human beings (because they would be misunderstood by cannibal consumers); the bathing of the feet of President Kaunda of Zambia in blood by members of his cabinet; the construction

performance of African governments unfavorably with that of colonial and settler-dominated governments, even suggesting that ordinary Africans would have preferred to be back under colonial rule.[124]

Given what they saw as endemic mismanagement and tyranny in African states, conservatives had little time for African leaders who demanded democracy and human rights in white-ruled states and complained about exploitation and inequality in the international economy. Their outrage at the seeming hypocrisy and double standards of these leaders (and their Western apologists) increased as Africa fell under military rule. Liberals, they complained, were silent and indulgent regarding the violence and usurpations of power in Nigeria and other black-ruled countries, while relentlessly assaulting Ian Smith and the white rulers of Rhodesia as a "minority government." Who, said James Burnham, were the African leaders to complain about "minority government"? For, "in all Africa, there is not a single government that can show a legitimate claim to representing anything more than a minority—in most cases a considerably smaller minority than in Rhodesia. . . . Africa is unique only in the rigor of its devotion to minority rule."[125]

Liberal silence on the violence in Nigeria in 1965 and 1966 provided, Elspeth Huxley declared, a perfect specific example of a double standard at work: "In a logical world, it would be hard to explain why Mr Smith who took over a country he was already legally governing without a shot, without a murder, a trial, or even a coup, is a wicked, lawless villain unfit to be negotiated with by decent men; whereas those who seize control of their country by force and shoot, arrest or exile the existing rulers, and then establish a military dictatorship, are immediately recognized as the praiseworthy heads of a respectable legal movement."[126] Huxley's comments provoked a complaint by a *National Review* reader that the comparison was unfair. The Nigerian coup, the reader argued, had been "the active expression of popular feeling," whereas Smith's Unilat-

---

by a political rival of a lyre made from the nerve fiber of the prime minister of Burundi's grandfather; the dumping of a handbag containing fetish objects into a public reservoir in Accra, Ghana, in order to induce drinkers of the water to vote for a particular election candidate; and a ban on daytime tom-tom playing in the Central African Republic. The Accra incident was widely reported and constituted evidence in a major trial. No sources were given for the other stories.

124. Molnar, "An Outsider Speaks," 146–47.

125. "Global Apartheid?" *National Review,* 18 October 1966, 1036.

126. "The Rope That Hanged Nkrumah," 269.

eral Declaration of Independence in 1965 (and the government he led) had no such support.[127] To this, Huxley replied that, while she did not support white minority rule, Smith's government was at least legally constituted, whereas the Nigerian government had come to power through "a violent and arbitrary act."[128]

Conservatives found the same hypocrisy in African positions on human rights. They complained that the only human rights Africans cared about were those of Africans infringed by whites. With this exception, Kenneth L. Adelman observed, "African leaders concede they have little interest in Western concepts of human rights."[129] For example (David Reed pointed out), President Nyerere of Tanzania was ever ready to denounce "racial injustices in South Africa," but a visitor to his country would quickly find that Nyerere himself had kept "black people under lock and key without trial, some for eight years now."[130]

In at least one respect, the conservatives' pessimistic view of African politics led them to be more accurate than their rivals about Africa's future. Specifically, they predicted the potential for military coups in Africa earlier and more clearly than most liberals. As early as 1961, Duignan and Gann wrote that in African states "power either must become highly centralized or anarchy is likely to ensue." It followed that "new independent nations may easily fall under army rule."[131] When they did so, conservatives declared themselves vindicated in having warned that Africa was not ready for democracy or self-government. Events in Nigeria, Senator Ellender reportedly said in 1966, proved that "the educational and cultural advancement of the African was in such a primitive stage that he could not govern himself nor operate the ordinary machinery of organized society, at least in the American or European sense."[132]

127. Letter from Robert J. Palmeri, 3 May 1966, 390, 435.

128. The *National Review,* 3 May 1966, 435. Huxley remarked that she did not believe "that the rule of a white minority in Africa can, or should, endure. Nor do I believe in the African nationalists's one-man-one-vote now. You reach compromises by reasoning with people, not by bludgeoning them."

129. "The Black Man's Burden," 89.

130. "The Rocky Road to Freedom," 232.

131. The army, they pointed out, was Westernized; it cut across "local and clan ties"; and, not least, it did "after all have the best weapons" ("The Case for the White Man," 18).

Writing of the January 1966 coup in Nigeria, Elspeth Huxley commented that the only surprise was that a coup had not occurred earlier ("Death in Nigeria," 163).

132. Cited in Grundy, "The Congressional Image of Africa," 12.

As long as military rulers were able to claim convincingly that they were ensuring order, they could attract favorable comment in conservative journals (as in David Reed's sympathetic account of President Mobutu of Zaire).[133] Usually, however, they were suspected of being simple dictators, and especially so when they used the liberal-enticing rhetoric of "nation building" and "development."

Independence and Nationalism

Other African governments than military ones did, however, attract conservative sympathy. They did so because they avoided the specific political vices that conservatives discerned in most states and because they confirmed conservative prejudices about the conditions for statehood and self-determination in Africa.

Biafra: Romantics vs. Realists

One of the strongest such prejudices, we noted above, was that in favor of "naturally" small, tribally based polities and against large, "artificial," and centralized states. In the early sixties, this prejudice had moved conservatives to support Katanga: in the late sixties, it moved them to equally partisan support of another secessionist movement, that of Biafra. This support was qualified only by "realist" concerns about backing pro-Western regimes (such as Nigeria had at least until 1967) and by a philosophical reluctance to get actively involved in obscure foreign disputes which did not obviously endanger American interests.

Conservatives were certainly quick to see parallels between Biafra and Katanga. In April 1967, James Burnham remarked that Nigeria seemed to be "on the verge of doing a Congo. The Congo analogy is, in fact, surprisingly complete. Eastern Nigeria, with its oil and its tribal distinc-

133. "When it comes to an iron will backed up by an iron fist, few are in Mobutu's league. Each time he speaks on the radio, life in the capital halts. The stern voice booms out in all government offices, shops and bars, as well as from car radios. Everyone hangs on every word. . . . However much he and other African presidents may posture in their roles as uncrowned kings, it can be argued that it is necessary at this stage of African development. . . . Beneath the carryings-on, there is method in what Mobutu is doing . . . trying to create a nation in a country of 250 quarrelling tribes" ("The Rocky Road to Freedom," 224).

tions, corresponds to Katanga with its copper. Eastern Nigeria resists domination by the northerners who control the central government in Lagos, just as Katanga resisted domination by the northerners in control of Leopoldville. Eastern Nigeria's Military Governor, the Ibo Odumegwu Ojukwu, corresponds to Katanga's Lunda chief, Moise Tshombe."[134] While it was true, the *National Review* admitted, that Ojukwu did not have the same backing from the ex-colonial power as Tshombe, yet he was "an equally formidable operator."[135]

Conservatives argued that the Congo and Nigeria were crucially similar in that they had been created "more for the convenience of colonial administration than for reasons of tribal feeling."[136] Like many liberals, conservatives such as Elspeth Huxley admired Nigerian democracy, but their instincts told them that such a huge state must be fragile and liable to break into fragments corresponding to tribal identity and tradition.[137] The January 1966 coup and its aftermath, they claimed, exposed the folly of trying to keep such artificial states in existence, especially one such as Nigeria which was really "four separate and largely hostile nations."[138] The Federation as established by the British had merely enabled one "na-

134. "Clouds over the Golden Horn," 342. Burnham wondered sardonically whether the United Nations would be sending a force to put down any secession that occurred.

American conservatives were not the only people to see a parallel. At the September 1968 meeting of the Organization of African Unity, President Mobutu of Zaire explicitly compared the Biafran secession to that of Katanga in 1960, arguing that both movements had enjoyed the support of "the neocolonialists" (Cynthia Kahn, "The O.A.U.: Hurrying Nowhere?" 2). Zaire, incidentally, was one of the most stalwart and vocal supporters of the Federal Military Government in Nigeria throughout the Biafran war.

135. Two weeks after the Biafran declaration of independence, the *National Review* commented that there were "uncomfortably close" parallels between the Nigerian conflict and the earlier situation in the Congo. In each case, "the most prosperous region . . . tired of political domination by less sophisticated tribes," had broken away ("Nigerian Breakaway," 625).

136. Ibid.

137. At the time of the 1964 elections, Huxley remarked: "There is no one-party state. This will be a pretty genuine election . . . the voters will be offered a genuine choice rather than a set of stooges" ("As Nigeria Goes," 1,106). But she also commented: "The crust of Nigerian unity is very thin and there are ominous cracks just under the surface."

138. Huxley, "Death in Nigeria," 163. "Nigeria [Huxley commented in 1968] is not a nation, never has been a nation and lacks even the makings of one" ("Sacred Cow," 962).

tion''—the Hausa-Fulani north—to make colonial subjects of the southerners.[139]

The theme of the artificiality of African states appeared again in much conservative writing on the civil war itself. When Biafra formally seceded, the *National Review* commented:

> There is little to be said for the federation. And what there is to be said will be said with assegais. Most Nigerians would undoubtedly find it more congenial if the Regions became separate states. Each Region separately is larger and more viable than many independent African states. Besides, the encouraging political and economic sophistication in much of Nigeria will bloom faster if regional leaders are not eternally occupied in squabbling with a ramshackle federation—which has bred little but corruption and top-heavy bureaucracy.[140]

In Elspeth Huxley's view, it had always been obvious that "the end of colonialism would spell the resumption of the ancient tussle for power between tribes and peoples that had been suspended by colonial conquest

139. As Huxley wrote: "This is a colonial situation, of course. The white colonialists have gone, the black ones have stayed, and now they are getting the same treatment, only with far more violence, bloodshed, and hatred" ("Death in Nigeria," 163).

The coup which had brought Ironsi to power had therefore been "an act of Ibo retaliation against the domination of the Hausa-speaking Northerners," a rejection of the "colonialism exercised by non-Negro Northerners." This was an unusual case of a Biafran sympathizer accepting the view of the January 1966 coup propagated by the Federal government and the northerners. Usually, Biafran sympathizers argued that the coup was national in character: the heavy involvement of Ibo officers in the action and their subsequent prominence in the military government were, in this view, coincidental and insignificant.

140. "Nigerian Breakaway," 625. Nothing that happened in the next two and a half years changed the journal's view of the significance of the conflict in Nigeria. In its obituary on Biafra, published in January 1970, the *National Review* commented: "The nations of Africa are still largely artificial constructs, agglomerations of traditionally hostile tribes glued together with the most watery of cements" ("The End of Biafra," 72). Elspeth Huxley, the journal's main writer on Nigeria, consistently took the same view. In August 1967, she wrote: "Whatever happens now Nigeria must be fragmented. This was inevitable. It was the colonial power that brought together the many separate and often hostile races, faiths, tribes and ill-assorted geographical areas into one hotch-potch state. . . . As soon as the British left, their creation began to crumble. This crumbling process is still incomplete, but it has come into the open" ("Biafra Libre," 896).

for little more than half a century. . . . A country so deeply divided as Nigeria by race, religion and history can be united by one means only, namely conquest."[141]

Given the diversity of Nigeria—and the special character of the Ibos— there was, Huxley concluded, "no valid reason why Biafra should not have been allowed its freedom from Lagos, just as Lagos was allowed its freedom from London."[142]

Conservative treatment of the war was consistently sympathetic toward Biafra. Like much liberal writing, it consistently emphasized tribal characteristics, especially those of the Ibos. A sympathetic conservative congressman remarked that the Ibo people were "the most advanced and educated of any in tropical Africa," and in fact much like Americans.[143]

As the war continued and when it ended, however, conservative commentary revealed a tension between strongly committed supporters of Biafra and the "realists" who, though sympathetic to Biafra, felt that the United States had, in both cultural and geopolitical senses, little interest in Africa. By the summer of 1968, even the "romantics" recognized that Biafra was likely to fail (though in fact it survived until January 1970). But, with great bitterness, they blamed the outside world for the imminent collapse. Biafra, said Huxley, had "failed to engage the sympathies of the outside world. . . . The genocide of Ibos will be incomplete. . . . Despite all their starving children and babies bulldozed into communal graves the Ibos will survive; but not their hopes of independence. Uhuru is for the strong, they are not strong enough."[144]

In appealing to conservative readers, Huxley used the ready, contem-

---

141. Much of the blame for the Nigerian tragedy, Huxley argued, could be placed on the British who, in Nigeria, central Africa, and elsewhere, had made of "federalism, i.e., centralism . . . a sacred cow" ("Sacred Cow," 962).

142. Ibid., 975.

143. Rep. Donald Lukens wrote: "They have many traits similar to Americans': initiative, a determination to pull themselves up by their bootstraps, a democratic tradition. They are, or were before the war, exceptionally prosperous. They have governed themselves throughout their history by electing their own leaders" ("The Right to Live," 79). Elspeth Huxley described the Ibos as "a lusty and quick-witted race of Negroes"—"energetic, resourceful, ambitious and persistent" ("Death in Nigeria," 163; "Biafra Libre," 896). In Huxley's view, there was no doubt about their courage and determination: "Whatever General Gowon's forces may do [she wrote in August 1967], these Ibos are not going to give in. They will die first" ("Biafra Libre," 921).

144. "Sacred Cow," 975.

porary parallel of the crushing of the "Prague spring" by Warsaw Pact forces: "It is the same drama: the crushing of a small nation struggling for freedom by a large one as determined as ever the Nazis were to apply a final solution . . . hopes of freedom for the East and Central European peoples, and hopes of survival for the Ibo nation, seem to have been snuffed out in a single week."[145] Huxley and conservatives such as Rep. Donald Lukens of Ohio wanted the United States government to endorse "the right of Biafra to live and to determine its own future for itself."[146]

But "realists" such as William F. Buckley, Jr., while sympathetic to Biafra, felt that Americans were "right to stay out of that political controversy." Buckley accepted that the world was callous toward the Biafrans—"such a damned gallant people"—and he too compared their treatment to that of the victims of Communist power (in this instance, the kulaks).[147]

Yet from beginning to end Buckley opposed involvement on the part of the United States. Americans, he observed, knew little about the Nigerian conflict and those who did made "arbitrary commitments."[148] The American government and the United Nations, Buckley and his *National Review* colleagues urged in June 1967, should not support either side in the war. They "should do nothing to aid [Gowon's] efforts to re-establish the *status quo ante*. The United States should not waste time, blood and platitudes in efforts to shackle together those who would be asunder."[149]

The same studied remoteness colored Buckley's comments on the eventual collapse of Biafra in January 1970. He acknowledged that the Biafrans had "fought brilliantly" and would have won and achieved nation-

145. "Sacred Cow," 962. Liberal supporters of Biafra often drew a parallel between the fate of the Ibos and that of the Jews under the Nazis. Not all, however, accepted this analogy, at least insofar as it implied the conduct of genocide by the Federal government.

146. Lukens, "The Right to Live," 78. This statement was made only seven months before Biafra collapsed.

147. "The suffering of the Ibo people [Buckley wrote] is on a scale unparalleled since the Communist starvations of the Kulaks in the mid-Thirties, and somehow nothing is being done about it ("Where's Biafra?" 924–25).

148. Ibid. In this article, Buckley noted that African problems were largely ignored in the United States as long as they did not involve whites. This general indifference, he suggested, explained why "so little attention [had] been given to the horrors of the Biafran secessionist war."

149. "Nigerian Breakaway," 625.

hood if they had been properly armed. Yet, he continued, nobody had done anything to help them and this was probably just as well: "Legitimate moral outrage must often be subordinated to national and international interests. And this is what happened in Biafra. It simply served no Western interests to support Biafra." American intervention would have set a bad precedent, and Nigeria was "especially important to the West, potentially the most prosperous and powerful pro-Western nation in black Africa." Rather abruptly, Buckley concluded: "But it's over now and our national interests have probably been well served by neutrality. . . . Conscience is not elastic, and one regrets deeply the necessity to attempt to stretch it for the sake of such abstractions as the virtue of centralization and sphere of influence politics."[150]

Despite differences about what outsiders should do, conservatives agreed about the general significance of the Biafran war. In their view, it proved that states such as Nigeria and the Congo were both unwieldy and unloved: in the long run, they were probably undesirable as well. They should be dismantled and replaced by states that corresponded to Africa's "natural" (that is, tribal) communities.

Beyond this shared assumption, conservative commentators (admittedly a small group) divided into those (such as Huxley) who positively admired aspects of African tradition and those (such as Buckley) who were mainly concerned about the harmful pretensions of the new African states to international stability and American interests.

To the former, the Biafran struggle had great symbolic importance and cried out for active involvement by outsiders. To the latter, Africa was of little diplomatic and still less cultural significance. Even their expressions of sympathy were sometimes couched in terms of the anti-Communist struggle. Ultimately, while sympathizing with the Biafrans, they felt that national interest dictated staying friendly with the Federal government, partly perhaps to limit Soviet influence in Lagos.

Yet even the growth of Soviet influence did not seem (at this point) to worry conservatives as much as it did earlier or later. Rather, they were inclined to concentrate on problems elsewhere. Americans, James Burnham concluded after a month's trip around the continent in 1967, should practice "a considerably stricter non-intervention in Africa for the supposed sake of either doing good or correcting evil. . . . [The Africans] have got to solve their own internal problems, including both one-man

150. "The End of Biafra," 72, 73.

one-vote and no-man no-vote . . . either they will solve the problems or the problems won't be solved."[151]

The problem in interpreting conservative writing on Africa, as on other political issues, is that much of it consists of criticism of the liberal orthodoxy, its authors' own values and preferences being implied or assumed. This characteristic makes it especially important to pinpoint the fundamental areas of difference between conservative and other writers on Africa.

The central assertion of conservatives, the contention lurking behind all the *National Review*'s anecdotes about African politicians bathing each other's feet in blood, throwing bewitched handbags into reservoirs, and so on, seems to concern the inevitability of culture and tradition shaping politics, and the extreme difficulty of changing, escaping from, or bridging the gaps between cultures. Institutions, in the conservatives' view, acquired meaning, authority, and stability from the cultures in which they evolved. Such cultures could not easily be changed, and therefore institutions (and philosophies) could not be lugged around from country to country like so much second-hand machinery.

Conservatives found liberals lacking in respect for both institutions and cultures. The main vices arising from this lack of respect and understanding were, in the conservative view, a naivety regarding rationality in human affairs and an arrogance regarding the export of institutions and values. Such, indeed, had always been the reaction of American conservatives to liberal proposals for exporting ideas and institutions (or—what came to the same thing—trying to induct large numbers of people of foreign culture into American institutions and culture).[152]

151. "The View from the Outside," 128.
152. For example, in the 1820s, John Quincy Adams (then secretary of state) rejected the idea that the "Spirit of '76" could be exported to the newly independent republics of South America. Adams, according to one historian, "did not consider the cause of the revolted colonies to be identical with that of the North American Revolution of his own boyhood. . . . He tended to see the Spanish Americans as 'an ignorant, miscegenated populace benighted by centuries of political and ecclesiastical tyranny, doubtfully capable of self-government.'" Fifty years later, similar doubts were expressed about the proposed acquisition of the Virgin Islands and Santo Domingo on the grounds that involvement in such tropical societies would poison American democracy by bringing into Congress people who, in the words of a contemporary critic, "have neither language, nor traditions, nor habits, nor political institutions, nor morals in common with us. . . .

While dismissive of liberal crusades abroad, conservatives nevertheless admired the colonial enterprise in Africa—an admiration founded on their sense that some cultures were better than others. In this connection, conservatives were inconsistent, to the same extent and in much the same way as liberals were when they expressed support for self-determination while also hoping that it would take certain directions. The conservatives were inconsistent in that, on the one hand, they proclaimed the distinctiveness of cultures and the perils of communication between them while, on the other, they asserted the superiority of one culture over others, less civilized. The tension between these commitments appeared quite clearly in differences in conservative assessments of African precolonial societies between those (like Elspeth Huxley) who saw them as having qualities lacking in European societies and those who frankly saw them as primitive and barbaric. This tension necessarily appeared also in discussions of modernization and of the colonial administrations that were responsible for such modernization.

In polemics against liberal supporters of decolonization, this tension was somewhat resolved. All conservatives abhorred what they saw as the liberals' betrayal of the necessarily arduous, long-term mission of European colonialism. On this they could agree. Those who felt that colonialism represented a desirable expansion of European cultural influence obviously deplored its destruction. The "romantics" like Huxley could also deplore it to the extent that, compared to the brusquer forms of modernization likely to occur under an African "nation-building" government, colonialism involved the kind of long-term cultural adjustment appropriate to contact between strong and distinctive cultures. The proposition on which conservatives could agree was that the political problem in Africa was a cultural problem. Since cultures were slow to change, this solution required patience, self-confidence, and a willingness to bear responsibility—all qualities that, in the conservative view, liberals scorned and, indeed, lacked.

The result was the tragedy of decolonization—a "tragedy" because it would harm all parties, and because it would lead to an infinity of further tragedies in postcolonial Africa. Such tragedies could only be reduced by a recognition that, for better or worse, African culture and institutions,

---

Sir [the senator concluded], if that were manifest destiny, then I should be seriously tempted to call it manifest doom." Both episodes are referred to in Pratt, "Anticolonialism in U.S. Policy," 293.

like other cultures and institutions, were persistent and powerful. Sanity would only return to Africa when political forms and development programs began to take account of the cultural facts of life. Such a change of view would also provide more appropriate standards by which to judge the behavior of Africans. They should, suggested Thomas Molnar, be seen as the victims of a betrayal and their behavior should be judged accordingly. Thus Frank Meyer, after surveying the disintegrated condition of the Congo in 1961, declared: "We should not blame barbarians if they act like barbarians when they are deserted by those who have taken upon themselves responsibilities for raising them to civilization, and in doing so, have disrupted and destroyed the ancient continuity of their pre-civilized mode of existence." In Africa and elsewhere, Meyer concluded, Americans should recognize "the stern necessity of a return to the truths of our tradition."[153]

This injunction sounded very like that voiced by the revisionist liberals discussed in chapter 4, but in reality its implications were quite different. For liberals, the injunction meant applying the same standards to all men. For conservatives, it meant defending the values of one culture in a world of competing, unequal, and sometimes mutually unintelligible cultures. Sometimes such defense would involve intervention, sometimes it would involve withdrawal. What it never involved was surrender of a sense of America's uniqueness or neglect of America's interests.

153. "Abdication of Responsibility," 218.

EIGHT

Conclusions

O n a trip to the Biafran war zone in March 1968, Lloyd Garrison of the *New York Times* found himself wondering why he was going. "The war," Garrison noted, "appeared to matter little to the outside world. And who these days cared about Africa's problems?"[1]

By the early seventies, indeed, the level of interest in Africa was clearly much lower than in the early sixties.[2] Southern Africa was (and continues to be) the great exception to this generalization. Periodically other regions and particular states appeared in the news—Uganda from 1971 until 1979, Angola in 1975–1976, Zimbabwe and the Horn of Africa in the late seventies, Chad in the early eighties. But for most Americans, Africa probably remained (as one writer suggested in 1978) "a monumental mystery—monolithic, distant, forbidding, and alien."[3]

However, it is important to distinguish between, on the one hand, the passing celebrity of a country in times of diplomatic crisis or internal strife, and, on the other, more enduring and fundamental generalizations about a continent. We can safely say that by 1970 outsiders had largely

1. "Biafra vs. Nigeria: The Other Dirty Little War," 37.
2. From a peak of 3,608 column inches in 1961, coverage of African news in the *New York Times* declined continuously to 955 inches in 1969. Coverage in *Time* showed a similar trend, going down from 748 inches in 1961 to 307 inches in 1969 ("The Changed Images of Africa in Some Selected American Media from 1930 to 1969" 125–36, 139–46). By 1963, the American media were employing fifty-nine correspondents in Africa; but this figure represented 9 percent of the number employed in Europe, 21 percent of those employed in Asia and Australia, and 26 percent of those employed in Latin America (Payne, "American Press Coverage of Africa," 46 [citing survey by John Wilhelm of the McGraw-Hill News Service]).
3. Randall M. Miller, "The American Discovery of Black Africa," 6. The fact was, declared the *New Republic* on the occasion of President Idi Amin's overthrow in 1979, that Africa was "still unknown to most [Americans]. It [had] not yet made any real impact on the Western mind" ("News from Uganda," 28 April 1979, 5).

made up their minds about the character of postcolonial Africa: after 1970, the expectation (contrary to Pliny) was of little new out of Africa. Moreover, the expectation of anything good was clearly much less than it had been in 1960. A fashion for gloom had replaced the earlier fashion for high optimism (but, some critics said, it was showing itself every bit as dogmatic and undiscriminating as its predecessor).

Again, however, it is useful to distinguish between the specific and superficial—the popular stereotypes of African states and politicians—and the more fundamental—in this case, the fundamental significance of Africa in the cosmology of American foreign relations. Stereotypes abounded, varying according to point of view: the variations often amounted to variations in label rather than variations in substance ("terrorist" versus "freedom-fighter").

But if we try a basic question—such as Why does Africa matter?—an interesting, if tacit, consensus can be found. This consensus, underlying liberal, radical, some conservative, and even occasionally some African-American commentary, defines Africa as a candidate for improvement. There is, in fact, a peculiarly moral quality to outsiders' approaches to Africa—an evangelistic strain, an assumption of the need to instruct, protect, and lead which marks off the continent from others.

Admittedly, this assumed mission to uplift is present in Westerners' (and often Easterners') relations with other parts of the third world, but nowhere else (I would suggest) has it been so consistently assumed and so little shaken as in outsiders' relations with Africa. Other continents have been recipients of gratuitous advice about the best interests of their inhabitants. Africa, however, occupies (as the historian John Lonsdale remarks) "a tender spot on our cognitive maps—both guilty burden and wayward child."[4] Its role in the slave trade, its recent colonial history, its poverty, the apparent fragility of its political systems—all make it attractive to those anxious to solve large social problems and those anxious to promote particular kinds of solutions. Africa seems a temptingly vulnerable patient, customer, or would-be convert.

The Issue of "Ethnocentrism"

Observing the facility with which foreigners—journalists and academics—assumed this posture toward Africa and took for granted the rele-

4. "The State and Social Processes in Africa," 4.

vance of their own ideas and institutions to African countries, critics formulated what has become a standard complaint about the "ethnocentrism" or "intellectual imperialism" of outsiders. The latter, according to the critics, improperly imposed their own models on Africa and applied their own standards to African politics.

One problem about this complaint concerns less the factual basis on which it rests—the fact that outsiders applied their own values and referred to their own experiences—than the logic of complaint. The critics of ethnocentrism often make their point by using crude examples of inappropriate technology (such as the famous snowploughs sent by the Soviet Union to West Africa) or instances of gross presumption concerning institutional transfer. Beyond such examples and a salutary, if elementary, injunction not to *assume* the practicality or desirability of intellectual and institutional transfer, the criticism is typically inarticulate on the larger philosophical issues it raises and unhelpful to the unfortunate outsider.

Suppose, as we have seen is generally true, that Americans have tried to apply their own ideas and standards to African politics. As a matter of logic, and even charity, we might ask how they could have done otherwise. The complaint sidesteps the simple question of how anyone can understand or evaluate *anything* without some prior set of meanings and values in their minds. It also, in directing itself particularly at Westerners, implicitly denies what anthropologists—the coiners of the concept of "ethnocentrism"—generally assert: that all societies are ethnocentric. If the anthropologists are right, then societies as well as individuals need some identifying and orienting concepts and values. If Americans err logically in applying ideas bred within their own cultures to Africa, we should expect Africans to be just as misguided, applying their home-bred concepts to American life.

Is the complaint about ethnocentrism, then, that Westerners are more inflexible than others about applying such concepts and values to foreign societies (if so, what is the evidence)? Is it that they impose their judgments more forcefully than others (in which case, the charge is really one of cultural imperialism, and requires some evidence of how such force is applied)? Or is the complaint essentially an expression of a reactive or defensive nationalism—a cultural equivalent of political nationalism, and an assertion of conceptual and moral self-determination? If it is the latter, it is obviously prone to the same problems of isolation inherent in other kinds of nationalism. Is its message that only native-born writers can legitimately write and reach judgments about a society—a message that, ironically, would enshrine rather than undermine ethnocentrism.[5]

My point here is that the charge of ethnocentrism, so strongly and frequently made, in fact ignores or denies the existence of real and fundamental dilemmas that even the most sensitive foreigners writing about a country face in going beyond the most literal reporting of "facts." The charge implicitly presumes that there is a known, correct position, a readily identifiable formula, for overcoming or minimizing ethnocentrism. It implies that there is a right way of seeing, interpreting, and judging developments in societies. But rather than identifying this perspective it merely suggests that it is available to insiders and is unlikely to be found or recognized by outsiders. As a line of criticism, therefore, the charge of ethnocentrism is commonly tautological (if everyone is ethnocentric) and incomplete (if it does not provide an appropriate standard, other than the implied standard of birth and citizenship in a suitable place).

Another, less philosophical problem raised by the charge of ethnocentrism is that it overlooks the impact of the supposedly passive and imposed-upon culture on the values and assumptions of the imposer. If there is one pervasive sound rumbling through the preceding chapters, it is that of cherished beliefs bending and buckling. Outsiders may well have gone out blithely expecting to be able to apply their own ideas and standards, but they often returned with their instruments bent and their spirits confused. They often found that the generalities they had taken with them were overgeneralized or inapplicable. At the least, they had to qualify their expectations and their standards and to be more specific about their meaning and application. In most cases, also, the experience of attempting to apply their beliefs in an unfamiliar setting led to the exposure of ambiguities or plain contradictions within this body of beliefs.

The Dilemmas of Liberalism

In the case of American liberals, for example, it is possible to discern at least six points of tension, revealed in arguments about such issues as the meaning of democracy in Africa, the nature of one-party states, and the

---

5. For a further development of this argument, see Staniland, "Democracy and Ethnocentrism."

political requirements for economic development. The tensions can be depicted thus:

1. A tension between respect for *national* self-determination and respect for *local* or *individual* self-determination. How far, for example, should liberals' sympathy for African nationalism go when, in particular cases, it was used as an ideological shield to protect illiberal treatment of regions, groups, or individuals within a country?
2. A tension between respect for national self-determination and a belief in the universality of certain moral and political values. How far did nationalism provide a mandate for autarky in all areas of political, social, economic, and cultural life? Was such autarky possible?
3. A tension between respect for national self-determination and an ambivalence about traditional African culture. What was the cultural substance of African nationalism? Was it (as in most nationalisms) a distinct linguistic and cultural heritage and a distinct historical experience? Or was it the developmental objectives of the elite? To which, faced with a choice, did liberals owe support?
4. A tension between belief in a strong, interventionist state, to promote economic development, and belief in private enterprise and laissez-faire.
5. A tension between belief in a strong state, for developmental purposes, and fear of the threat from a strong state to constitutionalism and political liberties.
6. A tension between respect for neutralism or nonalignment (as a diplomatic expression of self-determination) and a hope that African states would support liberal ideals in the Cold War.

Contrary to the assertions of critics of ethnocentrism, many liberals worried about which, if any, of these principles were applicable in Africa. Overall, they (more perhaps than any other group) also worried about the larger issue of applying their own principles and standards abroad. This type of issue was particularly acute for liberal Americans actually working in Africa—Americans such as those living in Ghana under the auspices of the Crossroads Africa. According to the sociologist Harold R. Isaacs, who visited such a group in 1961, these volunteers were greatly bothered by the problem of trying to adapt to local tastes and attitudes which they did not share or actually found repulsive. They anguished over such things as food (Ghanaian fufu versus American hamburger) and, more seriously, over whether they had any right to be upset about the bad sanitation, poor education, and prevailing attitudes toward women that they found in their hosts' villages.

Isaacs's response illustrates the thinking implicit in much liberal revisionist writing on Africa. People in such situations, he urged, should stop being defensive and self-denying. If they found that they were appalled by what they saw, they should not feel that they had to suppress this reaction: "By every value and standard which the American deems important, these things *are* bad, they *are* undesirable, they *are* negative, damaging to human decency and progress, and . . . one is entitled to think so clearly and firmly without regard to anyone's race, creed, color, or national sensitivity and, where it is important to do so, to confront the matter fairly and speak about it plainly." Isaacs concluded by suggesting that Americans in general needed "a new way of achieving a fair confrontation of values and goals between members of societies that are all in the process of change . . . the ethnocentrism of the fathers assigned all virtue to themselves, but the cultural ultra-relativism of the sons threatens to err just as badly in surrendering all virtue to others or suggesting that *anything goes.*" A rejection of ethnocentrism, he declared, "cannot be made to mean that we also get rid of our essential commitments to our own values, our right to have our judgments about ways of life and human relations. It simply means that we have got to learn to hold these values and rights in a new way."[6]

Such appeals for integrity clearly responded to an uneasy (and logically well-founded) sense that "relativism" could only go so far without destroying the moral identity of liberalism (or any other set of beliefs). But the question remained, How far? What was the "new way" of holding liberal values, and what was "fair" in confronting liberal values with others?

Dilemmas on the Left

Commentary by writers on the left also reveals serious differences over the applications of concepts and standards (as well as over strategy). Such differences concerned:

6. "A Rebirth of Self-Esteem," 24: emphasis in original. In a similar vein, Harvey Glickman called on the American liberal to "throw off his self-imposed guilt about imperialism, his wealth, and American race relations" ("When Africans and Americans Meet," 18).

1. The claims of self-determination and the extent to which self-determination (and nationalism) would assist the cause of advancing socialism;
2. the revolutionary potentials of the industrial proletariat and the peasantry in third world countries;
3. the relevance of the Soviet Union and the People's Republic of China as models for socialism in the third world;
4. the feasibility of advancing socialism within the established structure of nation-states, given the international preponderance of capitalism;
5. the compatibility of interests between the industrialized "north" (socialist and nonsocialist) and the agricultural "south."

By the late sixties, socialists had become as skeptical as liberals and conservatives about the possibility of progress in Africa. Both the Soviet Union and Western socialists were by this time wary of Africa as a continent where rapid advances and great innovations might be expected. As one writer declared gloomily: "Nowhere south of the Sahara is there a nucleus of creative revolutionary change; nowhere have the people been able to take their fate into their own hands. The subcontinent is left with no internal catalyst for change and remains subject to continued manipulation from abroad. . . . The peasantries are quiescent, galvanized occasionally by local or traditional rivalries of a negative kind."[7]

For some socialists, there were still bright spots. Tanzania was, at least for neo-Marxists, one such bright spot—a country that was avoiding the errors committed by such leaders as Nkrumah in Ghana, Sekou Toure in Guinea, and Modibo Keita in Mali.[8] In the seventies, Mozambique, Angola, Guina-Bissau, and Ethiopia raised similar hopes.

But if these hopes were to be realized, socialists obviously had to learn from earlier mistakes and misunderstandings. Unfortunately, the postmortems on failing or displaced socialist regimes did not show any unanimity about what had gone wrong or about feasible ways of preventing such weaknesses from appearing again.

7. Diamond, "The Biafran Possibility," 16.
8. Tanzania, declared Giovanni Arrighi and John S. Saul, was "the country in contemporary Africa where socialist aspirations figure[d] most prominently in the development equations" ("Socialism and Economic Development in Tropical Africa," 20). In Tanzania, another observer remarked, "a radical nationalist regime" was truly pursuing "economic self-reliance, social egalitarianism, and rural development" (Peter Waterman, "Radicalism in African Studies," 263–64).

African-American Dilemmas

Among African-American commentators, interest in Africa was more sustained chronologically than among the mainstream ideological commentators.[9] Again, however, some persistent disagreements or tensions are apparent, notably:

1. tension between the instinct to defend all African states as a matter of racial solidarity and the observation that African states differed in the quality of their leadership, their domestic politics, and their external policies;
2. tension between those who wanted a mainly domestic political strategy aimed at integration and pan-Africanists who wanted a strategy emphasizing international racial solidarity;
3. tension between those who perceived a parallel between colonialism in Africa and the situation of African-Americans, and those who did not.

As with other groups, closer acquaintance involved some shocks and some triumphs. Over a decade, it led to a more differentiated view of Africa and of African-American connections with the continent. Disenchantment sometimes occurred, as in the case of one African-American lawyer who commented on returning from West Africa: "It's hard to be romantic about Africa once you've seen it. You see the colonial mentality transposed into black heads. You see blacks exploiting blacks. It's not very pretty."[10]

Yet few travelers seem to have regarded disenchantment as any kind of loss. Rather, it was part of an experience of discovery which was only superficially a physical journey. When white Americans, such as Harold Isaacs and Russell Warren Howe, claimed that African-American experiences in Africa had only exposed deep differences between Africans and African-Americans, they were accused of trying to create divisions within the African-American community.[11]

9. This chronological difference in levels of interest is noted in Carson, "Black Power after Ten years," 114.

10. Roger Wilkins, "What Africa Means to Blacks," 137.

11. For this controversy, see Harold R. Isaacs, *The New World of Negro Americans*; idem, "A Reporter at Large—Back to Africa"; Howe, "Strangers in Africa"; Bond, "Howe and Isaacs in the Bush: The Ram in the Thicket"; Howe, "A Reply to Horace Mann Bond," 102, 104; Robert S. Browne, review, *Freedomways* 3, no. 4 (Fall 1963): 577–78.

However, the remarks that Isaacs and Howe reported do seem to have reflected a process of self-discovery which many African-Americans experienced abroad and which others than those they interviewed also described. Indeed, one important wing of African-American opinion was always skeptical about facile expectations of unity between Africans and African-Americans of the kind nurtured by pan-Africanists.

But Isaacs and Howe were clearly wrong if they meant to imply that familiarity with Africa had bred contempt on the part of African-Americans. Familiarity seems, rather, to have sharpened African-Americans' awareness of the paradoxical situation in which their history had left them. In discovering Africa, they also rediscovered the duality of allegiance that one of the greatest African-American writers had described so poignantly. "One ever feels," W. E. B. DuBois had written of the African-American, "his two-ness—an American, a Negro: two souls, two thoughts, two unreconciled strivings; two warring ideals in one dark body, whose strength alone keeps it from being torn asunder. The history of the American Negro is the history of this strife—this longing to attain self-conscious manhood."[12]

Conservative Dilemmas

Finally, incongruities, though not outright conflict, are also apparent in conservative commentary. Again, we can identify some persistent points of tension:

1. a tension between "romantics" and other conservatives over the desirability of modernization and the achievements of colonialism;
2. a tension between a hierarchical view of cultures and a belief in the value of cultural idiosyncrasies;
3. a tension between a belief in the Western civilizing mission and a belief in its cultural futility;
4. a tension between a general belief in self-determination and a reluctance to accept its application to African colonial territories (except at the "tribal" level);
5. a tension between a general preference for "strong" government and a scorn regarding African "dictatorship";
6. a tension between a belief in national and even racial identities

12. Quoted in Skinner, "African, Afro-American, White American," 381.

and a dislike of "racial solidarity" as manifested in African nationalism.

These tensions could combine to produce apparently incongruent positions. In the Nigerian case, for example, many conservatives admired
the "modernizing" energy and ambitiousness of the Ibo, while simultaneously urging support of Biafra because it showed the wisdom of using
tribal identity as a basis for statehood. Interestingly, they did not show
much enthusiasm for the cause of the northerners in Nigeria, who by
general consent really were traditionalists in mind and spirit. Equally,
however, they never came to terms with the argument that the Ibos were
at heart the most committed believers in *Nigerian* nationalism—Biafra
being merely a defensive entity created as a result of the expulsion of the
Ibo from other regions.

As regards postcolonial states in general, a striking feature of conservative commentary is its gradual evolution toward accepting their probable permanence. For a decade after independence and at every moment
of crisis in Africa, conservatives were ready to point to the artificiality of
African states and to urge (and, indeed, predict) their reconstitution as
"tribal" states.

In the early seventies, such urging began to fade, to be gradually replaced by a critique of the African states which resembled the general
conservative critique of the third world. Like other third world states,
African countries were criticized for their allegedly pro-Communist or
anti-American positions in international relations and for the authoritarianism, corruption, and wastefulness of their domestic politics. Implicitly,
however, they came to be accepted as a permanent, if unedifying, part of
the international scene.[13] The theme of imminent disintegration gave way
to a theme of immanent incompetence and incapacity.

13. Norman Roberts suggested in 1971 that the disdain for African cultures,
expressed in earlier references to black magic and witch doctors, had disappeared
from a wide range of publications by the late sixties. "Strong disapproval of the
African social structures which was apparent in the early sample years has disappeared. Though a trend to positive acceptance is not evident, a trend toward
acceptance of Black African cultures with more mild approval than implied disapproval is evident" ("The Changed Images of Africa," 202–04). Roberts found
that the theme of "primitivism" had largely disappeared (except in the columns
of *Time*) and that particularly radical changes had occurred in school textbooks.
His sample was drawn mainly from *Time, Newsweek,* the *New York Times,* and the
Department of State Bulletin.

Ideology and International Relations

Having surveyed some of the damage that Africa did to alien ideologies, we should ask in conclusion what we can learn from this case about the role of ideologies in the making of foreign policy and in international relations more broadly.

Any suggestions about this role are speculative. Very few policymakers appear in the preceding pages, and I have found no evidence of direct influence by any article or writer quoted on any decision concerning American policy toward Africa. Making a case for such influence would have to take a more circuitous route and would (I suggest) involve the exploration of institutions and processes that are routinely examined by sociologists and anthropologists and routinely ignored by students of international relations.

The individual chapters of this book offer only one element of such an exploration. They examine just the printed product and really constitute a set of essays in intellectual or ideological history. What we discover in the product are the key categories and metaphors that identify a community of discourse; but while the ideas and symbols are important, they are not themselves the community. In other words, we can hear the conversation, see what is distinctive about it, and understand the arguments that occur. But our understanding is quite disembodied: we do not see the speakers, observe their relationships, or see how they and others use their ideas and arguments to affect political decisions.

To go beyond an interesting but nevertheless limited piece of intellectual history requires a sociology or ethnography of international relations. As Ralph Pettman has remarked, there is currently very little traffic between sociology and the study of international relations.[14] Political scientists and economists dominate the field, with a resulting emphasis on "power" and "rational choice" as explanatory categories and to the exclusion of the social institutions—the "invisible colleges" and "communities of discourse"—which influence how we conceive (in this case) both our own and other societies.

14. "The sociological approach is a curiously neglected one, and sociological theories, concepts and research methods are rarely identified as such, either because they are simply not recognized for what they are, or because theorists and practitioners have chosen to ignore the source of what are really 'sociological' ideas. Sociologists themselves scarcely acknowledge the structure of international relations as a determinant of social affairs, while students of world politics neglect the importance of a sociological view" (*State and Class,* 12).

In international relations (as in science and art), there are "thought-worlds" that determine the adoption and dissemination of constructs and that assert values.[15] Without the ideas and beliefs articulated within these worlds, "politics" and "policy-making" are literally inconceivable. Consequently, while the case for influence by "intellectuals" cannot be made on the strength of the material and issues covered in this book, if the perspective advocated here is accepted, such influence is necessarily pervasive and inescapable. The table at which policymakers sit is like the platform on which, in Indian cosmology, the world stands: under it is a pyramid of arbitrary assumptions, untested and indeed untestable hypotheses, and imprecise measures—in the original imagery, it is "turtles all the way down."[16]

Ideologies are actually constructed on similar lines and play the same role—that of providing a (perhaps illusory) sense of order and a framework of meaning in a complicated and seemingly arbitrary world. They are not just crutches (though crutches, after all, have their uses): they are indispensable in providing the community of meanings and values on which collective action depends. But this "service" may be offered by competing ideologies. Although we have not sought in this book an "ideology of decision makers," we have shown that even if such an ideology exists, it is likely to be contested by others which are as comprehensive and as deeply cherished by those in the "thought-collectives" they define.[17]

The most obvious implication of this condition of ideological competition is that it cannot make sense to talk about an "ideology of American foreign policy," unless we can establish the existence of a distinct and self-sustaining pattern of beliefs and concepts among decision makers that is unaffected by the tide of ideological battle outside the castle walls at Foggy Bottom. Such a notion would make more sense if it referred to an official ideology that reflected a consensus within the public—a consen-

15. See Mary Douglas, *How Institutions Think* (Syracuse: Syracuse University Press, 1986), 17.

16. See Geertz, "Thick Description: Toward an Interpretive Theory of Culture," in *The Interpretation of Cultures*, 28–29. This view recalls E. H. Carr's remark that history is at least as much "a hard core of interpretation surrounded by a pulp of disputable facts" as a "hard core of facts" surrounded by a "pulp of disputable interpretation" (*What Is History?* [London: Macmillan, 1961], 18).

17. The term *thought collective* derives from the work of Ludwik Fleck: see Douglas, *How Institutions Think*, 11–16.

sus that, in turn, persistently favored one of the competing turtle-towers (for instance, liberalism).

In any case, simply to state the tenets of such an ideology would be a rather sterile exercise, without some consideration of the competition. Such consideration would inevitably raise the question of why one point of view has usually beaten the others, and why it has sometimes failed to do so. Without a more sophisticated account of how the ideological amoebas organize and propagate themselves (as American conservatives did for twenty years before 1980), we cannot answer such questions. We will never answer them if we assume that there is a simple, unchallenged relationship between "American political culture" and "foreign policy ideology." How does this relationship show itself in relation to, for example, South Africa or Central America?

To say that ideologies are necessary is not to say that they are virtuous or trouble-free, any more than we see bones as virtuous or trouble-free. Ideology, as Geertz remarks, "names the structure of situations in such a way that the attitude contained toward them is one of commitment."[18] Such commitment can create stress when the integrity of a turtle-tower is threatened. Are the threats serious? What parts of the structure do they threaten (essential beliefs or expendable positions)? What remedy or repair, if any, is appropriate?

The dilemmas bred by commitment create the drama—tragic or comic, depending on the reader's point of view—of the encounters described in specific chapters of this book. But the important question, surely, is how such dilemmas are resolved. Commitment is not just inevitable: it is desirable and essential for any determined political action. The crucial issue for a "thought-collective" is whether in a crisis of faith its leaders can separate the transient or tactical stand from the essential beliefs that give it identity and that actually inspire commitment.

The editors of journals of opinion and political organizers usually share the task of managing the relationship between symbolic and political commitments, of making sure that ideology and program—what we believe in and how we are going to achieve it—are congruent and mutually supportive. Some of the writers quoted here have been directly involved in this task. Certainly, their writings have been offered by editors in order to further a broader discourse, central questions in which are raised periodically by the emergence of new states.

18. "Ideology as a Cultural System," 71.

But the writers are not simply to be labeled "ideologists." If we were pursuing the ethnography of international relations proposed here, their ideological role would necessarily be a required object of study. We might, however, suggest in ending, as a compliment and even as a tribute to them, that they have themselves exhibited the ethnographer's skill, which, in Geertz's words, rests not on the scholar's ability "to capture primitive facts in faraway places and carry them home like a mask or a carving, but on the degree to which he is able to clarify what goes on in such places, to reduce the puzzlement—what manner of men are these?—to which unfamiliar acts emerging out of unknown backgrounds naturally give rise."[19]

19. "Thick Description," 16.

BIBLIOGRAPHY

Adams, Mildred. "Key Pieces in the African Puzzle." *New York Times Magazine,* 17 January 1960, 18, 75.

Adelman, Kenneth L. "The Black Man's Burden." *Foreign Policy* 28 (Fall 1977): 86–109.

"Africa in Curlers." *Africa Today* 11, no.1 (January 1964): 3.

The Africa League. *A New American Policy toward Africa.* New York: Africa League, February 1960.

African Studies Association. "Training and Career Opportunities for the American Specialist on Africa." *African Studies Bulletin* 2, no.4 (December 1959): 13–26.

"African Studies Association." *Science,* 17 May 1957, 998–99.

"Africa's Quiet Revolution." *Ebony,* June 1952, 94–98.

Aldridge, Dan. "Politics in Command of Economics: Black Economic Development." *Monthly Review* 21, no.6 (November 1969): 14–27.

"All the King's Horses." *National Review,* 25 February 1961, 102–03.

Allen, V. L. "Nigeria: Coup on a Tightrope." *Nation,* 7 February 1966, 143–45.

Almond, Gabriel A. "Making New Nations Democratic." *Current* 55 (January 1965): 19–24.

Alsop, Stewart. "Africa: The Riddle without an Answer." *Reader's Digest,* June 1961: 82–87.

"Americans and Africa." Editorial. *Life,* 4 May 1953, 178.

Apter, David E. "Some Economic Factors in the Political Development of the Gold Coast." *Journal of Economic History* 14, no.4 (1954): 409–27.

———. "British West Africa: Patterns of Self-Government." *Annals of the American Academy of Political and Social Science* 298 (March 1955): 117–29.

———. "Political Democracy in the Gold Coast." In *Africa in the Modern World,* ed. Calvin W. Stillman, 115–39. Chicago: University of Chicago Press, 1955.

———. *Ideology and Discontent.* New York: Free Press, 1964.

Aptheker, Herbert. "Africa and Imperialist Intellectuals." *Political Affairs,* October 1960, 32–40.

———. "Present Thinking in Socialist Countries." *Political Affairs,* December 1964, 43–52.

"Arming the Nigerians." *New Republic,* 22 June 1968, 158.

Arrighi, Giovanni, and John S. Saul. "Socialism and Economic Development in Tropical Africa." *Monthly Review* 21, no.1 (May 1969): 12–22.

Astrachan, Anthony. "A Guide to the Nigerian Elections." *Africa Report* 9, no.11 (December 1964): 31–32.

"The Atlantic Report—Nigeria and Ghana." *Atlantic Monthly,* November 1962, 22–31.

Axelrod, Joseph, and Donald N. Bigelow. *Inventory of NDEA Title IV and Title VI*

Language and Area Centers. Washington, D.C: American Council on Education, July 1961.

Ayorinde, Femi A. "The Racists' Role in the Nigerian Crisis." *Liberator,* September 1968, 16.

Baldwin, James. "Africa's Effect on the U.S. Negro." *Current* 13 (May 1961): 6–7.

Ball, George W. "American Policy in the Congo." *Africa Report* 7, no.1 (January 1962): 15–16.

Baran, Paul A., and Paul M. Sweezy. "Notes on the Theory of Imperialism." *Monthly Review* 17, no.10 (March 1966): 15–31.

Barrett, Lindsay. "A Message to Black Activists on the Nigerian Crisis." *Freedomways* 9, no.3 (Summer 1969): 212–20.

Bauer, P. T. "African Political Economy." In *The African Nettle: Dilemma of an Emerging Continent,* ed. Frank S. Meyer, 39–72. Freeport, N.Y.: Books for Libraries Press, 1965.

"Beats of the Heart of Darkness." *National Review,* 9 April 1963, 268.

Beckett, Paul. "Frantz Fanon and Sub-Saharan Africa: Notes on the Contemporary Significance of His Thought." *Africa Today* 19, no.2 (Spring 1972): 59–72.

Bellamy, Joan. "A Valuable Study of Neo-Colonialism." *Political Affairs,* February 1967, 58–65.

Berg, Elliot J. "Socialism and Economic Development in Tropical Africa." *Quarterly Journal of Economics* 78, no.4 (November 1964): 549–73.

Berger, Peter L. "The Third World as a Religious Idea." *Partisan Review* 50, no.2 (1983): 183–96.

Berki, R. N. "On Marxian Thought and the Problem of International Relations." *World Politics* 24, no.1 (October 1971): 80–105.

Bertolin, Gordon. "U.S. Economic Interests in Africa: Investment, Trade and Raw Materials." In *Africa and the United States,* ed. Jennifer Seymour Whitaker, 21–59. New York: Council on Foreign Relations/New York University Press, 1978.

Bird, Christopher. "A Soviet Ethnographer Visits Ghana." *Africa Special Report,* March 1958, 10.

"Birth of a Nation." *New Republic,* 18 March 1957, 5.

"Birth of an African Nation." *Ebony,* March 1957, 17–28.

Bishop, Robert L. "How Reuter's and A.F.P. Coverage of Independent Africa Compare." *Journalism Quarterly,* Winter 1975, 654–62.

Blumer, Herbert. "Society as Symbolic Interaction." In *Symbolic Interaction: A Reader in Social Psychology,* ed. Jerome G. Manis and Bernard N. Meltzer, 139–48. Boston: Allyn and Bacon, 1967.

Blumler, Jay. "Is 'Vanguardism' Enough?" *Current* 34 (February 1963): 39–42.

Bolter, Peter D. "The Congo . . . Seven Bloody Years." *American Legion Magazine* 83, no.4 (October 1967): 8–12.

Bolton, Frances P. Speech to the Ninth Annual Foreign Policy Conference, Colgate University. In *Africa Special Report* 1, no.7 (19 November 1956).

Bond, Horace Mann. "Howe and Isaacs in the Bush: The Ram in the Thicket." *Negro History Bulletin* 25, no.3 (December 1961): 72ff.

"Bourgeois Democracy in Eclipse." *Monthly Review* 10, no.10 (February 1959): 408.

Bowles, Chester. "Africa." *Collier's,* 10 June 1955, 40–44.

———. "Myths About Africa—And the Reality." *New York Times Magazine,* 16 June 1963, 8, 33–38.

———. *Africa's Challenge to America.* Westport, Conn.: Negro Universities Press, 1956. Repr. 1970.

Bracker, Milton. "Congo: Pulsing Heart of Africa." *New York Times Magazine,* 15 March 1959, 14, 106–07.

———. "The Congo Is Like This." *New York Times Magazine,* 21 August 1960, 16–17.

Bretton, Henry L. "Current Political Thought and Practice in Ghana." *American Political Science Review* 52, no.1 (March 1958): 46–63.

———. "Straight Thinking on Africa." *Nation,* 5 March 1960, 205–07.

———. "Congo and Emergent Africa." *Nation,* 15 October 1960, 241–44.

Brodie, Bernard. *War and Politics.* New York: Macmillan, 1973.

Browne, Robert S. "The Black Stake in Global Interdependence." *Review of Black Political Economy* 6, no.4 (Summer 1976): 408–19.

Brym, Robert J. *Intellectuals and Politics.* London: Allen and Unwin, 1980.

Buchanan, Keith. "The Negro Problem in the U.S.—An Outsider's View." *Monthly Review* 15, no.5 (September 1963): 235–45.

———. "When Hyenas Go Away." *Monthly Review* 16, no.5 (September 1964): 309–15.

Buckley, William F., Jr. "Uhuru-Ushuru." *National Review,* 9 May 1959, 38.

———. "Will the Jungle Take Over?" *National Review,* 30 July 1960, 39.

———. "Rx Africa: The Kennedy Doctrine." *National Review,* 25 March 1961, 170–71.

———. "Must We Hate Portugal?" *National Review,* 18 December 1962, 468.

———. "Where's Biafra?" *National Review,* 10 September 1968, 924–25.

Burnham, J. Bernard. Review of Moise Tshombe, *My Fifteen Months in Government. National Review,* 25 July 1967, 817.

Burnham, James. "Watch out for That Back Door!" *National Review,* 25 April 1959, 12.

———. "The Explosion of Africa." *National Review,* 20 June 1959, 140.

———. "Eurafrica or Afro-Asia?" *National Review,* 10 October 1959, 388.

———. "The Loneliest Men." *National Review,* 12 March 1960, 164.

———. "What Kind of War?" *National Review,* 9 April 1960, 228.

———. "What Is Ahead for Black Africa?" *National Review,* 22 October 1960, 240.

———. "At the Crack of Khrushchev's Whip." *National Review,* 5 November 1960, 272.

———. "The African Shambles." *National Review,* 28 January 1961, 45.

———. "Image in What Mirror?" *National Review,* 15 July 1961, 15.

———. "The United States, the United Nations, and Africa." In *The African Net-*

tle: Dilemmas of an Emerging Continent, ed. Frank S. Meyer, 243–53. Freeport, N.Y.: Books for Libraries Press, 1965.

———. "Global Apartheid?" *National Review,* 18 October 1966, 1,036.

———. "The View from the Outside." *National Review,* 7 February 1967, 128.

———. "Clouds over the Golden Horn." *National Review,* 4 April 1967, 342.

"Business as Usual." *Africa Today* 8, no.9 (November 1961): 3.

Calder, Ritchie. "Shinkolobwe: Key to the Congo." *Nation,* 25 February 1961, 163–65.

———. "Congo Drums Again." *Nation,* 24 November 1962, 339.

Campbell, Alexander. "Africa: A Continent in Ferment." *Life,* 4 May 1953, 9–10.

Campbell, J. E. "Struggle: The Highest Form of Education." *Freedomways* 8, no.4 (Fall 1968): 407–14.

Canada, Afroman U. O. "Pan-Africanism and Black Nationalism Are One." *Africa Report* 18, no.1 (January–February 1973): 34–35.

Carr, E. H. *The Twenty Years' Crisis, 1919–1939.* New York: Harper and Row, 1964.

Carson, Clayborne. "Black Power after Ten Years." *Nation,* 14 August 1976, 111–15.

Carter, Gwendolen M. "Danger Signs in Africa." *Africa Special Report,* October 1959, 3–14.

———. "The Character of the New States." *Africa Today* 7, no.7 (November 1960): 13.

———. "African Studies in the United States: A Report for Dr. Paul Miller, Department of Health, Education and Welfare." *African Studies Bulletin* 10, no.3 (December 1967): 96–108.

Cartwright, Marguerite. "Progress in the Congo." *Negro History Bulletin* 17, no.5 (February 1954): 125–26.

———. "African Odyssey: Ghana." *Negro History Bulletin* 20, no.8 (May 1957): 175–78.

———. "Travel Diary." *Negro History Bulletin* 24, no.2 (November 1960): 35–36.

———. "Zik Becomes Governor General." *Negro History Bulletin* 24, no.5 (February 1961): 104–09.

Chick, John D. "Nigeria at War." *Current History,* February 1968, 65–118.

———. "The Nigerian Impasse." *Current History,* May 1969, 292–308.

Chrisman, J. Eugene. "Jungle Doctor." *Negro Digest,* September 1951, 46–49.

Clain, Roger. "The Congo Freedom-Struggle." *Political Affairs,* August 1959, 56–58.

Clarke, John Henrik. "The New Afro-American Nationalism." *Freedomways* 1, no.3 (Fall 1961): 285–95.

———. "Africa: New Approaches to an Old Continent." *Freedomways* 11, no.3 (Third Quarter 1971): 298–305.

Clecak, Peter. "*Monthly Review*: An Assessment." *Monthly Review* 20, no.6 (November 1968): 1–16.

Cleveland, Harlan. "The U.N. in the Congo: Three Questions." *Africa Report* 8, no.2 (February 1963): 21–23.

Cloete, Stuart. "End of Era with Threat of the Jungle Taking Over." *Life,* 1 August 1960, 14–15.

Clos, Max. "Why the Africans Hate Tshombe." *New York Times Magazine,* 10 January 1965, 24–25, 70–73.

Cohen, Abner. *Two-Dimensional Man: An Essay on the Anthropology of Power and Symbolism in Complex Society.* Berkeley and Los Angeles: University of California Press, 1974.

Cohen, Bernard C. *The Public's Impact on Foreign Policy.* Boston: Little, Brown, 1973.

Coleman, James S. "Current Political Movements in Africa." *Annals of the American Academy of Political and Social Science* 298 (March 1955): 95–108.

———. "America and Africa." *World Politics* 9, no.4 (July 1957): 593–609.

Comte, Gilbert. "Are There Any Conservative Africans?" *National Review,* 20 May 1969, 491–502.

"Congo Drums Again." *Nation,* 24 November 1962, 339.

Coser, Lewis. *Men of Ideas: A Sociologist's View.* New York: Free Press, 1965.

———. "The Myth of Peasant Revolt." *Dissent,* May–June 1966, 298–303.

Coughlan, Robert. "Black Africa Surges to Independence." *Life,* 26 January 1959, 100–104.

"The Courteous Africans." *Crisis* 76, no.7 (August–September 1969): 272.

Cousins, Norman. "Report from the Congo." *Saturday Review,* 3 February 1962, 12–32.

———. "What Hope in Nigeria?" *Saturday Review,* 16 August 1969, 1617.

———. "The Grisly Aftermath." *Saturday Review,* 7 February 1970, 22.

Cowan, L. Gray. "Ten Years of African Studies." *African Studies Bulletin* 12, no.1 (April 1969): 1–7.

Cox, Richard. "The Strong Man of Katanga." *Reporter,* 30 March 1961, 22–24.

Craig, Gordon. "Political and Diplomatic History." In *Historical Studies Today,* ed. Felix Gilbert and Stephen R. Graubard, 356–371. New York: Norton, 1972.

Crocker, Chester A., and William H. Lewis. "Missing Opportunities in Africa." *Foreign Policy* 35 (Summer 1979): 142–61.

Cruse, Harold W. "Negro Nationalism's New Wave." *New Leader,* 19 March 1962, 16–18.

———. *The Crisis of the Negro Intellectual.* New York: Morrow, 1967.

Curtin, Philip D. "African Studies: A Personal Assessment." *African Studies Review* 14, no.3 (December 1971): 357–68.

Davidson, Basil. "Enlightened Colonialism: The Belgian Congo." *Reporter,* 27 January 1955, 34–39.

———. "Difficulties, Not Disillusionment." *Africa Report* 12, no.9 (December 1967): 27–28.

Dawn, J. Michael. "Toward an International Strategy." *Monthly Review* 19, no.11 (April 1968): 28–41.

de Madariaga, Salvador. "As Africa Comes of Age." *Crisis* 60, no.6 (June–July 1953): 346–48.

de Schweinitz, Karl. *Industrialization and Democracy: Economic Necessities and Political Possibilities.* London: Free Press of Glencoe, 1964.

Dean, Vera Micheles. "Democracy East and West." *Progressive,* July 1962, 18–21.

Diamond, Stanley. "Modern Africa: The Pains of Birth." *Dissent,* Spring 1963, 169–79.

———. "The Weight of the North." *Africa Today* 10, no.1 (January 1963): 4–15.

———. "The End of the First Republic." *Africa Today* 13, no.2 (February 1966): 5–9.

———. "The Biafran Possibility." *Africa Report* 13, no.2 (February 1968): 16–19.

Disdier, Albert P. "The Congo's Economic Crisis." *Africa Report* 5, no.6 (June 1960): 6–15.

"Divorce, Nigerian Style." *Reporter,* 30 May 1968, 8–10.

Dodd, Thomas J. "Congo: The Untold Story." *National Review,* 28 August 1966, 136–44.

"Dodd's Private War." *New Republic,* 18 December 1961, 3–4.

Douglas, Mary. *How Institutions Think.* Syracuse, N.Y.: Syracuse University Press, 1986.

Drake, Lyman. "African Studies Association Meets." *Africa Special Reports* 3, no.10 (October 1958): 2.

Drake, Francis Vivian. "Don't Decry Colonialism." *Reader's Digest,* August 1960, 65–70.

Draper, Theodore. *Ordeal of the U.N.: Khrushchev, Hammarskjold and the Congo Crisis.* New Leader Pamphlet, 1960.

———. "The Fantasy of Black Nationalism." *Commentary,* September 1969, 28–54.

———. *The Rediscovery of Black Nationalism.* New York: Viking, 1970.

Dressel, Carol A. "The Development of African Studies in the United States." *African Studies Bulletin* 9, no.3 (December 1966): 66–73.

Du Bois, W. E. B. "Black Africa Tomorrow." *Foreign Affairs* 17, no.1 (October 1938): 100–110.

Duggan, William R. "The New African Chiefs." *Review of Politics* 28, no.3 (July 1966): 350–58.

Duignan, Peter, and L. H. Gann. "A Different View of United States Policy in Africa." *Western Political Quarterly* 13, no.4 (December 1960): 918–23.

———. "The Case for the White Man." *New Leader,* 2 January 1961, 16–20.

Edeani, David Omazo. "Realities of Mass Emigration to Africa." *Crisis* 79, no.2 (February 1972): 41–45.

Edwards, H. W. "The Colonial War at Home: A Comment." *Monthly Review* 6, no.7 (November 1964): 447–52.

Emerson, Rupert. "American Policy in Africa." *Foreign Affairs* 40, no.2 (January 1962): 303–15.

———. *Africa and United States Policy.* Englewood Cliffs, N.J.: Prentice-Hall, 1967.

Emiola, Akintunde. "Diamond Was Prophetic." *Africa Today* 11, no.5 (May 1964): 6–7.

Emmanuel, Arghiri. "The Delusions of Internationalism." *Monthly Review* 22, no.2 (June 1970): 13–19.

"The End of Biafra." *National Review,* 27 January 1970, 72–73.

Feinberg, Richard E. *The Intemperate Zone: The Third World Challenge.* New York: Norton, 1983.

Ferkiss, Victor C. "Breakdown in the Congo." *Commonweal* 81, no.10 (24 November 1964): 325–28.

Feuer, Lewis S. "What Is an Intellectual?" In *The Intelligentsia and the Intellectuals: Theory, Method and Case Study,* ed. Aleksander Gella, 47–57. Beverly Hills, Calif.: Sage Publications, 1976.

Fierce, Mildred C. "Africa—Some Views and Previews." *Negro History Bulletin* 35, no.4 (April 1972): 78–79.

Foreign Aid." *Commonweal,* 6 January 1956, 343–44.

Forman, James. *The Making of Black Revolutionaries.* New York: Macmillan, 1973.

Foster, Badi G. "United States Foreign Policy toward Africa: An Afro-American Perspective." *Issue* (African Studies Association) 2, no.2 (Summer 1972): 45–51.

Frankel, Charles. "A Conservative Autopsy." *New Leader,* 20 July 1964, 5–9.

Friedenberg, Daniel M. "An African Notebook." *Commonweal,* 29 January 1954, 420–23.

———. "The Horatio Alger of the Gold Coast." *New Republic,* 8 April 1957, 16–18.

———. "An Economic View of Negro Independence." *Dissent* 7, no.2 (Spring 1960): 188–200.

Friendly, Alfred. "The Children Are Starving." *The New Republic,* 17 August 1968, 22–26.

Futch, J. D. "The Day of the Let's Pretends." *National Review,* 12 September 1959, 328.

Garrison, Lloyd. "Biafra vs. Nigeria: The Other Dirty Little War." *New York Times Magazine,* 31 March 1968, 36–47, 60–64.

———. "The 'Point of No Return' for the Biafrans." *New York Times Magazine,* 8 September 1968, 29, 84–95.

Garrison, Lloyd. "Odumegwu Ojukwu *Is* Biafra." *New York Times Magazine,* 22 June 1969, 7–9ff.

Geertz, Clifford. "Ideology as a Cultural System." In *Ideology and Discontent,* ed. David E. Apter, 47–76. New York: Free Press, 1964.

———. *The Interpretation of Culture.* New York: Basic Books, 1973.

George, John B. "How Stable Is Tanganyika?" *Africa Report* 8, no.3 (March 1963): 3–12.

Gershman, Carl. "The World According to Andrew Young." *Commentary,* August 1978, 17–23.

"Ghana: How U.S., British Press Fabricate and Distort News." *Liberator,* November 1961, 2.

Gibson, Richard. "African Unity and Afro-Americans." *Liberator,* August 1968, 16–18.

Glickman, Harvey. "Four Critiques of U.S. Policy in Africa." *Africa Report* 5, no.7 (July 1960): 13–14.

———. "A Melange of Biases on Angola." Review of *Views of a Revolt: Angola: A Symposium* (London: Oxford University Press for the Institute of Race Relations). *Africa Report* 7, no.6 (June 1962): 19.

———. "When Africans and Americans Meet." *Africa Report* 7, no.7 (July 1962): 17–18.

———. "Dialogues on the Theory of African Political Development." *Africa Report* 12, no.5 (May 1967): 38–39.

Gold, Herbert. "My Summer Vacation in Biafra." *Harper's*, November 1969, 63–68.

Goldberg, Harry. "Africa: Challenge to World Democracy." *American Federationist*, October 1959, 20–23.

Goldman, Phaon. "The Significance of African Freedom for the Negro American." *Negro History Bulletin* 34, no.1 (October 1960): 2–6.

Goldwater, Barry. "A Foreign Policy for America." *National Review,* 25 March 1961, 177–81.

Gonze, Colin. "Katanga Secession: The New Colonialism." *Africa Today* 9, no.1 (February 1962): 4–6.

———. "First Column." *Africa Today* 11, no.1 (January 1964): 2.

———. "Tshombe in Wonderland." *Africa Today* 11, no.7 (September 1964): 4–6.

Good, Robert C. "Africa's Gulliver." *New Leader,* 15–22 August 1960, 6–8.

Goodell, Charles E. "Biafra and the American Conscience." *Saturday Review,* 12 April 1969, 24–27, 102.

Gostev, M. "Nigeria: The Problems of Independence." *International Affairs* (Moscow), November 1960, 91–92.

Gould, Julius, and William L. Kolb, eds. *A Dictionary of the Social Sciences.* New York: Free Press, 1964.

Graham (DuBois), Shirley. "The African Personality." *Political Affairs,* September 1960, 13–19.

———. "The World We Live In." *Freedomways* 1, no.2 (Summer 1961): 115–77.

———. "What Happened in Ghana? The Inside Story." *Freedomways* 6, no.3 (Summer 1966): 201–23.

Greaves, William. "The First World Festival of Negro Arts: An Afro-American View." *Crisis* 73, 6 (June–July 1966): 313.

Greene, Fred. "Toward Understanding Military Coups." *Africa Report* 11, no.2 (February 1966): 10–14.

Grundy, Kenneth W. "Power in Nigeria." *Africa Today* 11, no.5 (May 1964): 14.

———. "The Congressional Image of Africa." *Africa Today* 14, no.1 (December 1966): 8–13.

Guérard, Albert. "To My African Friends." *Atlantic,* February 1960, 60–64.

"Guinea after Five Years." *Africa Report* 9, no.6 (June 1964): 3–6.

"Guinea—Balance Wheel in West Africa?" *New Republic,* 15 June 1959, 140.

Gunther, John. *Inside Africa.* New York: Harper, 1955.

Haines, Grove C. *Africa Today.* Baltimore: Johns Hopkins University Press, 1955.

Halberstam, David. "Mystery—and Tragedy—of Tshombe." *New York Times Magazine,* 12 August 1962, 7, 56–58.

Hallet, Jean-Pierre. *Congo-Kitabu.* New York: Random House, 1965.

Hammond, Dorothy, and Alta Jablow. " 'The African' in Western Literature." *Africa Today* 7, no.8 (December 1960): 8–10.

Hapgood, David. "Africa's New Elites." *Harper's,* December 1963, 4349.

Harrigan, Anthony. "America Needs a Realistic Foreign Policy." *American Mercury,* March 1962, 11–18.

Harris, James T., Jr. "Perspectives on the Congo." *Africa Today* 10, no.9 (November 1963): 16–17.

Hatch, John. "Africa between East and West." *Progressive,* January 1965, 19–23.

"Herskovits Report Calls for Imaginative U.S. Africa Policy." *Africa Special Report* 4, no.11 (November 1969): 7–12.

Hessler, William H. "The Agenda for Africa." *Reporter,* 23 June 1960, 33–37.

Hinden, Rita. "Emerging Africa: Is Democracy Possible?" *Current* 34 (February 1963): 36–39.

———. "Is It Time to Denounce the Dictators?" *Current* 48 (April 1964): 6–8.

Holder, Geoffrey. "It's All Africa This Year!" *Current* 27 (July 1962): 41–42.

Hollander, Paul. *Political Pilgrims: Travels of Western Intellectuals to the Soviet Union, China, and Cuba, 1928–1978.* New York: Harper and Row, 1983.

Hollinger, David. "Historians and the Discourse of Intellectuals." In *New Directions in American Intellectual History,* ed. John Higham and Paul C. Conkin, 42–63. Baltimore: Johns Hopkins University Press, 1979.

Holsti, Ole R., and James N. Rosenau. *American Leadership in World Affairs: Vietnam and the Breakdown of Consensus.* Boston: Allen and Unwin, 1984.

Houser, George M. "Leopoldville Revisited." *Africa Today* 7, no.8 (December 1960): 5–7.

"How to Cure the Congo." *National Review,* 14 August 1962, 88–89.

"How to Stop the Mau Mau." *Ebony,* March 1953, 88–89.

Howard, Charles P., Sr. "What Price Kasavubu?" *Nation,* 18 March 1961, 136–48.

———. "How the Western Press Defames Africa." *Freedomways* 2, no.4 (Fall 1962): 361–70.

———. "Katanga and the Congo Betrayal." *Freedomways* 2, no.2 (Spring 1962): 136–48.

Howard, Michael. *War and the Liberal Conscience.* New Brunswick, N.J.: Rutgers University Press, 1978.

Howe, Russell Warren. "Gold Coast into Ghana." *Phylon* 18, no.2 (July 1957): 155–61.

———. "George Padmore." *Encounter,* December 1959, 52–56.

———. "Prospects for Stability in Nigeria." *Africa Report* 5, no.1 (January 1960): 2–10.

———. "What Is the Congo?" *Reporter,* 16 March 1961, 23–28.

———. "Strangers in Africa." *Reporter,* 22 June 1961, 34–35.

———. "These Are the Africans." *Progressive,* August 1961, 11–13.

————. "A Reply to Horace Mann Bond." *Negro History Bulletin* 25, no.5 (February 1962): 102–04.

————. "Everybody's Problem Child." *New Republic,* 27 April 1963, 10–12.

————. "Racism in Africa." *New Republic,* 3 October 1963, 18–20.

————. "The Second Revolution." *New Leader,* 20 July 1964, 12–15.

————. "Nigeria's Civil War." *New Republic,* 16 September 1967, 16.

————. "A Talk with Sekou Toure." *Africa Report* 13, no.1 (January 1968): 49–53.

————. "One Nation, Divisible." *New Republic,* 7 February 1970, 15–17.

Howe, Russell Warren, and Sarah Hays Trott. *The Power Peddlers: How Lobbyists Mold America's Foreign Policy.* Garden City, N.Y.: Doubleday, 1977.

Hubbard, Margaret C. "The Threat of African Tribalism." *Atlantic Monthly,* January 1961, 45–47.

Hughes, John. "Africa Today." *New Leader,* 19 May 1958, 3–5.

————. "Nationalism in the Congo." *New Leader,* 16 February 1959, 7–8.

Hunt, Michael H. *Ideology and U.S. Foreign Policy.* New Haven: Yale University Press, 1987.

Hunton, Alphaeus W. "West Africa Today." *Political Affairs,* December 1959, 38–41.

————. "Guinea Strides Forward." *Freedomways* 1, no.1 (Spring 1961): 22–31.

Huxley, Elspeth. "Two Revolutions That Are Changing Africa." *New York Times Magazine,* 19 May 1957, 9, 69–70, 76.

————. "The Nationalist Tide Sweeps Africa." *New York Times Magazine,* 15 February 1959, 14–15.

————. "Africa's First Loyalty." *New York Times Magazine,* 18 September 1960, 14, 109–110.

————. "Disengagement in Africa." In *The African Nettle: Dilemmas of an Emerging Continent,* ed. Frank S. Meyer, 73–101. Freeport, N.Y.: Books for Libraries Press, 1965.

————. "Death in Nigeria." *National Review,* 22 January 1966, 163–64.

————. "The Rope That Hanged Nkrumah." *National Review,* 22 March 1966, 268–70.

————. "A Confusion of Colonels." *National Review,* 2 May 1967, 466–67.

————. "Biafra Libre." *National Review,* 22 August 1967, 896–921.

————. "Sacred Cow." *National Review,* 24 September 1968, 962–75.

————. "Motes in the Eye of Africa." *National Review,* 4 August 1972, 853–54.

Isaacs, Harold R. "A Reporter at Large—Back to Africa." *New Yorker,* 13 May 1961, 105–43. Repr. as "The American Negro in Africa." *Current* 15 (July 1961): 6–12.

————. "A Rebirth of Self-Esteem." *Current* 17 (September 1961): 18–24.

————. *The New World of Negro Americans.* New York: Viking, 1964.

————. "Portrait of a Revolutionary." *Commentary,* July 1965, 67–71.

Jack, Homer A. "Tale of Two Cities." *Crisis* 60, no.4 (April 1953): 217–53.

Jack, Homer A. "Eyewitness in Ghana." *Christian Century,* 3 April 1957, 416–18.

Jackson, James E. "The Meaning of 'Black Power.'" *Political Affairs,* September 1966, 1–9.

———. "National Pride—Not Nationalism." *Political Affairs,* May 1967, 43–48.

———. "Separatism—A Bourgeois-Nationalist Trap." *Political Affairs,* March 1969, 25–38.

Jenkins, George. "The Scholars' Paper Nigeria." *Africa Report* 12, no.5 (May 1967): 48–51.

Jervis, Steven. "A Letter from Nigeria." *Dissent,* July–August 1966, 418–20.

———. "Nigeria and Biafra." *Africa Today* 14, no.6 (December 1967): 16–18.

———. "Biafra Has Oil as Well as Starving Children." *New Republic,* 1 March 1969, 8–10.

Johnson, Christine. "Letter on the Ghana Coup." *Freedomways* 6, no.2 (Spring 1966): 152–58.

"Jungle Taking Over." *National Review,* 2 December 1961, 366–68.

Kadushin, Charles. *The American Intellectual Elite.* Boston: Little, Brown, 1974.

Kahn, Cynthia. "The O.A.U.: Hurrying Nowhere?" *Africa Today* 15, no.5 (October–November 1968): 1–2.

Karefa-Smart, Rena. "Africa Asks Questions of the West." *Ecumenical Review* 10, no.1 (October 1957): 43–55.

Karpat, Kemal. "The Reception of Western Political Institutions in the New Nations." Summary of the Proceedings of the Fourteenth Annual Meeting of the Western Political Science Association, University of California, Berkeley. *Western Political Quarterly* 13, no.3 (September 1960; supplement): 29–31.

"Katanga." *Africa Today* 10, no.1 (January 1963): 3.

"Katanga, the Committee, the U.N." *National Review,* 30 December 1961, 437–39.

Kennan, George. F. "History and Diplomacy as Viewed by a Diplomatist." In *Diplomacy in a Changing World,* ed. Stephen D. Kertesz and M. A. Fitzsimons, 101–08. Notre Dame: University of Notre Dame Press, 1959.

Kenworthy, Leonard. "Ghana: So Young, So Hopeful." *Progressive,* February 1958, 20–22.

Killens, John Oliver. "Explanation of the Black Psyche." *New York Times Magazine,* 7 June 1964, 37–38, 42, 47–48.

Kilson, Martin L., Jr. "Authoritarian and Single-Party Tendencies in African Politics." *World Politics* 15, no.2 (January 1963): 262–94.

———. "African Autocracy." *Africa Today* 13, 4 (April 1966): 4–7.

"The Kingdom of Silence: The Truth about Africa's Most Oppressed Colony." *Harper's,* May 1961, 29–37.

Kissinger, Henry A. *The Necessity for Choice: Prospects for American Foreign Policy.* New York: Harper and Row, 1961.

Klinghoffer, Arthur Jay. "Why the Soviets Chose Sides." *Africa Report* 13, no.2 (February 1968): 47–49.

Kloman, Erasmus H. "An African Program for the Africans." *New Leader,* 13 March 1961, 14–17.

Kohn, Hans. "Changing Africa in a Changing World." *Current History* 41 (October 1961): 193–216.

Kristol, Irving. "American Intellectuals and Foreign Policy." *Foreign Affairs* 45, no.4 (July 1967): 594–609.

Krosney, Herbert. "Senator Dodd: Portrait in Contrasts." *Nation,* 23 June 1962, 547–53.

Kuehnelt-Leddihn, Erik von. "How Europe Sees Foreign Aid." *National Review,* 21 November 1959, 484.

———. "The Mozambique Story." *National Review,* 9 April 1960, 232.

———. "Letter from the Congo." *National Review,* 18 June 1960, 393–94.

———. "Katanga's Case." *National Review,* 13 August 1960, 77.

———. "What About Katanga?" *National Review,* 21 October 1961, 266.

———. "Africa in Perspective." *National Review,* 18 May 1965, 424–26.

———. "The Afro-Asian Inferiority Complex." *National Review,* 23 August 1966, 836.

———. "Will Africa Make the Transition?" *National Review,* 17 October 1967, 1,114.

Kurzman, Dan. "Katanga Was Not Crushed." *Reporter,* 9 November 1961, 30–33.

Kwitney, Jonathan. "Nigeria in Focus." *New Leader,* 16 January 1967, 14–18.

Lake, Anthony. *The "Tar Baby" Option: American Policy toward Southern Rhodesia.* New York: Columbia University Press, 1976.

Lawrence, Harold G. "African Explorers of the New World." *Crisis* 69, no.6 (June–July 1962): 321–32.

Lee, Don L. "African Liberation Day." *Ebony,* July 1973, 40–46.

Legum, Colin. "The Future of Africa, II." *New Republic,* 17 October 1955, 13–15.

———. "The Tragedy in Nigeria." *Africa Report* 11, no.8 (November 1966): 23–24.

———. "Africa on the Rebound." *Africa Report* 12, no.9 (September 1967): 24–27.

Lejeune, Anthony. "No Comfort for the West." *National Review,* 14 March 1959, 586.

———. "Cult of the Messiah." *National Review,* 21 May 1960, 586.

———. "The Day Lumumba Died." *National Review,* 25 March 1961, 330.

———. "No Surrender in Rhodesia." *National Review,* 6 May 1961, 282.

———. "Africa without Fear or Favor." *National Review,* 21 September 1965, 833–35.

———. "Can Britain Stop Rhodesia?" *National Review,* 11 January 1966, 22–23.

Lemarchand, René. "How Lumumba Came to Power." *Africa Report* 5, no.8 (August 1960): 2–15.

Lens, Sidney. "The Bell Tolls in Africa." *Progressive,* November 1959, 16–20.

———. "The Revolution in Africa." *Liberation* 4, no.10 (January 1960): 8–11.

———. "The Birth Pangs of Revolution." *Progressive,* December 1961, 32–36.

Levering, Ralph B. *The Public and American Foreign Policy, 1918–1978.* New York: Morrow, 1978.

LeVine, Victor T. "Independent Africa in Trouble." *Africa Report* 12, no.9 (December 1967): 19–24.

Lewis, W. Arthur. "The Growing Pains of African Democracy." *Reporter,* 26 October 1961, 35–38.

———. *Politics in West Africa.* Toronto: Oxford University Press, 1965.

———. "Africa's Officers Take Command." *Reporter,* 24 March 1966, 33–36.

Lewis, Norman. "A Highlife or Two in Ghana." *New Yorker,* 23 November 1957, 134–56.

Lightfoot, Claude. "The Right of Black America to Create a Nation." *Political Affairs,* November 1968, 1–11.

"Like Father Like Son." Editorial. *Africa Today* 9, no.1 (February 1962): 3.

Lindsay, Kenneth. "Can There Be a Peace Settlement in Nigeria?" *Africa Report* 15, no.1 (January 1970): 14–15.

Lipset, Seymour Martin, and Richard B. Dobson. "The Intellectual as Critic and Rebel: With Special Reference to the United States and the Soviet Union." *Daedalus* 101 (Summer 1972): 137–98.

Little, Richard, and Steve Smith, eds. *Belief Systems and International Relations.* Oxford: Basil Blackwell in association with the British International Studies Association, 1988.

Lofchie, Michael F. "Political Theory and African Politics." *Journal of Modern African Studies* 6, no.1 (May 1968): 3–15.

Logan, Rayford W. "The Free World." *Negro History Bulletin* 14, no.7 (April 1951): 168ff.

Long, Richard A. "Race and Scholarship." *Liberator,* July 1970, 4–7.

———. "The Black Studies Boondoggle." *Liberator,* September 1970, 6–9.

"Long Live Nigeria." *Crisis* 77, no.2 (February 1970): 41–42.

Lonsdale, John. "The State and Social Processes in Africa." Paper presented to the annual conference of the African Studies Association. Bloomington, Indiana, October 1981.

Love, Kennett. " 'Saturday's Child' of Ghana." *New York Times Magazine,* 20 July 1958, 14–17.

Lovell, Colin Rhys. "Winds of Change in Southern Africa." *Current History* 41, no.242 (October 1961): 225–31.

Lukens, Donald. "The Time for Action on Biafra!: The Right to Live." *Reader's Digest,* May 1969, 77–79.

Lumer, Hyman. "U.S. Imperialism in the Congo." *Political Affairs,* September 1960, 1–12.

Lystad, Robert. "African Studies in the United States." *Africa Report* 11, no.8 (November 1966): 48–50.

Mander, John. "Britain's Vietnam." *New Leader,* 16 February 1970, 5–7.

Manners, Robert A. "Nations Growing up Overnight." *Saturday Review,* 18 April 1964, 48.

Mannheim, Karl. *Ideology and Utopia: An Introduction to the Sociology of Knowledge.* New York: Harcourt, Brace and World, 1966.

Marcum, John A. "Report from Guinea." *New Leader,* 1 December 1958: 3–6.

Marzani, Carl. "Reflections on an American Foreign Policy." *Monthly Review* 12, no.9 (January 1961): 481–87.

May, John Allan. "Little Red School House in the Jungle." *Negro Digest*, 9, no.6 (April 1951): 5.

McCall, Daniel F. "American Anthropology and Africa." *African Studies Bulletin* 10, no.2 (September 1967): 20–34.

McConnell, Grant. "Africa and the Americans." *Virginia Quarterly Review* 37, no.1 (Winter 1961): 34–50.

McKay, Vernon. "A United States Policy for the New Africa." *Current History* (July 1959): 1–6.

McKenna, Joseph C. "Elements of a Nigerian Peace." *Foreign Affairs* 47, no.4 (July 1969): 668–80.

McKinley, Edward H. *The Lure of Africa: American Interests in Tropical Africa, 1919–1939.* Indianapolis and New York: Bobbs-Merrill, 1974.

McQuade, Lawrence C. "The Showplace of Black Africa." *Yale Review* 49, no.2 (December 1959): 215–29.

Meisler, Stanley. "Breakup in Nigeria." *Nation*, 9 October 1967, 334–36.

———. "Pomp or Carnage." *Nation*, 26 August 1968, 132.

———. "New York's African Summer." *Africa Report* 13, no.9 (December 1968): 8–12.

Melbourne, Roy M. "The American Response to the Nigerian Conflict, 1968." *Issue* (African Studies Association) 3, no.2 (Summer 1973): 33–42.

Melnikov, Y. "U.S. Foreign Policy: Traditions and Present Trends." *International Affairs* (Moscow), October 1976, 87–95.

Merriam, Alan P. *Congo: Background of Conflict.* Evanston, Ill.: Northwestern University Press, 1961.

———. "The Congo's First Year of Independence." *Current History*, October 1961, 232–37.

Meyer, Frank S. "Abdication of Responsibility." *National Review*, 8 April 1961, 218.

———. "The Prickly Dilemmas." In *The African Nettle: Dilemmas of an Emerging Continent*, ed. Frank S. Meyer, 11–16. Freeport, N.Y.: Books for Libraries Press, 1965.

Meyers, Albert. "The Congo after 6 Years and a Billion in Aid." *U.S. News and World Report*, 18 April 1966, 65–67.

Miller, Randall M. "The American Discovery of Black Africa." In *African and Afro-American History: A Review of Recent Trends*, ed. James A. Casada, 6–12. Owerri, Nigeria: Conch Magazine, 1978.

Minogue, Kenneth. *The Liberal Mind.* London: Methuen, 1963.

Mittelman, James. "Some Reflections on Portugal's Counter-Revolution." *Monthly Review* 28, no.3 (March 1977): 58–64.

"Moise Tshombe, R.I.P." *National Review*, 15 July 1969, 685.

Molnar, Thomas. "The Truth about Angola." *National Review*, 7 April 1964, 280.

———. "African Paradox." *National Review*, 22 September 1964, 826.

———. "An Outsider Speaks." In *The African Nettle: Dilemmas of an Emerging*

Continent, ed. Frank S. Meyer, 132–53. Freeport, N.Y.: Books for Libraries Press, 1965.

———. "Rhodesia at the Crossroads." *National Review,* 2 November 1965, 971–72.

Monteiro, Tony. "James Forman's Pseudo-Marxism." *Political Affairs,* July 1973, 86–89.

Moore, Richard B. "Africa Conscious Harlem." *Freedomways* 3, no.3 (Summer 1963): 315–34.

Morgan, Charles, Jr. "Afrikaner Dixieland." *Nation,* 6 November 1976, 466–67.

Morgenthau, Hans. "United States Policy toward Africa." In *Africa in the Modern World,* ed. Calvin W. Stillman, 317–28. Chicago: University of Chicago Press, 1955.

———. *Politics among Nations.* 5th ed. New York: Knopf, 1973.

Morrison, Alan. "His Toughest Assignment." *Ebony,* October 1960, 32.

Morrissett, Ann. "Cold War in the Congo." *Liberation,* November 1960, 9–12.

Morsell, John A. "The Meaning of Black Nationalism." *Crisis* 69, no.2 (February 1962): 69–74.

Murray, Roger. "The Ghanaian Road." *New Left Review* 32 (July–August 1965): 63–71.

"New Labels for Old Products." *Monthly Review* 12, no.11 (March 1961): 545–52.

Newman, Edwin. "Independent Guinea's Morning After." *Reporter,* 13 November 1958, 24.

"Next Phase Coming Up." *National Review,* 27 March 1962, 190–91.

Niebuhr, Reinhold. "Imperialism in Perspective." *New Leader,* 14 November 1960, 7–8.

———. "The Negro Dilemma." *New Leader,* 11 April 1960, 13–14.

———. "Well-Tempered Evangelism." *New Republic,* 26 June 1961, 11–12.

Nielsen, Waldemar. "Africa Is Poised on the Razor's Edge." *New York Times Magazine,* 9 February 1964, 11, 61–62.

———. *The Great Powers and Africa.* New York: Praeger, 1969.

"Nigeria: Toward Democracy." *Africa Today* 13, no.4 (April 1966): 3.

"Nigeria Unshackled." *Ebony,* October 1960, 25–28.

"Nigerian Breakaway." *National Review,* 13 June 1967, 625.

"Nigeria's Civil War." *South Atlantic Quarterly,* Spring 1969, 143–51.

Nkrumah, Kwame. *Ghana: The Autobiography of Kwame Nkrumah.* Edinburgh: Thomas Nelson, 1959.

Noah, Monday Efiong. "The Nigerian Civil War and the Gullibles." *Africa Today* 17, no.2 (March–April 1970): 5–6.

Numada, N. "Marxism and African Liberation." *Political Affairs,* January 1961, 57–65.

Nwankwo, Nehe. "The Nigeria-Biafra War." *Liberator,* November 1968, 17.

Nye, Joseph S., Jr. "Verdict on Rotberg." *Africa Today* 13, no.4 (April 1966): 9–10.

O'Brien, Jay. "Portugal and Africa: A Dying Colonialism." *Monthly Review* 26, no.1 (May 1974): 19–36.

O'Connell, James. "The Scope of the Tragedy." *Africa Report* 13, no.2 (February 1968): 8–12.

O'Dell, J. H. "Colonialism and the Negro American Experience." *Freedomways* 6, no.4 (Fall 1966): 296–308.

———. "A Special Variety of Colonialism." *Freedomways* 7, no.1. (Winter 1967): 7–15.

O'Donovan, Patrick. "Ghana—Trial Run in Africa." *New Republic,* 18 December 1961, 10–11.

Oakes, John B. "Africa—A Continent Afire." *New York Times Magazine,* 3 January 1960, 9–13.

———. "Africa's 'Ordeal of Independence.'" *New York Times Magazine,* 31 July 1960, 7, 45–47.

Ofuatey-Kudjoe, W. "My Unwilling Brother." *Liberator,* June 1963, 10.

Ogunbadejo, O. "Ideology and Pragmatism: The Soviet Role in Nigeria, 1960–1975." *Orbis* 21, no.4 (Winter 1978): 803–30.

Okoye, Mokwugo. "Communism and African Perspectives." *Political Affairs,* April 1962, 47–51.

Oliver, R. P. Review of Prince Modupe, *I Was a Savage. National Review,* 17 May 1958, 476.

"Operation Smash, Phase III." *National Review,* 15 January 1963, 8–12.

Opubor, Alfred E., and Adebayo, Ogunubi. "Ooga Booga: The African Image in American Films." In *Other Voices, Other Views: An International Collection of Essays from the Bicentennial,* ed. Robin W. Winks, 343–75. Westport, Conn.: Greenwood Press, 1978.

Orick, George T. "Nigeria: A Study in Hypocrisy." *New Leader,* 1 January 1968, 7–11.

Ostrander, F. Taylor, and Winifred, Armstrong. "U.S. Private Investment in Africa." *Africa Report* 14, no.1 (January 1969): 38–41.

Oudes, Bruce. "The White and Green and the Rising Sun." *Nation,* 9 February 1970, 149–51.

Padmore, George. "Bloodless Revolution in the Gold Coast." *Crisis* 59, no.3 (March 1952): 172–99.

———. *Pan-Africanism or Communism? The Coming Struggle for Africa.* New York: Ray, 1956.

———. "The Birth of a Nation." *Crisis* 64, no.4 (April 1957): 197–207.

———. "The Press Campaign against Ghana." *Crisis* 64, no.10 (December 1957): 607–12.

Parker, Franklin. "Pass Carrying Requirements for African Negroes in Southern Rhodesia." *Negro History Bulletin* 23, no.7 (April 1960): 153–54.

———. "The Republic of Congo." *Negro History Bulletin* 25, no.3 (December 1961): 50–61.

Payne, William A. "American Press Coverage of Africa." *Africa Report* 11, no.1 (January 1966): 44–48.

Peffer, Nathaniel. "Colonialism: New Problems for Old." *Virginia Quarterly Review* 38, no.1 (Winter 1962): 71–78.

Perlo, Victor. "The Baran Memorial Volume." *Political Affairs,* February 1972, 63–56.

Persen, William. "Africa in Transition." *Worldview* 2, no.7 (July 1959): 3–6.

Pettman, Ralph. *State and Class: A Sociology of International Affairs.* New York: St. Martin's, 1979.

Petras, James. "The Roots of Underdevelopment." *Monthly Review* 18, no.9 (February 1967): 49–55.

Pittman, John. "The October Revolution and National Liberation." *Political Affairs,* November 1967, 27–38.

Ponomarov, B. "On National Democracy (Part II)." *Political Affairs,* September 1961, 47–57.

"Portuguese Africa." *Crisis* 67, no.2 (February 1960): 99.

Pratt, Julius W. "Anticolonialism in U.S. Policy." *Orbis* 1, no.3 (Fall 1957): 291–314.

Pye, Lucian W. "Culture and Political Science: Problems in the Evaluation of the Concept of Political Culture." In *The Idea of Culture in the Social Sciences,* ed. Louis B. Schneider and Charles M. Bonjean, 65–66. Cambridge: Cambridge University Press, 1973.

Quigg, Philip W. "The Changing American View of Africa." *Africa Report* 14, no.1 (January 1969): 8–11.

Rake, Alan, and J. D. Farrell. "Nigeria's Economy: No Longer a Model." *Africa Report* 12, no.7 (October 1967): 19–22.

Record, Wilson. *The Negro and the Communist Party.* Chapel Hill: University of North Carolina Press, 1951.

Reed, David. "In the Congo's Jungles, a Boom and a Ferment." *U.S. News and World Report,* 20 April 1959, 92–100.

———. "A Different Kind of Report on Africa." *U.S. News and World Report,* 18 May 1959, 96–100.

———. "The Rocky Road to Freedom." *Reader's Digest,* January 1973, 212–32.

"Rising Tide of Color." *Crisis* 67, no.5 (May 1960): 306–07.

Ritner, Peter. "Many Pictures but No Patterns." *Africa Today* 8, no.8 (October 1961): 14–16.

Ritner, Susan, and Peter Ritner. "Africa's Constitutional Malarkey." *New Leader,* 10 June 1963, 17–20.

———. "Africanism." *New Leader,* 22 July 1963, 26–27.

Rivkin, Arnold. "Principal Elements of U.S. Policy towards Under-Developed Countries." *International Affairs* 37, no.4 (1961): 452–64.

———. "The Politics of Nation-Building: Problems and Preconditions." *Journal of International Affairs* 16, no.2 (1962): 131–43.

———. "Nigeria: A Unique Nation." *Current History,* December 1963, 329–34.

Roberts, Norman Philips. "The Changed Images of Africa in Some Selected American Media from 1930 to 1969." Ph.D Diss. American University, 1971.

Robinson, Alma. "Africa and Afro-America." *Africa Report* 19, no.5 (September–October 1974): 7–10.

Robison, David. "The Price of One Nigeria." *New Leader,* 2 February 1970, 5–9.

Rogers, Harold. "The African Liberation Movement." *Political Affairs*, July 1973, 35–46.

Rosenau, James N. "The Study of Foreign Policy." In *World Politics: An Introduction*, ed. James N. Rosenau, Kenneth, W. Thompson, and Gavin Boyd, 1535. New York: Free Press, 1976.

Rosenblum, Paul. "Boa Constrictor in the Desert." *Africa Today* 10 no.2 (February 1963): 4–11.

Ross, David F. "Peace Is a Long Way off for Nigeria." *New Republic*, 5 October 1968, 13–14.

Rowan, Carl T. "How the U.S. Looks at Africa." *Ebony*, November 1961, 117–21.

Rudin, Harry R. "The Past and Present Role of Africa in World Affairs." *Annals of the American Academy of Political and Social Science* 298 (March 1955): 30–38.

———. "The International Position of Africa Today." *Annals of the American Academy of Political and Social Science* 306 (July 1956): 50–54.

———. "The Republic of the Congo." *Current History*, December 1962, 334–69.

Sale, J. Kirk. "Togo: The Lesson for Africa." *Nation*, 16 February 1963, 135–37.

———. "Freedom and/or Progress." *New Leader*, 13 September 1965, 23–24.

———. "After Colonialism." *New Leader*, 17 January 1966, 27–29.

Satterthwaite, Joseph. "The Challenge of the Hour." *Africa Special Report* 4, no.3 (March 1959): 9–12.

Schachter, Ruth. "Single-Party Systems in West Africa." *American Political Science Review* 55, no.2 (June 1961): 294–309.

Schechter, Daniel B. "From a Closed Filing Cabinet: The Life and Times of the Africa Research Group." *Issue* (African Studies Association) 6, nos. 2 and 3 (Summer and Fall 1976): 41–48.

Schneider, William. "Public Opinion: The Beginning of Ideology?" *Foreign Policy* 17 (Winter 1974–75): 88–120.

Schuyler, Philippa. "Behind the Congo Crisis." *National Review*, 13 August 1960, 76–77.

Segal, Aaron. "Africa and the United States Media." *Issue* (African Studies Association) 6, nos. 2 and 3 (Summer and Fall 1976): 49–56.

Sevareid, Eric. "Talking back to Africa." *Reporter*, 4 February 1960, 6.

Sheehan, Edward R. F. "It's Still the Heart of Darkness." *New York Times Magazine*, 30 October 1966, 30–33, 76–99.

Shepherd, George W., Jr. "The Birth of Ghana." *New Leader*, 11 March 1957, 5–6.

———. "Toward a Positive Program in Africa." *Progressive*, April 1959, 24–27.

———. "Biafra—The Issue Is Massacre." *Africa Today* 15, no.3 (June–July 1968): 3.

Shils, Edward. "Intellectuals." *International Encyclopedia of the Social Sciences*, vol. 7, 399–415. New York: Macmillan and Free Press, 1968.

———. "The Intellectuals and the Powers: Some Perspectives for Comparative Analysis." In *The Intellectuals and the Powers and Other Essays*, edited by Edward Shils, 3–22. Chicago: University of Chicago Press, 1972.

Simpson, George Eaton. *Melville J. Herskovits.* New York: Columbia University Press, 1973.

Skinner, Elliott P. "African, Afro-American, White American." *Freedomways* 5, no.3 (Summer 1965): 380–95.

Sklar, Richard L. *Nigerian Political Parties: Power in an Emergent African Nation.* Princeton: Princeton University Press, 1963.

———. "Nigeria/Biafra." *Africa Today* 16, no.1 (February–March 1969): 3–4.

Sloan, Pat. "Ghana without Illusions." *Political Affairs,* October 1966, 16–29.

Smythe, Hugh H., and Mabel M. Smythe. "Black Africa's New Power Elite." *South Atlantic Quarterly* 59, no.1 (Winter 1960): 13–23.

Songha, Wanyandey. "Marxism and the Black Revolution." *Liberator,* September 1969, 17.

Sonnenfeldt, Helmut. "Nigeria as Seen from Moscow." *Africa Report* 6, no.1 (January 1961): 9–10.

Spellman, A.B. "Interview with Malcolm X." *Monthly Review* 16, no.1 (May 1964): 14–24.

Spiro, Herbert J. "New Constitutional Forms in Africa." *World Politics* 13, no.1 (October 1960): 69–76.

———. *Politics in Africa.* New York: Prentice-Hall, 1962.

———. "Whose Problems?" *Africa Today* 12, no.2 (February 1965): 3–4.

Staniland, Martin. "Democracy and Ethnocentrism." In *Political Domination in Africa: Reflections on the Limits of Power,* ed. Patrick Chabal, 52–70. Cambridge: Cambridge University Press, 1986.

Stent, Angela. "The Soviet Union and the Nigerian Civil War: A Triumph of Realism." *Issue* (Africa Studies Association) 3, no.2 (Summer 1973): 43–47.

Sterling, Claire. "Can Nigeria Catch up With Its Reputation?" *Reporter,* 19 May 1966, 39–42.

———. "The Self-Defeating Civil War in Nigeria." *Reporter,* 10 August 1967, 23–30.

Stevenson, Adlai E. "The New Africa: A Guide and a Proposal." *Harper's,* May 1960, 48–54.

———. "The American Revolution in Our Time." *Progressive,* June 1960, 26–30.

———. "The Issue Is Peace." *Progressive,* November 1960, 8–11.

Stevick, Earl W. "The Teaching of African Languages in the United States." *African Studies Bulletin* 10, no.1 (April 1967): 16–21.

Stillman, Calvin W., ed. *Africa in the Modern World.* Chicago: University of Chicago Press, 1955.

Stirling, William L. "To Touch The Hand and the Land." *Africa Report* 13, no.9 (December 1968): 13–15.

Stolle, Jane. "The Congo: A Calculated Confusion." *Nation,* 23 March 1963, 252–54.

Strickland, William. "Documenting Congo Betrayal." *Freedomways* 7, no.3 (Summer 1967): 249–52.

"Summer in the Congo." *New Republic,* 20 June 1960, 5–6.

Suret-Canale, Jean. "Colonialism's Impact on Africa." *Political Affairs*, June 1962, 30–37.

Sutton, Francis X., and David R. Smock. "The Ford Foundation and African Studies." *Issue* (African Studies Association) 6, nos. 2 and 3 (Summer and Fall 1976): 68–72.

Sweezy, Paul M. "Modern Capitalism." *Monthly Review* 23, no.2 (June 1971): 1–10.

———. "Class Struggles in Portugal." *Monthly Review* 27, no.4 (September 1975): 12.

Tanner, Henry. "The Congo Is Still an Active Volcano." *New York Times Magazine*, 10 September 1967, 52–53.

Tas, Sal. "Report on French Africa." *New Leader*, 8 September 1958, 6–8.

"Tell the Truth." *Monthly Review* 17, no.2 (June 1965): 1–6.

"The Ten Biggest Lies about Africa." *Ebony*, May 1957, 58.

Thompson, Era Bell. "Freedom Comes to 83 Million Africans." *Ebony*, December 1960, 151.

———. "Progress, Africa's Untold Story." *Ebony*, June 1969, 74–85.

Thompson, W. Scott. "Nigeria." *Atlantic*, April 1967, 17–28.

"Those Katanga Freedom Fighters." *Nation*, 20 January 1962, 41.

Tonelson, Alan. "The End of Internationalism?" *New Republic*, 13 February 1989, 23–25.

Torgoff, Stephen. "Some Thoughts on Earl Ofari's 'Marxism, Nationalism, and Black Liberation.'" *Monthly Review* 23, no.5 (October 1971): 80–83.

"The U.N. and Africa." *New Republic*, 2 October 1961, 3–5.

"Up the U.N!" *Nation*, 6 August 1960, 61–62.

Uphoff, Norman T., and Harold Ottemoeller. "After the Nigerian Civil War: With Malice toward Whom?" *Africa Today* 17, no.2 (March–April 1970): 1–4.

Van Dongen, Irene S. "Angola." *Focus* 7, no.2 (October 1956): 1–6.

Van den Haag, Ernest. "The U.N. War in Katanga." *National Review*, 27 March 1962, 197–202.

Van Essen, Marcel. "The United States Department of State and Africa." *Journal of Human Relations* 8, nos.3 and 4 (Spring and Summer 1960): 844–52.

Walker, William D., III. "Drug Control and the Issue of Culture in American Relations." *Diplomatic History* 12, no.4 (Fall 1988): 365–82.

Wallerstein, Immanuel. *Africa: The Politics of Independence*. New York: Vintage Books, 1961.

———. "A Program for Africa." *New Leader*, 30 January 1961, 12–14.

———. "What Next in the Congo?" *New Leader*, 6 March 1961, 35.

———. "Congo Confederation." *New Leader*, 27 March 1961, 3–5.

———. "Africa out of Joint." *New Leader*, 15 May 1961, 27–28.

———. "Our Unfriendly African Friends." *New Leader*, 14–21 August 1961, 10–11.

———. "Nigeria: Slow Road to Trouble." *New Leader*, 23 July 1962, 15–18.

———. "An Africanist's Reply." *New Leader*, 10 June 1963, 21–22.

———. "African Unity Reassessed." *Africa Report* 11, no.4 (April 1966): 41–46.

———. "Ghana as a Model." *Africa Report* 12, no.5 (May 1967): 43–46.

————. "What Is Revolutionary Action in Africa Today?" *Africa Today* 14, no.3 (June 1967): 4–5.

————. "Looking back at African Independence Ten Years Later." *Africa Today* 18, no.2 (April 1971): 2–5.

————. "Africa, the United States, and the World Economy: The Historical Bases of American Policy." In *U.S. Policy toward Africa*, ed. Frederick S. Arkhurst, 11–55. New York: Praeger, 1975.

————. "Class and Class Conflict." *Monthly Review* 26, no.9 (February 1975): 34–42.

Waring, Ronald. "Angola: Terrorists on the Run." *National Review*, 11 September 1962, 189–91.

Waterman, Peter. "Radicalism in African Studies." *Politics and Society* 3, no.3 (Spring 1973): 261–81.

Weaver, Edward K. "What Nigerian Independence Means." *Phylon* 22, no.2 (Summer 1961): 146–59.

Weigle, Graham. "How to Deal with Africa." *National Review*, 3 December 1960, 345–46.

Weisbord, Robert. *Ebony Kinship: Africa, Africans, and the Afro-American.* Westport, Conn.: Greenwood Press, 1973.

Weiss, Herbert F. "The Tshombe Riddle." *New Leader*, 17 September 1962, 3–6.

Weissman, Stephen R. *American Foreign Policy in the Congo, 1960–1964.* Ithaca, N.Y.: Cornell University Press, 1974.

"We're on Their Side." *National Review*, 16 December 1961, 402–03.

Wesley, Charles H. "Resurgence in Africa's Historical Tradition and the American Reaction." *Negro History Bulletin* 24, no.4 (January 1961): 81–89.

Wesley, Charles. "Black Studies and History Week." *Negro History Bulletin* 35, no.2 (February 1972): 28–29.

West, Eleanor, and Robert L. West. "Conflicting Economic Interests of Africa and the United States." In *U.S. Policy toward Africa*, ed. Frederick S. Arkhurst, 153–84. New York: Praeger, 1975.

Weyl, Nathaniel. "The Ordeal of Negro Africa." *National Review*, 19 June 1962, 445–46.

————. "New Mythology of the Negro Past." *National Review*, 8 October 1968, 1,020–22.

"Where Reds Are No Problem." *U.S News and World Report*, 23 July 1954, 35–37.

"Where We Stand." *Monthly Review* 1, no.1 (May 1949): 1–2.

"Whose Drums on the Congo?" *National Review*, 16 July 1960, 7.

Wilkins, Roger. "What Africa Means to Blacks." *Foreign Policy* 15 (Summer 1974): 130–42.

Williams, Babatunde. "Where Does Nigeria Go from Here?" *Africa Report* 5, no.10 (October 1960): 3–15.

Williams, Chancellor. "African Democracy and the Leadership Principle." *Journal of Human Relations* 8, nos. 3 and 4 (Spring and Summer 1960): 819–30.

Williams, G. Mennen. "Diplomatic Rapport between Africa and the United

States." *Annals of the American Academy of Political and Social Science* 354 (July 1964): 54–64.

———. "Congo Realities and United States Policy." *Department of State Bulletin*, 24 June 1965, 798–805.

Wilson, Angene. "Taking Tarzan out of the Textbooks." *Africa Report* 13, no.5 (May 1968): 43–44.

Winston, Henry. "Padmore, the 'Father' of Neo-Pan-Africanism." *Political Affairs*, July 1973, 1–19.

Young, Crawford. *Politics in the Congo: Decolonization and Independence.* Princeton: Princeton University Press, 1968.

Zanzolo, A. "The Struggle for Nigerian Unity." *Political Affairs*, February 1969, 1–13.

Znaniecki, Florian. *The Social Role of the Man of Knowledge.* New York: Octagon Books, 1965.

Zolberg, Aristide. "One-Party Systems and Government for the People." *Africa Today* 9, no.4 (May 1962): 4–7.

INDEX

Academic community, 29–31
Adams, John Quincy, 262*n*152
Adams, Mildred, 37*n*56, 38, 39,
40*n*69
Adelman, Kenneth L., 255
Africa: American relations with
(1919–1955), 20–26; chieftaincy
in, 182–83; climate, 40–41; golden
age in, 181–82; institutions in, 59–
63; military coups in, 255–56; societies in, 42; traditionalism in, 60–
61; tribalism in, 61
Africa League, 120
African-Americans, 10–12; American
left and, 154–55; American Revolution analogy and, 194–97; Biafran
secession and, 205–09; black nationalists, 199–203; colonialism
and, 183–93; Congo crisis of *1960–
1961* and, 204–05; decolonization
and, 193–97; dilemmas of, 272–
73; individual trips to Africa, 203–
04; nationalism and, 197–203; nationalism in, 154–55; postindependence politics and, 203–13;
precolonial Africa and, 180–83
African bourgeoisie, 166
African economic behavior, 220–21
African elite, American liberalism
and, 107–09
African history: American conservatives and, 216–17; American left
and, 141–42
African languages, teaching of, 29*n*32
African leaders: American conservatives and, 253–54; American liberalism and, 104–06
African mind, 214–15
African news coverage, 265*n*2

African peasantry, 168–69
African proletariat, 167–68
African revolution: American liberal-
ism and, 66–68; American Revolu-
tion and, 119*n*63
Africans: American liberalism on, 58–
63; conservatism of, 214–15; driv-
ing behavior of, 59; economic be-
havior of, 220–21; patronizing
anecdotes about, 178–79; rational-
ity of, 58–59
African socialists, 164–65
African states, artificiality of, 257–58
African Studies Association, 31
African studies programs, 29–31
Aldridge, Dan, 211*n*121
Allen, George V., 22*n*7
Allen, Victor, 159*n*55, 165, 170
Almond, Gabriel, 114*n*48
Alsop, Stewart, 37*n*58, 39, 214
American capitalism, decolonization
and, 146
American Civil War analogy, Biafran
secession and, 133–34
American Committee for Aid to Katanga Freedom Fighters (ACAKFF),
237
American Committee on Africa, 31
American conservatives, 12–16; Afri-
can history and, 216–17; African
leaders and, 253–54; American liberalism compared to, 13*n*19; American Revolution analogy and, 229–
31; authoritarianism and, 250–51;
Biafran secession and, 256–62; colonialism and, 215–23; conservatism of Africans and, 214–15;
decolonization and, 223–31; dilemmas of, 273–74; independence and,